AIRCRAFT CARRIER
IMPERO

AIRCRAFT CARRIER IMPERO

THE AXIS POWERS' V-1 CARRYING CAPITAL SHIP

DAVIDE F. JABES AND STEFANO SAPPINO

FONTHILL

Fonthill Media Language Policy

Fonthill Media publishes in the international English language market. One language edition is published worldwide. As there are minor differences in spelling and presentation, especially with regard to American English and British English, a policy is necessary to define which form of English to use. The Fonthill Policy is to use the form of English native to the authors. Davide F. Jabes and Stefano Sappino were born in Italy and took their degrees in Italy and England (Davide F. Jabes, PhD in History, University of York); therefore, British English has been adopted in this publication.

Fonthill Media Limited
Fonthill Media LLC
www.fonthill.media
office@fonthillmedia.com

First published in the United Kingdom and the United States of America 2018

British Library Cataloguing in Publication Data:
A catalogue record for this book is available from the British Library

ISBN 978-1-78155-677-1

Typeset in 10.5pt on 13pt Minion Pro
Printed and bound in England

Acknowledgements

We would like to thank Enrica Anna Campagnoli for making available the Campagnoli archives and Luigina Campagnoli for sharing numerous period photos and documents.

We would like to thank the supervisors and archivists at the *Ufficio Storico della Marina Militare* and at the *Rivista Marittima*, those of the Central Archive of the State (ACS), at the Historical Archive INSEAN, the Historical Archive of the Ansaldo Foundation, and the Civic Museums of History and Art of the city of Trieste.

We are grateful to Richard Hunt Jr for the great work in reviewing the text; all the mistakes are, of course, ours.

This book would not have happened without the collaboration of many individuals, each one contributed in inestimable ways: Giampiero Galeotti, Dr Dieter Thomaier, Professor Gaspare Galati, Dr Lidia Calvano, Gen. Maurizio Sulig, Takács Zoltán, Dr Claudia Cerioli, Dr Carla Zilahi de Gyurgyokai, Ing. Filippo Bonfiglietti, Michela Fiaschi, Vittorio Catalano Gonzaga, Ing. Alessando Cominu, Dr Cristina Klarer, Alessandro Romanello, Niccolò Tognarini, Raffaele D'Aniello, Fabio Cubo, and Akos Gergely, Massimo Pontillo, and Angelo Taverna. Final thanks go to Rie, Irene, and Alessio; Lidia and Ginevra who supported and lived with husbands and fathers busy with the adult game of historical research.

Contents

List of Abbreviations

AA	Anti-Aircraft	*Antiaerea/o*
ACS	*Archivio Centrale dello Stato*	Italian State Archive
AR	*Ali ripiegabili*	Foldable wings
BUSMM	*Bollettino d'archivio dell'Ufficio Storico della Marina Militare*	Italian Navy Historical Office's Archival Bulletin
CRDA	*Cantieri Riuniti dell'Adriatico*	'United Shipbuilders of the Adriatic' Trieste and Monfalcone shipyards.
CSM	*Capo di Stato Maggiore*	Chief of Staff
CSMG	*Capo di Stato Maggiore Generale*	Chief of the Defence Staff
De.Te.	*Dezimeter Telegraphie o Dezimetertechnik*	German Radar
DG	*Documento Gunnarson*	Gunnarson document
DL	*Decreto Legge*	Decree
FFAA	*Forze Armate*	Military Forces
Gil	*Grande Incrociatore Leggero*	Large Light Cruiser, a 203-mm equipped warship with light armour
GN	*Genio Navale*	Corps of Naval Engineering (NC)
HMS	His/Her Majesty Ship	*Nave di Sua Maestà (britannica)*
HP	Horsepower	*Cavalli Vapore*
IMAM	*Industrie Meccaniche Aeronautiche Meridionali*	Name of aircraft industry, see Italian
INSEAN	*Istituto nazionale per studi ed esperienze di architettura navale*	'The Italian Ship Model Basin', established in 1927
IRI	*Istituto per la Ricostruzione Industriale*	Institute for Industrial Reconstruction established 1933
K	Knots	*nodi*
MAC	Merchant Aircraft Carrier	*Mercantile convertito a portaerei di emergenza*
MAS	*Motoscafo Armato Silurante*	Torpedo Armed Motorboat

NC	Naval Corps	*Corpi tecnici della Marina*
OKM (*Oberkommando der Marine*)	*Comando Supremo della Marina Germanica*	German Naval high command
RA or R.A.	*Regia Aeronautica*	Italian Royal Air Force
RAF	Royal Air Force	*Aeronautica britannica*
RD or R.D.	*Regio Decreto*	King's Decree
RM or R.M.	*Regia Marina*	Italian Royal Navy
RN or R.N.	*Regia Nave*	King's Ship
RS	*Regio Sommergibile*	King's submarine
SM	*Stato Maggiore*	Chief of Staff Office
TDS	Torpedo Defence System	*Sistema di protezione da siluro*
TNT	Trinitrotoluene	*Tritolo*
UP	*Ufficio progetti Ansaldo*	Ansaldo's Project Office
US	*Ufficio Studi Ansaldo*	Ansaldo's Design Office
USMM	*Ufficio Storico Marina Militare*	Italian Navy's Historical Office
USN	United States Navy	*Marina degli Stati Uniti d'America*
WT or W.T.	Washington Treaty	*Trattato di Washington*

Introduction

This book is devoted to the study of the last Italian battleship that was built, RN *Impero*, and its transformation to fleet aircraft carrier with features unique for that time.

Through original and unpublished documents, sources have been found regarding the transformation of the battleship to aircraft carrier, how it was conceived in order to accommodate jet propulsion weapons, and that both the German V1 and the previously unknown Italian DAACs (experimental rocket-propelled weapons from 1940) had been taken into consideration for this purpose. From this perspective, the importance of this finding shifts from naval history to naval strategy.

While studying the documents, in addition to the confirmation of a complete lack of collaboration among the Axis forces, as well as of understanding the respective priorities and joint interests, a disconcerting spy story was discovered, an event which occurred among allies in reference to one of the most classified of Nazi secrets.

Another interesting fact connected to the planning of the aircraft carrier is the analysis that concerns it; in fact, the project was only definitively shelved in 1944. This was just another demonstration of how the Fascist regime was unaware of military problems before the conflict began and subsequently was entirely incapable of adapting to the evolution of wartime events.

Finally, the material brought us to the Russian–German battlefront, when we examined the hull of the unfinished Russian battleship *Sovetsky Soyuz* as well as new information on its status and that of the TDS Pugliese, which allows for a definitive assessment of the efficiency of the latter.

The first chapters of the book present an overview of the political and military situation in Italy between the two World Wars; they also include the preludes to what brought about Italy's self-imposed diplomatic isolation and its decision to ally itself with Germany.

Subsequent chapters describe in detail the story of the plans of the aircraft carrier of the *Regia Marina* and the rivalry with the *Regia Aeronautica*, a rivalry that caused a lack of adequate preparation of the aircraft as well as a lack of collaboration with air and sea resources. Additionally, attention was brought to how much of an influence these circumstances had on the main war efforts at sea and how Italy and Germany ignored the recommendations and experience of the Japanese Navy, particularly with regards to its aerial components, until it was too late. Finally, the text goes through an in-depth examination of a period covering twenty years of the structure of political and military decisions of the Fascist regime, which saw the country ill prepared for the conflict.

The text is a collaboration of two authors: Davide Franco Jabes mainly described the general historic context and the collaboration among the Axis forces; and Stefano Sappino was responsible for the military history of the time frame between the years 1922 and 1941, as well as the research regarding the *Littorio* design and the *Impero* as aircraft carrier and analysed the story of one of the most significant schools of naval architects, the Ansaldo school, which Lino Campagnoli attended.

1

Historical Context

How Italy Joined the War and its Goals

For many nations, the fight against Nazi fascism was the essence of the Second World War, and for some, the war became an anti-fascist crusade. Ever since it began, fascism had proclaimed imperialist inclinations, although in the first ten years of government, it had steered clear of military 'adventures' (with the exception of the naval action in Corfu).[1] It therefore seems necessary to focus on the reasons that determined the entrance of Italy into the war at Germany's side, analysing the situation of the peninsula in the years after the Great War. It was in Italy that the first movement of the radical right came to power. This was surprising for many reasons, including the fact that Italy had been one of the victorious forces of the First World War, as well as because the country was governed by a constitutional monarchy.

Contrary to the Marxist movement and the liberal governments, the radical right appeared in Europe only after the conclusion of the First World War. The masses who largely fomented fascist actions were people and soldiers who had been disillusioned by the promises of the First World War. Italy, in fact, despite being one of the victors, considered itself among those nations that were penalised, betrayed, or 'wounded' by the international peace treaties.

Many Italians considered the liberal government corrupt and inefficient, at the service of regional or class interests. There was also a certain amount of bitterness due to the awful way the First World War had been run by the state government, as well as because of the lack of territorial gains, particularly after the enormous sacrifice of lives—approximately 760,000 men died on the battlefront or in internment.[2] The movement of the Italian *Fasci italiani di combattimento* was founded a year after the end of the war, and it developed a large base of popular support under the leadership of Benito Mussolini. Fascism was based on a programme self-described as totalitarian and, as the historian Emilio Gentile has written, it was presented 'as a radical alternative to the principles of equality, put into effect in the historic process of the assertion of the rights of man and the citizen which began with the age of Enlightenment and with the democratic revolutions at the end of the eighteenth century', and which, as Gentile continues, had the goal of establishing itself on the complete subordination of the individual to the state, as opposed to an individual or a particular social class.[3]

At the beginning of the parliamentary activity in 1922, the Fascist party was a minority in parliament: only after the March on Rome did King Vittorio Emanuele II nominated Mussolini as Prime Minister. Once in office, Mussolini established laws that allowed him to keep Fascism in power and to neutralised or killed his opponents. He obtained the dictatorship gradually and kept 'an ambiguous position between political terrorism and a policy of normalization' until the subversion of the constitution and the overshadowing of the King.[4]

Italy, as Japan had been during the First World War, had been a member of the Entente, and France and Britain did not take any initiative to stop the birth of an authoritarian government. The army supported Mussolini's foreign policy and his opposition to leftist politicians. The *Duce* had also attracted a significant consensus abroad, both from the radical right in Germany as well as in Eastern Europe and from some conservative elements in other countries.[5]

The Fascist ideology dangerously increased the likelihood of another great war through territorial expansion and the creation of an empire. The historian MacGregor Knox remembers that Mussolini said in a speech on the creation of the new elite in 1925: 'revolution and war, internal and foreign politics, interacted mutually'. Not always, the *Duce* continued, did one fight aggressively, but sometimes one needed to 'stagnate on the positions conquered for a long time. But the goal is: the empire'.[6] Mussolini further reiterated:

> [The State is thus] a will of power and empire: for Fascism, the tendency to the empire in other words to the expansion of the nations is a manifestation of vitality; its opposite or a foot at home is a sign of decadence...[7]

The feet of the Italians would thus tread in various foreign lands.

In a sense, Italian soldiers had no choice because the wars they had to fight for Mussolini and Fascism were almost entirely run on foot, as if they were a Napoleonic army.

If facts do not change over the course of time, their interpretation is subject to numerous changes. The emergence of China as a global superpower has an influence also in the historiographic realm; it is thus natural that the never-declared conflict between Japan and China, which started in 1937, should currently be reconsidered as the beginning of the war that according to the established date began in 1939 with the German attack on Poland.

On the contrary, some believe that the Second World War started with the Italian invasion of Ethiopia in 1935. This is a theory that is denied by those such as the English historian Evan Mawdsley, who did not believe that the war for East Africa was directly related to the conflict. According to Mawdsley, as Mussolini's African adventure had a beginning and an ending, and the ending occurred before the 'continuous conflict' of the Second World War, Italy did not take part in it.[8] Furthermore, aside from the success in prestige and propaganda, the conquest would not have been such until there would have been real peace in Ethiopia. However, this never completely occurred and those actions that were done to 'secure' the country can be considered criminal acts against humanity by Italy.

To return to the subject of the advantages of the political-military options available to Mussolini, from the Italian perspective, the choice to assault Ethiopia would turn out to be very economically involved and would also mark the beginning of the cooperation between Germany and Italy. The

Ethiopian campaign and the subsequent construction of a network of roads and railways seriously undertook Italian finances (as many know, the first 'concealed' tax in the price for petrol was introduced by Mussolini in order to finance part of the military operations in Africa). Through the assault on Ethiopia, a state that was a member of the League of Nations (the predecessor to the United Nations), Italy had isolated itself politically; thus, it was that the alliance with Germany, which occurred shortly after these events, reduced the possibility of complete isolation from public opinion in both countries. Yet the fear that Western forces had for a German rearmament would have easily allowed Mussolini to obtain various advantages.

In reality, the *Duce* already had another war in mind: that of Spain (1936–1939). After the success of the adventure in Africa, his popularity was at its peak and the other powers-that-be against this new initiative, from the monarchy to the military authorities, would not have had the ability to react with sufficient force.

The Spanish War, which caused many delusions because of the efficiency of the *Regia Aeronautica* in the skies, should not have aroused many concerns at sea given the proven inability of the bombers at altitude to target ships at sea and by submarines with outdated tactics and techniques.[9]

Additionally, whether the *Duce*'s intentions were to mould the new Fascist man through wars or to acquire ever greater prestige and power to the detriment of the monarchy, by now the fulfilment of the Fascist revolution seemed to go through a permanent state of war.

In Spain in 1936, the electoral coalition of the Popular Front was affirmed and an effort was made to revitalise it with the support of the socialists, the communists, and the radicals. Shortly after the victory of the Front, the military nationalists rebelled, and after three years of civil war, the nationalist general, Franco (commander of the foreign Spanish Legion in Morocco), won thanks to the direct assistance of Germany and Italy. Although it was essentially an internal Spanish fight, this war involved many European military advisers as well as some non-Europeans. Particularly because of the innovative use of some military weapons and techniques, the conflict was considered the prelude to the Second World War.

The war of Spain was a complete failure for Fascism, with the partial exception of the propaganda. If the battles for the conquering of the empire had committed the Italian economic resources, the Fascist's support of General Franco impoverished Italy to the point of it being impossible for the country to be involved in any other equivalent war effort. The new Spanish dictator did not offer any reward to his Italian counterpart, unlike Germany, which did obtain considerable benefits from the assistance give to the Francoists despite the fact that they had done business with the Republican antagonists.

Now that the Spanish Civil War had ended, it was time for Mussolini to find another conflict, another step in the fulfilment of *Mare Nostrum*, which was both complement and a goal for the realisation of the Fascist revolution.[10]

The annexation of Albania (in 1939) was convenient because, compared to the previous two conflicts, it would have employed a reduced amount of expenditures both of manpower and resources. The annexation of Albanian territory would have also allowed for a 'base' for the future conquest of Greece and, at the same time, it would have strengthened the Italian position with regard to the designs on Dalmatia. Subsequently, the deterioration of the general situation in Europe reduced the Albanian episode to a matter of small importance; in fact, just a few months later, Germany went to war against Poland on 1 September 1939.

The imbalances caused in 1919 immediately after the First World War were destined to create large internal trauma among the nations that recently formed and among those that had lost the conflict. One of the most important diplomatic agreements in the European continent at the start of the twentieth century was that between France and Tsarist Russia; however, with the advent of the Bolshevik revolution, everything changed. Among those nations that had won the First World War, France was the most interested in maintaining the status quo obtained in the post-war period, yet after 1919, only Poland remained as France's ally to East. Additionally, in the East, various 'cushion' states had formed from the Baltic to the Black Sea (in other words, from Finland to Romania), which the Western democracies considered a 'cordon' capable of blocking communist contamination.[11]

At the Treaty of Rapallo in 1922, the USSR and Germany reconciled, followed by a Baltic agreement against the feared Soviet expansionism, and in 1925, the Treaty of Lucerne brought Germany closer to the Allies.[12]

After the collapse of the four empires, there were many characters on the international scene, and each move on the international chess board would mobilise all the diplomatic services and would change its strategies and goals. In particular, the Fascist Italy of the '20s did not have a clear foreign policy: at times, it would opt for a revisionist policy of the Balkans alternated with a defence of the existing equilibrium in Western Europe. Great Britain traditionally pursued an easing of tensions among the European nations so that none of them would prevail over the other. In this aspect, London's diplomatic angle was against indefinite defence of the status quo, which was, in its opinion, too favourable towards the French. Nevertheless, the enactment of the Treaty of Lucerne was effective for several years. Some factors caused a change in the scenario, the first being the economic crisis of 1929, which caused serious social tensions and, more importantly, prevented the United States economy from continuing to operate for the economic balance of Europe.

Among the Allied powers, the United States was most in favour of an economic recovery for Germany; however, the persistence of the crisis caused a forced political and economic isolation for the United States.

A second factor was symbolised by Japan's aggressive policy starting from 1931; the country's expansionist action was never seriously opposed because of the economic crisis, which was at its peak at that time. Two years prior to Hitler's rise to power in Germany, the Japanese showed that it was possible to redraw the borders and the balance set up in the immediate post-war period, at least as far as the Orient was concerned.

While the economy of the richer nations had a tendency to restrict itself to national areas of interest, politics was globalising on an exasperating level. For example, both Russia and Great Britain were favourable to the emergence of Japan: Russia believed that sooner or later the Japanese would hurt British, French, and United States interests in the Orient, while London believed that the presence of the Japanese military in Manchuria would control and contain the Soviets.[13]

The last important factor was the success of National Socialism in Germany. The politics of the Third Reich, which aimed to subvert the international order, were favoured by a context marred by imbalance, mistrust, and revisionist projects in addition to the decisions by the various authoritarian regimes.

Italy, which until 1934 had been able to keep Germany distant from the internal affairs of Austria, changed outlook, as was said earlier, with the war of Ethiopia and the resultant politics of sanctions decided upon by the Western powers. From that time on, the Fascist regime entered the sphere of influence of National Socialist foreign policy. The League of Nations proved to be utterly incapable to stop the invasion of Manchuria by the Japanese and Italy's attack on Ethiopia. Quite possibly, this gave Hitler the courage to enact his policy of annexations, which began in 1938 with the *Anschluss*, the reunification of Austria with the Reich.

In September of that same year, at the conference in Munich between Germany, Italy, Great Britain, and France, a last and futile attempt was made to stop the race to war with Germany. The dismemberment of Czechoslovakia (the transfer of the Sudetenland to Germany) would have to satisfy Hitler's demands. The Soviet Union, which had been excluded from the Monaco agreement, began to fear that it would be isolated by Hitler's aggressive politics. Even though Germany had guaranteed that its demands had been satisfied at Monaco, in reality, France and Great Britain had resumed a frantic rearmament programme, albeit quite late compared to Germany. Shortly afterwards, in March 1939, while General Franco was winning the war in Spain, the Wehrmacht would go on to conquer Czechoslovakia, Bohemia, and Moravia without firing a shot, thus becoming a protectorate of the Reich.

As a response to Germanic expansionism, Mussolini decided to occupy Albania; however, at this point, Italian politics in the Balkans had been seriously compromised, with Romania and Hungary having entered the German area of influence.

New and precise land claims were made by Hitler to the Polish Government, then France and Great Britain decided not to make the same error they did in the past with Czechoslovakia, by guaranteeing protection for the entirety of Poland. Germany had gained advantages thanks to the stipulation of the non-aggression Molotov–Ribbentrop pact with the Soviet Union with which they established the division of Poland. Indeed, on 1 September 1939, Germany attacked Poland. Britain and France declared war on Germany on 3 September 1939. Thus began a war in Europe, which many saw as a progression of the conflict that had been interrupted in 1918 and for which the grounds had been laid by the collapse of liberalism as well as by the civil wars, the economic crises, the dictatorships, the paybacks, and the expansionisms, which had transformed the post-war period into a prelude to the new world conflict.

Mussolini's declaration of war on France and Great Britain was given on 10 June 1940 after nine months of non-aggression. If the police reports sent to the *Duce* at the beginning of hostilities pointed to the population's intense concern for the war and German aptitude to war, after the Wehrmacht's rapid victories in Norway, the Netherlands, and France, the monarchy, the military authorities, and public opinion appeared to have changed opinion.

Italy's joining the war at the side of Nazi Germany seemed to serve Italian interest; at that time, France was on the verge of collapse and Great Britain was isolated. As mentioned earlier, from 1936, Italy chose to align itself with Germany mainly because of the international isolation caused by the assault on Ethiopia initiated by Mussolini.[14]

Italian-German Cooperation: From 'Parallel War' to Subordination

> ... my unshakeable friendship with Italy and the *Duce* can certainly be considered an error on my part. In fact, it is abundantly clear that our alliance with Italy was more useful to our enemies than to us.... the greatest service that Italy could have offered us was to remain outside this conflict.

> To assure us of its abstention, no sacrifice, no gift on our part would have been great enough.… Our Italian ally has been a cause of embarrassment for us, everywhere.[15]

Although the authenticity of the text above is disputed, it nevertheless efficiently represents the thought process of Hitler as well as of a large number of German soldiers and officers.[16] In fact, there was a mutual prejudice about the Italian military abilities and a general aversion among the working class that was never diminished, regardless of the regime's efforts to the contrary. How then did the Italian–German cooperation proceed during the pre-war days and during the years of the war, regardless of the prejudices and negative conditions? In particular, what was the attitude of the *Regia Marina* towards their counterparts in the *Kriegsmarine* and *vice versa*?

Before responding to these questions, some necessary premises must be stated. The first concerns the preparation of the Navy compared to the Air Force and the Army. Of the three armed forces, the Navy was without a doubt the corps with the most advanced level of preparedness, and if a large part of the naval historiography underscores the 'high sense of duty and good preparation of the officers, the devotion and cohesiveness of the crews', it also admits that 'the British Navy was better trained'.

The war in Africa started late, and the reason for this is connected to the fact that Germany had lost its colonies during the First World War; therefore, only when Italy joined the war did the conflict reach African soil. Eritrea and Italian Eastern Africa (AOI) were very distant from Italy and had no hope of receiving supplies because of the English blockade. Nothing was done to prevent the collapse of the AOI, nor was it possible to attribute a plan to endanger Sudan (a country that was almost undefended) and its citizens to Great Britain. Briefly, the plan was to occupy a useless piece of land primarily to give journalists the chance to write articles on the Italian conquests and to await the final victory of the Germans in order to then sit at the peace table with the victors—all this without disrupting British sensibilities. Events transpired differently, and a short time later, the British, having become cognisant of the Italian inaction, reinforced Malta, which they assumed would fall along with all the Middle East.

The battle in North Africa was very difficult for Italy: the Italian forces had a considerable base in Libya and a larger number of soldiers compared to the British soldiers stationed in Egypt; however, the main problem was transportation of all supplies, ammunition, food, and petrol across the sea. Controlling the Mediterranean was crucial to the matter of supplies, and the Italian Army in Africa and the Italian–German Army at a later date entirely depended on the Italian Navy for the provisions that arrived from the Italian metropolitan territory. Even at the expense of great economic loss, the British were instead able to exercise continuous actions of disruption in the Mediterranean. Malta played a crucial role in this as aircraft departed from there as well as sometimes surface naval units, which intercepted the Axis' north–south routes.

Although plans had been made for the occupation of the island by the Italian Government, there was never a political desire to prepare such an attack. Despite Mussolini's desire to go to war, and as paradoxical as it may seem, the military aspect was secondary to his vision that was and essentially remained political.

At the beginning of the war, Italy had one of the most powerful naval forces of the world, in theory: two battleships and four almost ready to be pressed into service, numerous heavy cruisers, destroyers, and other minor units, as well as the second largest underwater force in the world (at least according to the amount).[17] The oil for the ships was in any event only available in limited quantities and was increasingly rationed as the war continued. Furthermore, the Italian Navy did not have its own aircraft carrier nor its own air force.[18] The Air Force did not have aerial torpedo squadrons and coordination with the Italian Navy was almost non-existent.

The British had a far superior fleet; however, they could only designate part of it to the Mediterranean. In between the two wars, Germany equipped itself with a ciphering system based on a machine called Enigma, whose messages the British were only able to decipher thanks to the creation of the computer device bombe, which decrypted Axis signals. The main problem for the Italian–German forces was the vulnerability of their shipping lane in the Mediterranean, which was constantly exposed to attacks from the British who would receive news regarding the resupply movements of the Axis through the bombe decoding system. ULTRA was the codename given to intelligence gained from these decoded signals.

Thus, Italian communications that went through Enigma were routinely deciphered and that is how part of the data of the *Regia Marina* fell into enemy hands.[19] From the beginning of the Ethiopian crisis, British plans envisaged an attack against Taranto, a main base of the *Regia Marina*; Admiral Andrew Cunningham completed the mission with success in November 1940.

Three battleships were damaged (one did not re-enter service), and the fleet was transferred to Naples and La Spezia, where the port facilities were more suitable to defending against attack.[20] A second naval defeat that occurred near Cape Matapan in March 1941 confirmed the British supremacy in the eyes of the Germans (who had been equally responsible for the events) and caused the issuance of extremely cautious directives for the fleet by Mussolini until it would be equipped with an aircraft carrier.

In the meantime, several important events occurred in North Africa. At the beginning of the conflict on 10 June 1940, the Italians had fifteen divisions in Libya, of which five were sent to Egypt. Mussolini was pushing for an attack, yet the Italian commander, Marshal Graziani, advanced with great caution only in September 1940, complaining to Rome about his problems with the procurement of supplies.[21] Graziani had succeeded Balbo who had been struck down at Tobruk from Italian anti-aircraft artillery.

Even though Balbo's presence could have not changed the situation on the ground, it is possible that his personality would have 'had a greater influence on the decisions and regarding the necessary measures to take in Northern Africa'.[22]

After years of praise from the Fascists, Graziani revealed his limits in Libya: it was one thing to fight against ill-equipped native forces with superior technical abilities, but it was an entirely different thing to engage the regular divisions of the British Empire.

The initial Italian advance did not meet any resistance: the British had abandoned their positions in good order without coming into contact with the enemy (moreover, the Italians advanced on foot while the British troops were motorised and could thus retreat with a certain calmness).

English General Archibald Wavell, commander of the troops in the Middle Eastern theatre, originally had only two divisions; however, had he wanted to reinforce the area, he could have brought more troops from the entire empire, from east of Suez, in particular from Australia, India, and New Zealand. In December 1940, a surprise attack hit the Italian positions, which were exposed on the Egyptian front in the desert.

The British surrounded a considerable number of enemy troops and rapidly pushed themselves ahead through Cyrenaica (a province east of Libya). By the beginning of February 1941, Wavell had conquered about half of the Libyan coast, establishing his headquarters behind Benghazi. Approximately 130,000 Italian soldiers and various pieces of equipment were captured, whereas the losses of the British Empire were insignificant.

After having 'faced' the British, directing operations from 'a Ptolemaic tomb of Cyrene, 30 metres deep and several hundred kilometres distant from the battlefront', Graziani was finally removed from his post after having lost the entire Cyrenaica and part of Sirtica.[23]

At the same time, the British Empire had won another victory 2,400 kilometres to the south, in Italian Eastern Africa (AOI). This war theatre was in a very marginal area and the biggest territory 'overseas' that was held by a European Axis force. With a large garrison of 90,000 Italians and 250,000 local troops under the command of the Duke of Aosta, Italian Western Africa constituted a threat for the neighbouring British colonies (such as British Somalia, Kenya, and Sudan) and for the passage of commercial ships through the vital artery of the Red Sea.[24]

On the other hand, the Italian colony was cut off from receiving supplies because of the English control of the Suez Canal. Addis Ababa fell on 6 April, and the Italian resistance quickly ended.[25] On 19 May, the Duke of Aosta surrendered in the mountain of Amba Alagi and the last regular troops commanded by General Nasi resisted at Gondar until 27 November 1941.[26] Thereafter, the British reinstated the monarchy of Negus Hailé Selassiè, in Ethiopia, he had already entered Addis Ababa on 5 May 1941.

After the winter victory in Egypt and Cyrenaica, the British Government made a serious error: the British forces could have completed the capture of Libya or at least consolidated their positions if Churchill had not moved some of his best divisions to Greece to support the government of Athens in its fight against the Axis.[27]

London's decision to intervene together with the Greeks had even more serious impact given the fact that Hitler decided to militarily assist the Italians in North Africa. In order to accomplish those tasks that the *Regia Aeronautica* could not do efficiently, several *Luftwaffe* units were sent to Sicily.[28] In the first months of the war, the island was strategically important both for its position and for the bombardments; additionally, it very close to the enemy base in Malta and the Luftwaffe could use the combat range from the various Sicilian airports, which allowed them to attack the enemy waterways.

The *X Fliegerkorps* had the double task of interrupting British traffic in the central Mediterranean and 'to act with bombardment units and minelayers against the Suez Canal'.[29] The German dictator had supported an offensive in the Mediterranean and in Africa ever since Italy joined the war effort, but its offers had been refused based on the principle of a 'parallel war' defended by the *Duce*.[30] When Mussolini accepted German assistance, it was already too late for an offensive action, and the Germans had to intervene in Libya, which was at risk of being entirely lost.

A more well-known fact is the involvement of the troops on the ground, initially just a couple of mobile divisions, the core of which would become known as *Afrika Korps*.[31] General Commander Erwin Rommel arrived in Tripoli in February of 1941. He had previously been noted for the excellent results obtained in France when he commanded the 7th tank division.

The German commander moved his scouting units towards the area of Sirte, and in March, he made contact with the British. On 1 April, Rommel attacked the British vanguards at Marsa Brega, defeating them and, after this initial success, he succeeded in reconquering Cyrenaica in fifteen days and laid siege to the Tobruk stronghold, which was land isolated and resupplied only via sea by the Royal Navy.

The British made several attempts to liberate the stronghold of Tobruk from the siege with the operations 'Brevity' and 'Battleaxe' in May and June 1941. Both the attempts to remove the Axis' siege on Tobruk failed, and Churchill, the British Prime Minister, replaced Wavell with General Auchinleck. After the last British offensive, there was a period of relative inactivity, during which both formations rebuilt their units.

Auchinleck began to prepare a new offensive for the liberation of Tobruk, while Rommel reinforced the defensive disposition. The garrison was constantly restocked via sea thanks to the superiority of the British Navy in that area of the Mediterranean, while the Axis was superior in its aerial abilities. The situation of provisions and restocking was particularly difficult for the Axis as they were losing a large number of ships to Allied attacks.

When Rommel decided to attack Tobruk in November 1941, Operation Crusader was launched, which proved a victory for Britain over Germany. Unfortunately for Auchinleck, external factors contributed to a change in the strategic picture: the Japanese attack that was in its infancy in December 1941 slowed down the Allies' efforts in the Mediterranean, immobilising numerous forces of the Commonwealth of Asia (Australian and New Zealander); furthermore, Hitler recalled the aerial corps from Russia, which were not usable due to the freezing winter conditions, and partially redirected them towards the African war theatre.[32]

In the autumn of 1941, over twenty U-boats were removed from operations in the Atlantic and entered the Mediterranean where they caused serious losses to the Royal Navy. In January and February 1942, Rommel reconquered most of Cyrenaica, repelling the British Empire forces. The important stronghold of Tobruk remained under siege for months, and ended on 27 November 1941, when the city was relieved by the Eighth Army during Operation Crusader following the surrender on 21 June after the results obtained at the Battle of Gazala (in May 1942).[33]

Although the *Regia Marina* still had considerable war potential and had been able to maintain the flow of supplies between Italy and Libya, the Air Force and particularly the Army had not been adequate in their conflicts with modern armed forces. Only the proximity of German units in Libya would give the Italians new capabilities on an instructive basis—by then, the parallel war so desired by the *Duce* had ended a year and a half prior.

Scenes from an Alliance

The alliance between Germany and Italy came to be for several reasons: the Italian adventure in Ethiopia and the international isolation that followed it certainly had the effect that some attribute to the rapprochement of Italy and Germany, not excluding the various missteps of international diplomacy and the mistakes of the Italian leadership. Among other matters, one asks oneself what importance did Germany give to the *Regia Marina*? Were the *Regia Marina* and its naval construction plans sufficiently attractive to the *Kriegsmarine* in a future war theatre scenario?

It has been said on many occasions that the German industrial apparatus was not even minimally comparable to the Italian one—it was superior in numbers and by tradition.

Furthermore, the German industry had been in competition with Britain since the second industrial revolution and had notably excelled in various fields.

The Italians came close often to important results as for radar and jet planes as well as other innovations both technical and doctrinal; however, these were realities that were not sufficiently developed in the pre-war period for reasons that had more to do with politics, the backwardness and fragmentation of the industrial system, and the rigid conservatism of the chiefs of staff rather than for the actual ability to materially obtain the desired results.[34]

What was therefore the main difference between the Germans and the Italians in research technology and testing of army exercises in the military field? In particular, in the naval department (the *Regia Marina* was, among the three Italian Armed Forces, the most powerful and most well-trained), was it perhaps Italy's power at sea that raised the German ally's hopes?

It was certainly one of the most important aspects, so much so that the fate of the war between the Allies and the Italian–Germans depended on control of the sea. Winston Churchill was trying to avoid a Japanese approach to the Italian–Germans, and he sent a message to the Japanese Minister of Foreign Affairs Yosuke Matsuoka in an informal way (it was hand delivered) through the British Ambassador in Moscow on 12 April 1941.

In this letter, written in a fairly direct tone, there were various issues listed according to points. In the first point, the British Prime Minister asked if the Germans would ever be able to invade Great Britain in the summer or autumn of 1941, without control of the seas and skies, and added: 'Would it not be in the interests of Japan to wait until these questions have answered themselves?'[35] For the fifth point, he focused on Italy, and asked: 'Is Italy a strength or a burden to Germany? Is the Italian fleet as good at sea as on paper? Is it as good on paper as it used to be?'[36]

The Prime Minister's questions were probably the same ones that the Germans asked themselves in the previous years as they considered the consequences of an alliance with Fascist Italy. From these questions, it is clear that the Italian naval forces emerge as an important factor in the calculation of political conveniences.

The Germans could not have been unaware of the more serious problems that plagued Italy, and particularly the armed forces; in fact, although bound by the Pact of Steel in 1939, the Italians had declared themselves unready to intervene in the event of a European war until at least 1942. When the situation appeared to deteriorate and pointed towards a war that would involve not only Poland, but also France and Great Britain, Ciano requested the compilation of the famous list of raw materials necessary for Italy to make it possible for the country to fight in the war. This request amounted to 16½ million tons of raw materials and various provisions.[37]

The Italian Navy, on its part, had already presented a lucid picture via Admiral Cavagnari's writings of the seriousness of the situation that would occur in case of war with the British and the French.[38] These warnings had also been given during the Ethiopian crisis by the Navy and Air Force sources, before all the endeavours of occupation of Ethiopia and Albania which would connect Italy to the most aggressive power of Europe and therefore definitely start the war.

On 9 August 1935, Mussolini requested plans in the eventuality of a war with the British Empire, alarmed for the new deployment of British Naval forces in the Mediterranean; on 13 August, the Chiefs of Staff met: *Regia Marina* and *Regia Aeronautica* stated they were not ready for a such a war; *Regio Esercito* stated it could deal with it.[39, 40]

Further communications from Chief of Staff Badoglio to Mussolini underline the utmost inferiority of the Italian fleet as well as the 'display' of superiority by the *Regia Aeronautica*, with old and worn-out aircraft that would not have lived through the first days of war.[41]

If these warnings had been given and the war had evolved in a negative fashion, much can be ascribed to Benito Mussolini who was the supreme decision maker in military matters. A few episodes will help us understand at which level one descended with regards to decision making for the military forces, including at an operational level. The first relates to the renovation work ordered for the reactivation of RN *Conte di Cavour*.

In April 1943, Mussolini would have the following response given to whomever requested that the useless refurbishment and modernisation of RN *Conte di Cavour* be stopped:

> … there are political needs and those of prestige towards the ally and the enemy which obligate us to the speedy operational return of RN *Conte di Cavour* ship … consequently no diversion of materials in the meaning indicated can be authorised as per the expressed instructions of His Excellency the Minister.[42]

The second episode concerns the task of choosing a heavy tank for Italy. General Caracciolo, who was in charge of the technical services, showed the *Duce* architectural plans for various possible heavy tanks. The episode is retold by General Caracciolo, here is how events transpired:

> Mussolini looked at the plans of the four types, he listened to my explanations, he again looked at the plans and then pinned his index finger on one of them and ordered: 'this one should be done'. And so it was.[43]

An absolute amateur in military matters, who relied only on himself and his 'unerring intuition' and loved showing off with theatrical gestures, would thus arrange the expenditure of hundreds of millions.[44]

Even in operational aspects during the tragic episode of Matapan, where initially it seemed that only RN *Pola* was in danger, it was Mussolini in person who gave the order to sink her if it would become impossible to retrieve her.[45]

At the peak of his career, Mussolini covered half of the ministries of the government, as Mack Smith records:

> Guido Leto, chief of police, complained that the *Duce* had no idea of the administrative issues, according to him, M. in his position as multi-minister, would sign orders that were contradictory even on the same day, since he had no time to read most of the documents that were brought to him for his signature.[46]

It thus follows that because the *Duce* was at the head of the three ministries of war (Air Force, Navy, and Army), the jealous independence of the individual armed forces and the lack of proper management of the generals couple with a Mussolini who did not 'want to establish a chain of efficient interforce authority (with real powers and a proper state government), capable of arranging programmes for war preparedness … both because he did not understand its importance as well as due to his clear aversion to give power to authorities that would limit his power'.[47]

Certainly, numerous (perhaps too many) generals pandered to the *Duce* and lied or allowed him to continue to delude himself concerning the true state of the armed forces. The Undersecretary of War General Federico Baistrocchi, although aware of the impossibility for Italy to conduct a quick war with the vehicles, the training, and doctrines available, nevertheless publicly declared in 1935 that 'a quick war was not only possible but certain and easy'.[48]

In 1933, when Balbo left the command of the aviation weapons to Valle, the number of aircraft in service was drastically reduced in a report by his successor (911 against the 3,154 declared aircraft); in fact, many of the aircraft were obsolete or not able to fly.[49] Besides, Valle did worse than that when General Pricolo replaced him in 1939, the aircraft that were delivered were noted in two charts, one regarding the entire air forces and the other to aircraft and their efficiency for war purposes. The total number of the first chart came to 8,258 aeroplanes and the second, 5,939. Nothing could be falser and deceitfully inflated and altered, 'after slimming down the list and subsequent check-ups, Pricolo can finally verify that the war efficient aircraft were 838 in total'.[50]

This does not mean that competent officials of high moral stature at all hierarchal levels did not exist: they were faced with a choice as to whether to express their dissent with conviction (assuming that conditions allowed them to do so) and be put aside (dictators and their sycophants do not like ideas that are not aligned with theirs, Admirals Thaon di Revel, Bernotti, and Ducci are examples of such behaviour), or perform their duty as best as possible within the limits of the system where they served.

Subsequently, in his meetings at Friedrichshafen in 1939 with *Grossadmiral* Erich Raeder, Cavagnari clearly expressed Italian availability in response to a German request to aggressively involve France and Great Britain on the Central Western Mediterranean and defended the position voiced by *Supermarina* concerning the priority commitment for supplies from Italy to Libya. Privately, the Germans came to the conclusion that, in case of a combined war, they would have to assure themselves the following:

> Italy does not go running after all sorts of prestigious targets (the protection of Libya or taking possession of Tunisia or Egypt), but that, in the interests of our common goal, she displays the most vigorous activity in the Western Mediterranean and, at the same time, persists in the strategic defensive in the Eastern Mediterranean.[51]

Aside for this agreement on principle, nothing else was accomplished at those meetings, a unified naval command was not established, and nothing was done to somehow connect the war theatres of the Atlantic and the Mediterranean.

For this purpose, Cavagnari and the Germans agreed to eventually send twelve Italian submarines to the Atlantic for the war on traffic, and a consistent exchange of information and operational concepts was expected, something which effectively did not happen at all.[52]

The basic reason for these failures and lack of collaboration can be found in the deep difference between the two dictatorial regimes that were pursuing different objectives. In regards to which, Santoni notes that Italian–German relations were not lacking in prejudice and jealousies; in fact, Hitler had started doubting the abilities of the Italian ally on the eve of the start of battle, while the *Duce* was envious of the more powerful ally to the point where he showed satisfaction in June 1940 when the French resisted Germany: 'Finally the Germans are wearing themselves out and will not arrive to the end of the war too fresh and strong'.[53] We leave it to the reader's judgment to decide which type of political and military collaboration could possibly work based on these conditions.

Japanese Naval Cooperation with Berlin and Rome: IJN Missions to Rome and Berlin

> *Between Japan, Germany and Italy there were truthfully many secrets, yet few problems in common.*[54]
>
> Admiral Nomura Naokuni

One of the first contacts in naval matters between Japan and Italy came about thanks to the sale of two armoured cruisers, *Nisshin* and *Kasuga* (this last one had been built by the Ansaldo company). It was 1904 when the two ships sailed from Italy, traveling towards the Land of the Rising Sun and becoming part of a fleet that faced the Russians at Tsushima.[55]

A concrete approach between Italy and Japan only occurred in the '30s; in fact, Japan's first expansionist plans towards China began in 1927–1929, after which a marked increase in Japan's diplomatic activity was noticed. While developing these plans, it was clearly evident that the armed forces were structured in a way that they could employ significant decision-making powers, side by side with part of the ruling class.

The first result of these projects was the creation of the puppet state of Manchukuo. Simultaneously to these initiatives, the Imperial Navy (*Kaigun*) postulated for the need of an expansion in domination of the area of the Western Pacific.

In the beginning of the '30s, the Army and the Navy laid down the law with ever more strength as proactive and propelling elements of the Japanese foreign politics to the detriment of those political components, such as Tenno and the Minister of Foreign affairs who had, at least until 1939, maintained their political positions prudent and moderate.

This is not to say that the Japanese Government was ignorant of expansionist ideas: the conflict against China in 1937 and the previous episode of Manchukuo had the approval and support also of civil components of both governments in power at the time, but a large part of it would have preferred to obtain similar results without armed contrast with the Western powers, as opposed to the military who approved of the option of armed conflict.[56]

Between the '20s and '30s, the idea had spread in the Japanese diplomatic circles that the Far East was going through a transformation and that its international equilibrium was changing in a deep way.

The Western countries had a less consistent military importance, while the Soviet Union, having established a strong Eastern army, was instead dangerously increasing its influence in the area. Based on these assumptions, a new role for Japan was developed.

The Japanese plan envisaged the creation of a new equilibrium in the Far East whereby the Land of the Rising Sun would be the only true military force able to guarantee stability. At the same time, it would operate in such a way as to gradually eliminate colonial interests of the European countries in the area.

The latter, and especially Great Britain, aware of the Japanese intentions, quickly understood that it was best to avoid an armed conflict with Japan considering the serious situation in Europe and of their uncertain military presence in the Orient. Until 1936, the Japanese Empire attempted to achieve its goal, at the same time trying to maintain discreet relations particularly with the Anglo-Saxon powers. However, by the end of the year, the situation appeared to have been compromised.

The manoeuvres of rapprochement between Italy and Japan were long and complex. At the beginning of the 1930s, the two nations had business relationships, economic interests, and diplomatic relations to the point of contrasting the two.

In China, Fascist Italy had promoted a policy of economic infiltration and a programme of technical military assistance.[57] Japan did not view this activity favourably, perceiving it as an interference in a territory that it considered its own natural area of expansion.

Italy, similarly to other European countries present in the Far East, observed the Japanese manoeuvres with fear and suspicion. In spite of that, the Italian Government decided to adopt a diplomatic view of cautious wait, continuing the economic infiltration of China while at the same time avoiding taking positions that were obviously anti-Japanese.

Also the Ethiopian issue was cause of friction between the two nations. In fact, the Italian colonial aspirations in Africa did not jibe with business relations between Ethiopia and Japan, which included, among other things, the provision of weapons. Nevertheless, in the first months of 1934, a slow and circumspect dialog began.

Some Italian individuals began to see the Japanese expansion in a new light: through its actions, Japan was endangering the interests of the European states in the Far East; it also emphasised their weakness and inability to coalesce in order to reduce Japanese demands, and questioned the role of Great Britain in the area.[58]

Based on these facts, and considering the military and economic force of Japan (the country had successfully exited the 1929 crisis before other industrial powers), an anti-Nipponese attitude on Italy's part with the goal of defending its interests in China would have been futile and perhaps counterproductive.

At that time, Italy needed to consolidate the markets in the Far East, yet a privileged relationship with Tokyo would have also allowed the Fascist government to play the role of moderator in the international controversies between Europe and Japan. Furthermore, the passive attitude exhibited by the European nations during the Manchurian Crisis could serve as a possible insight into Western reactions if Italy had considered and undertaken a colonial expedition

The attitude taken by Tokyo towards the Ethiopian conflict was proof of a nascent attraction between Italy and Japan.[59]

The events of 1935 were significant for bringing the two nations close, but also other circumstances worked together to make the convergence possible. The final deterioration of relations between Tokyo and London as a result of the conflict in China, the budding conflict with the United States, and the ever more threatening presence of the Soviet Union at the borders convinced the Japanese Empire to take what appeared to be the only way that would help it emerge from the isolation in which it had placed itself as a result of its foreign policy of expansion.

For Japan, it was therefore a priority to promote a policy favouring Italy, even before Germany, with the goal of also preventing an alliance between Russia and Germany. This theory was to be avoided as it would have placed Japan in dangerous international isolation. Additionally, on a military level, the understanding was similar: the Japanese Armed Forces observed Europe and were fascinated by Nazi Germany.

Since December 1936, and then with the official plans in September, November, and December 1937, the *Regia Marina* saw Japan as a natural rival of the Royal Navy for the control of the Indian Ocean.[60] In light of this grand strategy, an alliance with Japan would have made it easier for the ground forces to attack and defeat the British forces in North Africa and thus take control of the Mediterranean.

On 25 November 1936, Germany and Japan signed the Anti-Comintern Pact. The Italian wish to agree upon a similar pact with Japan was viewed with reservations by the latter. The efforts of German diplomatic representatives in Berlin and Tokyo with the goal of including Italy as an original signatory of the agreement and the outbreak of the war with China caused the Japanese to change their minds about including a third party in the pact.[61]

Shortly before Japan joined the conflict (on 7 December 1941), relations between Rome and Tokyo intensified and the number of Japanese military personnel increased considerably. Some military missions had the goal of increasing business exchanges while others were to study the conflict and its effects. It is important to note the presence of Japanese military observers in Taranto shortly after the attack of the British Royal Navy, quite possibly present in order to study the raid of the British torpedo bomber units in preparation for the attack on Pearl Harbor.[62]

The joint mission of the Japanese Navy and Army was received by Mussolini at a meeting on 19 May 1941.[63] The Japanese military had arrived in Europe between November and December 1940 with the goal of evaluating the status of German technology in the weaponry department. The visit, of what can be more appropriately called a board, was part of the agreements of economic, political, and military cooperation agreed upon at the Tripartite Pact undersigned a few months prior. Among the appointments of the mission, after the meeting at Palazzo Venezia, was an expected visit to the Western battlefront, as well as to some military installations and Italian aerial and naval bases. The delegates of the Imperial Navy represented the military in large numbers, totalling thirty-two officers.[64]

The members of the military delegation were led by Vice-Admiral Nomura Naokuni.[65] In the beginning of May, Admiral Nomura had sent to *Supermarina* (the Italian Naval Command) a substantial questionnaire that included eighty-three subjects to be evaluated. The questions represent an analysis of what was known about the *Regia Marina* (from the organisation to logistics, strategies, armaments, etc.). The members of the naval mission were headed by Rear-Admiral Abe. Three admirals (Giuseppe Fioravanzo, de Courten, and Ferreri) were dispatched by the Italian Navy Chief of Staff, Admiral Arturo Riccardi with 'the task of furnishing the Japanese delegates with all the information about organization, strategy, and tactics that they requested, without of course going into detail about matters of special secrecy'.[66]

In return, the Japanese delegation had to give data on *Kaigun*'s tactical doctrine to Admiral Fioravanzo. At the time, the greatest interest of the *Regia Marina* lay in the operations of the aircraft carrier, given that Mussolini had decided to convert the *Augustus* and the *Roma* having been forced by military evidence to admit the necessity for the conversions.[67]

The Japanese appeared interested in British combat techniques as well as combat manoeuvres and cruising formations, particularly of the attack of the Fairey Swordfish torpedo bombers against the ships anchored at Taranto the night of 12 November 1940.[68]

By way of introduction, it was taken into consideration that the features of the naval war in the Pacific could not be compared to the Mediterranean as the distances in particular would have removed the element of surprise attacks. However, there was clarity about one thing already in 1941, which, from a doctrinal point of view, the Japanese explained to their Italian colleagues:

> [After having pinpointed the enemy forces at sea through reconnaissance] it is a fundamental directive of the Japanese Navy that the prime objective of the carrier-based attack planes be the enemy aircraft carriers, since when these are sunk, the enemy's naval forces will be deprived of effective means of search, of launching torpedo planes and bombers, and of launching fighters for their protection. When the naval air forces are destroyed, one can say that approximately 50% of the war making potential of a fleet is destroyed.[69]

After this, more suggestions related to the defence of the aircraft carrier and the engagement of the enemy aerial fleet embarked had to be led in the so called 'pre-tactic phase', a phase that some call the 'pre-ballistic phase' given that the phase during which the enemy entered combat radius of the boarded Japanese aircraft was considered the 'tactical phase'.[70] Subsequently, there was a description of the standard procedures of navigation for these particular naval units as well as the formation for cruising and battle of the Japanese fleet. The most important of these descriptions, again, was regarding the position of the aircraft carrier regarding the main body of the fleet.[71]

That which interested the military men the most, we reiterate again, were the operations with the aircraft carriers, the tactical tenets connected to these units. Yet even while receiving this information, they always verified what they learned with the Germans, even though the *Kriegsmarine* for the aero-naval component was formed primarily by Japanese. In 1935, a commission of the German Navy received permission to inspect the aircraft carrier *Akagi*, which was being modernised again at the time at the Naval Arsenal of Kure.

This fact, certainly unusual due to the traditional secrecy of the Imperial Navy, allowed German technicians to gather precious information that contributed to better define the final plans of the aircraft carrier *Graf Zeppelin*.[72]

In fact, regardless of the consistent successes of the aviation of the Nipponese Imperial Navy, we remind the reader in particular of Pearl Harbor and of the destruction of the Force Z (namely battleship HMS *Prince of Wales* and battlecruiser HMS *Repulse*), the opinions of the military agents, and, in particular, of the naval *attaché* Toyo Mitsunobu and of commander Toyoda needed to be verified with what was discussed with the Germans.[73]

After all, the Japanese had been constantly underestimated by the Americans and the British, as both nations had no knowledge of the ability of Japanese aviators and of the objectives they had reached in the aero-naval field. Regarding the destruction of the Force Z, led by Admiral Sir Tom Phillips, naval historian Mark Stille wrote:

> The true nature of the Japanese air threat was unknown to Phillips and RN in general. The capabilities of Japanese aircraft and aviators were judged to be unimpressive, and probably not as developed as the threats that RN had faced in the North Atlantic and in the Mediterranean.[74]

Japanese military mission in Rome. (*Courtesy Fototeca USMM*)

We do not have any doubts regarding the professional merit and the analytical ability of the naval *attaché* at the Japanese embassy in Italy, at least if we keep in mind that a document written by Mitsunobu himself, which outlines his opinion on the events that brought about the fall of Fascism (written a few months later).[75] In this report, Mitsunobu effectively describes some of the problems that most afflicted Italian naval operations; according to the Japanese naval agent, in order to operate efficiently in North Africa, Italy needed to first be assured of its superiority in the Mediterranean:

> Instead, the naval operations of Italy in the Mediterranean were held primarily live with an armed escort for the reinforcement and resupply of the troops in Africa. Also, the British Navy operated with an armed escort of its convoys in the Mediterranean without trying to defeat the Italian fleet.[76]

Mitsunobu then continued to write that according to his opinion, after having studied the naval battles of Punta Stilo, Cape Matapan, Cape Teulada, etc., 'the collaboration between the Italian aviation and the Italian fleet was not sufficient':

> … the movement of the Italian fleet was always limited to the area where the Italian fighters could operate from land bases. Observing two aero-naval battles in the Straits of Sardegna and Sicily in the summer of 1942 during which English convoys suffered great losses, I observed that the Italian fleet and aviation fought almost independently. Furthermore, until this day no enemy battleship nor aircraft carriers have been sunk by Italian aviation.[77]

These observations of Mitsunobu implicitly bring us to the subject of the absence of aircraft carrier ships in the *Regia Marina*, even though they were said at a time when the use of an aircraft carrier was almost without any strategic value.

2

Regia Marina's Air Force Holy Grail: A Good Start and a Sad End

In 1920, the *Regia Marina* owned an organised and independent force of hundreds of aeroplanes, a set of air force bases, and a solid experience in terms of pilots, tactics, and strategies developed during the First World War.

Twenty years later, the *Regia Marina*, one of the five strongest navies in the world, entered the Second World War with no pilots, no naval air force of its own, and, in a context of difficult collaboration with the *Regia Aeronautica*, without having ever had aircraft carriers.

Why is it that in the 1918–40 timeframe the *Regia Marina* did not develop a strong naval aviation and doctrine? Why had Italy never built aircraft carriers? In three long years of war of attrition against the Royal Navy, the air power deficiencies at sea were, if not decisive, certainly significant.

In 1941, forced by the lessons learned at war, Mussolini finally demanded the immediate conversion of two liners in aircraft carriers, the future RN *Aquila* and RN *Sparviero*. Too little, too late, but, above all, the burdens to guarantee an effective naval air force were not removed.

Meanwhile, another path was developing: since 1941, a study had begun to convert the latest *Littorio*-class battleship, RN *Impero*, into a fleet carrier. The unique characteristic of such a transformation would have enabled RN *Impero* to act as aircraft carrier and as a carrier of rocket/jet weapons.

The political and military context, the hope to balance the conflict through new weapons, and the Ansaldo's *Ufficio Studi* (hereinafter 'US', Design Office) technical and design abilities will guide us to uncover, on the base of newly discovered documentation, the characteristics of one of the most innovative warships ever conceived during the Second World War.

The First World War

During the First World War, the *Regia Marina*'s air force expanded significantly, starting from the institution of the '*Sezione Idro Aeroplani*' ('Seaplanes Section') in Venice, 1912.[1] In 1913, Admiral Paolo Thaon di Revel being Chief of Staff, the aeronautical services were an independent section and the '*Scuola di aviazione Marina*' in Venice ('*Regia Marina* Air Force academy') was created. That same year, Captain Alessandro Guidoni performed in La Spezia a series of torpedoes trials launching from seaplanes, experiments that had inconclusive results due to the limitations of the vehicles of the time and the technical characteristics of the torpedoes.[2]

The initial war experiences demonstrated that the naval air force was very useful in exploration, reconnaissance, and antisubmarine missions. Consequently, new naval air force bases were established (in Venice, Taranto, and La Spezia), new support ships deployed (RN *Elba*, RN *Quarto*), and the number of pilots increased.

In September 1916, the organisational effort seemed to go beyond the *Regia Marina*'s resources: all its aeronautical services were given to the '*Ministero della Guerra*' ('War Department'), with the agreement that the War Department would progressively replace the *Regia Marina* personnel with its own.

An important clue of the necessity for a close cooperation between the *Regia Marina* and the *Regia Aeronautica* was provided by the disappointing outcome of this agreement. In 1917, the air services returned to the *Regia Marina* to guarantee successful results thanks to a staff with naval experience; further experiments of torpedo launching from an aeroplane were conducted.[3] A squadron of torpedo bombers was created in 1918 to attack ships at harbour or at sea.[4]

The First World War demonstrated the ability of performing attacks with aircraft launched from ships (Cuxhaven raid, 25 December 1914) and to torpedo ships (a Turkish merchant sunk by a Short 184 seaplane launched from the seaplane carrier HMS *Ben-My-Cree*, 12 August 1915). The first catapult used during the First World War was in the USN: on 5 November 1915, a seaplane was launched from the catapult installed on board the USS *North Carolina* (an armoured cruiser). The first two real aircraft carriers, HMS *Eagle* and HMS *Argus*, were launched before the end of the First World War.

Dive bomber Caproni Ca.5 launching torpedoes in 1917. (*Courtesy Fototeca USMM*)

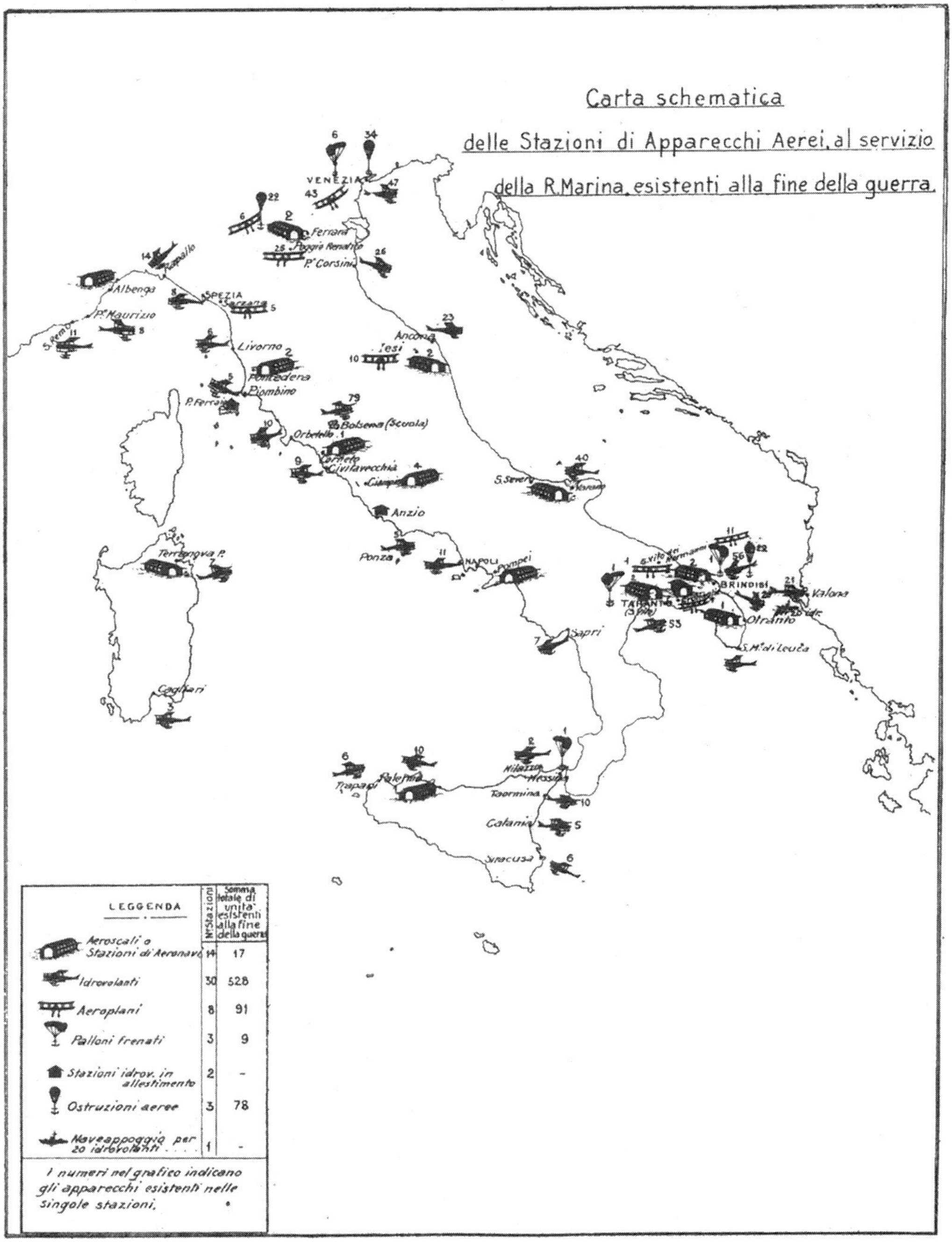

Regia Marina's naval aviation bases at the end of the First World War. (*Courtesy Rivista Marittima*)

At the end of the war, *Regia Marina*'s air service counted thirty-five bases, 638 aeroplanes (552 seaplanes and eighty-six ground-based bombers and fighters), 227 pilots (278 were the pilots belonging to the *Regio Esercito* (Italian Army) air force), and a force of 3,098 elements, plus ninety-six pilots and 961 elements assigned to the forty-six airships. The number of newly instructed pilots per year was fifty naval aviators.[5]

A total of 2,177 bombing raids, 3,467 reconnaissance or recognition missions in enemy territory, 9,433 search and attack on sea, 10,385 anti-submarine surveillance flights, and 1,107 air defence or attack missions were completed. The losses had been of 392 aircraft, of which forty seaplanes were shot down in combat (compared to 130 Austro-Hungarian vehicles of the same type destroyed). A total of 112 people (thirty-eight officers) were lost.[6]

A total of 1,630 aircraft were built for the *Regia Marina*, and 893 of these were stricken off for inefficiency or damage, proof of a too fast and probably too diversified development of technology.[7]

Douhet, Fascism, and the *Regia Aeronautica*'s rise

In the 1920s, the radical ideas of General Douhet emerged, stating the air force's absolute value and the necessity to integrate all existing air force branches into a single entity. Against this vision, in a heated debate, were Admiral Bernotti, Rear-Admiral Valli, and Captain Fioravanzo. They emphasised the enormous disadvantage of a fleet forced to fight against an enemy provided with a well-organised air force trained to war at sea and under a single command.[8]

Meanwhile, the *Regia Marina* had formalised its air force organisation: on 30 September 1920, the *Regia Marina* Air force was instituted, with a force of 939 men (fifty-nine officers).[9] In the limited framework of the available economic resources after the First World War, duties of naval aviation were identified: reconnaissance missions; reconnaissance in direct support to the fleet; torpedo attacks; and protection of the fleet. This was a doctrine not dissimilar to those developed in the navies that already had operating experiences with aircraft carriers.[10]

The importance of aircraft as weapons embedded in the naval formations had been clearly recognised, particularly with reference to the danger of the torpedoes, with a minimum complement estimated at 264 aircraft in peace times and 800 in case of war.[11]

The post-war demobilisation led to a radical reduction of the *Regia Marina*'s ships, writing off four old battleships and fifteen cruisers; the naval staff went from 120,000 men in 1919 to 34,000 in 1920. The fleet composition would have a decisive impact, along with the strategic assessment of France as a probable enemy, in the successive building decisions and programmes.

At the same time, a line of thought defined large warships as obsolete elements in comparison to airplanes, subs, and light, fast vessels, these ones no subject to treaty limitations; more balanced thinkers were instead in favour of an integrated strategy harmonically using all the available components.

In this context, in spite of the opposition of the *Regia Marina*, due to budgetary requirements, RN *Caracciolo* super-dreadnought was cancelled, as well as the reconstruction plans for RN *Leonardo da Vinci*, which had sunk due to Austro-Hungarian sabotage in Taranto and had been brilliantly salvaged.[12 13]

Similarly, the studies for the conversion of RN *Caracciolo* into an aircraft carrier were abandoned; such a conversion could have brought a precious experience in aero-naval operations and cooperation between forces.

In Great Britain, the problem was tackled in a more practical and less theoretical manner, thanks also to the greater availability of funds: from July 1919, the 'Post-war Questions Committee' had been formed. This committee was presided by Admiral Phillimore, who had confirmed the enduring merit of the capital ship. The committee made abundantly clear that aero-torpedoes had great importance for the fleet, to the point to recommend the building of two aircraft carriers.[14]

In July 1920, the British naval chief of staff, based on the experiences on the HMS *Eagle*, decided that a minimum of five aircraft carriers were necessary for the Royal Navy, even though there was still uncertainty as to which would be the best architectural naval solutions to choose.[15] With the testing completed, both in the wind tunnel and in an operational manner, the decision was to adopt an island on the flight deck. Thus, in 1924, Great Britain had three working aircraft carriers and three were being converted from other types.[16]

Japan had started its piloting courses for marine officers in 1912. During the First World War, it used a transport ship, the *Wakamiya Maru*, which had been modified as a seaplane carrier (with the ability to transport two assembled and two disassembled seaplanes); this ship participated in operations against German territories in China.[17] Through their experience with the *Wakamiya Maru* and observing the Royal Navy, the Japanese realised the importance of including some aircraft carrying ships in a modern navy.[18]

The construction plans of the fleet for 1918 and 1920 did in fact include the construction of an aircraft carrier. In 1920, Japan asked its traditional British ally for technical assistance in developing its naval aviation. So it was that between 1921 and 1923, the mission sent by the Royal Navy to technically assist the Japanese Navy was very useful for the development of the Imperial Navy's carrier force. Each aspect of on-board aviation was examined, from the training of the crew to the design details of the first aircraft carrier to the planning of her aircraft. The Washington Naval Treaty limited the size of the vessels, but not, in theory, the number of aircraft carriers that could be built.

Beyond theory, the political reality in Italy was quickly leading to a change that would have biased the military development. At the end of the First World War, many former pilots found themselves deprived of a role and began to join associations ideologically close to the Fascist movement.

Mussolini was a politician who understood and took advantage of the communicative potentialities of strong aviation as a symbol of a society projected in the future, free of traditional ties but founded on technology and rationality.

To the statements of the head of the Fascist movement, 'An Italian aviation, that will include a Fascist aviation' received more and more strong support from the aircraft industry (Caproni, Macchi, Capa, Salmoiraghi, Breda, and Bezzi (Ansaldo)).[19]

The great '*Adunata Aeronautica Nazionale*' on 27 and 28 March 1921, organised by the future prominent Fascist Bottai, saw the presence of all Italian aeronautic stakeholders with the only absence of the *Regia Marina*, which had its own men and vehicles.[20]

By the end of 1922, after the March on Rome and widespread illegal Fascist occupation in the north of Italy, Benito Mussolini was legally entrusted with the formation of a new government, and in this role, he would act with a non-Fascist-dominated Parliament support for almost two years before becoming a full-fledged dictatorship after the 1924 elections.[21]

Quickly, on 24 January 1923, a Royal Decree created the new '*Commissariato per l'Aeronautica*' ('Aeronautics Commission') and General Ruggero Piccio was appointed Head of the *Regia Aeronautica* at the joint dependencies of the War and Navy Departments and Mussolini himself, who at the same time took the role of Minister of the new Air Force Department. This organisation merged the efficient naval aviation with the non-existent civil aviation and the aviation of the Army, the latter poorly integrated from a military point of view.[22]

The beginnings of the new Army were uncertain. When Fascism came to power, there probably were 1,000 aeroplanes, some of which were unusable, and approximately 500 pilots (according to Mussolini's exaggerated lies, they had no aircraft and only a dozen pilots).[23]

The *Duce* of Fascism's wish to slander the management of the liberal governments is consistent with the propagandist position of creating a legend according to which Fascism worries for the fate of the soldiers who were forgotten after the Great War; it also raises the lot of the entire Air Force, including the pilots, and through Mussolini becoming one of them, it shines as the perfect metaphor for the national relaunch.[24]

All requests from the *Regia Marina*—aimed to save a well-organised specialisation deriving from the war experiences—were met with strong hostility from the newly born *Commissariato*.[25] Nevertheless, great Admiral Thaon di Revel, Minister of the Navy, managed to secure the naval air force specialities already established (recognition, fighting, bombing, and torpedoing).[26]

An example of results obtained thanks to the Grand Admiral's pressure was the contest for a 'torpedo seaplane for the high seas' in 1922; this brought about the production of the S.55, which played a role of patrol seaplane at long range until 1938. Even though torpedo launches had been tested, the aeroplane never had this weapon as a standard armament.

Formally, the requirements for naval aeronautics would have been dictated from the *Regia Marina* and taken up by the new Army. The path that would lead to the conception of the aircraft carrier and their pilots and aircraft as separate entities had been opened.

On 28 March 1923, the *Regia Aeronautica* was instituted; it encompassed the air forces previously belonging to the *Regia Marina* and the *Regio Esercito*: auxiliary air forces dedicated to the *Regia Marina* and the Army were created inside the *Regia Aeronautica*. Staff and vehicles belonged to the new-born force, but their operational use was under responsibility of the *Regia Marina* and the Army.[27, 28]

On 9 June 1923, Grand Admiral Thaon di Revel, who had previously expressed himself in favour of the aircraft carriers, asked the Admirals' Committee to evaluate the convenience of the aircraft carriers and the best type of units to select.[29, 30]

The directives of the Grand Admiral were very clear, the aircraft carrier had 'to have the possibility of carrying from the first days of the hostilities a decisive, rapid, violent, uninterrupted offense, pushed until the end against the enemy bases, its industrial and logistic centres, its population centres, its communication lines…' and it greatly differentiated itself from the prevalent assessments on the immediate ability of the aircraft based on land to quickly bring an offense on land targets directly from their bases.[31]

The Admiral's Committee would answer, reasonably, that the amount of vehicles necessary would be very large, while the necessity of directly participating in the war at sea, remained very strong.[32]

The new unit, to be regarded as 'experimental', had to dislocate less than 10,000 tons (to avoid Washington Treaty limitations), carry at least twenty aircraft, have a long range, a speed no less than 30 knots, and be exclusively used as an aircraft carrier, and not as scout, allowing a cutdown of protection and armament, in line with the simulations and the choices of the Royal Navy at the time.[33, 34]

Aeroplanes, and the solutions connected to take-off and landing, would have had to come from the *Regia Aeronautica*.

The *Comitato Progetto Navi* was in charge of further developments for the ships; the first draft was ready in February 1924 and full plans for the aircraft were completed in December 1924; in the meantime, the war games in August 1924 demonstrated the difficulties of coordination with the *Regia Aeronautica*, particularly when its staff was not trained to operate at sea. Great Admiral Thaon di Revel himself stressed the importance of an aircraft carrier, given the war game results.[35, 36]

A complete summary of the *Regia Marina*'s thought process at the time can be seen in the writings of Commander Giuseppe Fioravanzo, the winner of the contest for officers announced by the *Regia Marina* with the title 'On the opportunity of building aircraft carrier ships or of cruisers of the Trento type'. Fioravanzo was one of the most brilliant thinkers of the period between the two wars.[37] His idea considers with precision the opportunities offered by an aircraft carrier and the risks for a fleet lacking in them, as well as the features necessary for the aeroplanes of embarked aviation. Indeed, when the Second World War broke out, the problems were still holding at the level described by Fioravanzo.

The unit that was judged as minimally necessary was a fast aircraft carrier of at least 15,000 tons, two were needed to guarantee a sufficient amount of aircraft also to be used as 'strike' on distant targets. The weaknesses and inconsistencies of the proposed alternatives were pinpointed correctly as the aircraft carriers and the Gil (the large light cruisers, as the *Trento* were then called) were destined to operate as a task force.[38]

However, Fioravanzo appeared doubtful due to the existing challenges for the use of the aerial torpedoes; he recommended a compromise for the equal use of resources of an aircraft carrier and a squadron of destroyers. In this aspect, the lack of practical experience was felt, while these had been carried out by the Royal Navy in September 1919, and in September 1920, these experiences caused Admiral Roger Keyes to theorise about the use of the torpedo to slow down the enemy force and bring it to action even while retreating from the range of the British guns.[39]

When Fioravanzo went on to examine the usefulness of the aircraft carrier in the context of a limited budget and a war against France, the only possible enemy at the time, he correctly stated that it was not possible to give priority to the aircraft carrier rather than to the Gils and the light forces.

Essentially, this would be the position that the *Regia Marina* would have taken until the crisis of 1935 with the British Empire as the conditions discussed above would not have changed.[40] The strategic picture outlined was not complete in regard to one of its most important assumptions: that of the development of naval aviation in all its specialities.

On 8 March 1925, Great Admiral Thaon di Revel resigned from the position of Minister of the Navy in protest against the new '*Stato Maggiore Generale*', an entity coordinating the three services, always to be chaired by the Head of the *Regio Esercito*.[41]

The Great Admiral's resignations risked igniting an avalanche effect, with many first ranked, selected, and strong-minded naval officers ready to resign, first of them being the

Regia Marina's Chief of Staff Admiral Ducci. Admiral Thaon di Revel himself asked his men to remain to help build the new *Regia Marina*.[42]

On 4 May 1925, the new law for the *Regia Aeronautica* warranted thirty-five air squadrons for the *Regia Marina* (on paper: only nineteen squadrons were in existence, all ground-based), but stated that the construction of the airplanes and their characteristics were to be regulated by specific agreements between the two services.[43]

With Great Admiral Thaon di Revel's resignation, the *Regia Marina* lost the main supporter of the development of naval aviation and the construction of aircraft carriers, and the Great Admiral's ability to select officers of great value as his staff. Negative effects would develop very quickly when the Admirals' Committee was asked to choose whether to build aircraft carriers or traditional warships.

On 11 August 1925, Mussolini, being Head of Government and Minister of the Navy, chaired an Admirals' Committee meeting; the plans for a hybrid carrier/cruiser drawn by General (NC) Rota were rejected for being 'not convenient compared to a classic cruiser and not a substitution for a true aircraft carrier'.[44, 45] The construction of a true aircraft carrier was nevertheless set aside in the same meeting, being described as 'useful but not mandatory for the Italian Navy'.[46]

The Admirals statements during this meeting, constrained by a limited budget and considering the same operational weaknesses the Royal Navy was experiencing, were

Above left: Great Admiral Paolo Thaon di Revel.

Above right: Admiral Romeo Bernotti. (*Courtesy Rivista Marittima*)

anything but in favour of the necessity of the aircraft carriers, with the exception of General Rota, allowing Mussolini to sum up with the sentence 'the aircraft carrier is therefore unanimously discarded and the context of our discussions is now clearer'.[47, 48]

When evaluating the findings of the Admirals' Committee in 1925, it is necessary to pay attention and not to jump to simplistic conclusions such as 'The Admirals did not want the aircraft carriers', as is assessed even in serious historic analyses.

The evaluations were done in the context of the technology available at the time and with fragmented information (for example, it is evident that at the time the general opinion of the Admirals Committee, as in USA, was that the *Nelson*-class battleships would be a hybrid battleship/aircraft carrier), budget limitations were known to all; in fact, an aircraft carrier would not just be 'one more ship', but a ship 'instead of' one or more ships that were absolutely essential in a scenario where the only enemy in consideration was France and the obsolescence of all the major units of the *Regia Marina* was an incontrovertible fact.[49]

On 2 September 1925, the Air Force Commission was formally transformed in to the Air Force Department.[50]

The fairy tale of the *Duce* as pilot is one of the masterpieces of the Fascist talent for propaganda, a tale that was confirmed with the attainment of a pilot license by the dictator in 1937 (even though the airplanes piloted by the *Duce* had double commands and an excellent pilot flying next to the 'passenger' Mussolini, ready to take control).[51]

For Mussolini, aviation represented the possibility 'to use the prestige and popularity of aviators moulded by the war as efficient mechanisms in a prolific culture of consent activated to spread the nationalist religion of the homeland'.[52]

During the first years of Fascist management of the *Regia Aeronautica*, the young Air Force was exposed to the direction of Finzi (vice-commissioner) and Mercanti (general specialist), who were accused by the press (not yet subjugated to the regime) of speculation, cronyism, and excessive concessions to Fascist circles.

In 1924, Finzi's responsibility for the murder of the Member of Parliament Matteotti ended the period of the 'method of the arrow'—in other words, career advancement without merits other than Finzi's personal trust.[53]

The inadequacies of this management were numerous, so much so that the Army forced a general on Mussolini, Bonzani; he would be capable of reorganising and correcting Finzi and Mercanti's actions, thus giving the *Regia Aeronautica* a semblance of an Army. In November 1926, Bonzani was dismissed by Mussolini because, although he had filled his role well, he had not properly used the weapon for Fascist propaganda.

Budget and Requirements

Were the economic resources needed for a balanced development of the *Regia Marina*'s capabilities really available, while its warships in service, all built before the First World War, were quickly aging? Great Admiral Thaon di Revel in 1923 believed Italy could maintain its fleet 'as currently constituted', gradually replacing the obsolete ships, excluding new 'construction of great ships'.[54]

In spite of the emphasis on the support of military development, Fascism continued to keep a firm grip on budget control, at least until 1935.[55] The budget thus only allowed for a choice between the first *Washington*-type cruisers and one aircraft carrier at an equal expense. In 1924, the construction of an aircraft carrier was therefore reduced simply to a budget matter.[56]

In any event, the Great Admiral himself had hesitations in recommending the construction of a major unit (which he estimated would have to be a unit of about 25,000–30,000 tons, even though Fioravanzo's plans for the 15,000-ton carrier were available) instead of one or two modern cruisers, a type of unit the *Regia Marina* was desperately in need of, while its capital ships, the battleships of 'Giulio Cesare' and 'Andrea Doria' classes were inferior to France's (the probable enemy), opposing units of the same type.[57]

Furthermore, a building capability issue influenced the possibility to build ships over 200 metres long as large shipyards were not available. Between 1924 and 1931, only three shipyards in Genoa and Trieste had the needed capacity, but considering their building schedule, no slot was available for an aircraft carrier without first enlarging a shipyard.[58]

In the argument on the usefulness of an aircraft carrier compared to a cruiser (or two aircraft carriers against a cruiser and a squadron of destroyers) weighted the evaluation of the effectiveness of torpedoes carried by airplanes. The *Regia Marina*'s opinion was not positive and differed from the experience already developed by the Royal Navy in 1919 in the first attempts of torpedo attacks against warships at anchor and at sea (1920).[59]

A fleet composed of cruisers and destroyers was still preferred on the assumption that the probable enemy was France (and its Balkan allies). A war based on traffic protection, offensive action of light units, and Jutland-style confrontation between opposite battle lines was then the guideline for building.

Building against the Wrong Enemy

Did an Italian naval strategy (doctrine and shipbuilding) actually exist in the 1920s, given the economic constraints and the signing of the Washington Treaty? The answer lays in identifying the future possible enemy; at the time, Italy thought it was France, which reciprocated this attitude. There were historical reasons of disagreements regarding colonies and borders, enhanced by the alliance network (e.g. Kingdom of Yugoslavia), built by France to encircle Italy.

France always considered the naval parity with Italy stated by the Washington Treaty as a humiliation given its need to manage a worldwide colonial empire; parity was only accepted as the French naval theory attributed scarce importance to the larger warships, the only types limited by the treaty.[60]

Tension between the two nations was constant throughout the '20s, and it was a direct reason for the two nations not to sign the 1930 London Treaty (even if, for practical effects, both nations followed its rules).

Naval construction in the '20s and '30s was therefore beyond the Fascist propaganda, centred on answering to the new *Marine Nationale*'s buildings: France started the first Washington cruisers, Italy answered with RN *Trento* and RN *Trieste*; France built a strong submarine fleet, and so did Italy; France launched new heavier cruisers and the *Dunkerque* battle cruiser (laid down 1932), Italy opposed with the Zara-class and rebuilt two dreadnoughts to modern standards (RN *Conte di Cavour* and RN *Giulio Cesare*).

When France went with 'super destroyers', Italy replied with fast, very light cruisers.[61] The competition carried on up until the attempt of an Italian–French naval agreement in the first half of the '30s, which was never reached.-

The balance of force is broken when Germany started building 'Pocket battleships' (*Deutschland* (laid down 1929)), and France answers with a second battle cruiser (*Strasbourg* (laid down 1934)), followed by Italy with the first two modern 35,000-ton battleships (*Littorio*-class (laid down 1934)).

A clear example of Italy's will to maintain a balance of forces with France is the proposed 1928 naval programme, which at the beginning included one Bonfiglietti-type aircraft carrier, then ruled out in favour of the four heavy cruisers of the Zara-class in answer to the equivalent French units.[62]

New Warships Approved from 1922 to 1933		
	Italy	France
Battleships/Battle cruisers	-	1
Heavy cruisers	7	7
Light cruisers	12	12
Destroyers	46	70
Submarines	54	79
Total	119	169

After the Washington Treaty, the Washington-type cruisers are the warship types the navies were playing with, struggling against the limitations and trying to adapt the specifications to the different needs. This Italian–French rivalry is especially clear upon examining the building timeline for these warships, starting from 1922:[63]

Italian and French Cruisers Built between the Two Wars				
Laid Down	Name	Displacement (Tons)	Main Armaments	Speed (Knots)
1922	*Duguay-Trouin*	7,000	8 × 155	33
1923	*La Motte-Picquet*	7,000	8 × 155	33
1923	*Primauguet*	7,000	8 × 155	33
1924	*Tourville*	10,000	8 × 203	33
1925	*Trento*	10,000	8 × 203	35
1925	*Trieste*	10,000	8 × 203	35
1925	*Duquesne*	10,000	8 × 203	33
1926	*Suffren*	10,000	8 × 203	31
1927	*Colbert*	10,000	8 × 203	31
1928	*Alberto di Giussano*	5,000	8 × 152	37
1928	*Alberico da Barbiano*	5,000	8 × 152	37
1928	*Bartolomeo Colleoni*	5,000	8 × 152	37

1928	*Giovanni delle Bande Nere*	5,000	8 × 152	37
1928	*Foch*	10,000	8 × 203	31
1929	*Zara*	10,000	8 × 203	32
1929	*Fiume*	10,000	8 × 203	32
1929	*Dupleix*	10,000	8 × 203	31
1930	*Gorizia*	10,000	8 × 203	32
1930	*Cadorna*	5,000	8 × 152	36
1930	*Diaz*	5,000	8 × 152	36
1931	*Pola*	10,000	8 × 203	32
1931	*Montecuccoli*	7,000	8 × 152	37
1931	*Algerie*	10,000	8 × 203	31
1931	*Bertin*	5,000	8 × 152	34
1931	*La Galissoniere*	7,000	8 × 152	31
1931	*Jeanne de Vienne*	7,000	8 × 152	31
1932	*Duca d'Aosta*	8,000	8 × 152	36
1933	*Bolzano*	10,000	8 × 203	35
1933	*Attendolo*	7,000	8 × 152	37
1933	*Eugenio di Savoia*	8,000	8 × 152	36
1933	*Luigi di Savoia Duca degli Abruzzi*	9,000	10 × 152	34
1933	*Giuseppe Garibaldi*	9,000	10 × 152	34
1933	*Georges Leygues*	7,000	9 × 152	31
1933	*Gloire*	7,000	9 × 152	31
1933	*Maresellaise*	7,000	9 × 152	31
1933	*Montcalm*	7,000	9 × 152	31

The *Regia Aeronautica*'s Years of Records

While the naval competition with France was going on, which role did the new *Regia Aeronautica* play? The *Regia Aeronautica* was by now the Fascist's showcase Army, under the command of a man of qualities and power such as Italo Balbo, who was appointed Secretary of State for the Air Force in November 1926.

The aviation policy of the new minister was based on Douhet's theory of 'Dominating the air', yet this would no longer be a military Air Force ruled by the ventures of the individual ace fighter pilots of the First World War, but rather a new large-scale weapon that 'develops as a solid and qualified system of men and vehicles through which excellence stands out as a common feature'.[64]

This new air force, according to Douhet's predictions, could have completely modernised the pre-existing war scenarios. The nation that would succeed in securing control of the skies would be able to destroy entire enemy cities by using incendiary and chemical bombs until a complete surrender was given.

For this reason, the creation of a large aerial bombardment fleet was the *conditio sine qua non* of success, a choice that could have reduced the Navy's and the Army's auxiliary air forces, at this point reduced to secondary roles.

In the historic period in which this theory was expressed, the large bombers had yet to come; not even the construction of the big four-engined planes of the Second World War and the terrifying bombings that followed achieved the results imagined by Douhet.

The air power developed in a much more well-structured and flexible way, beginning with the support of the ground troops to the aerial division of the aircraft carriers. It is only during the years of the Cold War and the proliferation of missiles and nuclear warheads that Douhet's theory was proven.

Balbo's choice to use Douhet's ideas was partially because of his reputation and because of his abilities as a polemicist. Balbo therefore wanted Douhet to write for the *Rivista Aeronautica* magazine. The goal was to present again the theory of 1921, already expressed in *The Command of the Air*, strengthening the Air Force's demands at the expense of the other two services and further asking him to condemn any collaboration with the land and sea forces.

In order to accomplish this, Balbo guaranteed Douhet quite a large space in printed newspaper and several times attributed the new direction of the *Regia Aeronautica* to Douhet's ideas on condition that he would not criticise the actual developments of the *Regia Aeronautica*. In fact, Balbo's Air Force followed Douhet's theory only insofar as its goals and its strict refusal to collaborate with the other armed forces are concerned; yet at the same time, he never gave the attention Douhet wished to give to the development of bomber aircraft.

With sportsmanlike vision, following various records in the air, Fascism will only be able to grasp some aspects of Douhet's lucid and rational analysis, such as the immense and imaginative assets connected to flights and to pilots (Balbo's Atlantic cruise is the most famous event).

From a technical point of view, similar preference was given to spectacular aspects such as the speed records (the Schneider Trophy) and the cruises to South and North America by Italo Balbo (1930 and 1931)—many of the aircraft used were of the same types as those used in the war ten years later.

There is no doubt that there was a very close relationship between the *Regia Aeronautica* and Fascism: the Fascist symbol instead of the tricolored cockades on the wings of the aircraft, the aviation presented as 'favourite of the regime', the *Regia Aeronautica* as 'Fascist wing', the paintings, the symbols, and the declarations of Fascist saturation are numerous.

To illustrate and differentiate from the other armed forces, the crew members of the aeronautic cruises wore a black shirt under their flight suit, something that an officer of the *Regia Marina* would have never done. Furthermore, the *Regia Aeronautica* recognised the very Fascist Italo Balbo as its founding father, even though it was a relationship based purely on convenience where the aerial forces tried to take the most advantage from its connection to Fascism, initially for its consolidation as an independent force and subsequently for its expansion.

Its efficiency was marred by the development of too many prototypes and different models, as well as by having encouraged a very strict independence from the other armed forces. This brought about a lack of serious cooperation between the forces and, above all, the lack of an air force capable of operating efficiently at sea as a support for the fleet.

The following crisis will, in all respects, modify the politics of the Italian Government.

Rio de Janeiro, 15 January 1931. The Italian Naval Division and the '*Stormo Atlantico*' at the entrance of Guanabara bay. (*Courtesy BAUSMM*)

Italo Balbo in New York, 1930. (*www.futurodaunavita.sm*)

3

Projects and Ships: 1912–1930

1912 Guidoni's RN *Piemonte* Conversion Project

The plan was to build, at the stern of the old *Piemonte* cruiser, a wide hangar and a tilted deck of approximately 40 metres. The take-off of the aeroplanes would have had to take place through disposable undercarriages—they would be recovered after splashdown. At the beginning of 1912, the Royal Navy managed to launch take-offs from the HMS *Africa* and HMS *Hibernia* (moving at 15 knots) with similar solutions. The Royal Navy cruiser HMS *Hermes* was converted into a seaplane carrier in 1913 and the former liner HMS *Campania* was converted between 1914 and 1915.[1] HMS *Hermes* was sunk by a U-boat and another ship was laid down in 1918 and commissioned in 1919 as HMS *Hermes*, which was the world's first ship to be desgined as an aircraft carrier.

RN *Elba* Seaplane Carrier

The modifications to the protected cruiser *Elba*, already a support ship for observation balloons, envisaged the removal of the main superstructure, the main armament and part of the secondary one. A new platform at the bow and a hangar at the stern were added. The modified ships could carry three or four Curtiss Flying Boat seaplanes and a *Draken* balloon.

The transformation proved to be insufficient due the lack of space to host warehouses and workshops.[2] The ships remained in active service until 1916.[3]

RN *Europa* Seaplane Carrier

In January 1915, the *Regia Marina* obtained the funds for the purchase and transformation of a merchant ship destined to replace RN *Elba*.

The ship, named *Quarto*, was owned by a ship-owner from Genoa; it had been built in Britain (in 1895) and had sailed as *Manila* under the British flag and as *Salacia* under the German flag.

The purchase (740,000 Lire) was closed and the ship delivered to the *Regia Marina* on 6 February 1915. The conversion work lasted three months; two shelters, positioned fore and aft,

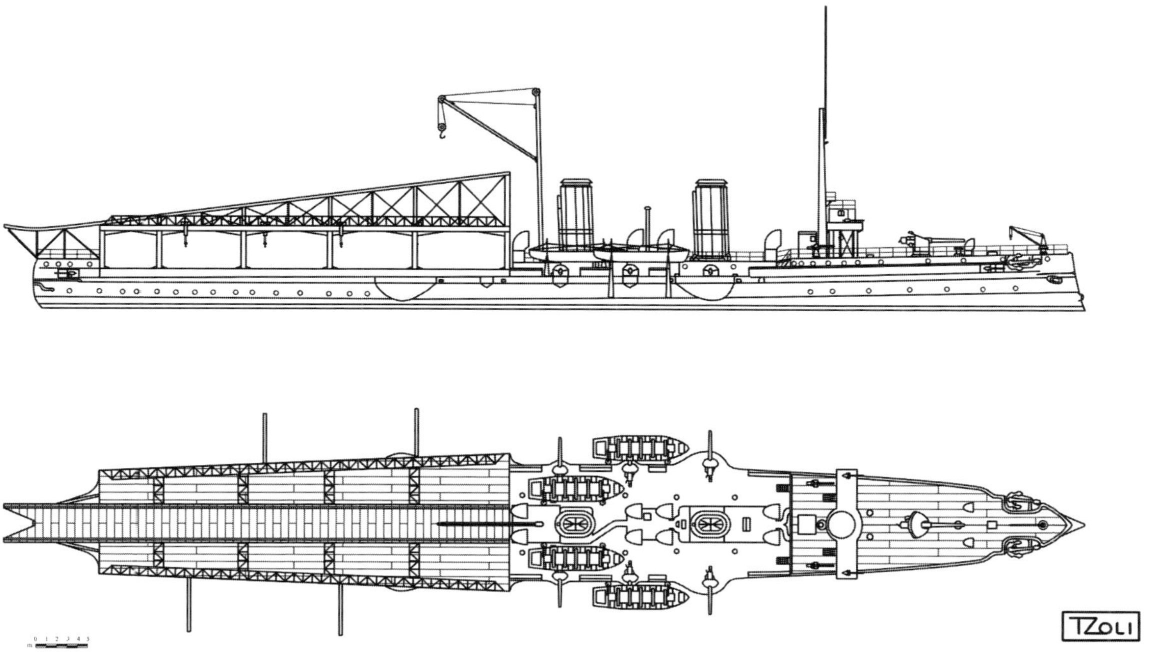

RN *Piemonte* as an aircraft launcher. (*Drawing by Tzoli*)

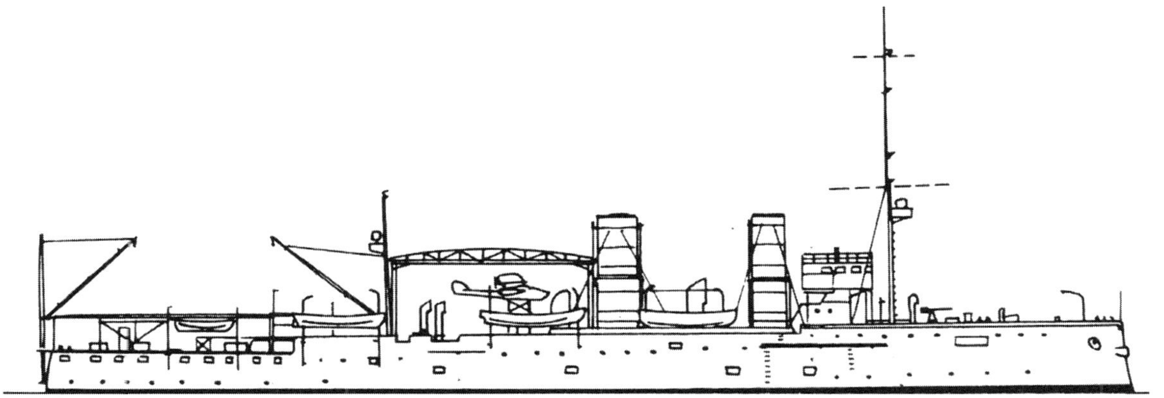

RN *Elba* in 1915. (*Courtesy Rivista Marittima*)

RN *Europa* at Valona, 1918. (*Courtesy Fototeca USMM*)

allowed for a total of eight seaplanes of medium dimensions. The needed services for their management were available on-board.

The speed (12 knots) was far from the desired one (18 knots).[4] The ship remained in service up to October 1919 and was written-off on 5 January 1920.

RN *Miraglia* 'Aircraft Carrier'

This unit, a ferry under construction acquired by the *Regia Marina*, would become the first catapult endowed ship. Launched in 1923 with the name of *Giuseppe Miraglia* and the official classification of 'aircraft carrier', it was equipped with two Gagnotto-type catapults at bow and at stern and had a total of eleven M.18AR seaplanes.

During the fitting, the ship had an accident that caused her to rest on its side on the bottom of the harbour because of a wrong weights distribution and insufficient stability. Once it was recovered, the outfitting works were delayed so much that the engine testing was only possible on 9 June 1927. She entered service in November 1927.

Stability remained a problem to control with careful attention. The only important missions, besides the training ones, were the participation in the Ethiopian war and the occupation of Albania.

The on-board airplanes were progressively replaced with the CANT 25AR and later by Ro.43 (1938); the tests for the new *Littorio*-class seaplanes were conducted on-board RN *Miraglia*; subsequently utilised as a barracks ship, it was taken out of service in 1950.

RN *Miraglia* (*Courtesy Fototeca USMM, Priore collection*)

The CANT 25AR (foldable wings) on board of a *Condottieri*-class cruiser. The aircraft was in service until 1937. (*Courtesy BAUSMM*)

RN *Caracciolo* Conversion Proposals

At the end of the First World War, the *Regia Marina* had two hulls apt to be converted into aircraft carriers, RN *Leonardo da Vinci*, sunk in Taranto for an explosion of the munitions depot due to Austro-Hungarian sabotage and later salvaged, and RN *Francesco Caracciolo*.

RN *Leonardo da Vinci* was completely empty and its structures seriously damaged from the explosion, while RN *Caracciolo*, empty and with no armour, was available; the plan of transforming her into a fast merchant ship (31,000 tons, 15,000 of useful capacity, 16.5 nodes, 17,000 hp, 14,000 miles at 10 knots) had been abandoned by the *Società di Navigazione Generale Italiana* that had acquired the hull.

RN *Leonardo da Vinci*, for which no conversion plan to aircraft carrier has been found so far, was dismantled in 1923; RN *Caracciolo*'s plans for an aircraft carrier conversion are in the Ansaldo archives, in two versions, each with two variations. A plan for a conversion to a liner, perhaps requested from the '*Società di Navigazione Generali Italiana*' itself, is also present. It seems probable that the conversion proposals were presented to the *Regia Marina* without success.[5]

Project 'A' Aircraft Carrier: Pg 582

The Pg 582 design envisaged a continuous flight deck ship, 185 metres long and with an average width of 25 metres. Under the flight deck, a large space nearly completely opened is present, under which is a closed hangar that is connected through an elevator to the flight deck.

All the flight deck superstructures, including the bridge and the charting room, were collapsible inside the deck.

The flight deck size is compatible with take-offs and landings with landing gears. Sixteen boilers, in three groups, were connected to the four axes, for a speed no less than 28 knots. Smokes were discharged at the stern. Eight double AA guns were the only armament.

The draught was 7.5 metres, and displacement was probably lower than the battleship; an armoured belt was probably present.

Project 'A' Aircraft Carrier: Pg 581

Version Pg 581 envisaged a flight deck directly on a hangar open on its sides.

Project 'B' Seaplane Carrier: Pg 580

Project Pg 580, in its two variations, was for a seaplane carrier. The flight deck was 135 metres long, starting from the stern, for a width of 25 metres. The command tower was at the end of the flight deck, and two AA twins and boat accommodations were placed astern.

There were twenty-two boilers for 100,000 hp and four shafts, with a presumable speed of 30 knots and an estimated displacement of 20,000 tons.

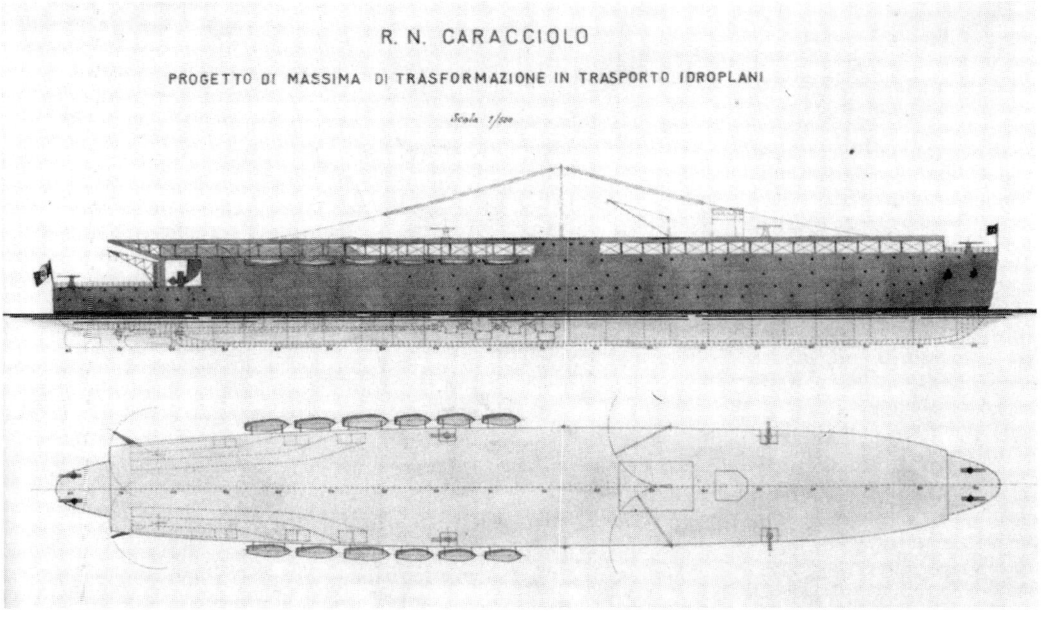

RN *Caracciolo* PG 582 external view. (*Courtesy Rivista Marittima*)

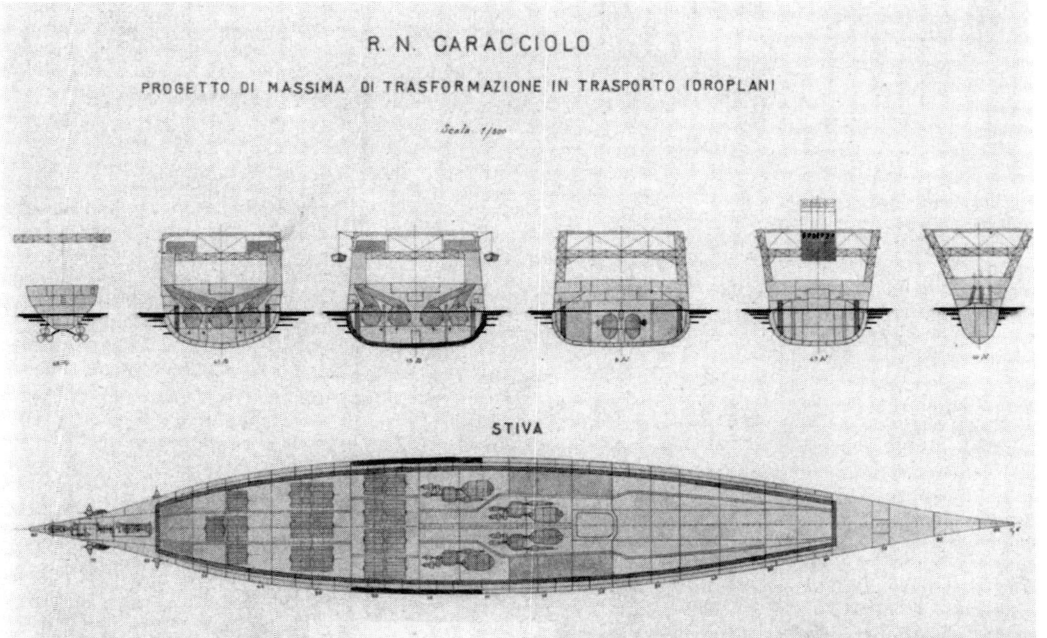

RN *Caracciolo* PG 582 sections. (*Courtesy Rivista Marittima*).

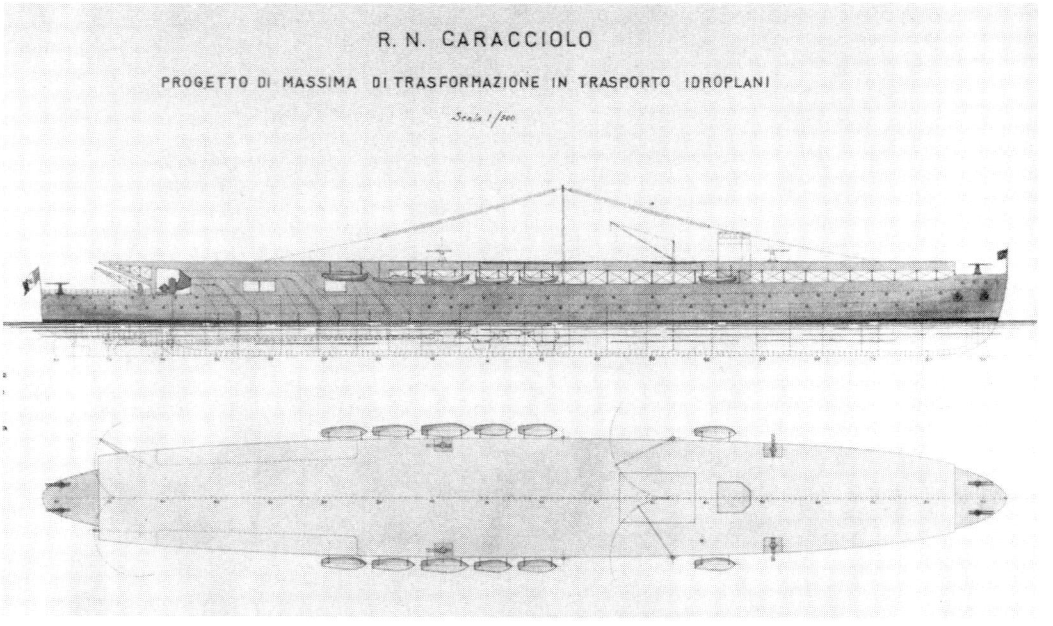

RN *Caracciolo* PG 581 external views. (*Courtesy Rivista Marittima*)

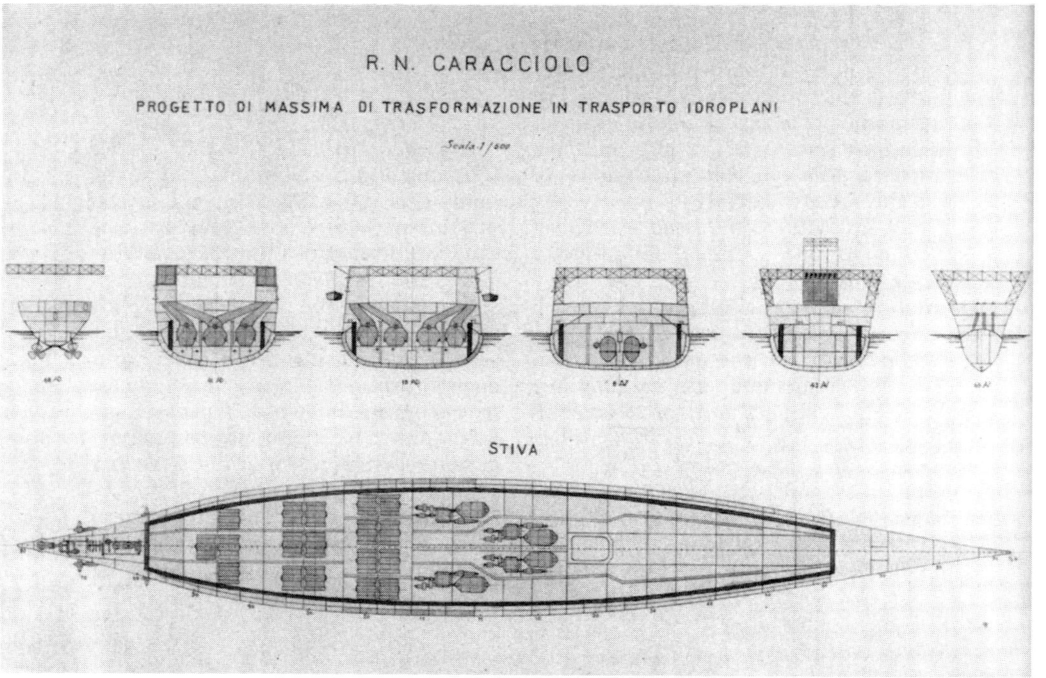

RN *Caracciolo* PG 581 sections. (*Courtesy Rivista Marittima*)

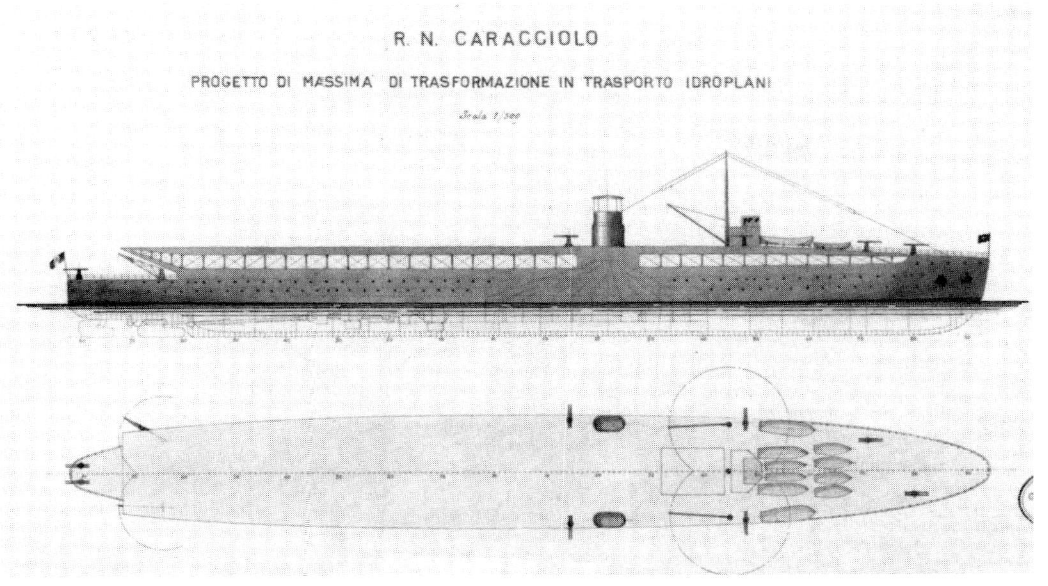

RN *Caracciolo* Project 580. (*Courtesy Rivista Marittima*)

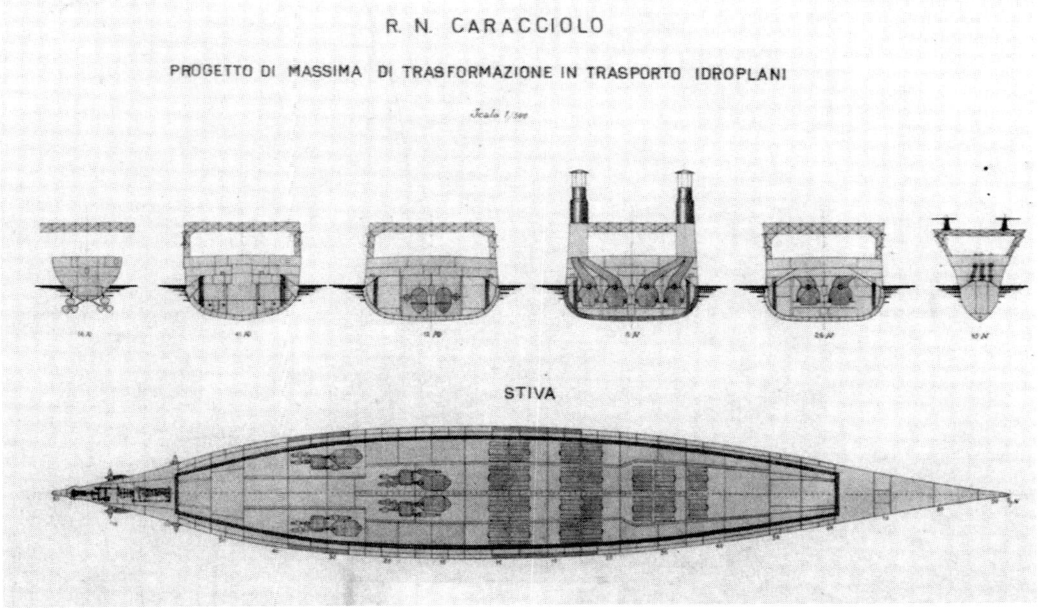

RN *Caracciolo* as a seaplane carrier. (*Courtesy Rivista Marittima*)

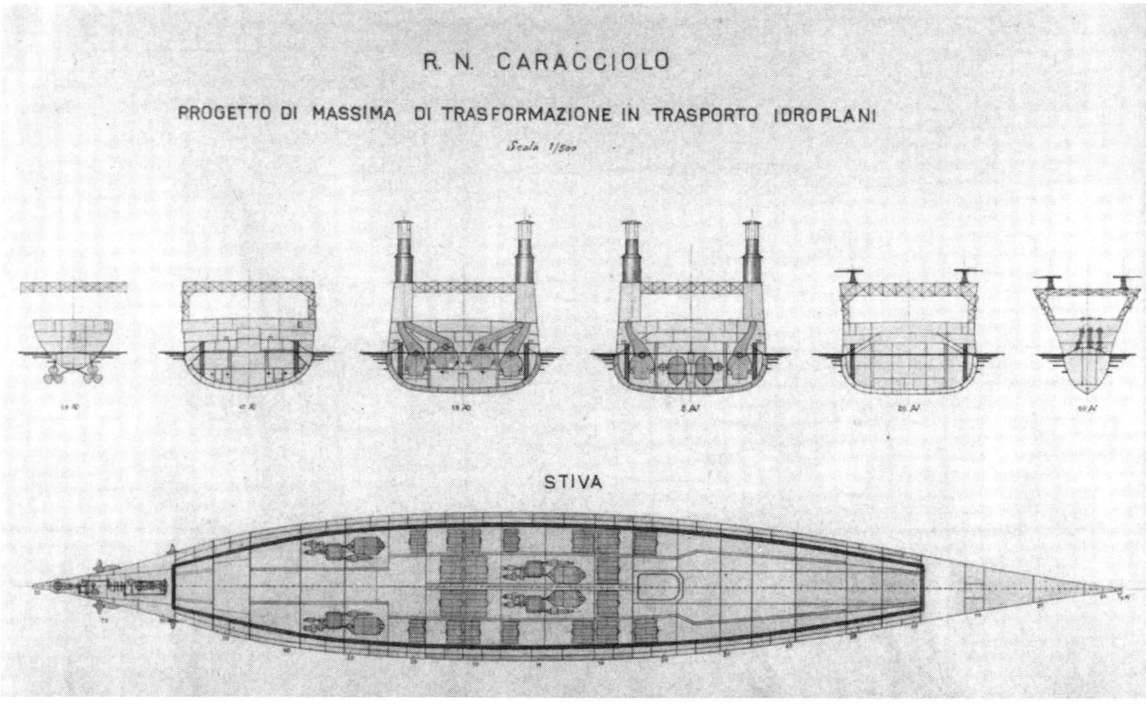

RN *Caracciolo* design Pg 579. (*Courtesy Rivista Marittima*)

TAVOLA IX - Variante al progetto di massima «B». Profilo.

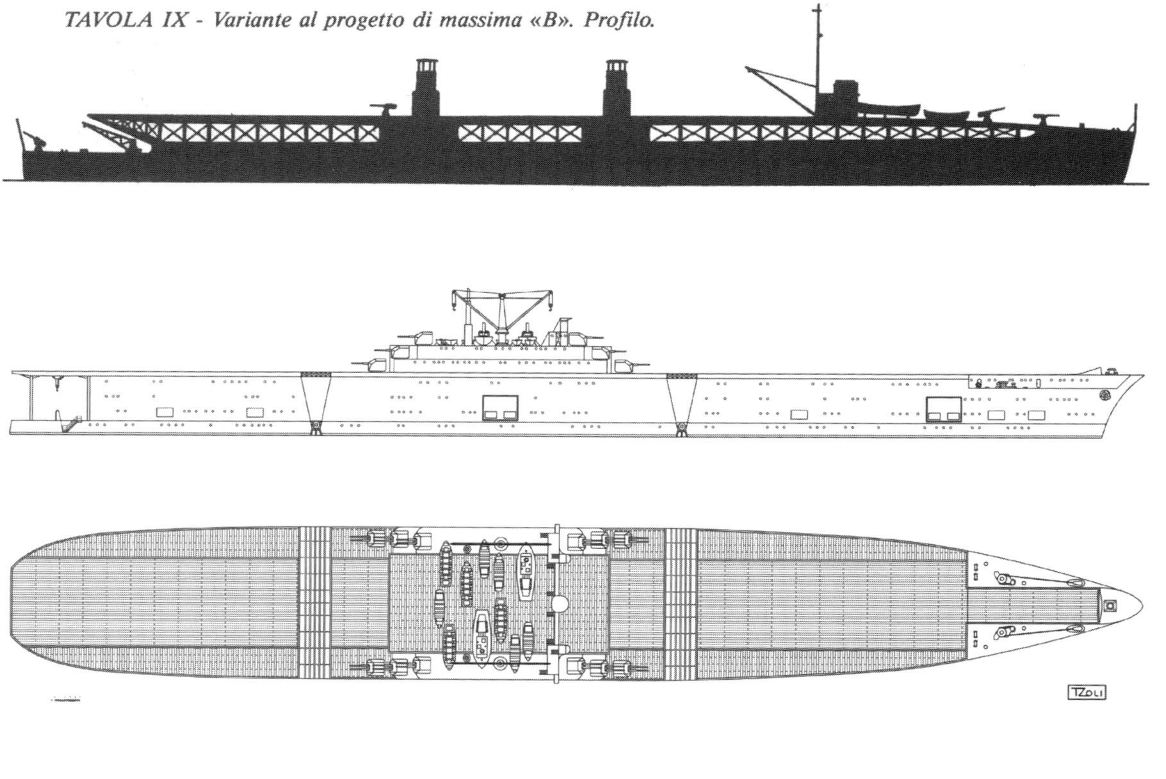

The Pg 579 variation had twenty boilers (twelve large and eight small) and four funnels at two sides of the deck. The speed was probably 20 knots.

The *Caracciolo* hull, retained in reserve by the *Società di Navigazione Generali Italiana* in Baia, was dismantled in 1927.[6]

Giuseppe Fioravanzo's Design (January 1921)

This proposal calls for an 'anti-aircraft cruiser': 11,000 tons, length 170 metres, width 21 metres, draught 6.5 metres, 70,000 hp and 30 knot, eighteen 102-mm or sixteen 120-mm, and sixteen fighters. A continuous flight deck, 175 metres in length and 21 metres wide, would have run on the entire length of the unit, funnels were to be placed on the sides. The proposal was not considered by the *Regia Marina*.

Giorgio Rabbeno's Proposal

The Rabbeno design was proposed on *Rivista Marittima* in January 1923 and is particularly interesting due to the technical solution presented as well as the author specifying the need to constitute 'offensive divisions, with a strategic aim, before the tactical one'.[7]

The air group was seven large (operation range 500 km) seaplanes bombers and twenty fighters/scouts, for 16,000 tons and a speed of 22 knots.

The dimensions would have been a length of 218 metres, a width to the waterline of 28 metres and a draught of 3 metres at full load.

The reduced draught, and the presence of propellers on the sides, was in order to ease manoeuvres in shallow waters, like current-day units for amphibious operations. Twenty-four guns in twin turrets were present, calibre unknown.

Rabbeno proposed an amazing articulated hull, with three sections connected via hinges (to be carefully verified in the Froude's tank) of 88, 70, and 60 metres each. The hangar, 155 metres long, 24 metres wide, and 9 metres high left a 20-metre free space at stern for the recovery of seaplanes.[8]

1924's Study for the Admirals' Committee

This design, made by the '*Comitato Progetti Navi* ('Naval Design Committee') is the answer to the request made by the Admirals in 1923.[9] The specs are as follows:[10]

Air wing:

16 bombers, 15-m wingspan (foldable), 24 fighters, 7.5–10.5-m wingspan.
6 'exceptional' bombers, 25-m wingspan (foldable) or 8 15-m wingspan (foldable), 24 fighters, 7.5–10.5-m wingspan.
168 × 28-m flight deck.

Cranes, warehouses, and aeronautic workshops.
12 152 × 50 in twins, two of them at stern on both sides.
36 knots.

A complete design was developed by 1924.[11]

Hybrid MAS Carrier: Aircraft Carrier (1924)[12]

A study by Colonel de Vito, developed upon request of the Admiral's Committee in 1923, presents a hybrid unit in three versions:

Project A) normal displacement of 10,500 tons, 200,000 cv at a speed of 40 knots.
Project B) 6,800 tons of normal displacement and a speed of 38.5 knots for 150,000 cv (with engines that were apparently identical to the cruisers of the 'Trento' class), 850-mile range at 38 knots and 2,400 miles at 24 knots. She was armed with eight 152-mm L. 50, eight 102-mm L. 50 anti-aircraft weapons, and 10 MAS (armed torpedo motorboat).
Project C) Derived from Project B, but with a completely empty flight deck, collapsible funnels as for the USS *Langley*, and the possibility of embarking fourteen to sixteen aircraft instead of the MAS. Total of 7,500 tons and other features as in 'B'.

For the 'A' and 'B' solutions, sea ramps were planned to be placed astern for the MAS, while in 'C', two cranes on an expandable deck would fulfil the function needed when the unit is used as a transport for MAS.

General (NC) Giuseppe Rota's Hybrid Carrier-Cruiser (1924–25)

This unit, designed in 1925, had a displacement of 12,480 tons and dimensions of approximately 170 × 23 metres; it reflected the operational uncertainty of the times. The continuous flight deck (with collapsible bridge and funnels when needed, and side smoke diversion) of 90 metres approximately, left space for two quadruple 203-mm turrets; twelve 40-mm guns were disposed along the sides; and a large slide to the stern allowed for the direct recovery of the seaplanes. The air group is evaluated as having eighteen to twenty aircraft.[13]

It is possible that the use of aeroplanes with landing gears was foreseen, considering that testing was conducted with arrest cables, near the small town of Monte Celio.

This solution would have been out of the boundaries of the Washington Treaty as a cruiser, as it would have been equipped with a flight deck so it would have been free to scale up to a 27,000-ton ship.[14]

Her cost gap with a Trento-type classic cruiser is low (120 million Lire (€16.5 million 2017): 152 million Lire (Trento) against 172 (Rota)); Rota's design was rejected in the Committee meeting of 11 August 1925.[15]

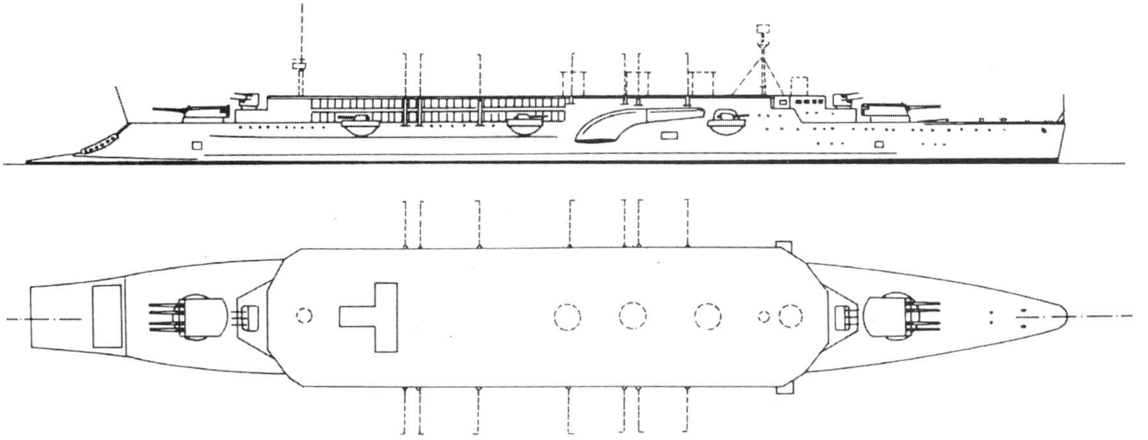

Above: The Rota's design. (*Courtesy Rivista Marittima*)

Below: The model of Rota's cruiser/aircraft carrier (aft) preserved at the *Museo di La Spezia*. (*Stefano Sappino*)

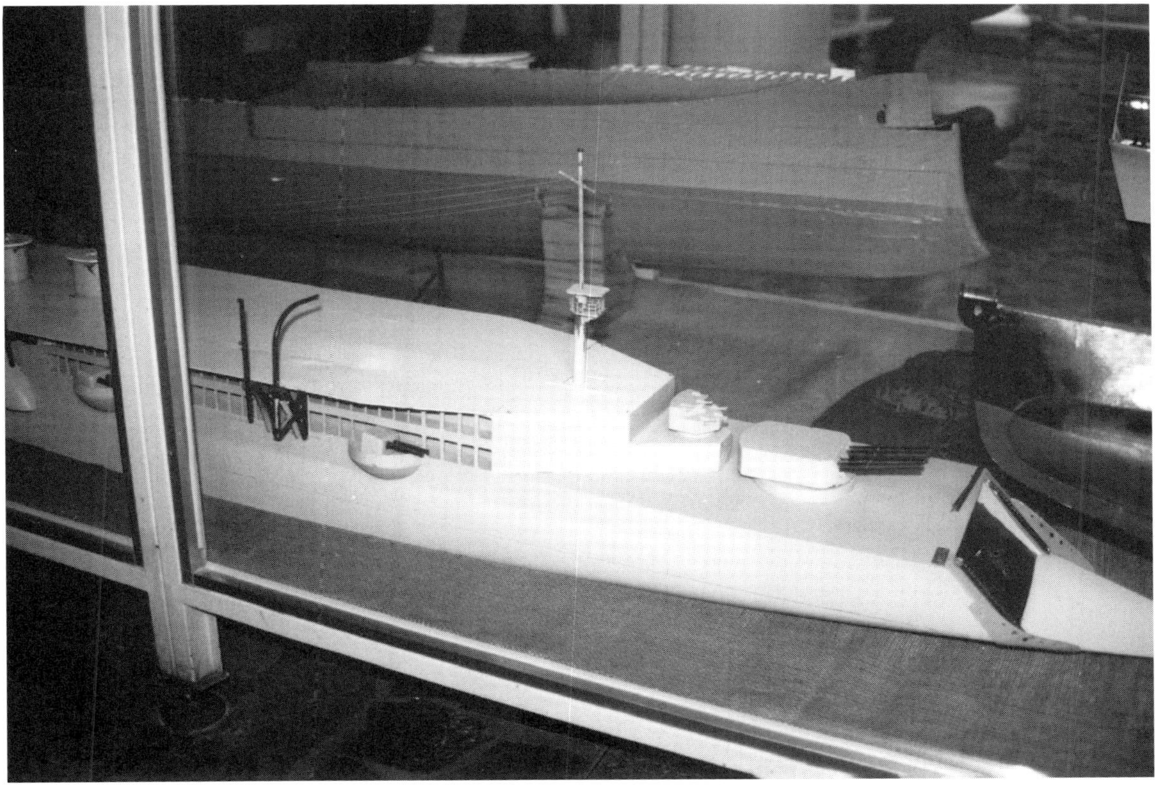

General Alessandro Guidoni's Catamaran Carrier (1926)

This design, definitely futuristic, is a revisitation of General Guidoni's 1912 concept; it required the connection of two destroyer hulls with a continuous flight deck and hangar, for a total of 3,500 tons, with a draught of 3 metres.

A power of 80,000 hp is created from a mix of four marine diesel engines, for a cruising speed of 14 knots, and ninety-six aeronautical internal-combustion engines that would have thrust the unit up to 33 knots.

The air group was ten heavy bombers, nine fighters, and six scouts; the armament was of four single 152-mm, two at bow and two at stern, two 76-mm L. 50 AA, and two 533-mm TT.

The flight deck had a length of approximately 100 metres and a width of 38 metres; a bow catapult would have enabled take-off directly from the hangar.[16]

It is worth noting that General Guidoni was perfectly aware of the experiences developed in other navies in the meantime as far as aircraft carrier operation were concerned. The General's death in 1928 placed an end to this design.[17]

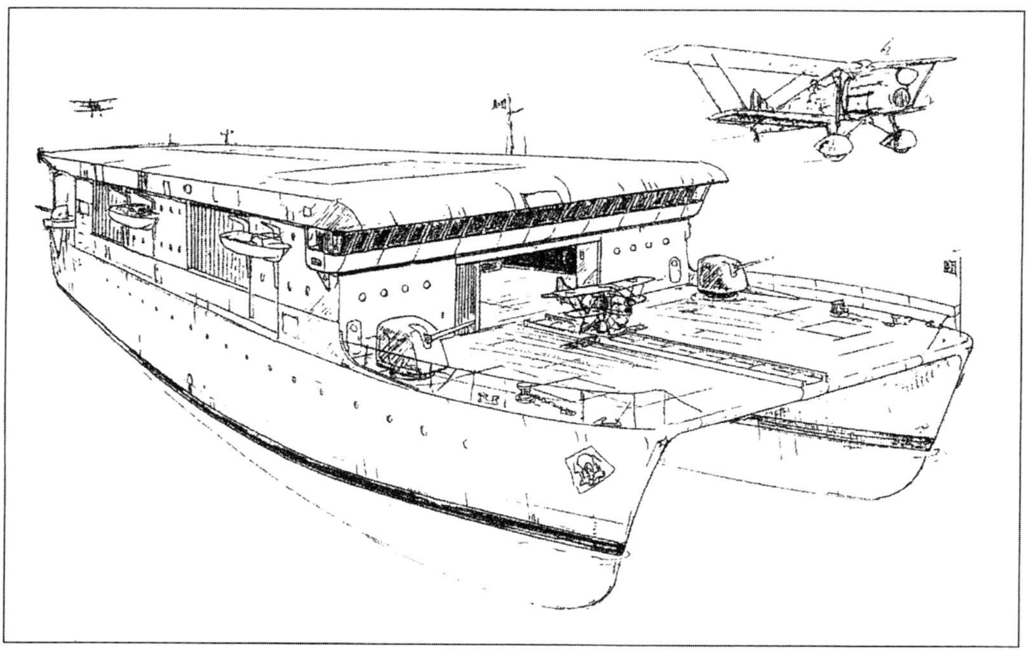

A depiction of the Guidoni catamaran aircraft carrier. (*Courtesy Dr Harrauer*)

4

Dark Times Coming

A Series of Relinquishments

The agreement between the *Regia Marina* and the *Regia Aeronautica* regarding aircraft and responsibilities was immediately disregarded by the opposition of the *Regia Aeronautica*, indirectly inspired by Mussolini and directly by Balbo.

In 1925, the *Regia Marina* intended to expand its air force to forty-five squadrons, in addition to the embarked ones, of course after the needed agreement with the *Regia Aeronautica*. The squadrons had to be placed along the Italian Libyan and Aegean shores and were to include bombers, torpedo bombers, fighters, and tactical reconnaissance planes.[1]

The *Regia Marina*'s strategy clashed with the wishes of Italo Balbo, a prestigious Fascist and the new person responsible for the *Regia Aeronautica*: he, too, was seeking parity with France, and the only way to achieve this, given the budget limitations, was to shrink the auxiliary air forces.[2] His air voyages, the transatlantic flights, held wild appeal for the Fascist regime due to its publicity opportunity, and his personal relationships with Mussolini made him an enemy who could not be politically contested by the Admirals of the *Regia Marina*. Although he immediately had all the powers equivalent to that of a minister (who formally was still Mussolini himself), he would receive political instructions from him; general military strategy was markedly absent.[3]

In 1927, the naval squadrons were reduced to nineteen, with the possibility to be raised to twenty-four by mid-1928.[4] Two memorandums from 1928 issued by Balbo's office stated that the tasks of auxiliary forces for the *Regia Marina* were not to include bombing and fighting and had to therefore be reduced to fifteen squadrons. 'The unity of the *Regia Aeronautica*' was not renounceable: even the observer on a reconnaissance plane had to be always under orders of his squadron commander; furthermore, the *Regia Marina*'s auxiliary air forces were to be stripped of traffic protection and coastal defence duties. No aeronautic command hierarchy was admissible outside the *Regia Aeronautica* (thus creating the seed for an independent structure).[5, 6]

To keep safe the autonomy of the new-born Army, a misleading use of Douhet's doctrine was made, not to build a strong doctrine for the air force but to defend the role and the life itself of the new department and avoid a roll back to the previous organisation, an air force divided between the Army and the *Regia Marina*. No effort to implement one of Douhet's strongpoints, the vehicles' standardisation in two types, fighters and bombers, was put into effect.[7]

At the same time, and to answer a *Regia Marina* request for aerial cover at sea from ground-based aeroplanes, the *Regia Aeronautica* said it would have been ensured by a seaplane specifically designed as fighter; considering a total autonomy of 900 km and the transfer time to and from operational zone, the real coverage was estimated in no more than sixty minutes, given the distance of the fleet was not excessive (100 km, 54 miles).[8] Even against their own data, Mussolini and the *Regia Aeronautica* continued presenting Italian geography as a 'Natural Aircraft Carrier': a good propaganda statement, but a military lie.

Admiral Bernotti, deputy chief of staff and an expert of air force operations, having personally taken part in two of Italo Balbo's famous cruises, tried to bring back attention to the issues of aerial squadrons for the *Regia Marina* and of the aircraft carrier, without success. It is possible that because of his opinion on the matter, which touched upon the delicate political balance between the *Regia Marina* and the *Regia Aeronautica*, after twenty-two months, he was 'promoted' as commander of a destroyer's squadron. In his own words: '… with the end of (my) role at the Chief of Staff office, the study of the project for aircraft carriers was abandoned only to be attempted again at a later date, in vain'.[9]

To further worsen matters, the role of General Chief of Staff, which had been created in 1925 and was a body that should have mediated and built military strategy, by 1927 had been already reduced (by Royal Decree on 6 February 1927) to an advisor, (now open to officers from all the services), forced to correspond with the various army branches through their ministerial offices (in other words, Mussolini), while war plans were to be reported to Mussolini alone.

The General Chief of Staff of the Army could instead communicate directly with all the state authorities. At the same time, in case of war, the General Chief of Staff was no longer the Head of Supreme Command; his office was limited to six officers directed by one colonel. Italy would not have a Supreme Command until 1940.[10]

On 27 January 1928, in a decisive meeting between the *Regia Marina* and the *Regia Aeronautica* on the topic of the aircraft carrier, with all the stakeholders present, the *Regia Marina* was defeated: Balbo's request for a reduction of naval auxiliary air force was approved (eighteen reconnaissance squadrons, twelve medium-range seaplanes, and six long range). The *Regia Marina*'s offensive aerial capability was no more. In the meeting, Admiral Bernotti gave a clear speech on the dangers a fleet operating far from its bases would face, like 'a blind person fighting against a person able to see', but was silenced at the end by his Chief, Admiral Burzagli, after the *Regia Aeronautica* Head of Staff stated: '…to us, the Mediterranean Sea is a puddle'.[11, 12]

This outcome was surely influenced by Italo Balbo's political weight, and by the fact that Mussolini had let his opinion on the matter be widely known beforehand as he expressed in his answer to a well-documented note sent him by Admiral Bernotti in 1927.[13] Again, in 1929, Mussolini's position on the aircraft carrier problem was reported: 'The Naval Projects Committee is studying the aircraft carrier, but the need for this type of ship has not been recognised yet by HE the Minister [of the Navy, Mussolini]'.[14]

Of the fifteen squadrons the *Regia Aeronautica* assigned to the *Regia Marina* auxiliary air force in 1929, one should have been for 'strategic reconnaissance' and two embarked. The *Regia Marina* officers were to be excluded from piloting functions.[15, 16]

However, the number of squadrons assigned was only theoretical as on 1 July 1929, including aircraft that were being repaired and reparable, there were twenty-one S.59 and 123 S.59bis (which could be used as reconnaissance aircraft, but were unable to defend themselves against enemy fighters), four S.55 for distance reconnaissance and four on order; for the embarked divisions, there were eleven M.18, plus seven on order, and fifteen M.7ter, both very outdated. The theory against this plan can be thus summarised (without counting the rate of replacement expected to be of sixty-five aircraft per year):[17]

July 1929	Theoretical	Actual
Close reconnaissance	218	144
Distant reconnaissance	8	6
Embarked	32	35

Balbo tried to get the same result with the *Regia Esercito*, but found stronger opposition thanks to the traditionally relevant role the Army had. In the end, he was forced to ask for Mussolini's direct intervention to unlock the new Air Force law, with a note on 16 June 1930.[18] With the new law, further limitations were set on the operational side for the auxiliary air forces.

In April 1930, the *Regia Marina* had tried through General Chief of Staff Badoglio to come to a conclusion regarding the size of its air forces. With a typical response of compromise, he assigned the 60 per cent to the *Regia Aeronautica*, 25 percent to the Army, and 15 percent to the *Regia Marina*. Unfortunately, there was no precise data regarding the total of *Regia Aeronautica*'s aircraft.[19] Badoglio's proposal was accepted by Mussolini on 15 April 1930.[20]

On 6 January 1931, a new law regulated the *Regia Aeronautica*; interestingly enough, the hierarchy's dependence on the on-board aircraft and a possible aircraft carrier was left to direct agreements between the two services. In any event, the *Regia Marina* had lost any negotiating power with its counterpart.

Once again, in 1932, General Chief of Staff of the *Regia Marina* Admiral Gino Ducci addressed the issue of the vagueness of the responsibilities, which needed to be solved in order to allow adequate studies to be made from his office: Badoglio, still General Chief of Staff, was interested. Ducci detailed the tasks which at that moment the naval aviation would have to take on. It was also detailed that even in the optimistic prediction that the *Regia Aeronautica* had 120 squadrons available, the percentage assigned to the *Regia Marina* would leave six of the necessary bases uncovered.

The General Chief of Staff's response was favourable on a formal level, yet vague at a practical level. Finally, in February 1933, the *Regia Aeronautica*'s answer became public: thirty seaplanes for strategic reconnaissance and ninety-two for short-range reconnaissance, with a conversion plan that brought them all to an autonomy of 2,000 km by 1938. It is hard to know for certain whether the numbers on paper matched the actual forces, given the unreliability of the data given by Balbo to his successor Valle at the end of his term (911 against the declared 3,154) that did not take into consideration the features of the aircraft as they related to technical advancements; at the time of the handover, the amount of the *Regia Aeronautica* for the *Regia Marina* was twenty squadrons, of which six embarked, with a total of 133 S.59bis, forty-five S.62bis and S.78s, and twenty-one Ca 111.[21, 22, 23]

The total inadequacy of ground-based aircraft to operate in action at sea pushed the *Regia Marina* to issue fall-back guidelines as equipping aircraft for distance reconnaissance with bombs, torpedoes, and smoke dischargers and using (admittedly without hope of effectiveness) embarked seaplanes as partial protection for the squadrons without aircraft carriers.

The same regulations also offered a completely non-realistic picture of operational conditions assuming that the aircraft could act without opposition. There was also total awareness of the necessity to achieve direct and reliable communications between naval and aerial components; in fact, direct communication between ship and aircraft would only become possible in 1943.[24, 25]

The aircraft carrier denial is no longer a military topic, but a way for the *Regia Aeronautica* to maintain full control of 'everything flies', and for the *Regia Marina* it was a way to get back its much-needed naval aviation. [26]

In Japan, which would go on to develop the best aero-naval doctrines prior to the Second World War, while the Washington Treaty restrictions remained in effect, they remained open to more operational directives that saw the carriers as reconnaissance providers, enemy detection, and anti-submarine control for the protection of the main battle fleet, composed by the units considered most important—the battleships.

In the beginning of the '30s, aviation technology reached a point where the carriers were seen as mobile platforms for the attack of enemy fleet (in the *Kaigun* plans namely the US fleet), and they were given a more important role compared to that of the previous decade.[27]

The debate between those who were in favour of the battleship strategy and those who were not lasted until the beginning of the Second World War and beyond; however, already by the beginning of the '30s, the importance of carrier combat had been acknowledged.

The next debate about doctrine was open to proponents of the dispersion of the carriers in order to have a greater chance of survival and between those who proposed to unite them in formation in order to have a 'greater striking force'. Ultimately, those for carriers' task force won, despite fear of their vulnerability.

On 6 November 1933, Mussolini was once again Minister of the Navy, and on 1 June 1935 accepted the resignation of the Chief of Staff of the *Regia Marina*, Admiral Ducci, who was pro-aircraft carrier, and replaced him with Admiral Cavagnari, at the time past undersecretary of state for the Navy. With this move, in addition to removing an admiral who was pro-aircraft carrier, Ducci who diverged with Cavagnari also about this issue, Mussolini was now Minister for both the Navy and the Aviation with undersecretaries who were also chiefs of staff.[28]

Additionally, Cavagnari assured that Admiral Bernotti, who was better qualified and would have been a better choice, would not have any important positions. Bernotti, who was a deep thinker, did not fail to voice his opposition to the easy lines of thinking and the wishes of the regime, with precise strategic and technical observations (including the necessity of having an aircraft carrier). For this reason, he was unpopular with Mussolini and the regime.[29]

The rigid division of duties, the lack of coordination between forces, and the absence of a real strategy for the forces produced, therefore, the paradoxical effect to strengthen the extreme wings of the two services, the supporters of the naval arm and those of aerial supremacy.

Mussolini thought it was still possible to take some time before deciding on the aircraft carrier topic, waiting for the outcome of Geneva's international disarmament conference in 1932. However, the conference failed, and in 1934, no final decision was taken on the detailed Vian-Bonfiglietti aircraft carrier proposal meanwhile designed. In a few months, the reality of the Anglo–Italian crisis would emphasise the price of this series of delays.

1930s Naval Aircraft

The reconnaissance squadrons are equipped with the not entirely satisfying Savoia S.59 and the on-board airplane is still the M.18 (thirty-two to thirty-five units).

With a financial plan in 1933–34, the situation should have improved, with the adoption of the S.62bis in two reconnaissance squadrons and a total of eleven squadrons for maritime reconnaissance. Furthermore, the embarked airplanes should have reached a total of forty-nine aircraft.[30]

The *Regia Marina*'s dissatisfaction of the overall situation was great, so the helicopters were considered (but the *Regia Aeronautica* promptly specified that they would never be part of the *Regia Aeronautica*) and the autogyros, with take-off and deck-landing trials in 1935 on a deck built on RN *Fiume*'s stern.

The outcome was positive and for some time the preliminary *Littorio*-class plans envisaged a flight deck at the stern for six autogyros.[31] The *Regia Aeronautica* managed anyway to confirm its authority on 'everything that flies' claiming the aircraft: the two autogyros were later wrecked in accidents.[32]

Subsequent developments lead up to the IMAM Ro.43 as embarked reconnaissance airplane and the CANT Z.504 as reconnaissance aircraft. These would have been the vehicles available at the beginning of the Second World War.

A series of contests launched in 1938 and 1939 to identify new aircraft to embark failed due to the contradictory requirements requested.

1935–36: Mussolini's First Crisis with the British Empire

The critical situation of the aero-naval cooperation and the opportunity and necessity to develop aircraft carriers and naval aviation were not limited to the military realm nor to that of the Fascist regime; in fact, precise discussions and arguments were held with Mussolini present at Parliament in March 1935.[33]

The Fascist foreign policy, and consequently the development of military components (with more serious results), continued to proceed in an overtly vague way; Mussolini—after having come to agreements, including military agreements, with France as an anti-German measure and the understanding of Stresa with France and Great Britain, starting from the Mediterranean crisis connected to the action in Ethiopia—did not want to choose a battlefield, hoping that the attitude assumed by both sides (the Western forces and Nazi Germany) would determine which battlefield would be more convenient, and wanting Italy to weigh in as the deciding factor at the last minute.[34, 35]

Above: Savoia S.59bis during the western Mediterranean cruise, 1934.

Below: Macchi M.18. (*Courtesy Rivista Marittima*)

Above: Savoia S.62bis. (*Courtesy Rivista Marittima*)

Below: A CANT Z.501 of the *Ricognizione Marittima*. (*Courtesy Fototeca USMM*)

On the other hand, Great Britain's stance towards Nazi Germany as regards to France's and Italy's will to place limits on German expansionism was very ambivalent, effectively removing itself from the safeguard of Austria's independence and shortly afterwards signing the Anglo-German bipartisan naval agreement to the consternation of France and Italy for this clear violation of both the Treaty of Versailles and the Stresa agreements.

In May 1935, the *Regia Marina* composed a draft of an optimal five-year plan (1936–40) for the fleet, for a total of 300,000 tons to be built in two phases, 1936–37 and 1937–41, and included three aircraft carriers, four battleships, four cruisers, twenty-four destroyers, twelve scouts, and fifty-four submarines, with the goal of obtaining a harmonious formation of the forces.[36]

In 1935, the unforeseen crisis with the British Empire, ignited by Italian goals in Ethiopia, suddenly modified the criteria and assumptions of the Fascist regime military policy and set again the aircraft carriers and the naval air force at the centre of the stage but also the beginning of an erratic and unbalanced foreign and military politics.[37]

On 5 July 1935, the Admiral's Committee unanimously expressed, looking at the changed international situation, the unconditional necessity of having a squadron of aircraft carriers destined to tactical operations with the fleet.

On 9 August 1935, Mussolini requested plans in the eventuality of war with the British Empire, alarmed at the new deployment of British Naval forces in the Mediterranean, and on 13 August, the Chiefs of Staff met. The *Regia Marina* and the *Regia Aeronautica* stated that they were not ready for such a war, while the *Regio Esercito* stated it could deal with it.[38, 39]

The *Regia Marina*'s Chief of Staff wrote to Mussolini a direct letter stressing the inability for the *Regia Marina* to do nothing more than act as 'naval guerrilla' and pointed out the availability, on the British side, of six aircraft carriers and 220 aeroplanes: a threat, escorted from the fleet, for any point of the national territory, a menace actually correspondent to the British plans:

> … had been a war with Italy over the Abyssinian crisis of 1935–36, it was the intention to use the carriers for attacks on Italian bases, not to retain them for future reconnaissance or for achieving air superiority.… Admiral Ramsey planned to use his carriers for bombing attacks on Port Augusta and the Catania air base as well as to launch a general assault on the Italian fleet base at Taranto with bombs and torpedoes.[40, 41]

Further communications from Chief of Staff General Badoglio to Mussolini underline both the utmost inferiority of the Italian fleet as well as the 'ostentatious display' of the superiority of the Regia Aeronautica with old fashioned and worn aircraft that would not have been able to survive the first days of war.[42] The international evaluation of the effectiveness of the very eye-catching Regia Aeronautica varied from the appreciation of the French and Germans to the more prudent approach of the British who were sure of the ship's ability for anti-aircraft artillery while still fearing the bombers.[43]

In truth, in a meeting on October 1935, Vice-Minister (the Minister being Mussolini) and Head of the *Regia Aeronautica* General Valle declared—while answering a direct question from Admiral Ducci—that in the event of a war, no more than five airplanes with light bombs were available against Alexandria.[44] Mussolini nonetheless maintained an attitude of

General (NC) Umberto Pugliese. (*Courtesy Rivista Marittima*)

self-assurance, perhaps counting on intelligence information that pointed to low AA ammo reserves for the British ships.

On 4 September 1935, Admiral Cavagnari, Vice Minister for the Navy, asked the *Comitato Progetti Navi* to prepare a design for a 14,000-ton and 38-knot aircraft carriers; the 'aircraft carriers topic', always to be intended only as far as the ship was concerned, given the rigid divisions between the services, and not as part of an integrated strategy, remained at the top of attention due the state of tension with the British Empire and the need for clarifying the political context before taking important choices for the evolution of the naval forces.[45]

The project remained confined within the *Regia Marina*: when General (NC) Pugliese asked to involve the *Regia Aeronautica* to jointly solve the air force/aircraft carrier interactions (issues by then resolved in the navies already equipped with carriers) and to ask for the aircraft's specifications, Admiral Cavagnari denied his approval, well aware of Mussolini's beliefs, as the *Duce*, on December 1935, after an Admirals' Committee meeting, answered Admiral Ducci, telling him that the *Regia Marina* required aircraft carriers: 'Or for what I think, that is, the aircraft carriers in the Mediterranean are useless, or for what S. E. Ducci says, that is there is no money, the aircraft carriers will not be built'.[46, 47]

The study regarding the aircraft carrier continued. In September 1935, the Comitato Progetti Navi asked specific questions; the *Regia Marina*'s staff answered them, demonstrating a good theoretical knowledge of the topics, but Cavagnari still maintained secrecy about the study.[48]

In March 1936, General (NC) Pugliese and the naval architects, having defined the general plans and carried out the Fraude tank and underwater resistance trials on scale models, stated that it was now mandatory to involve the *Regia Aeronautica* to solve specific technical points. Cavagnari this time authorised the involvement of the aviation industry, but still asked to keep the project classified, while informing his *Regia Aeronautica* counterpart, General Valle, in general terms.[49] Two exponents of the private aviation industry, engineers Zappata and Caproni, were involved in the project and the general specifications for two aeroplanes were settled; however, the involvement of *Regia Aeronautica* pilots to determine the characteristics of the flight deck and the landing techniques, including the stopping cables, still remained an unresolved need.

General Pugliese's efforts to better define the operational goals of the aircraft carrier units (Mediterranean or Ocean) collided with the need of Admiral Cavagnari to maintain an open line of communication with the *Regia Aeronautica*, despite the difficulties.[50]

Finally, on 12 July 1936, Admiral Cavagnari formally informed the *Regia Aeronautica*, requesting General Valle's cooperation. General Pugliese, on the other hand, thought that the *Regia Marina* could go on with the building of the aircraft carrier, estimating the open issues could be solved with the newly opened collaboration, since construction could not start before 1937.[51]

The duration of the crisis pushed the *Regia Marina* to propose the transformation in aircraft carriers of the liners *Roma* and *Augustus* (27 July 1936) to quickly acquire the most needed experience with aero-naval operation: a request refused due to military and economic reasons.[52]

The situation remained stalled, due to uncertainty on the final approval of the aircraft carriers features and the *Regia Aeronautica*'s reluctance to collaborate in something seen as a menace to its own integrity still being the *Regia Aeronautica* doctrine that the aircraft carriers were necessary for oceanic operations only.[53, 54] Mussolini's frequent quote about the necessity to have sea outlets on the ocean and the strictness of the opinions of the *Regia Aeronautica* brought the *Regia Marina* to continue talking, for deceptive reasons, about the aircraft carrier in the area of interest of the ambitious study of the 'escape fleet' (from the Mediterranean Sea).[55]

Even within the *Regia Marina*, the project of the aircraft carrier was subject to criticism from those who held that the displacement was too low for a balanced unit and from those who instead believed that the low level of protection was not compatible with operational use.[56] The horizontal protection had been abandoned because it was too heavy; its minimum estimate was 150 mm.

The concern for protection on the deck proved correct as the *Illustrious* aircraft carrier of the Royal Navy with an armoured flight deck of 76-mm showed great abilities to survive bombings.

While the Ethiopian war had significant impact on the international relationships, two more crises called the *Regia Marina* to heavy duty: the prolonged operations related to the Spanish Civil War (December 1936–April 1939) and the occupation of the Kingdom of Albania (April 1939). While almost no loss had been suffered, they had a toll on the warship's wear and on Italy's financial equilibrium.

The operational experience accumulated—in the context of a 'pirate war' as was with the Spanish war, which caused much moral discomfort to the men *Regia Marina* had involved—did not bring about an update in procedures and tactics, despite the lack of effectiveness of the strategy of submarine ambushes and of the torpedo launching devices.[57]

Whether combining the two endeavours (the conquest of Ethiopia and taking part in the war in Spain) had worsened the strategic situation of Italy on a global scale and rendered the naval component even more important is well said in a document of then Captain Maugeri, subsequently responsible for the Secret Service (SIS). According to Maugeri, the military position had drastically worsened with the economy becoming ever more dependent on international traffic. This would have led to a conflict with Great Britain exclusively of a naval nature, rightly appreciating the importance of Malta and the collapse of control in the central Mediterranean on the Italian side in case of retreats in Libya. The analysis further predicted the enormous traffic of supplies that would become indispensable with Libya, and it was noted that the Libyan ports were highly inadequate to the task.[58]

The fact that the 1928 relinquishment forced on the *Regia Marina* (not allowing it to have independent naval air squadrons) shows all its seriousness in the '30s, preventing the development of a cornerstone programme, the aircraft carrier, with independent staff and experience.

The 'Torpedo War': Why Italy Started the Second World War with Fifteen Aerial Torpedoes

During the First World War, the *Regia Marina* had already experienced aircraft torpedo launching through modified Caproni bombers, and from *Regia Marina*'s call for competition for torpedo bombers in 1922, there derived the double hull Savoia-Marchetti S.55; further trials were conducted in 1924 using the M.14.[59]

The 1923 and the 1928 laws regulating the *Regia Aeronautica*'s structure acknowledged that torpedo bombers were inherent to the naval war and therefore part of the *Regia Marina*'s

Savoia Marchetti S.55M. (*Courtesy Rivista Marittima*)

auxiliary air force; the first torpedo-equipped squadron was instituted at La Spezia, using the S.55.

The experiments carried out were positive, and the *Regia Marina* put together a manual of procedures for attacks that 'would be examined by the office of the Chief of Staff of the *Regia Aeronautica*'. The torpedoes used were modified spoils of war; furthermore, the *Regia Marina* had obtained a license for the Norwegian aircraft torpedo and had ordered the Whitehead torpedo factory in Fiume to create a weapon suitable for launches from aeroplanes.[60]

On 6 January 1931, a new law stated that the torpedo bombers were 'attack planes', and they were therefore to be removed from the naval auxiliary air force. The successive agreements (on 29 May 1933 and 1 September 1935) established that a certain number of aircraft had to be equipped as torpedo bombers and that the weapon's prototypes were the responsibility of the *Regia Marina* while the mass production of torpedoes was assigned to the *Regia Aeronautica*.[61]

The controversy between the *Regia Aeronautica* and the *Regia Marina* moved on in a 'suicidal' way from the hierarchical dependence of the aircraft to the specifications for the 'torpedo' weapon.

In 1936, the *Regia Marina* identified the ideal specifications for torpedoes: drop altitude of 100 metres and aeroplane speed at launch 300 km/h; the *Regia Aeronautica* rejected (October 1936) these specifications, requesting a drop altitude of 350 metres and aeroplane speed of 500 km/h. As a result, the situation was blocked until 1938, when even more extreme specs were detailed from the *Regia Aeronautica* side, for a weapon with a mostly aerial trajectory, a kind of torpedo bomb.[62, 63]

Further agreements led to testing of the torpedo prototype according to the *Regia Marina*'s specifications, the testing of which was interrupted in February 1938 due to the loss of a sample torpedo and the resulting bureaucratic issues between the production company and the *Regia Aeronautica*. Thus, the exact number for the minimum amount of successful launches necessary for the trial was not formally achieved (the *Regia Aeronautica* refused to consider as valid the successful launches done privately by the company).

At the meeting of the Joint Chiefs of Staff on 26 January 1939, the bureaucratic debate about the economic responsibility of the torpedoes regarding the order of thirty units was brought up: the *Regia Marina* considered them final while the *Regia Aeronautica* considered them still experimental.[64]

The project stalled after the last classes, which trained the Air Force personnel in torpedo launching in July 1936, all the while the debate, based on memos between the two branches, continued without any intervention from the Chief of Staff (demonstrating how little his decision counted) or by the Minister of the two services, Mussolini himself.[65]

In August 1938, when Germany started discussing a deal for 300 torpedoes with Whitehead, and a similar order was placed by the Romanian Navy, the *Regia Marina* tried to unblock the situation, directly interesting General Badoglio, Chairman of the Joint Chiefs of Staff.[66, 67]

On 18 November 1939, the situation was still blocked because of the issue of economic responsibility for the torpedoes.[68] Badoglio received the following answer from the *Regia Aeronautica*: 'General Valle says the Regia Aeronautica considers the aerial torpedo as a lesser weapon, as up to now its efficacy as a war instrument is very uncertain'.[69]

General Valle accepted that thirty torpedoes had been built for training purposes, but refused to sustain the costs. The incredible story reached Mussolini, at last, and General Valle stated that 'The *Regia Aeronautica* doesn't trust the weapon'.

On 6 September 1939, in a meeting chaired by Mussolini with three vice-ministers of the three services, General Valle suddenly declared the impossibility for the *Regia Aeronautica* to sustain a war, given the available fuel reserves (forty days of war only), the insufficient number of aircraft, the number further decreased by the 200 sold to the Kingdom of Yugoslavia (to be directly taken from the fighting squadrons). Mussolini's reaction was as follows: '40 war actions would be enough to win it, since the war is going to be a blitzkrieg…'[70]

Even though Italy had what was needed for years, only fifteen torpedoes were available in 1939, and finally, in November 1939, the *Regia Aeronautica* requested, based on contractual clauses, to divert fifty torpedoes from the German order and begin the mass production of S.79 torpedo bomber (seventy aircraft under construction), forced by the *Regia Marina*'s pressures and the evidence of the torpedo's effectiveness. The first squadron of five torpedo bombers would have been ready only in August 1940.[71]

Is there any justification for such behaviour? According to the direct testimony of General Pricolo, who replaced General Valle at the end of 1939, there was the 'constant worry that the development of the torpedo planes, sustained by the *Regia Marina*, would cause a dependency of the aircraft from the *Regia Marina* due the fact they were to be operated at sea'.[72]

One should not think that in other countries the collaboration between Navy and Air Force, embarked or ashore, was easy either. In Great Britain after the First World War, the elimination of the Royal Naval Air Service and the birth of the RAF caused a concern that the development of the torpedo would fall into oblivion.[73]

The effectiveness of the collaboration between the Royal Navy and the Coastal Command was criticised after the drills of 1931 precisely because of the inability of the latter to adhere to what was requested for the naval actions.[74]

The Royal Navy's requests to have an assurance of availability and control for ground-based aeroplanes were refused by Minister Inskip; operational control of the latter was passed on to the Admiralty only in April 1941, while still considered part of the RAF.[75, 76] All of these challenges did not compromise the development and implementation of an efficient doctrine for the embarked aircraft in the Second World War.

What level of collaboration was there between the *Luftwaffe* and the *Kriegsmarine* in the Reich? From the start, the organisational fragmentation at the *Luftwaffe* did not allow for a united vision for the Army even though the principle that aviation would have to fight in ground battles dominated all other ideas.

In 1934, Admiral Raeder had requested sixty-two squadrons of various types for the naval aviation, and Göring had promised he would deliver them, specifying that they would be part of an organic department, the *Luftwaffenkommando VI*, which would be under the *Kriegsmarine* for tactical command purposes.

The first chief of the General Staff of the *Luftwaffe* was Lt-Gen. Walter Wever (September 1933 to 3 June 1936).[77] Wever had very carefully read *Mein Kampf* (it was practically his strategic bible) and was of the opinion that Germany's main enemy was Russia.

Besides, Hitler had written that he did not want a revenge war against France and Great Britain, for this reason, the *Luftwaffe* would have to be built for a war against the Soviet Union. There was no opposition to this assumption that Germany would be involved in a large-scale land war.

Therefore, the debate on a strategic level moved from the discussion between those who wanted long-range bombers and those who wanted for the use of short- and medium-range bombers (which would be used as support for the Army, Hitler and Göring's position on the matter).[78]

The result was that the *Luftwaffe* 'largely focused on warfare over land rather than water'; it never had a significant task in improving the maritime air power even though, during the war, it gradually showed itself as being ever more important.

Hermann Göring further complicated matters for the already slim forces of the *Seeluftstreitkräfte* (Naval Air Arm). He was the commander-in-chief of the *Luftwaffe* who did not want to cede command of the aerial forces for the *Kriegsmarine* ('all that flies belongs to us'), thus depriving the *Kriegsmarine* of the strategic control of an important asset.[79]

In 1939, the squadrons that had been promised to the *Regia Marina* were reduced to only thirteen and they too would soon disappear, and just like with the *Regia Marina*, the German Naval Command only had limited jurisdiction on reconnaissance seaplanes and embarked aircraft.

When Hitler than authorised the start of a war to economically cripple Great Britain, thus blocking maritime trade, the *Kriegsmarine* was ready with submarines while the *Luftwaffe* was only able to carry out short-range missions (*Kanalkampf*) and did not have any long-range aircraft able to patrol the Atlantic.[80] The situation was partially solved by adapting a civil airliner designed for *Lufthansa*, which was quite successful (the Fw 200 Condor), there was still a clear separation between the two armies, Air Force and Navy.[81]

During the war, a few occasional specific cases of collaboration for some surface operations and the activities of the U-boats did occur and the *Luftwaffe* did not oppose the construction of aircraft carriers, given the oceanic nature of operations. Yet the *Graf Zeppelin*, launched in 1937, was never operational, both because of the interruption of work in 1940 and because of the impossibility to finish them after 1942, when, for a brief period of time, there was renewed interest in the aircraft carrier, which should have led to several new construction and conversions.

5

1930–40 Projects

Admiral Bonfiglietti's Projects (1928)

In 1928, a five-year naval programme was planned again, and it included aircraft carriers. In May 1928, the detailed specifications were established: the *Comitato Progetti Navi* developed a first design on 6 June 1928, and later a detailed project. All the documentation of the fully detailed project is today owned by General (NC) Filippo Bonfiglietti's heirs.

The specifications were for a 15,000-ton (to stay in WT limits), 28–29-knot, four twin 152-mm L. 53 Ansaldo 1926 turrets and eight twin 100-mm L. 47, and armour similar to the Condottieri-class cruisers ship.[1] The initial intention to adopt diesel engines, limiting the exhaust, was abandoned, as they never materialised. The engines were therefore similar to the Trento-class, with 70,000 hp, a 1,800-mile range at 29 knots, a 3,400-mile range at 22 knots, and a 4,200-mile range at 20 knots.

Given these specifications, the proposed design had the specs as follows:

Forty-two aircraft constituted the air group: twelve Fiat B.R.1 bombers with foldable wings, twelve IMAM Ro.1 scouts (six with foldable wings), and eighteen Fiat CR.20. The flight deck, 220 metres long and 30 metres wide at the largest point, had a 10-metre-long, 10-degree tilt at stern to ease landing. Three elevators connected the hangar with the flight deck, and no catapults or arrest cables were provided (but the possibility to install them if needed was taken into consideration in the plan).

The armament, besides the four twin 152-mm L. 53 was twelve 100-mm L. 47 OTO in twin turrets and four twin 37-mm L. 54 placed on the island; a 90-metre-long Pugliese system (5.10 metres in width) was the torpedo defence system, asymmetrically built to compensate the island's weight, completed by a triple bottom.

Armour was designed this way: side armour (all Ni-CR plate); 60 mm, starting 1.65 metres below waterline up to 2.85 metres above, 90 metres in length; avio fuel deposits protected by 50-mm armour; hangars: 20-mm side armour; horizontal protection; flight deck, 35-mm armour; second level, 15-mm armour; hangar deck, 40-mm armour and 60 mm at the fourth level.

The expected crew was 1,112 men, of which seventy-eight officers were divided between *Regia Marina* and *Regia Aeronautica*.[2]

The absence of catapults is significant; General Bonfiglietti judged them 'considerably complicated, an encumbrance and, according to some, could cause a delay in launch operations'.[3]

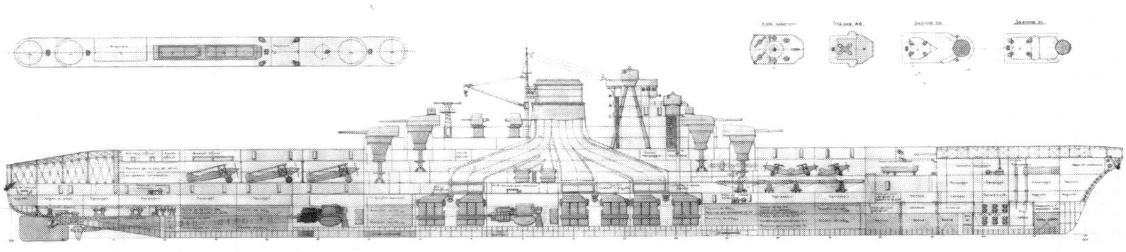

General (NC) Bonfiglietti's project. (*Courtesy Ing. Filippo Bonfiglietti*)

Above: General (NC) Bonfiglietti's model. (*Courtesy Ing. Filippo Bonfiglietti*)

Below: General (NC) Bonfiglietti's model, stern detail. (*Courtesy Ing. Filippo Bonfiglietti*)

During 1929–31, four versions of this project were drawn. The 1931 'D' proposal was rather different, with a much smaller island moved aft to ease the operations of landing and funnels on the side. Specifications for this variation were a 200 × 28-metre flight deck, 26 knots for a displacement of 11,500 tons, and a thirty-aeroplane air group (expandable to forty-two with the use of foldable wings). Armaments of four 120-mm L. 50 twins and four twin 100-mm L. 47. The Pugliese system was not present due to hull size limitations.[4, 5]

MARICOMINAV 1932 (Vian-Bonfiglietti)

This study, dated from 1928 to 1932, seems to have been known to Mussolini, in his position as Minister for the Navy, according to Admiral Bernotti's memories.

Specifications were for a ship of 15,000–16,000 tons, four 152-mm and seven 100-mm, all singles mountings, for a speed of 32–35 knots. Air group was forty to forty-five aircraft, eighteen fighters, twelve scouts, and the balance attack aeroplanes.[6]

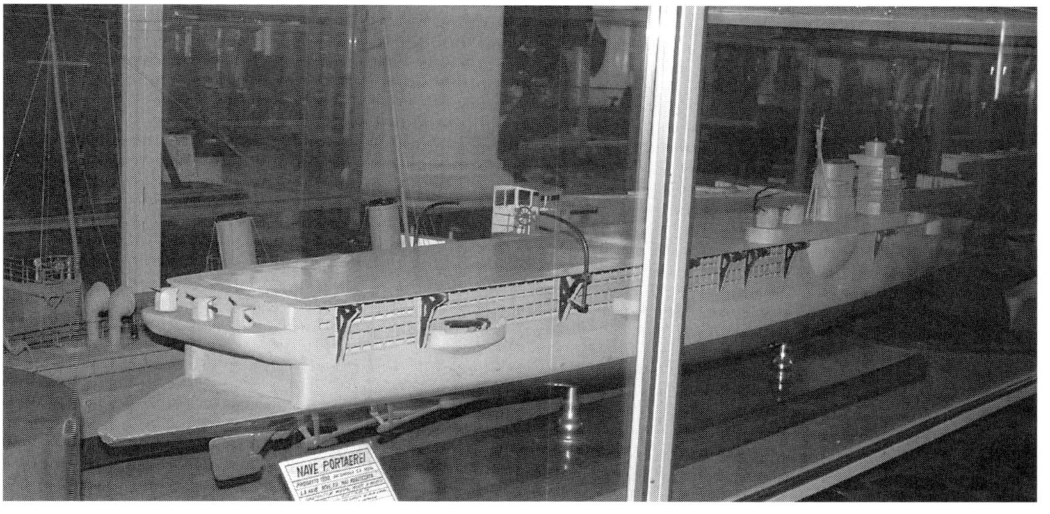

Above: The model of the 16,000-ton aircraft carrier by the *Comitato Progetto Navi*, 1932 (aft). *Museo Tecnico Navale di la Spezia*. (*Stefano Sappino*)

Below: *Comitato Progetti Navi* 16,000-ton carrier, line drawing. (*Courtesy Rivista Marittima*)

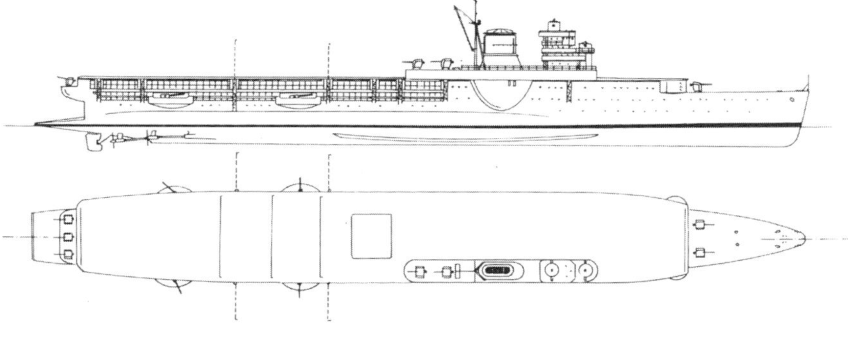

Conversions: Unfulfilled Expectations

The Conversion of the Rex and Conte di Savoia Liners

Between 1931 and 1934, plans to convert the two large liners, the *Rex* and the *Conte di Savoia*, to aircraft carriers with an air group of thirty seaplanes were studied by the *Regia Marina*.[7]

The design, by Captain Giuseppe Magagoli, was for a seaplane carrier equipped with two decks, at bow and stern, and two hangars.

The stern hangar, on two levels, allowed for thirteen S.78 seaplanes to be launched with two Gagnotto-type catapults. The bow hangar, on two levels, hosted twelve scouts or fighter seaplanes, to be launched with two 11-metre fixed catapults. A 'Hein mat' solution was present to recover the seaplanes. A small hangar between the two funnels hosted four further fighters. Two twin 120-mm turrets were the armament.

This solution was not satisfactory as a large and fast unit, capable of operating with the fleet, was actually slowed down by the need to recover the seaplanes at slow speed.

Furthermore, the need to use the seaplanes clearly showed a lack of alternative solutions on the side of aviation industry from that era, as well as the slowness of the two armed forces and of the industry in abandoning an operational concept (the seaplane), by then obsolete and unsatisfactory.

An additional study, aimed at modifying the ship into an 'aircraft carrier' with minimal modifications with thirty to thirty-four seaplanes, some with fixed wings and some with foldable wings, was blocked in its preliminary stage in October 1934.

Conversions of Egeo-Class Merchant Ships

In 1934, the *Regia Marina* studied a MAC-style conversion to support convoys; the request, made to Captain Malagoli, was for units with four to six seaplanes to be catapult launched and recovered via the 'Hein mat' solution.

The Egeo-class motor vessels (3,220 tons, with a speed of 14 knots) were considered. The design was for a ship able to launch up to five CANT 25AR, armed with two 120-mm L. 45 and two 76-mm L. 40. The conversion time during wartime was estimated, in 1934, for twenty days.[8]

Andrea Doria BB-Class Conversion

During the Ethiopian crisis, the conversion of the old dreadnoughts RN *Andrea Doria* and RN *Caio Duilio* into aircraft carriers was considered, then immediately aborted due to the speed and hull features as it happened with RN *Leonardo da Vinci* and due to economic constraints.[9]

1935 MARICOMINAV: Pugliese Project

A plan for a hybrid cruiser of 8,000–8,500 tons presented by the *Comitato Progetto Navi* was rejected by the Admirals' Committee on 4 July 1935 because the unit was not suited to be used as a real aircraft carrier, nor did it have ideal features for a war.[10] In addition, it was inferior to the other cruisers. The committee reserved the right to discuss the issue again once the plans related to the contests announced had been carried out.

In the same session, the Admirals' Committee voted unanimously in favour of the need for a real fleet aircraft carrier, which would operate tactically with the fleet at sea. Although it was late compared to other nations, this was the last possible moment in which the decision could be made for the availability of one or more aircraft carriers and a naval aviation with a minimal operational experience level by the beginning of the '40s.

The relationship with the *Regia Aeronautica* and Mussolini's thoughts have already been described: he was not capable of steering politics and military preparedness. There is no doubt though that the *Regia Marina*'s priorities were very clear, at least at the top advisory board.

In September 1935, work on a unit of 14,000 tons was started by the *Regia Marina*'s Chief of Staff and the *Comitato Progetto Navi*. The resulting project is described in the report made by General Pugliese to the committee itself.[11] The opposing requirements of high speed (38 knots) and limited displacement are underlined as critical.

The hull would have been long to favour speed and the engines of 160,000 CV (157,748 hp, eight boilers and four turbines on four shafts) would allow 36 knots with a peak of 38 knots. A solution for the diesel motors, long promised by the national industry but never actualised, would have brought significant improvements.

Protection would be limited to 60 mm at the waterline. The horizontal armour necessary for the flight deck (estimated at 150 mm) was rejected in order to keep within the specifications. The protection was a double hull, which included a compartmentalisation every 3 metres, working on a draught level of 4.5 metres; the engines were protected by a triple bottom.

As proof of the persistent uncertainty regarding operational use, the armament included two triple turrets of 152 mm at the stern and the bow of the island; the anti-aircraft weaponry was based on a total of ten 90-mm L. 50 singles, two were placed at the outer deck and two groups of four in the forward area of the flight deck (196 metres long), where it narrowed down from 30 to 18 metres.

The air force section was, for reasons already described, the least defined, with forty-two embarked aircraft (eighteen for torpedo bomber, torpedoes, and reconnaissance and twenty-four fighters), which would all be parked in the hangar. The models identified by the

Sections of 1936's aircraft carrier after underwater protection trials. (*Courtesy Rivista Marittima*)

expert air force industrialists were the Ca.165 and the CANT Z.1012; however, the dimensions of the areas necessary for managing the aeroplanes had not been defined.

Maximum length 221 metres
Waterline length 206.9 metres
Waterline width 25 metres
Displacement at trials 13,000 tons
Draught 4.50 metres
Flight deck length 196 metres
Flight deck maximum width 30 metres
Catapults 1 or 2, one for the fighters and one for the bombers, both on the flight deck.
Range of 4,000 nm at 25 knots fully loaded.

A solution using the non-existent diesel motors would have brought a speed of 32 knots and an increase of the embarked aircraft to fifty.

The repeated efforts of General (NC) Pugliese failed to force a final definition of the specifications, also given the relationships with the *Regia Aeronautica*, which defined an aircraft carrier 'unnecessary' in the Mediterranean Sea.

Conversion of the Liner Roma—1936 project

The liner *Roma* had been built in 1926; its engines, on four shafts, were originally built for the battleship *Cristoforo Colombo* of the Caracciolo-class.

The plan was for a partial conversion in a 23,000-ton ship, with a hangar placed over the original 145-m long weather deck; there would also be a flight deck, leaving fore and aft space for guns. The flight deck was 195 metres in length and 27 metres in width, in the last 50 metres it was reduced to 5 metres, which was provided for a catapult. Air group estimated it could hold thirty aircraft (non-foldable wings).

Armament was limited to singular AA pieces, probably 100-mm L. 47.

The engines were to be diesel, similar to those already on board the liner *Augustus* (28,000 hp and 18 knots). This solution would also allow for less smoke.

To the hull was unaltered but the added bulges as TDS, resulting in a widening to be compensated by increasing the engines' power.[12]

Conversion of the Roma Liner: Pg. n° 796 by Ansaldo (Gagnotto chief designer)

A second, more radical conversion plan for the *Roma* was developed by Colonel (NC) Luigi Gagnotto, who was detached to the Ansaldo shipyard for this purpose.

Colonel (NC) Luigi Gagnotto developed the plans for the apparently well-performing aircraft carrier. She would have had two overlapped flight decks: the lower one (165 × 19 m and at least 5 m in height) for take-offs, with two catapults; the wooden upper one (162.5 × 29 m) for landings as in the Japanese Navy *Akagi* and *Kaga* and HMS *Furious*.

Two catapults angled at 15 degrees on both sides were to be used for the launch of heavy aircraft, even though the lower flight deck was empty and available for regular take-offs. The two elevators were to be used for bombers (aft) and fighters (forward).

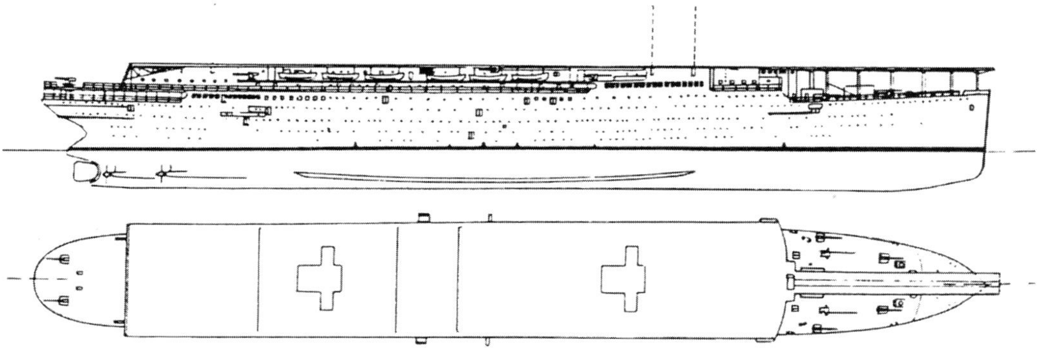

The *Roma* liner 1936 conversion design. (*Courtesy BAUSMM*)

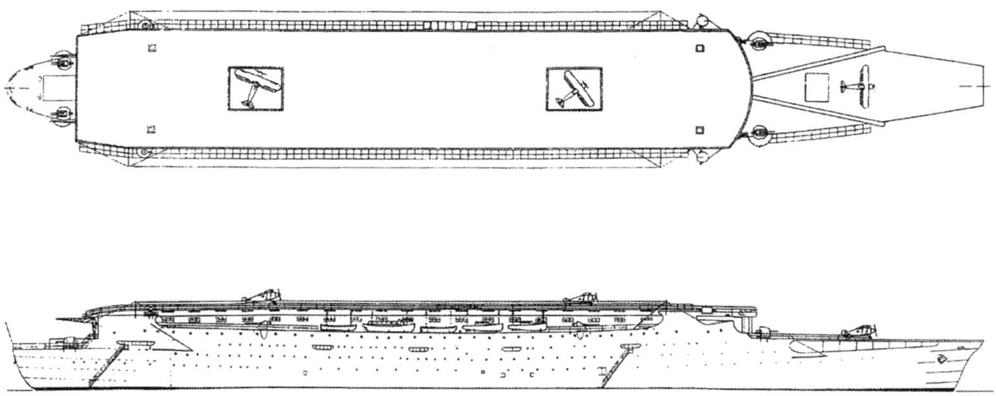

Ansaldo-Gagnotto conversion project. (*Courtesy Rivista Marittima*)

The original hull of the *Roma* would be lengthened, after the trials on models in the Freude tank, by 8.5 metres at bow and 4.5 metres at stern.

Engine replacements (diesel) and hull modifications should have allowed for a 26-knot speed and a range of 10,000 metres at 26 knots, allowing her to sail with the Fleet. The air group was formed by fifty-six aircraft, all with foldable wings: eighteen bombers, thirty fighters, with eight to be assembled.

Armament was four 120-mm L. 50, and four twin 100-mm L. 47. Crew was seventy-six officers, 100 non-commissioned officers, and 660 sailors and airmen. Construction time was optimistically estimated as taking a year's time.[13]

The plan was considered again during the Danzig crisis. The *Roma* was recalled from New York in September 1939; the Fiat diesel engines were not ready (and they would not have been for the duration of the war): when the non-belligerent status of Italy was declared, a lower priority was assigned to the project.[14, 15]

1935's Breakout Fleet

In 1935, the *Regia Marina* studied the possibility of establishing an oceanic presence, including a new naval base to be built in Chisimaio (Italian Somalia). Initially, the plan called for three 22,000-ton aircraft carriers, armed with four twin 152-mm turrets, fore and aft of the island. With the two new planned 45,000-ton, nine 406-mm in three triples, good AA battleships (UP41 Ansaldo design), such a task force would have permitted the full development of an integrated operational doctrine as already occurred in Japan, the USA, and the British Empire.

The 'oceanic' plan, perhaps because its implementation was not realistic, was not hindered by the *Regia Aeronautica*, which even promised 100 to 120 aircraft of various types with air group staff to be embarked on the aircraft carriers.

In 1936, the programme was cut down to two and then a single 14,000-ton carrier, with a 38-knot speed and an air group of twenty-four fighters and eighteen attack aeroplanes.[16] No TDS was provided as the hull would not allow space for the Pugliese System.

A further reduced design was proposed by Ansaldo in 1936, a seaplane carrier resembling the Japanese *Chitose*, with two fore catapults and three 152-mm twin turrets, for 9,000 tons. These plans were later sold to the Soviet Union.[17]

Still in 1939, two 15,000-ton aircraft carriers were proposed.[18]

RN Bolzano Conversion

An initial conversion to aircraft launcher of RN *Bolzano* was researched at the end of 1938 during the Sudeten crisis.

The conversion plans envisaged the elimination of the forward superimposed 203-mm turret and a complete amidships rearrangement to make space for a flight deck with four catapults, slightly inclined towards the bow, one fixed and enclosed in the flight deck and three abeam of the hull.

A small island limited to the bridge, the fire direction, and two funnels was placed starboard. The twelve-embarked aircraft (probably Ro.51) would have been parked on the deck, since a hangar was not included in the plans. The end of the Sudeten crisis and the loss of the trial aircraft put an end to this project.[19]

6

Five Years to the War

Japanese–German Naval Cooperation

While Italy was involved in the debate between the *Regia Marina* and the *Regia Aeronautica*, a different nation had started, possibly in time, to build aircraft carriers: Germany, with two units planned for the *Graf Zeppelin*-class.

The *Kriegsmarine*, aware of its total lack of experience, had sent two missions to Japan (which included *Luftwaffe* officers), one from September to December 1935, exclusively to obtain information, procedures, and plans for aircraft carriers and naval aviation.[1]

After the signing of the Tripartite Pact, a large Japanese naval mission (comprised of at least twenty to thirty officers) was permanently assigned to Germany in order to facilitate the exchange of information in areas of mutual interest.

The *Kriegsmarine* obtained information on radio communications between ships and pilots, techniques and procedures for deck landing, and a significant quantity of technological solutions, as well as the possibility of joining a cruise on the *Akagi*, with observers, to assist in all flight operations, both day and night.[2] Special attention was also given to the crew training plan and to the quality of officers in command of the aerial divisions, as well as to the planning of command facilities on the island.[3]

On a practical level, the Japanese also provided approximately 100 plans for equipment and flight systems.[4] The collaboration went so far as to obtain a visit (expressly requested by Hitler) to the super-secret *Yamato* battleship by Admiral Wennecker, the German naval *attaché* in Tokyo, in October 1942.[5]

On the other hand, the visit to the HMS *Furious*, open to the public in the summer of 1935, by one of the participants in the mission to Japan had almost no effect with regards to useful information gathered.[6]

Japan did not stop looking for as much information as possible from its allies. In 1936, the Japanese naval *attaché* in Rome, Commander Hiraide, asked and obtained from Admiral Somigli (on 15 January 1937), in the name of their common aversion to Communism, all the details regarding ships that had been sold by Italy to the Soviet Union.[7]

No Way: Italy Renounces the Building of Aircraft Carriers

After the combined manoeuvres of 1929–30 revealed significant issues, there was an attempt to create the basis for an operational cooperation between *Regia Marina* and *Regia Aeronautica*. In 1934, the *Regia Marina* released the procedures for combined sea and air actions, and in 1938, the *Regia Marina* and *Regia Aeronautica* agreed upon the communication procedures (that would remain complex and tragically inadequate for the duration of the entire war).

In 1935, for the first time, an aerial bombing of a ship, the old armoured cruiser RN *San Marco*, was attempted from an altitude of 3,000 metres, with small 50- and 100-kg bombs: the test was a complete failure.[8]

The *Regia Aeronautica*'s insistence in bombing at high altitude ignored—in addition to practical results—even the precise documentation of the problems connected to it, which was also reported in detail during parliamentary discussions of other nations and was thus public knowledge.

The experience of the war in Spain was also concealed; this war had demonstrated the inefficiency of high-altitude bombings, with no damage done by the *Regia Aeronautica*, next to Franco's insurgents, against the Republican trade traffic at sea.[9]

The British Empire and France were now seen as probable enemies and a war scenario with the British Empire, France, and Russia against an Italian–German alliance was by now under consideration by the Joint Chiefs of Staff, on explicit indication of Mussolini, until the 'Easter Agreement' between Italy and the British Empire on 16 April 1938.[10]

The aircraft carriers, of which two units were still included in the naval plan of 1937, were postponed to 1940–41 with an actual availability of 1943–44, again essentially because of budget issues as well as other construction plans already underway.[11]

The approved 1937 building plan, however, was very different. It called for two more *Littorio*-class battleships (RN *Roma* and RN *Impero*), twelve *Capitani Romani* light cruisers, and sixteen submarines. The aircraft carriers remained out of the building plans, even in the new strategic scenario.

Any construction plan would have had to deal with the shortage of raw materials, both in terms of iron and for the minerals needed for steel at high strength. In 1938, 52 per cent of the 400,000 tons of metal material was assigned to the Navy and only 8 per cent was given to the Army.[12]

In the well-known, but often partially reported, speech at the Chamber of Deputies on 15 March 1938, Admiral Cavagnari formalised the responsibilities for the naval building planning decisions, in a very clear way, in the writer's opinion:

> The *Regia Marina* persists instead in the decision not to construct aircraft carriers. Foreign observers … marked and criticised what appears like a weakness of our fleet. National strategists lengthy discussed this topic in the past and, for sure, naval strategist concurred in asking a positive solution of the problem.[13] Now I must declare that once more Mussolini, who had to decide between the opposite opinions, was, naturally, right.[14]

As a result, all interested military parties were on board to the point of eliminating the chapters about aero-naval cooperation from the textbook of the Naval Academy. One should not think that this position, required by political needs, relied on the incompetence or the blindness of the management at the *Regia Marina*; in fact, in mid-1938, it was clear that ground-based support of the *Regia Aeronautica* at sea would not be enough even according to the best conceivable conditions. In the discussion about the aero-naval component of the *Littorio*-class, Admiral de Feo said as follows:

> The on-board presence of aircraft in the largest quantity possible is a real necessity even if the organization of the naval coastal aviation would in the future achieve improvements, both in number and dislocation, to the point of giving more assurances with regards to the speed of intervention compared to today.[15]

Notwithstanding the statements articulated by the necessity to align their choices with the regime, the studies regarding aircraft carriers, as well as the important projects of the Comitato Progetto Navi, continued and some were even presented to Mussolini.[16]

In the meantime, the implementation of the organisation of the auxiliary air force of the *Regia Marina*, which was required by the law of February 1937, was very slow: only on 15 November 1939 was the inspector for naval aviation named (a role defined by a 1931 law), and his purviews defined on 19 February 1940.

All aircraft, even the embarked ones, were under the command of the Head of Aeronautic Services of the Naval Forces, an official of the aero-naval forces who was part of *Supermarina*. The embarked crew constituted the 'flight department' of the ship and depended on the highest ranking official, whether he was an observer from the *Regia Marina* or a pilot of the *Regia Aeronautica*, with the responsibility of independent decision maker of the use of the aeroplanes.[17]

Both the ground-based reconnaissance seaplanes and the embarked ones were not capable of fighting in combat, thus the very restrictive rules for their use; those on board would have to go to the land bases after having completed their mission, as recovering them at sea during an operation was unlikely. The *Regia Marina* Command was well aware of the operational limitations of this situation, and tried to embark as many aeroplanes as possible:

> … within the rules of engagement of the 2nd Division, it is said that the service of tactical exploration cannot be assured due to the lack of aircraft carriers. The fact that such a ship does not exist does not reduce the usefulness of the service of tactical exploration and therefore everything possible should be done with the existing means to assure it be done in the best way possible.[18]

In the meantime, the equilibrium outlined in the naval department by the Washington Treaty and by the subsequent London Treaties was falling apart in 1936, particularly after Tokyo's refusal to confirm that it did not have warships with calibres higher than 356 mm under construction.

The policy of Great Britain and France in the second half of the '30s aspired to steadfastly keep Italy and Germany separate, with partial success. In fact, Italy adhered to the London Treaty on 2 December 1938 and bilateral accords of a naval nature were signed in 1937 by

Great Britain and Germany and Great Britain and the USSR. This agreement was then decried by Germany in 1938 mentioning the policy of surrounding pursued by Great Britain.[19]

The last decisive ventures undertaken by the *Regia Marina* to once again discuss the strategic situation of the relations with the *Regia Aeronautica* and to again obtain control of the naval air force, triggered by the sad episode of the torpedoes, occurred in March 1939 and November 1939.[20] This time, the *Regia Aeronautica* was apparently not against the aircraft carrier project to the point where it acquired twelve models of fighters Caproni F.5 earmarked for naval fighters, modifying it with foldable wings, reinforced landing gear, and arrester.

In November 1939, the Head of the *Regia Aeronautica*, Valle, was replaced by General Pricolo; he, too, was not very amenable to collaboration with the other forces and the twelve fighters were dispatched to the defence of Rome.[21]

The distance between the needs of the imminent war and reality is clearly expressed in the Chief of *Regia Marina* Staff memorandum dated 12 October 1939 and titled '*Aviazione per la Regia Marina*'.[22] In the document, the available forces are listed (they were only called to scouting duties, as per the *Regia Aeronautica*'s statements): 138 against a theoretical 185 ground-based aircraft, and seventy out of seventy-three on-board, against a need, considering the Mediterranean Sea only, of 334 aeroplanes.

In the same document, the evaluation of operating necessities (anti-submarine surveillance and vigilance, convoys and fleet protection, tactical scouting, reserve forces, and losses replacement) is as follows:

Mediterranean: 768.
Red Sea and the Indian Ocean: 96.
Embarked airplanes: 102.
Missions on bases: 25.
Total: 991.

The other 'fundamental issues' to tackle before the now imminent war were as follows:

1. To improve the model for scouting aeroplanes.
2. To increase the stability of the squadron's organisation.
3. To improve the seaplane's bases and equipment.
4. To define adequate and separate oil and fuel reserves for the naval aviation.
5. To establish fighter squadrons for the naval bases' defence.
6. To establish squadrons of torpedo bombers.
7. To adopt and to apply training and cooperation criteria between the *Regia Marina* and *Regia Aeronautica* truly consistent with the necessities of the maritime war.

The international situation was deteriorating, yet Italy had military plans for a war that it expected to start after 1942.[23] Germany started the war on 1 September 1939; on 10 June 1940, Mussolini, tragically assuming that the war had already decided in Hitler's favour, declared war on the British Empire and France.

Aircraft Carriers and Aircraft 1 December 1939			
	Great Britain	United States	Japan
In service	7/257	5/428	6/394
Under construction	7/311	2/169	1/168
Undergoing conversion			2/106

The *Regia Marina* entered the war with no aeronautical staff and no aircraft carriers, and Italy did not have an aeroplane able to operate from aircraft carriers or to protect the fleet from its catapults; additionally, the cooperation between the *Regia Marina* and the *Regia Aeronautica* proved seriously deficient. Nonetheless, the *Regia Marina* was the force that could lose the war in a single day if defeated: the African front depended entirely on its ability to keep open the logistic lines across the Mediterranean.

7

Who is to Blame?

Any defeat requires culprits, no matter if real or imaginary. The lack of radar and aircraft carriers, as well as inadequate naval tactics and technology (a doctrine for night fighting, industrial weaknesses, and loose standards in ammo and shell production, excessively cautious behaviour at sea) are the most common ones in charge of the *Regia Marina* and its admirals. Let us examine the points as far as the aircraft carriers and the naval air force are concerned.

The admirals 'refused' the aircraft carrier. This does not fit with the evidence. As we have seen, the point has never been to have or not to have an aircraft carrier, rather an integrated naval air force. Since 1923, with the institution of the *Regia Aeronautica*, the *Regia Marina* had no real control over the doctrinal and technical development of the aircraft and their use. This situation progressively worsened, with the full support of the Fascist government, up until the situation described at the beginning of the war.

The *Regia Aeronautica* explicitly denied the need for a naval air force, the need to discuss an integrated strategy with the *Regia Marina*, and even the usefulness of the torpedo bombers. If we recall that the laws requested the *Regia Marina* and *Regia Aeronautica* jointly discuss and agree over the *Regia Marina*'s specific needs, we have a good chance of understanding what actually happened.

Some authors refer to the 1925 Admirals' Committee to demonstrate that the *Regia Marina* did not want an aircraft carrier. These authors forget that the real question then was whether they should build an experimental aircraft carrier, a hybrid cruiser-carrier, or the first modern cruiser 'with the available funding and according to the current strategic view, which means considering France as a probable enemy'. As the Italian Fleet was aging, with all of its cruisers built well before the First World War and the capital ships already inferior to the French ones, it is easy to identify these opinions as a case of historical insight.

Budget constraints and construction limitations of the time are often forgotten by those who perform evaluations limited only to the type of units built. We have seen how questionable decisions evaluated retroactively, such as the rebuilding of the four units of the Giulio Cesare and Andrea Doria classes, took a long time in the shipyards, precisely during the time frame when one or more aircraft carriers could have been built. However, during that time frame, the likely enemy was France, therefore the strategic priorities were different or it was the long uncertain period of international fascist policy.

The industrial abilities also represent a physical limitation that is impossible to ignore: in 1939, Italian production of steel reached 2.4 million tons against 13.4 million tons produced in Great Britain and the 22.5 million tons produced in Germany.[1] These resources had to be shared, as was mentioned earlier, among the armed forces. When Fascism was in power, the industry itself went through a process of provincialism in terms of research and production methods.[2]

In the Admirals' Committee of 4 July 1935, during the crisis of the British Empire, the unanimous writings related to the aircraft carriers were as follows:

> The test … made clear that the unanimous opinion of the Committee regarding the absolute necessity to have an aircraft carrier with a flight deck for the *R. Marina*. The Admirals are of the unanimous opinion that only through these ships being part of the Fleet can there be a guarantee of a quick use of the airplanes of the various specialities in the middle of a naval operation. And that the inferiorities of the *Regia Marina*, due to the lack of aircraft carriers, are made worse by the comparison to other Navies who do have these types of ships. It therefore votes that this serious omission be fixed as soon as possible and that the first example of aircraft carrier should be dealt with an extraordinary budget allocation.

No admiral resigned in protest of the 'wrong policies' (an argument to 'demonstrate' they were incompetent or culpable). This shows a fundamental lack of understanding of the historic and organisational context. Let us for a minute forget the fact that they were included in a dictatorial regime, whose head was, most of the time, Prime Minister, Minister of War, of the Air Force and the Navy, as well as Commander in Chief: we will return to this subject later.

The missing point here is that the admirals acted to preserve the operational efficiency of the *Regia Marina* within the rules (written and unwritten) of the system they belonged to. This meant, most of the time, to follow the rule of the lesser evil. The evidence for the need of aircraft carriers and a naval air force was fully highlighted by the crisis with the British Empire in 1935–36.

Nonetheless, the building plan presented by the *Regia Marina*, which included aircraft carriers, was not approved and no effort was made from the political powers to overcome the declared *Regia Aeronautica*'s hostility and doctrinal weaknesses once the crisis was over. Additionally, two admirals resigned, one in 1925 and the other in 1934: Great Admiral Paolo Thaon di Revel to protest against the prevalence of the Army in the newly instituted Joint Chiefs of Staff, a fact that, as it actually happened, would lead to an inconclusive way to drive the need of strict cooperation between the services at sea, and Admiral Ducci, always a supporter of the aircraft carrier, against the naval politics of Admiral Cavagnari. No similarly significant episode of the resignation of high ranking officers is registered in the *Kriegsmarine* (whose lack of naval aviation is an even worse case, given the *Graf Zeppelin* fleet aircraft carrier availability).[3]

Even if the ability of the national electronic industry to produce the needed primary components was lacking, it is irrefutable that the importance of radar technology was largely underestimated both from the strategic and industrial point of view. If it is true that Guglielmo Marconi's experience, clearly demonstrating the ability to detect position and movements at short distance, was interrupted by his death (and was certainly not a secret, being his company a British firm) and that the Regia Marina consistently financed Professor Ugo Tiberio's studies at Leghorn Naval Academy, everything was subject to the availability of imported, not state of the art components that the national industry was unable to build.

Furthermore, MARINELETTRO (the department in charge of the studies) was always downsized, and subject to conflicts with the company in charge of the actual construction of equipment, the SAFAR. Only in October 1939 did the first prototype, based on Telefunken electronic components, give satisfactory results, just to face the SAFAR inability to build it. In the end, the 'Gufo' EC 3 navel radar, based on Philips components, was still in the experimental phase when war was declared.

A clear statement of the different industrial strength involved is made by G. Galati:

> Overall, Italy invested a total of about sixty thousand dollars of that time for the development of the radar, with teams consisting of very few researchers and technicians. This is a derisive amount, orders of magnitude lower than the billions of dollars and the thousands of researchers and technicians (including those employed in the production) committed by the USA.

The analysis by the *Regia Marina* and the *Regia Aeronautica* of the first series of war experiences led to the conclusion that the British forces were not in possession of radar technologies; interestingly enough, the French were able to conceal their own progress in the field after the armistice. The studies and the industrial mobilisation on the topic was thus stopped until the end of 1940.

The root of the problem, which on the one hand caused the *Regia Marina* to develop plans for ships without aircraft and on the other for planes that could not operate efficiently at sea, was the choice to create an independent air force in 1925; this was a choice that would gradually distance the two directions of armed forces, which should have converged.

The political prevalence of the *Regia Aeronautica*, seen as an arm of the regime and propaganda, on the *Regia Marina*, extremely loyal to the King (as the tragic days of the Armistice will demonstrate), allowed the first to elude its responsibilities (doctrinal and organisational, certainly not for the lack of valour of its men, which has been demonstrated several times) way beyond the beginning of the war.

Nor can we compare the British experience whereby the Royal Navy, although deprived of its aerial branch in 1918, later to regain it in 1938, determinedly proceeded with the building plans for aircraft carriers and the collaboration between the two armed forces: the equilibrium between the two armies was, after all, not in the hands of a dictator.

One can say that Italy, regardless of the almost completed RN *Aquila*, had (like Germany, in fact) a capable ship that would have been able to oversee an aerial component, if it were to exist. Yet it never happened, neither with the aircraft nor with the necessary very intense training of the pilots.[4]

The *Regia Marina* developed a fleet and a doctrine for the war that would have to be fought 'somewhere in the Mediterranean and against someone' as Faldella says, without wanting nor able, given the instability of the political leaning, to truly define the military of its plans, often neglecting the technological and doctrinal advancements happening elsewhere particularly in the Orient where Nippon Kaigun with enormous efforts and in secret had reached high levels of excellence in its aero-naval operations.[5]

The effect of the accumulation of roles had negative effects on the chain of command; for the *Regia Marina*, the responsibilities of *Supermarina*, the central command in Rome, were always run by the adjunct General Chief of Staff in the name of the CSM, an admiral often on a lower level and less senior to those Admirals who were in command at sea.[6]

The General Chief of Staff, in contrast, received a decrease in power from 1927 in such a way as to not be able to execute his role, he was incapable of settling the rivalries among the various armed forces or setting up and expecting an effective collaboration between them, which would have to be verified in the field through the necessary drills.

The command system, in which Mussolini was Prime Minister and minister of the three armed forces and the Undersecretaries who performed the actual roles, eliminated the necessity for institutional debate and allowed a policy of one on one relations between Mussolini and the Undersecretaries, often also the CSM of the armies, who would reward relational abilities and avoided open conflicts.

The organisation of command during war times was even worse:

> One cannot imagine a worse organisation than the Command, nor Mussolini could have undertaken more serious personal responsibilities. The same establishment of the Supreme Command was ratified only on 29 May 1940 on a system that was thin and certainly inadequate for the onerous tasks in a coalition war.[7]

The astonishment of accredited historians is surprising, perhaps anxious to avoid assigning responsibility; to this day, they attribute the lack of decisions to the different armed forces and not to whom, for political reasons and to maintain power, created a chain of command where none, except himself and his loyal politicians, had the possibility to make decisions outside of their limited areas of expertise.

From a military perspective, these shortcomings, together with the *Regia Aeronautica*'s inflexible desire to control everything that flew, symbolised one of the most significant failures of the management at the time.

The collaboration between forces both in Italy and in Germany was very weak in the aero-naval departments. Negotiations would occur between consistent armies unbeknownst to the other ones. The slowness by which the Germans provided devices as well as the possibility to duplicate their radar technology to Italy and the *Regia Marina* shows a serious lack of appreciation on the part of the Germans of the situation in the Mediterranean, notwithstanding the concurrent complaints regarding the war abilities of the *Regia Marina*, an absence that also came, as written by Admiral Weichold (head of the *Kriegsmarine* in Italy), with the fact that German strategic conceptualisation was primarily ground-based.

An essential breach in the collaboration also showed itself in the intelligence field, where the existence of ULTRA was never even speculated upon, and the Axis allies preferred to chase irrationally non-existent traitors instead of coldly examining the weak points of their own systems.

From a political perspective, the Fascist regime had shown behaviour typical of dictatorial systems, meant to maintain power while encouraging rivalries among various stakeholders—in this case, between the three armed forces and an extremely fragmented industrial system.

The responsibilities of the person in the senior position, Benito Mussolini, are enormous. Not only because he was Prime Minister, Minister of the Three Armed Forces, and Supreme Chief of the Armed Forces, thus formally responsible for decisions, but also for having voluntarily ignored on multiple occasions factual evidence reported him by military directors, directors whom he himself had appointed.[8]

The gradual slide of Fascist Italy in the German sphere after the Conference of Stresa and its political consequences of constant decline of available choices and the highly amateur behaviour exhibited by Mussolini as Supreme Commander are well described by Alberto Santoni.[9]

The erratic international political scene, the illusion of being able to play a cornerstone role in the equation without actually having to commit oneself, the inability to strategically direct (over the needed period of years or decades) both allies and the political industry (the basis of any military demand), and the deranged gamble of joining the war while relying on its imminent conclusion are clear elements in identifying Fascism's ultimate responsibility of the events.[10, 11]

8

The War

It is not the purpose of this text to discuss the evolution of the naval war in the Mediterranean in all of its aspects. We will limit ourselves to discussing the episodes that were important to the outcome of the missions, such as the absence of aircraft carriers, of an independent naval aviation and an efficient coordinating body between *Regia Marina* and *Regia Aeronautica*, until the moment when their functioning brought to the decision to proceed with the construction of aircraft carriers.

An important aspect, given that the War in the Mediterranean was essentially a war of convoys, should be reported on a preliminary level because it is directly connected to the thoughts related to the political management of Italy. Mussolini had the ease of deciding the day and hour of the country's entry into the war; however, only on 7 January 1940 were the merchant ships outside the Mediterranean alerted about the danger of war.

With such short notice, 212 steamers for a total of 1,216,637 tons were lost—in other words, 35 per cent of the entire merchant navy—this was the greatest naval defeat of the entire war for all combatants.[1, 2]

At the same time, the preparation of the Army in Libya was completely inadequate. The *Regio Esercito* stated on 23 June 1940 that it had 13,000 men, 1,250 auto vehicles, 40,000 tons of provisions, 18,000 tons of petrol, 1,700,000 artillery shells, 48,000,000 rounds of small arms ammunition, and 800,000 mortar bombs in readiness in Italy, and all of this equipment needed to be shipped to Libya (this was independent of the possible dispatch of new big units to Libya), and the *Regia Aeronautica* had urgency to ship 5,000 tons of various materials among which were 20,000 aviation petrol drums. The war for the *Regia Marina* immediately became a war of convoys.[3]

Enemy Forces in Home Waters: *Marine Nationale*, Genoa[4]

On 14 June 1940, the 3rd Squadron of the French Navy bombarded Genoa. the 3rd Squadron had set sail out of Toulon the evening of the previous day under the command of Admiral Duplat. Overall damage to the city was light and nine civilians were killed.

The action, which began at 4.30 a.m., was done by two groups: the first (heavy cruisers *Algerie* and *Foch* and six destroyers) was supposed to act against the metallurgical plants and the deposit of naphtha at Vado; and the second (heavy cruisers *Dupleix* and *Colbert* and two

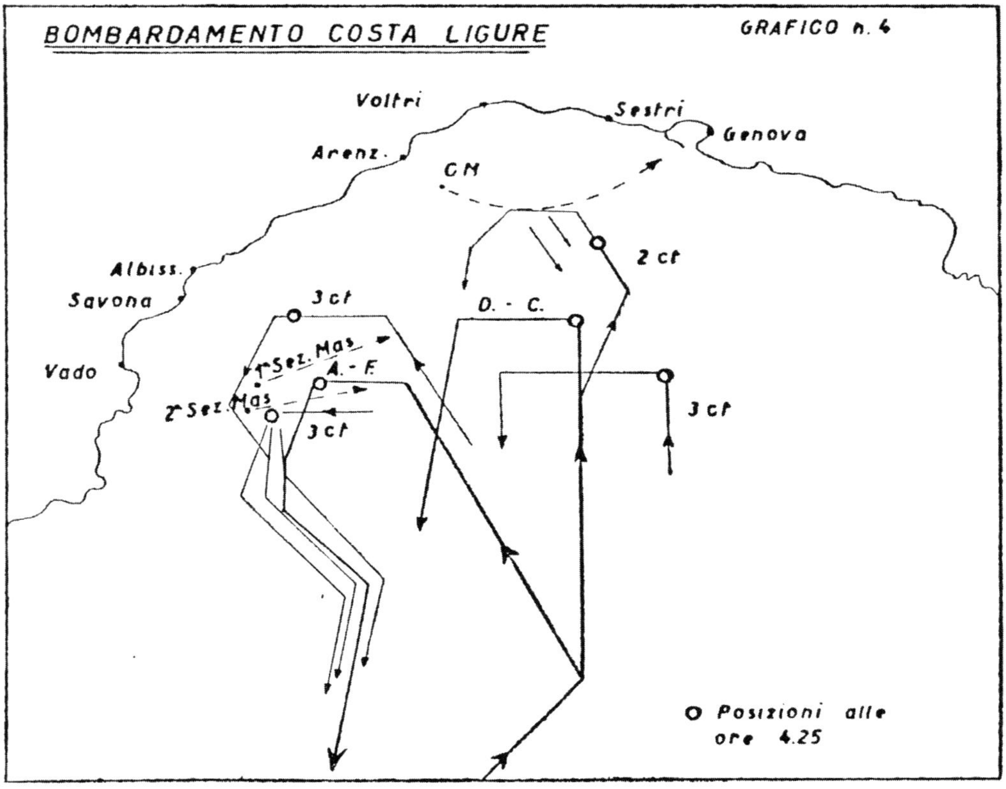

French action against Vado and Genoa. (*Courtesy BAUSMM*)

destroyers) against the city of Genoa. The action was engaged by the coastal artillery from an armed *Regia Marina*'s train by the torpedo boat RN *Calatafimi* and the 13th squadron MAS. One 152-mm hit of a coastal battery damaged the French destroyer *Albatros*, causing twelve deaths.

The damage caused by the naval bombardment was rather light: the French fired about 1,500 shots and the Italians 300. A night attack by the French bombers against Novi Ligure's airfield and Vado's oil storages resulted in the loss of one aircraft. The ten S.79 vehicles of the Italian aviation sent to attack the French squadron on its way back to Toulon did not spot the enemy also because of the poor visibility. The Italian Fleet did not intervene as it was then located in the southern bases of the peninsula.

Royal Navy: Action off Calabria

The encounter (9 July 1940) is well known. This inconclusive action was conducted by Admiral Cunningham and Admiral Campioni, who were in command, by common willing, given that the main mission on both sides (convoys escort) had already been accomplished.

As usual in British practice, Force 'H' exited Gibraltar on the morning of the 8th. Given the position of the Italian Fleet, this action was contrasted with aircraft and submarines. It is likely that the HMS *Escort* was damaged and then sunk 80 nm east of Gibraltar by RS *Marconi* on 11 July.

Thanks to the deciphering of important messages, *Supermarina* were able to gauge the British intentions, but were still unsure when exactly they were to occur; *Supermarina* concluded that the British groups were going to shell Catania, Siracusa, and maybe Augusta.[5] Almost the entire *Regia Marina* fleet was used to escort a five-ship convoy, knowing of the forthcoming meeting.

An initial British force presence was confirmed by radio goniometric analysis on 7 July, 60 nm north of Ras el Tin and a second force 45 nm east of the first, heading to Malta. Admiral Campioni initially manoeuvred to counter a possible bombardment of Bengasi, then was advised of the real British intentions thanks to *Supermarina* deciphering British radio traffic, and struck a heading 65 nm south-east of Punta Stilo.[6]

Admiral Cunningham was informed of the *Regia Marina* units at sea on the morning of 8 July, and then the sighting was then confirmed from aerial reconnaissance and manoeuvred (leaving the convoy escort duty) to intercept them on the route for Taranto (it is worth noting that the routes to Messina, Augusta, and Naples remained open to Admiral Campioni).

The meeting points for the two fleets were only 60 nm apart. The British fleet was attacked nineteen times by Italian bombers, with a hit on-board the HMS *Gloucester*.[7] These attacks were performed unhindered, given only two Gladiators were on board the HMS *Eagle*.

Before the battle, the Italian fleet was shadowed by a British Sunderland. Admiral Campioni's request for a fighter squadron brought no results.[8] The asymmetrical position of the two fleets is clear here, with the Italian reconnaissance aircraft exposed to aircraft carrier based fighters, while the long-range British counterparts were able to stay and follow Italian moves usually undisturbed.

On 9 July, the Italian reconnaissance was unable to find the British fleet, while an aerial torpedo attack from HMS Eagle (1.15 to 1.26 p.m.) was conducted against Regia Marina's heavy cruisers. The attackers released the torpedoes at the distance of 1,000–1,500 metres from a 20–30-metre altitude. No hit was scored.[9]

Finally, a reconnaissance aeroplane found (1.30 p.m.) the British fleet 80 nm north-east of the Italian fleet. Admiral Campioni headed for the enemy's position. Three seaplanes were catapulted, and an action by ground-based bombers was requested.[10]

It is not the goal of this work to describe the tactical phase of the battle; we will limit the description to the air force contributions during and after the battle.[11]

During the ballistic phase, a torpedo plane attack from the HMS *Eagle* was performed against the Italian heavy cruisers, with no results.[12] At 4.30 p.m., Admiral Campioni again requested a *Regia Aeronautica* action.

During the night of the 10th, an aerial torpedo attack was done against the ship at anchor in Augusta, sinking RN *Pancaldo* (a destroyer, later salvaged and put in service again).[13]

In the meantime, Cunningham, on his route back, was attacked by the *Regia Aeronautica*'s ground-based bombers (a total of 126 aeroplanes), with some splinter damage and no direct hit.[14, 15] During the route back to Alexandria, the ground-based aircraft based in Dodecanese and Libya executed thirty-one attacks, without direct hits.[16]

Which information did Admiral Campioni received from reconnaissance during the battle? From 4 to 5.50 p.m., there was nothing but an erroneous signal, which gave the

RN *Trento* and RN *Bolzano* in action at Punta Stilo. (*Courtesy Rivista Marittima*)

The RN *Conte di Cavour* opens fire on the British formation. (*Courtesy USMM, Collezione ANMI*)

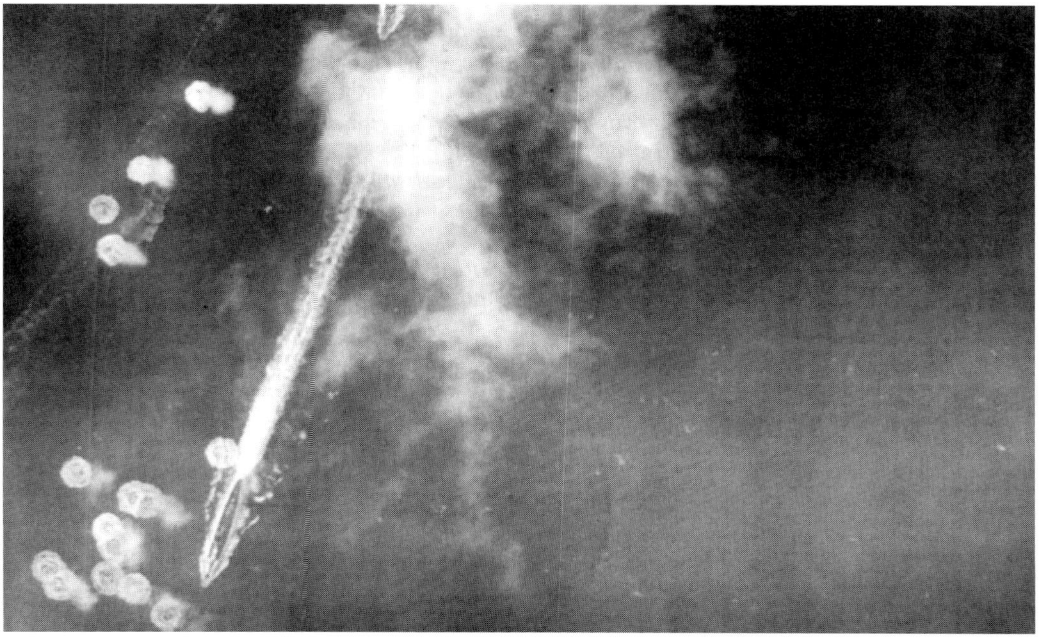

The *Regia Marina*'s light cruisers under attack by the 30th Squadron of the *Regia Aeronautica*. Note the white bows for the purpose of aerial recognition. (*Courtesy Rivista Marittima*).

Mediterranean Fleet a heading to the west. During his route toward the Sicilian bases, he reported 'a continuous series of aerial attacks' on his fleet from 4.45 to 9 p.m.[17] They were the *Regia Aeronautica*'s bombers.[18]

In Admiral Campioni's words:

> … no acknowledgement was given to my request to attack the Mediterranean Fleet, but a message at 16.15 from Taranto ensuring that 24 airplanes were sent; the attacking planes high altitude made it almost impossible to identify them before they were in the right position to release bombs; all the agreed upon signals were made to ensure the national ships were identified. Furthermore, the great difficulty in having timely aerial attacks during a fight was confirmed; the British forces were left undisturbed before the battle, while they used the [carrier] based aircraft to attack before and after the ballistic phase. The advantages of an aircraft carrier for defence and attack is evident, and the immediate construction of such a ship is desirable.[19] These considerations have greater value the farthest the distance from the national bases. The presence of an aircraft carrier would ensure having fighters and torpedo bombers during the tactical phase. [Carrier] based airplanes would be able to lead the ground based ones against enemy forces without mistakes, knowing the exact tactical situation. I believe the aircraft carrier should have building priority as opposed to the oceanic cruisers [the *Costanzo Ciano*-class].[20]

A total of about 500 aircraft and 2,000 bombs were used by the *Regia Aeronautica*, and only four aircraft were lost.[21]

General Giuseppe Santoro, under Chief of Staff of the *Regia Aeronautica*, writes in his text: 'The results were undoubtedly disproportionate to such a large display of force … this

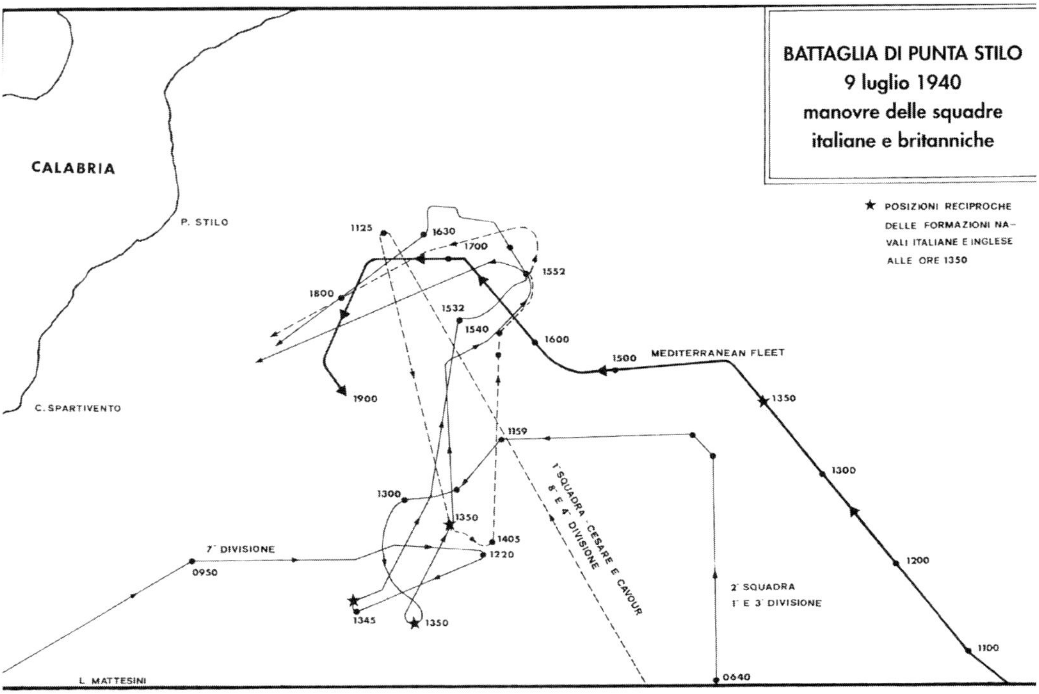

Action off Calabria. (*Courtesy USMM*)

should have been one of the practical demonstrations of the illusion of bombing at high altitude'.[22]

One could think that the political and military leadership should have taken note of the unsatisfactory action and triggered the necessary actions. Instead, we have the following note from the diary of Galeazzo Ciano:

> The true controversy on the subject of naval combat is not between us and the British, rather it is between the air force and the navy. Cavagnari maintains that the *Regia Aeronautica* action was entirely absent during the first phase of the battle and that when it finally arrived, it was directed against our ships who endured six hours of bombings by the 79 [Italian bombers]. Also other information contradicts the brilliant reports of the *Regia Aeronautica*. I confess to being sceptical as well. Mussolini is not. This morning he said that in three days he annihilated fifty per cent of British naval resources in the Mediterranean. Perhaps a bit exaggerated.[23]

Capo Spada

As an example of insufficient collaboration between commands, one can list this fortuitous encounter in which were involved the light cruisers RN *Bande Nere* and RN *Colleoni* (the latter was lost in the action), with the British HMAS *Sydney* (a light cruiser) and the destroyers HMS *Havock*, HMS *Hyperion*, HMS *Ilex*, HMS *Hero*, and HMS *Nasty*. The operation's original goal was to bomb the area of Sollum, in the operational perimeter of the Italian command of the Aegean (De Vecchi de Valcismon was Governor and Commander of the Armed Forces based in Rhodes).

The Rhodes' Command was supposed to provide aerial reconnaissance; however, the operation did not provide results on 18 July and was not carried out on 19 July due to technical reasons, this caused a surprise rendezvous between the two fleets. Moreover, the Governor did not hesitate to notify that 'he would accept orders from the Supreme Command only'.

Subsequently, *Regia Aeronautica*'s attacks damaged the HMS *Havock*. Shortly after this action, Conte de Vecchi, the Governor of Rhodes, was removed from his position.

Operation 'Hats'[24]

The goal of the mission (29 August to 6 September 1940) was to send Cunningham the reinforcements he had requested (a fast battleship, a second aircraft carrier, and more cruisers), after the action off Calabria. This was also a lost opportunity for a battle in which the *Regia Marina* could have been the superior force. This was the last mission during which the Mediterranean Fleet did not have units equipped with radar available; subsequently, the Royal Navy moved the HMS *Valiant* and the HMS *Ajax*, which both had radar, to the Mediterranean.

During this mission, the British 'B' force, which had departed from Gibraltar, was never attacked even though Italian observers had sent alerts regarding their exit from port as well as by the reconnaissance aircraft south of Ibiza and west of Sardinia, and again four times on their way back. Force 'F' departed from Gibraltar with Alexandria as its destination met with Force 'I' at 8 a.m. on 2 September south-west of Malta, which came from Alexandria.

During the approach route of the Mediterranean Fleet to the meeting point, she was sighted at 2 p.m. and at 4 p.m. by Italian reconnaissance, regardless of the fact that the Gladiators were constantly in flight above the British formation and exposed to aerial attacks; at 10.15 a.m. on the 31st, HMS *Eagle*'s reconnaissance sighted the Italian Fleet, which had gone out *en masse* from Taranto, Brindisi, and Messina to intercept the Mediterranean Fleet.

Supermarina's orders, however, aimed at intercepting the enemy if in route towards the Italian coast and probably to avoid a night battle, recalled the fleet to the centre of the Gulf of Taranto while it was already on the interception route with the British Fleet, which would have brought about battle with the Mediterranean Fleet at 6 p.m. on the 31st.

Further *Supermarina* orders, on 1 September, moved the Italian forces to once again search for the enemy north of the Malta–Zante line; the mission was aborted because of a storm from the north that made the operational use of the destroyers impossible, so the fleet returned to Taranto. The storm was much lighter in the south where even the *Cornwall*, a merchant vessel hit by aircraft, was able to get to Malta.

The bad weather prevented a proper reconnaissance from being carried out on 2 September, yet elements of the Mediterranean Fleet were sighted south of Malta and were attacked by aeroplanes, while the next successful sighting occurred on 3 September at 5.30 p.m. to the east, in the passage between Crete and Cerigo.

During the day of the 2nd, the Mediterranean Fleet was attacked five times by Italian aircraft, without results and with the loss of four aircraft.

On the way back, the Mediterranean Fleet attacked the airfield at Rhodes with Swordfish, losing four aircraft but destroying two S.79 on the ground. The Mediterranean Fleet was attacked three times on the morning of the 4th by bombers, without results.

A similar mission was undertaken by the Mediterranean Fleet from Alexandria to Malta by convoy escort at the end of September, the Italian Fleet sortied in full force at sea, without encountering the enemy. The reconnaissance was hindered by bad weather. On 1 October, the situation was clear, but on 2 October, it was clear that the Mediterranean Fleet was already returning to Alexandria. The three aerial attacks endured by the British were without results, and during the second attack, the Italians used torpedoes against a moving warship for the first time.[25]

During these missions, Italian reconnaissance was precise and efficient despite the presence of fighters on the British aircraft carrier. The missions of the *Regia Aeronautica* were ineffective and *Supermarina*'s orders were not very aggressive.

The discontent of the Italian Fleet due to the missed rendezvous with the enemy was high, to the point where Admiral Iachino sent a memorandum to the General Chief of Staff about the need for more active behaviour in the war.

Supermarina asked the Supreme Command for precise directives, being aware of his officer's and the men's disenchantment; the response, dated 16 September and signed by General Badoglio, compared the two Fleets forces, the goals obtained until then (the successful defence of traffic towards Albania and Libya was rightfully mentioned in first place, given that, according to the authors, being the *Regia Marina*, the service that 'would have been able to lose the war in only one day' as was Admiral Jellicoe's position in the First World War), and maintained that 'it is absurd to conceive a battle as a means in itself. It is not worth discussing'. He then confirmed the usefulness of a 'fleet in being' aimed to battle with the enemy when necessary.

The British appreciation of the situation was entirely different. In fact, Cunningham writes:

> The arrival of the *Valiant*, the *Illustrious*, the *Calcutta* and the *Coventry* symbolised not only a significant increase of our forces but it also assured us an aircraft carrier to maintain fighters such as the Fulmars in the skies during the day time hours, while the fleet was in navigation. We also had two big units equipped with radar. Until then we had to rely on our eyes to discover enemy aircraft … now however we could rely on a device which sounded the alarm when attacking vehicles were still at 40–50 mg distance … we dominated the air above the skies of the Fleet.

Taranto (Operation Judgment)[26]

The Royal Navy's actions against the Italian units at anchor in Taranto (on the night of 12 November 1940) are well known: in this work, we dwell on the aspects of aero-naval cooperation and some strategic elements that are not always emphasised.

The attack with carrier-based aircraft had been studied by the British, as we saw, since the Ethiopian crisis and the idea was quickly reconsidered at the start of the war.[27] A test of the British ability to attack ships at anchor was already done in Dakar with the torpedoing of the French battleship *Richelieu* on 8 July 1940, using magnetic torpedoes.[28]

The date established for the attack on Taranto was 21 October 1940 (anniversary of Trafalgar), then moved to 11 November because of a fire that broke out in the hangar of the HMS *Illustrious*. The attack would have been launched at the same time as a complex operation of supply and convoy transit (Operation MB8) also to support the Greek front, and was comprised of an attack on the canal of Otranto by a division of cruisers. Intense reconnaissance was arranged to assure the best possible information.

The strategic aspect was further motivated by the necessity to aid Greece, a new ally after the Italian aggression, as well as to try to open the Gibraltar–Alexandria route, after the British occupation of Crete, thus avoiding the long circumnavigation of Africa.

This activity was noticed by the Italians and the enemy's intent to carry out intense aerial attacks was expected.

On 6 November, the English squadron, composed of four battleships, one aircraft carrier, and several destroyers exited Alexandria with the goal of escorting the convoys headed to Malta and Suda: a division of cruisers then caught up with it.

It was sighted several times by the Italian reconnaissance and attacked by bombers, though without results. At 10 a.m. on the 10th, bolstered by units from Gibraltar, RN moved north east of the Ionian Islands to cover the merchant vessels returning from Alexandria and was once again attacked by bombers without results.

The next day, the embarked Fulmars were able to successfully keep away Italian reconnaissance aircraft, an aspect crucial in order to cover HMS *Illustrious*'s position, which was moving to launch the attack. At the same time, the ships destined to the raid on Taranto detached themselves from the British ship.

The information available to *Supermarina*, starting from the 6th, said that there was significant radio traffic in the Aegean and an absence of the Mediterranean Fleet at Alexandria on the 7th, while the exit from Gibraltar of the HMS *Barham*, HMS *Ark Royal*, three cruisers, and eleven destroyers *en route* for the east had been ascertained on the 7th, the Italian Fleet was placed under alarm, torpedo boats were sent to the Gulf of Otranto, and a squadron of destroyers sent to patrol the lower Ionian.

At 3.20 p.m. on the 8th, a group of two battleships, one aircraft carrier, numerous cruisers, and fighters were sighted at 146 miles of 120 degrees from Capo Passer with a heading 195 degrees at 16 knots. Force 'H' was divided into two groups, the most advanced group included a battleship, an aircraft carrier, two cruisers, and eight destroyers approximately 70 miles north-west of Algiers. *Supermarina* prepared for the night a patrol with destroyers and torpedo boats in the Sicily canal and another with torpedo boats in the lower Ionian. The MAS were not used because of inclement weather. Torpedo bomber units were also moved to the Sicilian bases and an ambush of three submarines was prepared south-east of Malta.

On the 9th, the reconnaissance, even though heavily contrasted by the enemy's fighters, signalled that the Mediterranean Fleet was cruising in several groups south and south-east of Malta, while Force 'H' was sighted reunited and navigating at high speed and had been attacked by twenty bombers with no results; likewise, the aerial attack done by the HMS *Illustrious* against Cagliari also had no consequences.

During the night of the 9th, new patrols of torpedo boats and MAS as well as submarine ambushes were prepared, the latter between Sardinia and Tunis and south-east of Malta.

On the 10th, and in addition to the news coming in from Crete, reconnaissance sighted many groups of units moving south and south-east of Malta, one of which was attacked by bombers, and in the western Mediterranean. The fleet was on a three hours' notice and the night patrols had been undertaken again.

On the 11th—aside from a few small groups of units to the east and to the south-east of Capo Passero—reconnaissance, as extended as it was, had not been able to find the British main group. What was certain was the return of the HMS *Ark Royal*, a cruiser, and five destroyers to Gibraltar. Taranto was under regular and constant observation by British reconnaissance. On the night of the 11th, at 11.30 p.m., the attack on Taranto began—it was led by twenty-one Swordfish.[29]

The port was defended by twenty-one gun batteries with 101 guns, sixty-eight groups of AA complexes (fixed and floating), 109 light machine guns (fixed and floating), twenty-seven spherical balloons, thirteen aero-phonic stations (of which two were connected to projectors), twenty-four spotlights, and 4,200 metres of anti-torpedo nets for a depth of 10 metres.[30]

Of the original ninety balloons, only twenty-seven remained due to the difficulties in replacing those that had been torn by the bad weather that had lasted until the day prior—it was also because of the lack of hydrogen. All the anti-aircraft artillery was ready to fire: barrage fire with the ship's AA was excluded to avoid revealing their position, but free firing against visible targets was allowed, as well as the use of projectors to blind the pilots.

The listening network (thirteen stations) had signalled aircraft noise earlier between 9 and 9.30 p.m. (in the area of Santa Maria di Leuca) and again at 10.25 p.m. (probably caused by the first British group) and the alert had been given; at 10.50 p.m. the alarm sounded, followed by the start of barrage fire.

During the first wave, RN *Conte di Cavour* was hit by a torpedo under the keel (Willamson and Scarlett), then their aircraft was shot down by the battleship's AA fire, and RN *Littorio* was hit at bow on the starboard side (Kemp-Bailey) and at stern on the port side (Swayne-Buscall); in the second wave at 11.25 p.m., RN Caio Duilio was torpedoed at bow and again RN *Littorio* a bit at stern from centre starboard (Hele-Carline or Torrens-Spence-Sutton).

The actions against the fuel depots and the bombings on other units had no effect (the two bombs that hit the destroyer *Libeccio* and the cruiser *Trento* did not explode) and the attack

Damage to the RN *Conte di Cavour* caused by the explosion of a torpedo under the keel. (*Orizzonte Mare*)

caused little damage to the seaplane base. Two British aeroplanes were shot down. The magnetic torpedoes, set for a depth of further than 10 metres in order to pass under the nets (for this reason, some of them ended up in the mud of the harbour), caused the following damage:

Regia Nave	Damage	Actions	Return to Squad
Littorio	Leak at starboard bow, 15 × 10 metres; Leak at starboard, 12 × 9 metres, almost entirely contained by the Pugliese system; Leak at stern, left side in the steering gear compartment, 7 × 15 metres.	Beached at 6.25 a.m.	Under repairs in Taranto from 11 December to 9 March 1941
Caio Duilio	Leak at starboard in the keel under forward deposits, 11 × 7 metres–both flooded.	Beached at 4.45 a.m.	Transferred to Genoa 26 January 1941 returned to Taranto 16 May 1941
Conte di Cavour	Leak under forward deposits, 12 × 8 metres–the entire bow was flooded.	Beached at 5 a.m., crew forced to abandon her	Brought to Trieste on 22 December 1941 for refitting and partial rebuilding, once the reconstruction was almost concluded did not go back into service as it was abandoned after the armistice and then sunk in Trieste

The British raid in the canal of Otranto was entirely successful, having destroyed a convoy, notwithstanding the reaction of the light escort units.

Admiral Cunningham did not order another attack the following night, as previously planned, because of a worsening in weather conditions.[31]

The Italian fleet was moved to Naples (and some units to Palermo) until the deployment of anti-torpedo nets deep in the seabed had been concluded and returned to Taranto between the end of March and the beginning of May 1941.

During the route back, the Mediterranean Fleet was the subject of a tenacious search on the 12th, the 13th, and the 14th; however, the aircraft carrier's fighters easily downed three reconnaissance aircraft. On the 13th, it was again sighted north of Marsa Maruth and attacked by torpedo bomber units without results.

The combination of the inability to fight off the reconnaissance aircraft, easily downed by the embarked Fulmar, as well as the absence of an Italian fleet aircraft carrier (which would have allowed to go out at sea with aerial and reconnaissance cover), together with a possibly excessive caution in the presence of huge enemy movements, even though not entirely well known, brought about a situation whereby British action had not caught the major Italian units by surprise, but at anchor.

The results of the action at Taranto were rightly praised, but largely overrated both from the historic literature as in action; in fact, the damaged Italian battleships stayed out of service for a few months only, aside for RN *Conte di Cavour*, and the Italian fleet returned to Taranto, its best strategic position, five to six months after the attack.

Also, the supposed acquired British moral superiority is not confirmed by the facts. Five days after Taranto (on 17 November), the *Regia Marina* was at sea to counter British Operation White, causing it to fail, and on the 27th, there was the Battle of Cape Teulada (Spartivento).[32]

Cape Spartivento

Regarding this, during which the HMS *Berwick* was damaged by two 203-mm hits, the contribution of the air forces for both sides was quite different. On the British side, there was the operation from the aircraft carrier during the tactical phase and again after the ballistic phase had ended; from the Italian side, ground-based operations were carried out with significant delays (at least two hours), while the performance of catapulted reconnaissance aircraft was good albeit not perfect.

Both commands judged the Italian firing as superior.

Speaking of this action, this is how the Historic Office of the Italian Navy expressed itself:

> We don't believe we should linger on the subject (of aerial collaboration) … given that it has already been clearly proven that all of the inconveniences were a result of:
> 1) A wrong system with which the operational relations between the Navy and the Air Force had been set up during the period before the war;
> 2) A lack of aircraft carriers which did not allow the Italian fleet to count on an efficient protection while at sea and a quick Air Force involvement on the tactical field.
>
> In 1941 and the subsequent years, various initiatives were taken to improve this regrettable situation, however they did not bring satisfactory results.[33]

The ease with which significant British forces were practically undisturbed for two days in the centre of the Mediterranean and the way the Taranto harbour was kept under control by British reconnaissance is a black mark on the control that the *Regia Marina* and *Regia Aeronautica* were able to maintain in that critical section of the sea. The uncertainty regarding the position of the British forces, which were present with all major units located in the Mediterranean, ultimately brought about greater damage than an actual clash with one of the opposing formations, with the decision to avoid having the battle squadron go at sea.

In any event, the British success at Taranto did not change their logistic options. Of the twenty-one British supply ships destined for the Middle East that left Britain on 18 December 1940, sixteen sailed around the Cape and only five risked the Mediterranean.

The Cape of Good Hope continued to be used even though it involved as much as a four-month round trip for the ships involved.[34] Nor did it assist the other theatres redistributing the British naval forces: after the persistent requests of the Admiralty, Cunningham only freed up HMS *Ramillies* and HMS *Berwick* to face the German corsairs in the Atlantic.[35]

The attack had no effect on the convoys between Italy and Libya, which actually increased the amounts transported without suffering any losses. The first losses only occurred in December

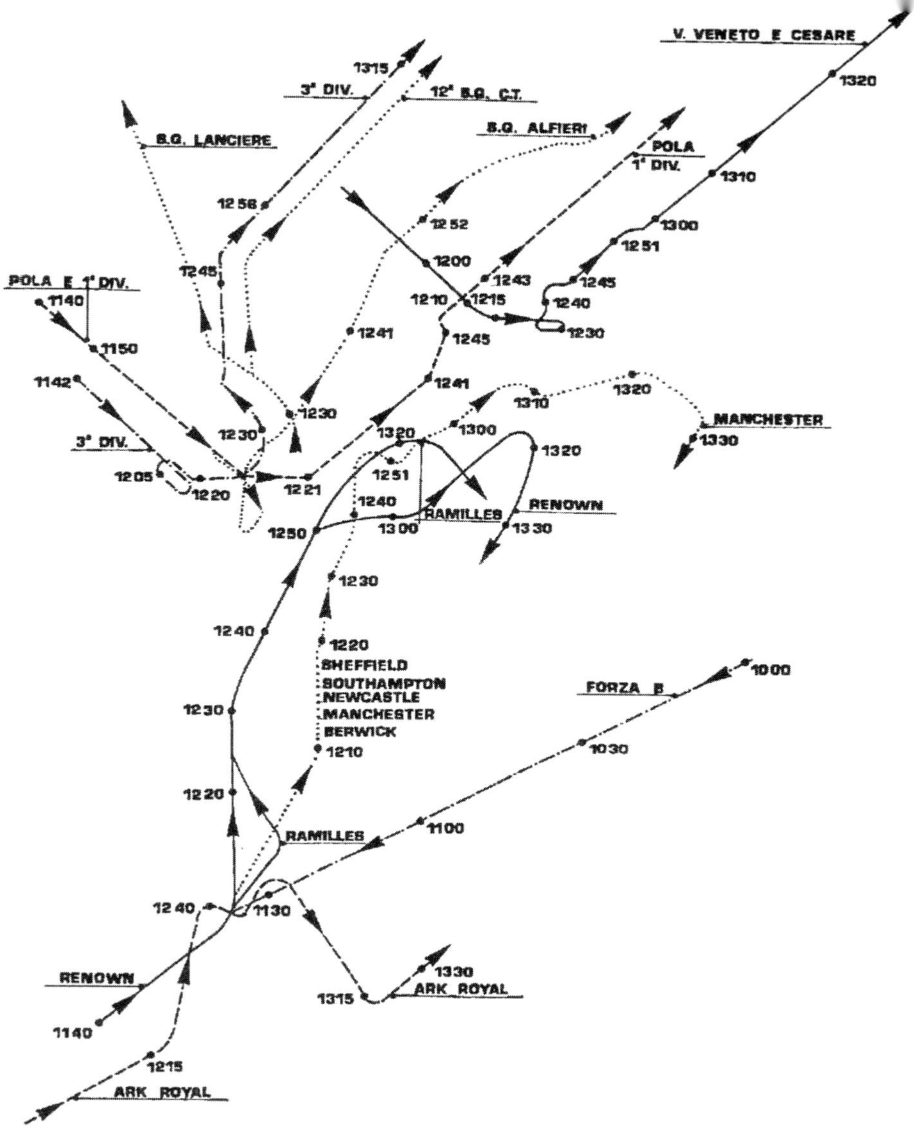

Cape Spartivento. (*Courtesy BAUSMM*)

1940, and amounted to two merchant vessels.[36] Also with the ULTRA's help, the losses in Libya were negligible in the first quarter of 1941, allowing the Axis forces to launch the offensive in April 1941.[37]

The most serious consequence was probably the exclusively political decision to allocate a large quantity of the limited Italian resources to refurbishment and modernisation of the already obsolete RN *Conte di Cavour*.

The flaws that came to light while containing the flooding, also because of an incomplete watertight seal of the minor elements of the bulkheads, were instead a subject of careful review, which were effective during torpedo damage suffered at a later date.

From a political standpoint, Mussolini suddenly changed his mind about the idea of an aircraft carrier, even assuming the authorship for the project, and so at the meeting of ministers of 7 January 1941, he said:

> Also on this occasion I must bemoan not having carried out my idea to build an aircraft carrier, but the entire Regia Aeronautica including the Chief of Staff was against it, maintaining the pointlessness of these types of ships in the Mediterranean. Now we see who was right![38]

On 8 December 1940, Cavagnari had been removed from his post as undersecretary of the Navy and replaced with Admiral Riccardi, shortly after he had shared his assessment of the situation in a detailed memo on 2 December, clearly touching on the subject of the merit of aircraft carriers as a key element from a strategic and tactical aspect and the failure of aero-naval cooperation. Evidently, if we recall Cavagnari's speech at the Senate about aircraft carriers before the war, Mussolini was always right, even when he was wrong.

Royal Navy: Genoa (Operation 'Grog')

The bold action of the British Force 'H' against Genoa on 9 February 1941 perhaps represented the best chance the *Regia Marina* had to meet with a clearly superior force a British Squadron far from its bases. The two fleets passed within only 30 miles of each other during the retirement of the British after the actions.[39]

The risky mission was planned with the goal to hit the Italian battleships damaged in Taranto and, on the basis of erroneous intelligence information, in the shipyard in Genoa. In reality, only RN *Caio Duilio* was undergoing repairs in Genoa (joined later by RN *Giulio Cesare*, which had been lightly damaged in the bombing of Naples); RN *Littorio* had remained in basin in Taranto. There was also the fear on the part of the British that Franco would release control of the Balearic Islands to Mussolini during their impending meeting.[40]

On the first try, aborted because of the worsening of the weather, Force 'H' had raised anchor from Gibraltar the evening of 31 January under the command of Admiral Sommerville (HMS *Renown*, HMS *Malaya*, HMS *Ark Royal*, HMS *Sheffield*, and ten destroyers), with the goal of attacking the morning of the 2nd, the dam of Tirso in Sardinia with torpedo bombers and Genoa the following morning.

The attack on the dam occurred as expected, without results and with one downed aircraft, and it was followed by a forced retirement of the British team because of the inclement weather.

During this raid, Force 'H' had been sighted by the aerial reconnaissance south of the Balearic Islands, and *Supermarina*, believing that it was possible it was going to attack Sardinia, had given the alarm to the fleet—an alarm that subsided after it was determined that the enemy was on its way to its base and out of range.

A repeat of the operation was established for 6 February (the next full moon) by Sommerville and the Admiralty, which would allow time to repair the damage suffered by the destroyers due to the heavy seas. The mission included a false departure towards the Atlantic and a new route (with a northern approach) to the Balearic Islands in addition to a series of measures designed to give the impression that the target was once again Sardinia.

At dawn on the 9th, HMS *Ark Royal* launched an attack against Livorno and La Spezia at a distance of approximately 70 miles from those cities—one aircraft was lost.

In the meantime, *Supermarina*, immediately informed about Force 'H''s departure by intelligence in Gibraltar, had correctly judged the possibility of British action in the Tyrrhenian Sea and ordered the moving of the 3rd Division (RN Trento, RN Trieste, and RN Bolzano, with three destroyers) from Messina to La Spezia and one aerial reconnaissance up the the Minorca meridian (and not, as was usual for these types of reconnaissance missions, named S.10, up the western end of Majorca, not supposing that there would be an action against the high Tyrrhenian); at 9.15 a.m. on the 8th, orders were given to remove the anti-torpedo nets of the battleships (RN Vittorio Veneto, RN Giulio Cesare, and RN Andrea Doria) and to be ready to go out to sea.

Between 11.40 a.m. and 3.35 p.m., *Supermarina* received various reports of encounters with enemy aircraft; however, the reconnaissance had not sighted anything due to the low visibility. At 2.30 p.m., a sortie was planned for the three battleships and the 5th Division of cruisers at 5.30 p.m. This sortie actually occurred from 7 p.m. to meet up with the 3rd Division and reach 50 miles (later reduced to 10 miles) west of Cape Testa by dawn the next day, waiting for the results of the reconnaissance. The British force was correctly estimated as two battleships, one aircraft carrier, and several destroyers. Submarines were also dispatched to the Strait of Sicily.

While not excluding a possible action against Genoa, it was assumed that, given the locations where enemy aircraft had been sighted, Force 'H' was south of the Balearic Islands.

The assessment of *Supermarina* correctly supposed the possible directions of British action; therefore, the instructions given to the battle squadron (positioned north of Asinara) would allow for intervention both in the south and in the Gulf of Genoa.[41]

The request to repeat the S.10 reconnaissance was disregarded because both seaplane and ground-based reconnaissance aircraft were not available, impeded by the rain that rendered the airports unusable. The reconnaissance planned for the next day concerned areas south of Calvi, and news arrived at 7.40 a.m. regarding aerial raids on Livorno and La Spezia and a sighting at Portofino of the major British units in route for Genoa occurred at 8.52 a.m.—a previous sighting at 7.33 a.m. had erroneously classified the units as friendly (which were not supposed to be in the area).

At 8.55 a.m., Admiral Iachino, lacking information regarding what was happening and therefore still assuming that the enemy was west of Sardinia, gave the order to catapult the Ro.43 of RN *Bolzano* and that of RN *Trento* at 9.35 a.m. in the same area. The two planes on board RN *Vittorio Veneto* were unusable due to a catapult malfunction, and so the Italian squadron remained with only one more usable reconnaissance plane, the one on board RN *Trieste*.

The shelling of Genoa is not a subject of this book, but it is interesting to evaluate the reasons of the missed encounter of the two fleets, notwithstanding the favourable intercept position of the Italian forces.

A message about the Genoa shelling reached the fleet at sea at 9.13 a.m. and arrived in the hands of Admiral Iachino at 9.50 a.m., when the British squadron was already on the way back at a speed of 22 knots.

The Italian Fleet, now heading north, received a series of imprecise or mistaken communications mentioning that the British squadron was on a westerly route, when it was really south-west, and the news of a squadron escorted by aeroplanes near Minorca on a course of 270 degrees at 18 knots (two British destroyers had been left in the area as a diversion, a mission that they partially accomplished). At 12.35 p.m., Admiral Iachino ordered to catapult the last available aircraft to explore from its position the French coast and then towards Spain to verify whether the enemy was retreating close to the French coast.

At 12.44 p.m., the Italian fleet was on course to intercept the British off Toulon, information from *Supermarina* regarding the position and course of the aircraft carrier and other three

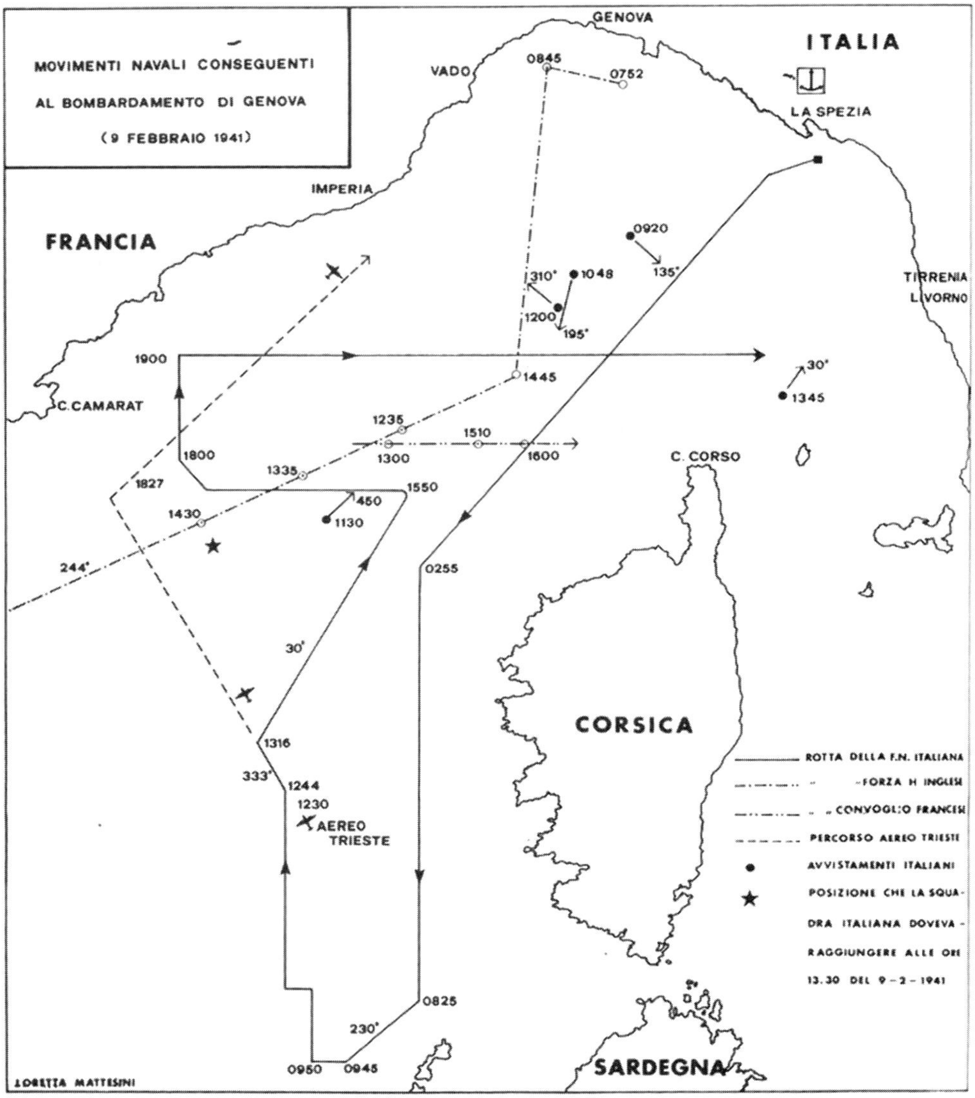

Movements of Italian and British fleets and the point of the missed encounter. (*Courtesy BAUSMM*)

enemy units, together with the lack of news from the reconnaissance aircraft in the Gulf of Genoa, gave the impression that the British squadron intended to head across a short distance from the western Corsican coast.

The reconnaissance aircraft of RN *Trieste* did not signal anything, confirming the likely course of the British towards south. The Italian course was therefore changed for north-north-east at 1.07 p.m., only thirty minutes to the contact with the British formation, and indeed it passed by the Italian formation at 30 miles distance.

The battle seemed to be imminent, particularly after a signal at 2.05 p.m. concerning British units present at 11.05 a.m., 70 miles west of Cape Corso on a course of 45 degrees. At 3.32 p.m., an oil tanker was sighted, and then at 3.38 p.m., various ships as well. RN *Vittorio Veneto* was ready to open fire at 32,000 metres. It was, however, a French convoy that had been intercepted and identified at 1 p.m. by Force 'H' and had then continued on.

The Ro.43 on board the RN *Bolzano*, 27 November 1940. These aircraft were the eyes of the fleet throughout the war. (*Courtesy fototeca AUSMM*)

Again at 3.32 p.m., *Supermarina* signalled that an aircraft carrier, two cruisers, and nine destroyers had been spotted 65 miles west of Cape Corso at 1 p.m., without communicating the course. At this point, Admiral Iachino correctly evaluated that the only possibility to encounter the enemy was by taking a westerly course at 24 knots with the destroyers and at 30 knots with the heavy cruisers.

At 4.45 p.m., the crew of an Italian aircraft that had been downed by British fighters without having seen the ships was rescued.

At 5.55 p.m., confirmation was again received about the sighting, at 12 p.m., of an aircraft carrier, two battleships, and other units 40 miles north-west of Cape Corso on a route of 310 degrees (from the torpedo boat *La Masa* that had retrieved the crew of a CANT Z.506, which had sighted the British squadron at 12 p.m., but had been shot down by the fighter before it was able to communicate).

By 6 p.m., the possibility of encountering the British squadron was considered unlikely, and the Fleet patrolled the gulf of Genoa during the night.

The analysis of the action shows that the aircraft catapulted from RN *Trieste* passed only 20 miles from the British Fleet, while the delays in communication caused the use of the other two reconnaissance aircraft towards South.

From the point of view of the air force's contribution, 191 aircraft (plus three embarked) participated in the operation on the Italian and German side.

A CANT Z.506 squadron. (*Courtesy BAUSMM*)

The news of the bombing of Genoa was immediately passed to the *Regia Aeronautica* command, which had the choice of attacking immediately or attacking after the position of the British fleet had been determined.

One aircraft squadron spotted and attacked the British formation at 1 p.m. (at 12.20 p.m. according to the British), but only notified of the event after landing at 3.16 p.m.

Another group signalled having attacked two cruisers at 2.30 p.m. in an area where there were no ships except for two MAS, which reported having been attacked by aircraft when they returned. Again at 3.07 p.m., a *Regia Aeronautica* group attacked a naval complex without results; it was later determined that it was the French convoy.

Consistent aerial formations did not find anything, having been sent to areas where there was no presence of British units (those sent to the Balearics, the only *Regia Aeronautica* force trained for operations at sea, and those of the German *X Fliegerkorps* with seventy aircraft).

Force 'H', thanks to the presence of aircraft carriers and radar, was able to shoot down two CANTs, which allowed the British force to hide its position and course, and was attacked only once by two Br.20s that released two bombs, far off the HMS *Ark Royal* stern at 12.20 p.m.

The missed encounter of the two fleets was mainly due to the inadequacy of the aerial reconnaissance and to the availability of fighters over the skies of the British Fleet. The carelessness and mistakes made by the *Regia Aeronautica* and an incredible inaccuracy both in the identification of the warships and the lack of efficient communications between the two services contributed to a lost opportunity by the *Regia Marina*, which would have met with superior forces a British fleet far from its bases.

The presence of a British squadron in home waters and the fact that it was able to leave unharmed was deeply embarrassing to the Italians and a point of controversy; the lack of cooperation and integration between the various commands was very obvious. Both the CSM of the *Regia Aeronautica* and of the *Regia Marina* expressed their clear irritation with strong memos.[42]

The Germans, who shared joint responsibility for the failure in terms of sighting the British forces, also had strong reactions; Goebbels described Weichold, *Kriegsmarine*'s Head in Italy, as 'purple with rage'.

Conference of Merano

At the conference of Merano of 26–29 March 1941 the situation of the Axis forces in the Mediterranean was jointly examined; in the meantime, the Cyrenaica had been lost and it was vital to keep traffic routes towards Libya opened, being that it was the only ground front between Great Britain and the Axis.

The analysis of the *Regia Marina* emphasised the drastic difference in operational conditions between the Mediterranean and the Atlantic. In the first, the strength was usually in favour of the British after the night at Taranto. The British did not use raiders against the convoys, while the operations of the main British fleet were always being held in a position of superiority and after accurate reconnaissance.

The risk of losing the supply lines with the troops in Africa, in case the naval battle had a negative outcome, was therefore something to avoid and forcing the enemy to maintain the maximum amount of naval forces was advantageous.

The *Kriegsmarine* received a request for assistance in the critical sectors of the *Regia Marina*: anti-aircraft vehicles, long-range reconnaissance seaplanes, and oil, as the initial supply was almost finished. No requests for operational cooperation were made.

Admiral Fricke's report at the beginning of the conference focused exclusively on the theatre of the Atlantic Ocean and the North Seas; the offensive strategy was based against merchant traffic through corsair ships, submarines, mines, and the air force while bemoaning the latter's lack of training necessary for war at sea.

The next day, Admiral Riccardi presented the thoughts of the Italian delegation, emphasising the unfavourable conditions of the Mediterranean Sea for submarines and mines. The discussion was based on the eventuality of making the Strait of Sicily impenetrable to the British, while still keeping it open to Axis traffic, and about the neutralisation of Malta as an air base. However, Admiral Raeder reiterated the importance of the war on the Atlantic, basically retracing the failed strategy of the First World War, admitting the possibility of excluding Great Britain from the Mediterranean with a succession of actions (including Spain joining the war) geared to neutralise Malta and Alexandria—the latter was supposed to be brought back within range of the ground aviation with the advance of the *Africa Korps*, which was about to be transported to Africa.[43]

For the purposes of the campaign against Greece, whose traffic with Egypt was almost undisturbed, Raeder cited the possibility of using one of the fast battleships of the *Littorio*-class together with groups of destroyers to attack the convoys and, at the same time, attract the British fleet in the range of action of the *Regia Aeronautica* (not considering the British habit of escorting convoys with at least two battleships).

The conference did not result in a 'unified' strategy nor was the radar issue, which will be discussed at length in a chapter on the subject, touched upon at all.

The situation of military politics was rapidly evolving, German troops were peacefully entering Romania and Great Britain was sending the first convoys of troops towards Greece (on 4 March), implementing a strategy of slowing down of the advance in Libya in favour of a containment of the Axis' advance in the Balkan peninsula.

The British attempt to seize an island on the Italian Dodecanese (Castelrosso) failed utterly, while 68,000 men were being transported to Greece from 4 March to 24 April with a system of biweekly convoys from Egypt.

To counteract this traffic, encouraged by the Germans and drawing upon an idea developed independently by Admiral Iachino at the end of February, where he once again examined the plans for an offensive against the traffic that would have to be executed by a fast battle squadron. In the notes to the German command, *Supermarina* emphasised that, because of the strategic situation, it was necessary to guarantee aerial protection and the neutralisation of the airports in Malta and Greece.

Gaudo and Matapan[44]

On 19 March, Admiral Weichold sent the German evaluation of the situation, according to which the Mediterranean Fleet had only one efficient battleship (the HMS *Valiant*); this evaluation was done based on two reports of aerial attacks of the *X Fliegerkorps* according to which two battleships were hit by one or two torpedoes, reports that would later emerge as erroneous.[45]

On 15 March, Admiral Iachino was called to Rome to discuss the details of a double offensive action against important British convoys, which would be held at the same time as an operation of Xª MAS boats against the bay of Suda, base of British cruisers and destroyers. The operation, initially to be held on the 24th, was postponed to the 26th to provide time to make the necessary agreements with the *X Fliegerkorps*. It was led by RN *Vittorio Veneto*.[46]

The collaboration with *X Fliegerkorps*, for the first time on a tactical field, included the boarding of German communication personnel on the *Vittorio Veneto*. A group of

The original plan of the operation that led to the Matapan action; the stop of British merchant traffic thanks to ULTRA, detected by Axis' reconnaissance, caused the plan to be modified with the entire Italian formation grouped south of Crete. (*Courtesy USMM*)

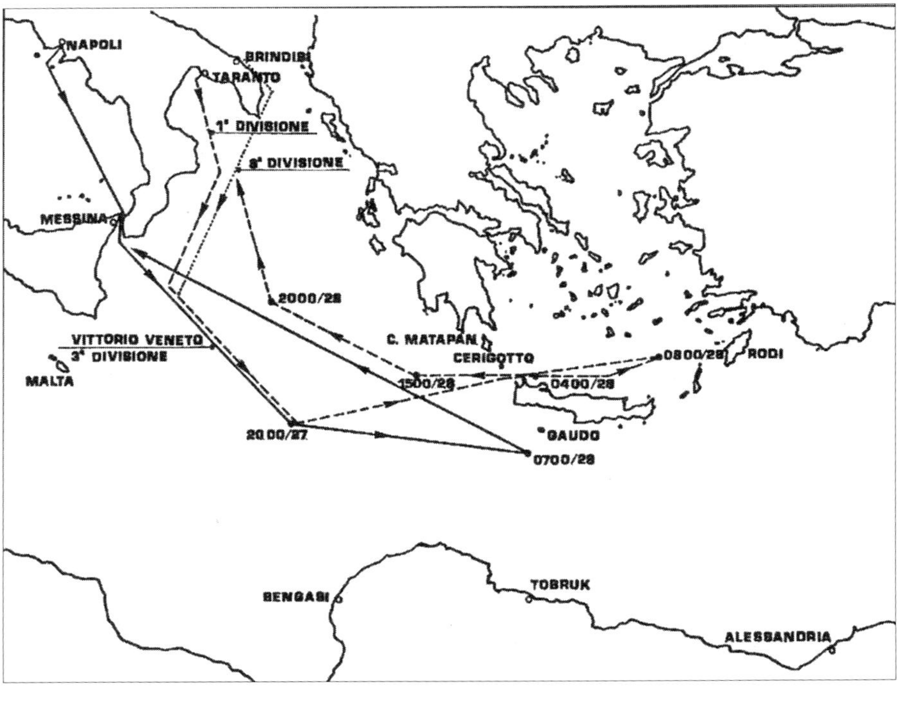

cryptographers of the *Regia Marina* was also embarked to ensure that the deciphering and the immediate use of intercepted enemy communications.

The following is the schedule of agreements:

Regia Aeronautica	*X Fliegerkorps*
Day X-2	Day X-2
Afternoon: Reconnaissance of the vessels coming from Alexandria to the Piraeus in the canals of Caso and Cerigo	
Afternoon: Reconnaissance on Alexandria and Suda (previously resp. *X Fliegerkorps*)	Morning: Reconnaissance on Alexandria and Suda (previously resp. *Regia Aeronautica*)
Day X-1	Day X-1
Reconnaissance sectors between meridians of Siracusa and Malta until Bengasi from morning until when necessary	Night, attacks on Malta airports
Reconnaissance south east gulf of Taranto until 300 miles from Taranto, from morning until when necessary	Protection of naval forces at sea from two hours after dawn to two hours before sunset.
Reconnaissance Alexandria and Suda (afternoon)	Blockading east of Malta with fighter planes.
Reconnaissance of the vessels coming from Alexandria for the Piraeus in the canals of Caso and Cerigo (afternoon) instead of two antemeridian reconnaissance south of Crete and on the vector of Caso–Alexandria canal	Aerial reconnaissance between Cyrenaic coast and eastern Crete
	Morning: reconnaissance on Alessandria and Suda bases
Day X	Day X
Bombing at dawn of the Crete airports and protection of the Fleet with fighter planes near Crete from 7.30 a.m. on (previously from 7 a.m. for an indefinite amount of time)	Reconnaissance east of Sicily between parallels 32°30 and 35°, to meridian 25° east (from the morning)
Reconnaissance of southern Aegean basin, including Suda (beginning at dawn)	Protection of naval forces until two hours before sunset west of the meridian 21° east and north of parallel 36°
Reconnaissance of the Caso–Alexandria–Greece vector (beginning at dawn)	Staging in Sicily of a combat group of approximately twenty aircraft
Reconnaissance south of Crete (beginning at dawn) followed by reconnaissance of the vector Gaudo–Alexandria	
Armed offensive reconnaissance starting from dawn until 10 a.m. in the area near Crete until the 22° east meridian (previously armed reconnaissance to protect naval forces starting from dawn)	
Staging of bombers and torpedoes (Aegean aviation) starting at dawn	

These arrangements did not fully satisfy Admiral Iachino, who obtained the promise of protection for day-X by CR.42, which would alternate every twenty minutes on the fleet, the maximum time allowed by their autonomy, even with auxiliary tanks.[47] The entire force of the *Regia Aeronautica* in the Aegean, the only force that could intervene on the Italian side in that area, was represented by nine S.79 and seven S.81 for bombing, five aero torpedoes, fifteen CR.42s and eight CR.32s, and eight reconnaissance aircraft.

The modifications that occurred between *Supermarina*, *Superaereo*, and *X Fliegerkorps* (underlined in the table) were not communicated to Admiral Iachino.

The order of operations, with separate arrangements for reconnaissance and air force protection, was sent by wire on the evening of the 23rd in Naples where Iachino was with the *Vittorio Veneto* and on the 24th and the 25th to the 'Egeo' command (the Dodecanese Islands) and to the *X Fliegerkorps* via radio.[48] It is not the purpose of this text to fully describe the course of action, which is well-documented and represents the first episode of ULTRA's operational activity in the Mediterranean, leading to an accurate British preparation that as first measure interrupted convoys' traffic, the main target of the operation.[49, 50]

After the inconclusive clash between the Italian and British cruisers (interrupted by a first aerial attack on RN *Vittorio Veneto* while she was chasing the British cruisers), who then retreated towards their own battle line. The aerial attacks from the aircraft carrier caused the torpedoing of RN *Vittorio Veneto* and then of RN *Pola*, followed by a fortuitous night encounter between the division of cruisers of Admiral Cattaneo and the British battleships—an encounter that caught the Italians completely by surprise and caused an almost total destruction of the Italian division.

Dwelling on the subject of aerial signals, the notice of the unavailability of two of the three British battleships was contradicted by another report of the *X Fliegerkorps*, which, based on an examination of the photos taken during the attack on a British formation on 24 March, notified on 26 March the presence in the attached formation of three *Queen Elizabeth*-type battleships and one *Formidable*-class aircraft carrier. This report was not forwarded to Admiral Iachino as Admiral Riccardi in Rome concluded it contradicted the detailed previous reports.[51]

On the first day of the mission, the *X Fliegerkorps* escort failed while a section of the Italian fleet (three cruisers and one destroyer) was sighted by a Sunderland; it stayed in sight of the Italian formation for approximately half an hour, and its messages were deciphered on board the *Vittorio Veneto*.[52]

The planned aerial reconnaissance on Alexandria (2 p.m. and 2.35 p.m.), also intercepted by the *Vittorio Veneto*, reported three battleships and one aircraft carrier in port.

The new evaluation of the situation (the British main force probably intact and the Italian units sighted) was the subject of a meeting on the 27th at *Supermarina*. The outcome did not intend, probably for political reasons, to postpone the mission, only to change the plan by cancelling the foray to north of Crete as no convoy was actually present in the Aegean (the convoys had been stopped by the British, warned by ULTRA).

At 6.35 a.m. on the 28th, an aircraft launched from the *Vittorio Veneto* sighted the British cruisers of the *Orion* division, and the Gaudo battle began, during which the main calibres of RN *Vittorio Veneto* straddled the British cruisers several times, with damage from near misses.[53]

In the area of the battle, the Italian naval forces should have been escorted by fighters from the base in Rhodes; however, no Italian plane was sighted. At 9.13 a.m., Iachino received a message from one of the reconnaissance planes that had spotted one aircraft carrier, two battleships, nine cruisers, and fourteen destroyers at 7.45 a.m.—a sighting that he correctly evaluated was of his fleet.

At 10.50 a.m., RN *Vittorio Veneto* surprised the British cruisers at 23,000 metres—they retreated at full speed, covering themselves with a smokescreen. At 11.18 a.m., the Italian battleship was attacked from British torpedo bombers (which had previously been targeted by the 'B' Force friendly fire), without results (while the British thought that one torpedo had hit the target). The British attack was disturbed by two reconnaissance Ju 88s, the only Axis aeroplanes that would appear above Italian naval forces. One of them was shot down during the attempt.

At 11.40 a.m., Iachino was informed by Rome that the aircraft for reconnaissance and the protection of the fleet had returned to base due to the weather conditions. Having received confirmation from his own reconnaissance by RN *Bolzano* that there were no enemy transports—and knowing with certainty about the presence of an aircraft carrier in the area, confirmed at 11.47 a.m. by *X Fliegerkorps* and continuously under observation by British reconnaissance—Iachino decided to return.

Thus a series of aerial attacks on the Italian fleet began: at 12.07 p.m., three torpedoes were aimed at RN *Bolzano*, and at 2.30 p.m., 3.01 p.m., 3.17 p.m., 3.26 p.m., 3.40 p.m., 4.20 p.m., 4.30 p.m., 4.44 p.m., and 4.58 p.m., bombing commenced from aircraft at high altitude, almost all without effect.

At the same time, information was received concerning enemy ships in the area. At 2.25 p.m., a battleship, an aircraft carrier, six cruisers, and five destroyers were sighted 79 miles east of the *Vittorio Veneto* (from two Italian torpedo planes, which unsuccessfully attacked the aircraft carrier), but the report was considered not credible and therefore not confirmed by *Supermarina* to Iachino (who had received the message and given the identical assessment).[54] Then, at 3.04 p.m., a radio goniometric detection of the presence of a unit that was transmitting orders to Crete and Alexandria located 170 miles south-east of the *Vittorio Veneto* was made, and the position was confirmed at 4 p.m. by German reconnaissance, after the torpedoing of RN *Vittorio Veneto*.

At 3.19 p.m., RN *Vittorio Veneto* was attacked at the same time by planes at altitude and torpedo planes of the HMS *Formidable* who hit her with a torpedo at the depth of the outboard port propeller (the attacking aeroplane was shot down); after emergency procedures, the battleship was able to continue on its course at 16 knots, later increased to 19 knots and then decreased to 15 knots. The attack had been ordered by Admiral Cunningham, who was aware that he would not be able to make contact with the enemy without first having succeeded in limiting the speed of the Italian fleet.

At 4 p.m. and at 5 p.m., Iachino asked *X Fliegerkorps*' fighters to protect the squadron and received confirmation by *Supermarina*. However, no plane was sighted. On the British side, aerial reconnaissance was able to track the movements of the Italian groups, with the only mistake of confusing two light cruisers of the *Abruzzi*-type with two battleships of the *Cavour*-class. They described the formation taken by the Italian fleet with precision.

After 3.50 p.m., Axis reconnaissance did not spot any British ship. No reconnaissance on Alexandria was ordered to verify the ships actually in the harbour. The cryptograph departments on board did, however, decipher messages from the British that ordered air torpedo attacks after sunset (the message actually came from *Supermarina*, too, well after the attack at 8.59 p.m.). At 8.05 p.m., *Supermarina* gave information that the enemy ship, which was the headquarters of a complex command centre, was 75 miles away, at 110 degrees of the *Vittorio Veneto* (in truth, it was 20 miles closer—because of the errors associated with the radio goniometric point, this uncertainty was not given over to the commander at sea).

Mattesini ran an in-depth analysis on the efficacy and precision of communications between the commands involved, given their importance for the purpose of subsequent decisions that lead to the destruction of the *Zara* division.[55]

At 6.50 p.m., a request was once again issued for *X Fliegerkorps*' fighters as British aeroplanes had already been sighted by the Italian formation. At 7.28 p.m., the attack began, countered with the aid of smoke dischargers, spotlights, and AA fire. RN *Pola* was hit amidships by a torpedo and lost all power, yet remained in good buoyancy condition. At 9.50 p.m., the news reached Admiral Iachino who had started navigating at 19 knots.

The decision to send Admiral Cattaneo's squadron to assist the *Pola* and the following events have been the object of careful studies, yet it is worth remembering that when the decision was taken, the British fleet was believed to have one only battleship and to be distant enough. Furthermore, at the time, it was believed that the British did not have radar. It is also noteworthy to underline that the possibility that the *Pola* would be caught by stronger forces while it was being towed was brought up to Mussolini who gave the order to sink the cruiser in such a case.

At 8.30 p.m., Admiral Iachino requested the intervention of fighters for dawn of the next morning at the expected location of the fleet and at 9.56 p.m. for the expected position of RN *Pola* and a squadron of destroyers from Messina to join Admiral Cattaneo's division.

During the night, the *Orion* division detected via radar the immobilised RN *Pola*, but not the division of Admiral Cattaneo; they probably detected for a brief time three destroyers of the *Zara* division, confusing them with British destroyers of Commander Mack's squadron, who were also searching for the Italians.

Zara-class cruisers. (*Courtesy Vittorio Catalano Gonzaga*)

Cunningham's Fleet had also detected the immobilised RN *Pola* via radar, while Commodore Edelsten had, completely unexpectedly, visually sighted the *Zara* division, followed by an immediate close-distance shooting (3 or 4 km) from the big calibres of the Mediterranean Fleet. RN *Pola* was then sighted again at night, initially confused with a unit of the *Littorio*-class after the order to scuttle her and part of the crew was already in the water. HMS *Havoc* opened fire on her, and while the crew on board fought the fire, some of the men in the water reboarded RN *Pola* and assisted with the blaze. HMS *Jervis* took her crew off and the *Pola* was finished by British torpedoes.

RN *Zara*, still floating despite the devastating damage suffered, was sunk by the Italians once the impossibility of rescue was determined at 2.30 a.m. under orders of Commander Corsi, approved by Admiral Cattaneo—both later died at sea.

RN *Fiume* remained with two working boilers for a bit, then the fires and the flooding caused the end of the ship. Captain Giorgis, who had been wounded, died at sea. Of the four destroyers that tried to cover the cruisers with a smokescreen, two survived, one unharmed and one seriously damaged (RN *Gioberti* and RN *Oriani*). RN *Alfieri* was hit in the engines and immobilised, and during the battle she returned fire and torpedoes against the British. Captain Toscano sunk with the ship, refusing to leave the bridge after having given the order to abandon ship. RN *Carducci* was immobilised during the attempt to place the smokescreen and it was sunk by the crew, the latter partially rescued together with her Captain Ginocchio after five days at sea.

During the return of the Italian fleet, five Ju 88 appeared at 6.23 a.m., followed by German fighters and, finally, when they were already at the Gulf of Taranto, by Italian aircraft. The aerial protection was carried out only when it was, for all intents and purposes, useless.

The British fleet was attacked during the return by one squadron of sixteen Ju 88 that attacked the HMS *Formidable* without hits, but with many near misses. During the operations that immediately followed, the HMS *Bonaventure* was attacked and probably damaged by the RS *Dagabur* and then sunk by the RS *Ambra*.

From the point of view of aero-naval cooperation, Operation Gaudo was a total failure: there was no aerial protection for the fleet and the reconnaissance gave only modest results. The situation was further exacerbated by the inexcusably complex chain of communication between the *Regia Marina* and the *Regia Aeronautica* and of the lack of coordination with the *X Fliegerkorps* and the *Regia Aeronautica* in the Aegean—both put to the test for the first time in aero-naval operations.

The lack of initiative in confirming the news of the attack by two Italian torpedo planes on the British aircraft carrier is inexplicable. A squadron of Italian torpedo planes 'escorted' a presumably British formation for more than an hour. Some aircraft of the *Regia Aeronautica* of the Aegean did not use the expected frequencies for their communications, therefore they were not received directly by RN *Vittorio Veneto*. While direct communications between the squadron and German aviation was possible, the inter-Italian communications that went through the various chains of command could take up to four hours.

The aftermath analysis is interesting from various standpoints. First of all, Admiral Iachino, who met with Mussolini on 31 March, received confirmation that the operation was necessary, mainly for political reasons. Mussolini stated that the lack of aero-naval cooperation was at the core of the failure and that this state of affairs was intolerable. As a result, it was necessary for the fleet to always be accompanied by an aircraft carrier. The order to proceed with its construction had already been given and it was estimated that she would be ready in a year; in the meantime, the fleet would be able to operate only in a combat radius of the ground-based fighters.[56]

It was necessary to go through a naval disaster—alleviated only by the brilliant performance of RN *Vittorio Veneto*, which survived very serious damage—to overturn the 'political' concept of military doctrine that had been maintained for years by the *Regia Aeronautica* with the support of indifference of the head of the Fascist regime.[57]

The Regia Aeronautica did not give up trying to avoid an embarked aviation in any possible way because of this. Again, in 1942, a document for Mussolini titled 'Aircraft carrier ship', edited by the Office of the Minister of Aviation, vehemently argued against the possibility of embarked aircraft and about their disadvantages concerning ground-based aircraft, maintaining the impossibility of deck landing also for the Re.2000 fighters. It seemed almost as if the writers of the document were ignorant of what had occurred in the war theatres until that moment.[58]

The immediate consequences were as follows:

1. The beginning of the conversion of two ocean liners *Roma* and *Augustus* to aircraft carriers, respectively RN *Aquila* and RN *Sparviero*.
2. While waiting to improve relations between the two services, the *Regia Marina* was instructed not to operate beyond the limit of 100 mm from national airports, in other words, to give up any efficient operation.[59]
3. The order was given not to risk any night encounters—given the fact that it was known that the British had radar—until they would be equipped with radar.[60]

Operation Halberd

This episode, which followed the instructions given after Matapan, represented a missed chance to intercept an important British convoy to Malta and conflicted the precedent, an event during which the *Regia Aeronautica* attacked with determination and the *Regia Marina* took a very prudent approach according to the new instructions. Aerial reconnaissance instead showed the known limits of precision and identification of the enemy forces.

The operation was, from the British side, very large. In order to guarantee passage of 81,000 tons of supplies and 2,600 embarked men on fast steamships, HMS *Rodney* and HMS *Prince of Wales* were added to Force 'H' in Gibraltar, in addition to submarine shields and the traditional divertive action of the Mediterranean Fleet that went out with three battleships, which were accompanied by cruisers and destroyers, without being detected.[61]

The force used to escort the convoy consisted of three warships, one aircraft carrier, five light cruisers, and eighteen destroyers. On the Italian side, RN *Littorio* and RN *Vittorio Veneto* weighed anchor from Naples under Admiral Iachino's command with three heavy cruisers, three light cruisers, and fourteen destroyers.

The British operation was immediately known in Rome and countermeasures were taken, including the deployment of submarines and aircraft. The first sighting of the British group reported the presence at sea of the HMS *Furious*, which let the Italians believe that there were two aircraft carriers at sea, but this was not confirmed by subsequent sightings.

The *Regia Aeronautica* performed a series of very determined torpedo bombers attacks, which led to the torpedoing of the HMS *Nelson*, probably attributed to the commander of the 36° *Stormo*. The British battleship reduced speed to 15 knots, and although judged as battle ready, it did not have good manoeuvring abilities (it returned to service after seven months). The information regarding the supposed successes of the attacks (which, as we shall see, were widely overestimated) were not transmitted to the *Regia Marina* commands until the aircraft returned to base.

The Italian fleet, although it did not have final information regarding the composition of the British forces, came close to a distance of 40 miles, always shadowed by British reconnaissance, deploying in battle formation and then changing course at 2.30 p.m., evaluating the conditions of the encounter as unfavourable (visibility was only 10 km in the direction of the British fleet and better in the direction of the Italian one). It was also decided that aerial coverage was not in accordance with the guidelines given after Matapan.

As soon as credible information was finally received about the composition of the British fleet by RN *Trento* reconnaissance, and regarding the estimated damage inflicted by the aerial attacks (one cruiser sunk and one battleship and two cruisers torpedoed), the course was once again changed. However, *Supermarina* ordered the fleet to stop, given that there was still much uncertainty regarding the enemy's composition.

In the meantime, Admiral Sommerville had decided—in order to avoid contact between the Italians and the convoy—to attempt an interception before dark with his three battleships, two cruisers, and six destroyers. HMS *Ark Royal* would have to remain with the convoy and attack with torpedoes as soon as possible. However, the condition of HMS *Nelson* did not allow her to follow the fleet, and therefore it remained at the end of the convoy. The British action was ordered to return when evidence was received that there was no possibility of contact before dark. The subsequent actions of aircraft and submarines had limited results (one British merchant vessel was sunk, and one Italian submarine and one torpedo boat were lost).

The operation was an irrefutable success for the British, both from a strategic and a tactical point of view. The restrictive directives imposed on the Italian fleet at sea showed their colours in the damaging restrictions they caused. Although the *Regia Aeronautica* acted aggressively, reconnaissance did not give complete and correct information regarding the composition of the British fleet.

The *Regia Aeronautica*'s assessment of the damage inflicted was not reliable, as seen in the following chart:

	Italian	British
Actual	RS *Adua*, RT *Albatros* sunk, 21 planes, of which 10 due to lack of fuel and 1 due to friendly fire	Steamship *Imperial Star* sunk, HMS *Nelson* torpedoed, 4 planes.
Enemy Estimate	12 planes, in addition to the two sinking	2 torpedoes from the submarines; from the airplane's torpedoes, 3 cruisers and two steamships sunk, one aircraft carrier, six cruisers, one destroyer and an undefined unit damaged

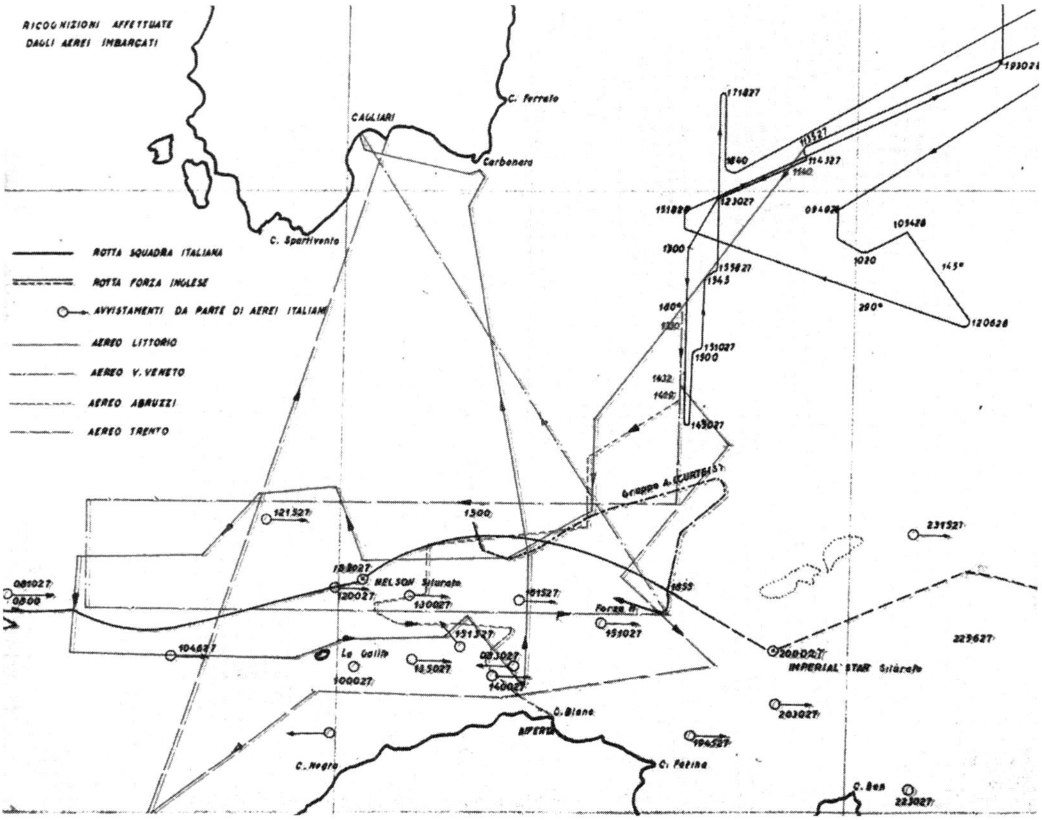

Movements as reported in Admiral Iachino's report. (*Courtesy BAUSMM*)

The *Regia Aeronautica* used a total of 241 aircraft in fifty-eight separate operations, including reconnaissance, using twenty-four torpedoes and eight bombs. Communication between fleets at sea and aircraft was extremely difficult and there were long delays in relaying communications concerning sightings. What followed was the usual controversy between the two services, alleviated only by the operations under way (the installation of the radio apparatus on board the aircraft 'in agreement with the manufacturing abilities of the national industry') and of the aircraft carrier under construction: two operations that would never end up being used in an actionable way.

The importance of the presence of the aircraft carrier was also crucial this time—not only did it cause a cautious approach of the Italian fleet, which was afraid of a torpedo attack not countered by its fighters, but it avoided a battle between the Italian and the British fleets, which would have seen superior forces on the *Regia Marina*'s side.

There were more victories and defeats for both sides in the Mediterranean, the convoys continued to supply the African front until the very last moment, even when the Allies' aerial and maritime superiority was total, but these facts are not within the scope of this book.

9

Wartime Studies and Conversions

Rex, *Conte di Savoia*, and *Roma*

During the war, after the action off Calabria, where the inability of the *Regia Aeronautica* to identify ships at sea was clearly demonstrated, Admiral Cavagnari proposed again the emergency conversion of two great ocean-going liners as they, with their 27 knots, could have been included in the battle line. The proposal was rejected due to opposition of the Merchant Navy concerned with 'the high economic value of the ships'.[1] The conversion, estimated to take about a year, would have been done by removing the superstructures, adding a hangar and a continuous flight deck, of approximately 260 by 30 metres, and an air group of approximately fifty aircraft.[2]

The *Roma* was instead considered for conversion to a fleet aircraft. The engines would have been replaced, and a flight deck of 218 metres in length and a maximum width of 27 metres, restricted to 20 metres at the island, was envisaged. Two hangars were also specified, the upper one more than 150 metres long, 26 metres wide, and 6 metres in height and the lower one 157 metres long, 18 metres wide, and 4.1 metres in height.

The solution was noticeably different from the one planned in the Gagnotto 1936 project and it appears to be similar to the *Ark Royal*, or to the one presumably adopted in the model for the conversion of RN *Impero* into an aircraft carrier located at the Museum of Venice (see Appendix I).[3]

RN *Aquila*

Despite the fact that, ever since the start of the war, the Supreme Board of Defence had decided not to start building ships of a displacement above 5,000 tons, war evidence pushed Mussolini, only after Matapan, to request the immediate conversion of two ships already available into aircraft carriers.[4]

After the leaders of the *Regia Marina* changed, work began on the conversion of the *Roma*, which had been idle for a while in Genoa, while a decision was being made.

The directives given by the Chief of Staff were for a study that would limit the conversion time to eight to ten months, given the large amount of designs already done. After only two

RN *Aquila*'s model tested in the wind tunnel. (*Courtesy BAUSMM*)

Above: The Bozzoni-Ansaldo project for the conversion of the liner *Roma*. (*Courtesy USMM*)

Below: The liner *Roma* ready for launch, 24 February 1926. (*Courtesy Aldo Cavallini via naviearmatori.net*)

weeks, the *Regia Aeronautica* communicated that it did not have aircraft or studies underway suitable for use on an aircraft carrier.[5]

The study was commissioned to General (NC) Gustavo Bozzoni in collaboration with Ansaldo ('Bozzoni' project, Ansaldo UP 188, June 1941).

The project was completed in June 1941; underwater protection included bulges, the maximum width of the ship's hull reached 30 metres, and a double bottom would have to be filled with cement.[6] The resulting reduction of speed would be contained with new engines, which would take it to a top speed of 30 knots.[7]

There was no hull protection; the minimum was estimated during the design phase (according to Bozzoni, the designer) to be at least 200 mm on the sides and 100 mm on the flight deck; these values were not compatible to the conversion.

Features of the Bozzoni project (dimensions in metres):

Length between perpendiculars	202.40
Length at the waterline	208
Max. length flight deck	223.50
Max. width at bulges	28.80
Max. flight deck width	25.20
Height of construction of flight deck	23.00
Displacement at max. normal load	23,500
Draft at max. normal load	6.96

For this project, the final configuration planned for a 25,000-ton displacement and a hangar on one level; therefore, the air wing decreased to only thirty-four fighters.

After Matapan, the final decision was taken on 6 July 1941 (and the *Regia Aeronautica* notified that it would 'carefully restart' the studies for aeroplanes with foldable wings), initially based on the original project by Bozzoni and with an estimated completion time of about eight to nine months starting from availability of materials.[9] Conversion work started on 15 July 1941 at the Ansaldo's Genoa shipyards.

The first complete conversion project is dated September 1941, while the final one, after the meetings with the German and Japanese Navies, is dated February 1942. Trials for different flight deck types were done between September 1941 and April 1942.[10]

The modifications done on the hull of the *Roma* included the application of long bulges (130 × 9.5 metres), modifications to the length of the hull and the structures at prow and stern, and modifications to a small internal compartmentalisation, which when completed was also improve hydrodynamics and speed.

Specifications of the aircraft carrier *Regia Nave Aquila* (as in 1943):[11]

Overall length	231.4
Length between perpendiculars	204.75
Length at the waterline	210.65
Max. flight deck length	211.6
Flight deck width	26.0

Max. width	35.75
Max. width at the waterline	29
Flight deck moulded depth	23.50
Draft at max. normal load	7.39
Metacentre Height	2.80
Standard displacement (tons)	23,350
Displacement at normal load	26,700
Displacement at full load	27,800
Displacement with max oil load	28,800
Displacement at test load	26,700
Max. speed	30 knots
Autonomy	5,550 miles at 18 knots, 1,580 at 29 knots (at max. oil load)
Island	55 metres in length, max. height 25 metres above the flight deck
Radar	EC 3/ter Gufo, rotating 360° with the range finder. Range 30 km surface and 80 km aerial.
Air group	Normal 38, Maximum 51 aircraft RE.2001/O.R. 'Falco II'. 26 in hangar, 15 suspended in the hangar, and 10–12 on deck. 66 expected if with foldable wings.
Hangar	160 × 18 × 5.5 metres, four sections (32, 25, 25 and 35 metres in length) divided by fire door walls
Elevators	Two 5 tons, 14 × 13 metres
Catapults	Two 23-metre Deutsche Werke for 2.5 tons at 140 km/h or 3 tons at 30 km/h. 9 launches in 9 minutes, then 50 minutes needed to refill the compressed air.
Deceleration cables	Four, DEMAG type
Armament	
Ansaldo/O.T.O. Mod. 1938 135 L.45	8 singles in shields; elevations +45° to -7°, range 19,600 metres, 6 rounds per minute, availability expected for August 1942
Ansaldo/Terni 65 L.64 1939 semiautomatic	12 singles in shields, elevations +80° to -10°, range 7,500 metres, 20 rounds per minute; availability April 1942, not yet honoured in April 1943
Breda 20 L. 65 mod. 1935	132 in sextuples, range 5,000 metres. Available in April 1943, twins used until that date
Range Finders	1 at 36 metres above sea level, connected to the 135 L.45 fire direction; two pairs on the bulwarks for the 65 L.64
Boats	9
Protection	
Horizontal	Plates of 60–80 mm. on munitions and fuel deposits; 30 mm for the rudder
Underwater	Bulges in reinforced concrete of 400–800 mm
Crew	1,532 men, of which 347 airmen
Engines	8 boilers and 4 turbines, 140,000 cv normal power, 151,000 cv maximum (engines from the Paolo Emilio and Cornelio Silla cruisers)
Shafts	4, propellers with four blades.

The protection in reinforced concrete had been tested on scale models, and a wood-planked flight deck was planned.

During the fitting of RN *Aquila*, there were numerous contacts with the German and Japanese Navies, with the purpose of gathering as much technical and operative information as possible. While the *Kriegsmarine*, which had planned the *Graf Zeppelin*, a design strongly based on the information received from the Japanese, could provide assessments and technical material, the Japanese were more generous with operational details, of which none of its European allies had experience. It is interesting to note that in discussions with Allied counterparts the 'Bozzoni' plan was used as a basis of discussion.[12 13]

The collaboration with the *Regia Aeronautica* remained troublesome until General Pricolo was removed and replaced with General Rino Corso Fougier on 15 November 1941, Fougier being more inclined to a realistic collaboration with the other armed forces.

The go ahead was given for a series of tests for aircraft landings first in Orvieto and then at S. Egidio di Perugia with runways that were as long as flight decks and were equipped with arrestor cables. The entire aero-naval programme merged into a specific organisation, the *Organizzazione Roma*—OR.

By 15 October 1942, the *Aquila* transformation had been going on for a year, and only the bulges and the armour plates in the planned areas were assembled; delays were due to the changes requested by the installation of the catapults coming from Germany and the lack of manual labour. The expected date of completion had shifted to July 1943.[14] As far as the air groups were concerned, manufacturing of the fighters was stated to start in December 1942 with a batch of fifty planes.

Testing for take-off and landing was run near Perugia where a catapult and arrestor systems were installed. Five G.50s (of which one was a two-seater) and two lightened Re 2001 fighters were set up for the tests run at the end of October 1942. These fighters had already passed the tests on a duplicate of the landing deck prepared in Genoa by Ansaldo. On 1 December, manufacturing of the fifty planes planned for RN *Aquila* began.[15]

Due to the aerial raids on Genoa, which heavily damaged the workshops, RN *Aquila* was moved to the Ansaldo shipyards and their anti-aircraft defence was increased; the incomplete hull of the cruiser *Cornelio Silla*, with a fake wood flight deck, was moved in her place.[16]

Original plans called for the installation of eight radars (three of the bulky type 'Felino'), which would have, in any event, allowed for a warning of only ten minutes prior to the arrival of enemy aircraft. This impressive arrangement was then reduced to four, of which three were of the German Seetakt.[17] This arrangement was then further reduced to only one, with the plan to install a second one.[18]

In January 1943, RN *Aquila*'s status, as described by the Chief of Staff of the *Regia Marina*, was the following:[19]

Engine testing at sea planned for 15 June 1943.
Testing for all other arrangements September 1943.
60 embarked aircraft, 26 in the hangar, 24 suspended from the hangar ceiling, 10 on the flight deck.
Aircraft: Ro.63 for night reconnaissance, modified Re 2001/O.R. as night fighters and Fiat G.50b N for daytime reconnaissance.

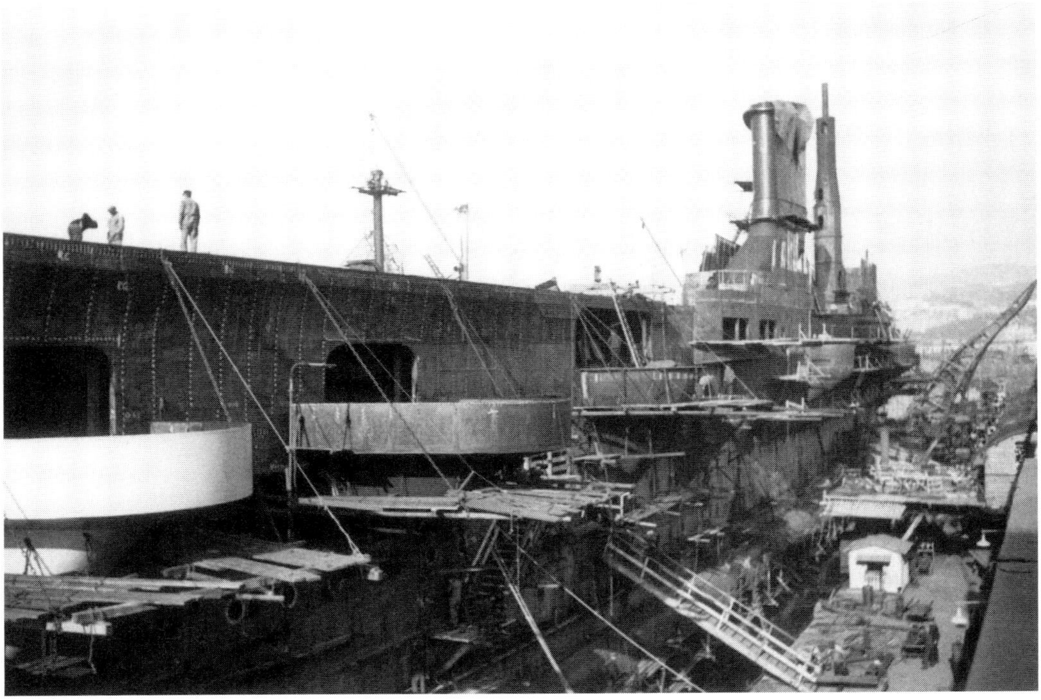

RN *Aquila* in Genoa. (*Courtesy Fototeca AUSMM*)

An Arado at testing deck landing in Perugia. (*Courtesy Fototeca AUSMM*)

The incomplete RN *Cornelio Silla* cruiser as aircraft carrier mock up. (*Courtesy Archivio Storico Ansaldo*)

RN *Aquila* at the Ansaldo shipyard in 1942. (*Courtesy Archivio Storico Ansaldo*)

By the time the work was interrupted, RN *Aquila*'s readiness state was 99 per cent for the hull, 98 per cent for the engines, and 70 per cent for the fitting. Weaponry was very behind schedule and only a few machine guns (German) had been installed.[20]

After the Armistice, the Germans dismantled the ship of anything that could be useful and then used her as storage, moving RN *Aquila* to the pier of Calata Canzio.

Chariot Attack on the *Aquila*, Spring 1945[21]

The nearly completed carrier is often described as having been sunk in shallow waters inside Genoa's harbour by German action or a joint *Regia Marina* and Royal Navy chariot sabotage. Nonetheless, an IWM picture shows her being moved via manual reaming at the end of April to mid-May 1945. In any case, she was found floating on 16 June 1945, when the harbour was returned from the Allied authorities to the *Regia Marina*.

In an aerial reconnaissance picture taken on 4 April 1945, RN *Aquila* was found blocking the narrow passage between the outer harbour and the inner one (Bacino della Lanterna). The ship was slightly inclined and had some visible damage to the bulges. After the move, the unit was moored at Calata Bettolo pier, where it was found on 16 June 1945. No direct bomb damage was visible in any of the available pictures.

The chariot attacks (Operation 'Toast') made on 18 April 1945 had little effect, as one of the two British-built chariots had to abandon the mission due to battery problems and the other (Tenente di Vascello Nicola Conte and Sottocapo Evelino Marcolini, the latter with serious problems with his aqualung) left the charge on the harbour bottom, possibly 10 metres below RN *Aquila*'s keel. It is probable the charge was responsible for the bulge damage found when the Allies entered Genoa.[22]

RN *Sparviero*

In 1942, the decision was made to proceed with the conversion of the almost-twins of the *Roma* and the liner *Augustus*, which was confiscated on 1 July 1942; initially, the plan was to obtain a sister for RN *Aquila*, with a more spacious hangar, up to ninety-eight aircraft (with foldable wings) or several more than those on the *Aquila* (if with fixed wings). The more spacious hangar would have required an increase in the size of the bulges, also built with reinforced cement.

The general complexity of the situation and the refusal of the *Kriegsmarine* to give material, a refusal motivated by the momentary upswing of the German plan to build aircraft carriers, caused the fall back on a simpler conversion aimed at traffic defence.[23]

The embarked aircraft should have been the reconnaissance IMAM Ro.63, but the minimal supply of the much-needed German motor Hirth caused the production of only six samples with the unsatisfactory Isotta Fraschini Beta engines.

The specifications of the final project (January 1943) are as follows:[24]

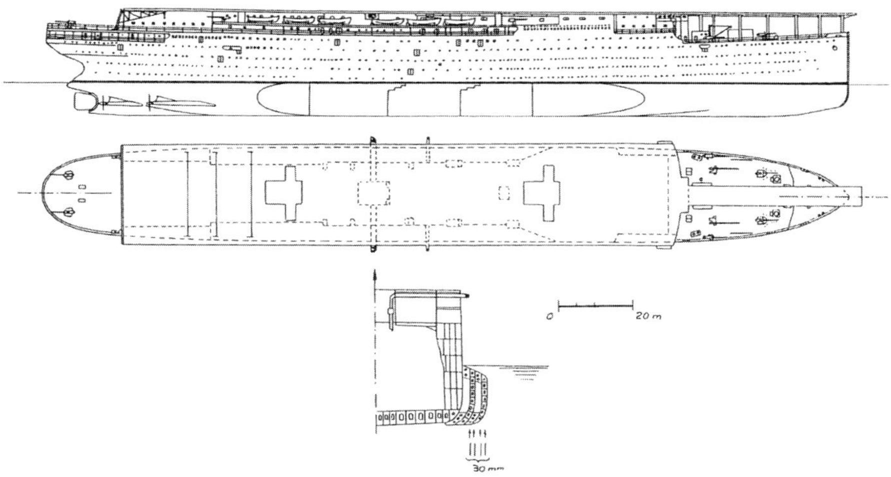

Plans for the RN *Sparviero*. (*Courtesy Rivista Marittima*)

Overall length	216.65 (metres)
Length between perpendiculars	206.18
Length at waterline	202.43
Max. length flight deck	180 (estimate)
Flight deck width	25.24
Max. width	34
Moulded depth at flight deck	23.00
Displacement at full load	28,000
Draft at full load	9.2
Max. speed	18 knots
Autonomy	6,000 miles at 18 knots
Island	Possible a small island at starboard bow
Air group	35 Re.2001/OR 'Falco II'.
Elevators	Two
Catapults	Two (possible)
Armament	
Ansaldo/O.T.O. Mod. 1938 135/45	8 shielded singles; elevation +45° to -7°, range 19,600 m., 6 rounds per minute, available for August 1942
Ansaldo/Terni semiautomatic 65/64 1939	12 shielded singles, elevation +80° to -10°, range 7,500 metres, 20 rounds per minute; proposed available date April 1942, but still not yet in production in April 1943
Breda 20/65 mod. 1935	22 sextuples, range 5,000 metres.[25] Available in April 1943, twins used until that date
Horizontal	
Protection	60–80-mm plates.
Underwater	Bulges, reinforced concrete
Crew	1,420
Engines	Four diesel Savoia/M.A.N. 28,000 cv on four axis

The name of the unit, initially *Falco*, was finalised as RN *Sparviero*.

RN *Bolzano*

A second conversion project was developed after RN *Bolzano* was torpedoed on 13 August 1942, receiving such serious damage as to make it clear that there was no possibility of refurbishing her as heavy cruiser.

Therefore, the conversion plan to a fast aircraft launch ship/transport (3,500 tons of materials) was considered.

The entire artillery would have been replaced, and a boiler room would need to be removed as would the superstructures, to make space for a bridge where twelve Re 2001/OR fighters could park up and be launched via two catapults placed at bow.

The optimistic estimated time for the conversion was for five months only.

The weaponry would have been composed of ten pieces of 90-mm L. 50 and 20 pieces 37-mm L. 54 in twins. The speed would have been lowered to 25 knots. The plan was quickly abandoned given the slowness of the launch of the planes and the low priority on the assignment of building material compared to escort units.[26]

Oil Tanker Conversions

The conversion of some of the modern motor tanks into aircraft launch ships was considered at the same time as the conversion of the *Bolzano*. Their slow speed (14 knots for the *Sterope*) would have required the replacement of the installed diesel engine with a more powerful one. The installed bridge would have had to allow for launch without catapults but not for the landing of aircraft. The air group was composed of ten aircraft.

The ships considered were the *Sterope*, the *Sergio Laghi*, and the *Giulio Giordani*.[27]

The flight deck would have been 150 metres long, 23 metres wide, and then tapered to 21 metres towards the bow. The expected height of the flight deck at the waterline was 10 metres. No island was planned and the bridge placed at the bow under the flight deck. In any event, this project was not fulfilled.[28]

Re 2001 OR Fighter

All of the projects for aircraft carriers carried out during the war called for the embarkation of the Re 2001 OR fighters (*Organizzazione Roma*, a body created for the conversion of the *Roma* to aircraft carrier). The specifications of this single-seater, retractable landing gear, fixed wing, and metal construction were as follows:[29]

Wingspan	11.00 metres
Wing surface	20.40 metres^2
Length	8.36 metres
Height	3.15 metres
Empty weight	2,806 kg

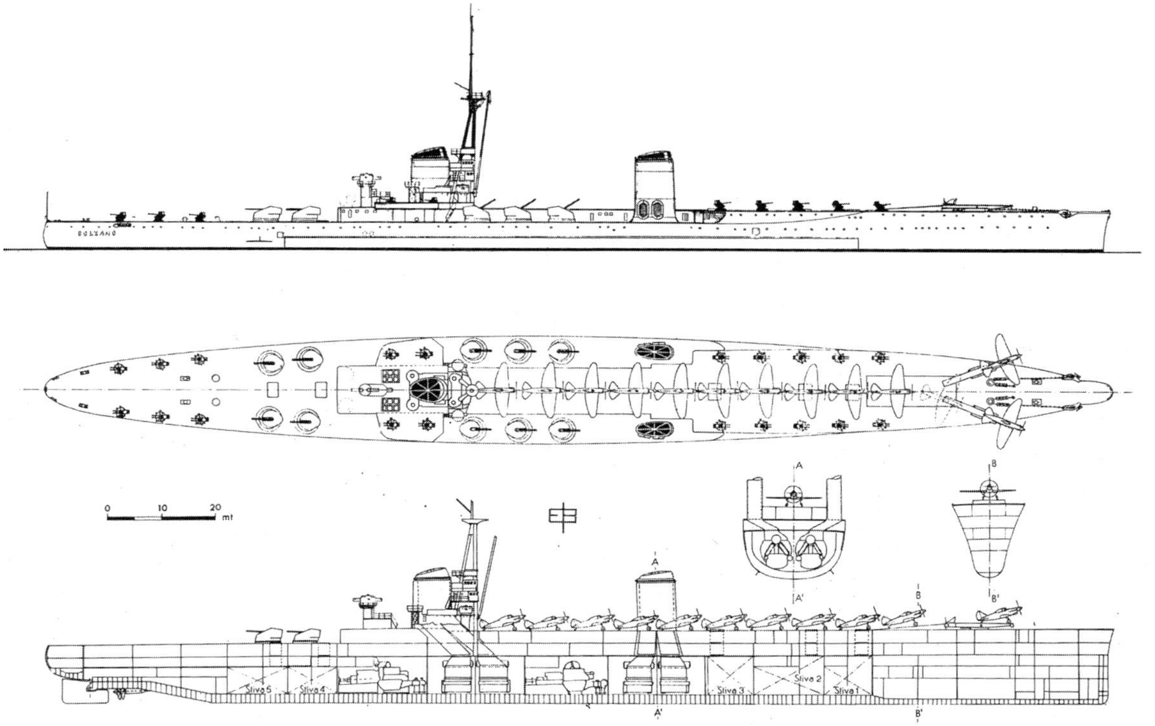

The 1942 project for the conversion of the damaged heavy cruiser RN *Bolzano*. (*Courtesy Rivista Marittima*)

Reggiane 2000 trial take-off, to be used aboard the *Littorio*-class battleships, from the RN *Miraglia*; a similar solution would have been implemented on board the RN *Bolzano* as converted to cruiser AA/aircraft launcher. (*Courtesy Rivista Marittima*).

Weight at maximum load	3,891 kg
Engine	Alfa Romeo A. 1000 RC 41 (Daimler Benz 601 with permit), twelve cylinders on line of 1,165 hp
Maximum speed	545 km/h at 5,500 metres; cruising 470 km/h; minimal with wing flaps 120 km/h
Highest Altitude	Max. 11,000 metres; climbing at 6,000 metres in six minutes and thirty seconds
Autonomy	1,165 km, no auxiliary tanks
Weaponry	Two 12.7-mm Breda-SAFAT machine guns forward, fixed with 350 rounds per barrel; two 7.7-mm Breda-SAFAT machine guns at the wings, 600 rounds per barrel; two bombs of 360 kg (or a bomb or a torpedo under the fuselage, max. weight 600 kg)

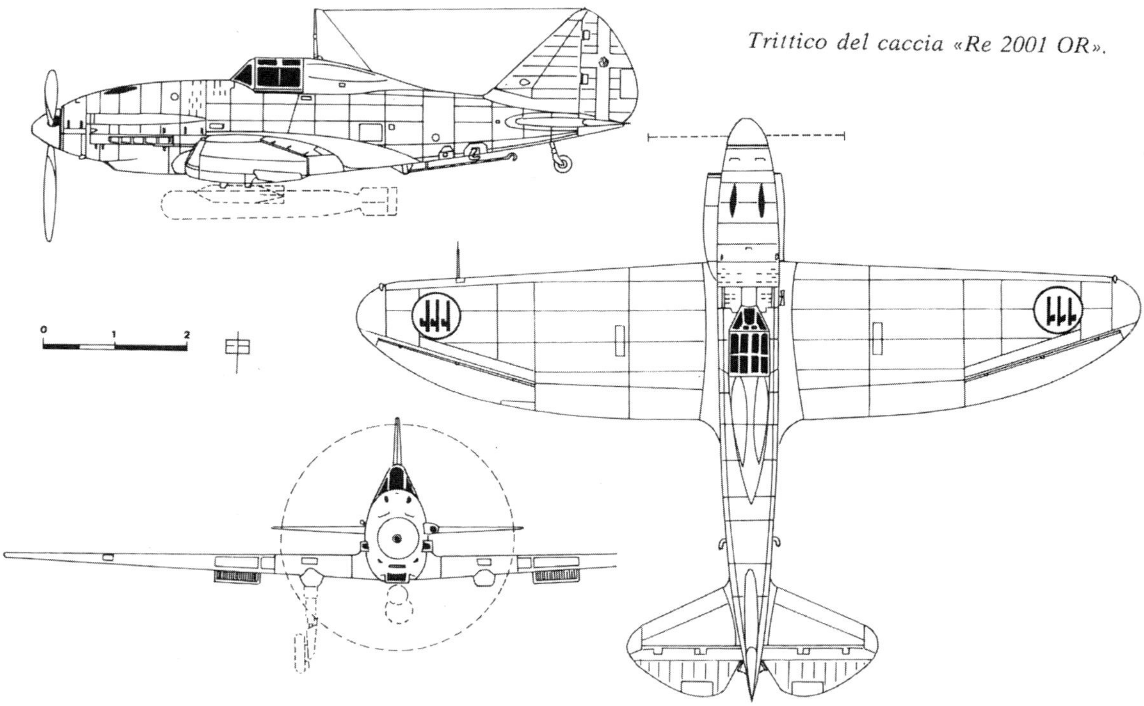

The fighter Re.2001 OR. (*Courtesy Rivista Marittima*)

10

RN *Impero* Fleet Carrier

Genoa and its Naval Architects

The history of the Genoese shipyards is tied to the story of the Republic of Genoa as an economic military power on the Mediterranean, which for centuries had commercial and business relationships with all the powers of the time. It ceased to exist because of the French Napoleonic invasion and was then annulled at the congress of Vienna, becoming part of the States of Savoia.

Even after the creation of the united Italian state, Genoa maintained its cultural, historic, and lingual traits. It was culturally open to exchanges with foreign countries, both commercial and knowledge wise, and the city also became the headquarters of numerous navigation companies and kept very close relations with Great Britain—for geopolitical reasons.

In the second half of the nineteenth century, through a gradual restructuring of the shipyards and heavy industry of Liguria, small workshops and garages formed around the Ansaldo S. A. Company. The organisation of the shipyard lay on those who had practical 'knowledge', and the specialised workmen, sent to Great Britain for training, were a vital cog in the running of the shipyard—also from a managerial point of view.[1]

It is not surprising that the shipyard paid these 'masters of the nautical art' when there was no work, instead of losing them and seeing them move to Leghorn, Trieste, or Marseille.[2] If the management of the training of the workforce was excellent, the prospect of a big industry could not be left in the hands of the 'shipyards' foremen', and so a strange overturning of roles was observed whereby the foremen forcefully joined the strategic decisions of the shipyard, creating enormous damage due to their lack of managerial impartiality.[3]

Under the direction of Perrone, at the beginning of the 1900s, the policy of the shipyards changed radically: careful attention to investments, cautious planning, and revised internal dynamics were better suited for a modern business chain of command.

The increase of personnel inflicted by the First World War required a choice that would leave a mark on the culture of the Ansaldo world: the internal training of all employees, be they workmen or managers. Perrone wanted to take an approach similar to Taylor's and this proved to be a winning choice.[4] In the nineteenth century, the Ansaldo of the '80s had 2,000 employees, and in 1914, it became a titan company in six production areas and had more than 30,000 employees.

Development was halted, however, during the post-war demobilisation, during which a gradual standstill of orders was experienced as well as a crisis of organisation that was no longer adequate for the new industrial methods.

The presidency of Cavallero (1929–1933), later CSM, brought significant military commissions to Ansaldo at a time when unemployment was rampant in Italy.[5] The Cavallero presidency ended because of the so-called 'scandal of armours', which related to low-quality material that was used to supply the *Regia Marina*.[6]

Under the direction of Agostino Rocca, who came from the United States and was managing director starting in 1935, an extensive reorganisation was applied, and from an industrial point of view, a massive renovation of machinery was done; the cornerstone of shipyards shifted to the specialists; management performed the job of planning; and control and the scientific committees belonging to the various operational components were the heart of technical choices.[7, 8]

In 1936, the *Reale Scuola di Architettura Navale* (the School of Naval Architecture) was merged with the Department of Engineering. The economic events brought about a symbiosis between the school and the shipyards to the point where many of the educators were also part of the management (whoever wanted to work at Ansaldo had to be trained by the company).[9]

At the same time, the company's attention to training, as well as after work and helpful activities, the mediation that the management held with Fascist politicians, the actual direct assistance given to the workers during the war, and the gradually worsening life conditions associated with it made the factory a non-politicised place both in relation to the regime as well as later on during German occupation and the liberation.[10, 11]

The sectors of the offices of naval studies and naval projects remained deeply 'Ansaldian', yet the same did not occur with other Ansaldo components in the shipyard world; open and able minds such as Achille Piazzai succeeded in keeping the doors of the school-shipyard open in order to guarantee the continuity of specialised training.[12]

Specialised Naval Training in Italy before 1936[13]

Until 1936, the year when, by decree, the Naval School merged with the Department of Engineering, the 'naval architects' had to leave the *Regia Scuola Superiore Navale* of Genoa.[14] Contextually, the training of specialists was done by Ansaldo and other companies in the field; Ansaldo managers were teachers at the naval school, and until 1936, students were obligated to go to the shipyard from 15 July to 4 November—an inalienable stage—as part of their practical training.[15]

Already from the second half of the nineteenth century, learning English was mandatory. A large segment of Ansaldo designers appear as having already been 'hired' by the shipyard from the first years of technical high school as '*medagliati*'. This condition was unique to the shipyard: choosing and training the best and most promising young people and connecting them to the company from the first training steps.

Among the many that came out of the school are Vittorio Cuniberti, creator of the dreadnought, and Giuseppe Rota, director of the *Vasca Navale* of Genoa (Freude Tank) and of INSEAN, as well as designer for RN *Dante Alighieri*.

Naval architects of the pre-1936 era were certainly students who had graduated from the *Scuola Reale Navale* in Genoa, to which a doctorate likely followed; the engineers who graduated the universities of the kingdom were obligated to attend two years of naval training before working in the field, then taking on the role of designer-builder.

The Naval Architect Campagnoli

Lino Enrico Campagnoli was born in Genoa in 1911 to Giuseppe and Luigia (*née* Bruschi), the youngest of four brothers. His father had been 'chief of boatyard' since the end of the nineteenth century at Ansaldo ('*U Bacan*'—'the chief' in old Genoese)—his home life was impregnated with the life of naval construction, the sea, and navigation.

Due to family and personal problems (he had a stutter), Campagnoli was sent to the Ansaldo School of naval training after middle school—it was his fall-back option. In truth, he advanced very well in the technical studies and was admitted to the course of 'Naval architecture', which he completed at twenty-one years of age.

In the meantime, the young Lino realised that if he 'sang' the first word, the stuttering defect disappeared, so he took it upon himself to do that, curing himself of this important (at the time) lingual and communication skills deficiency in just a few years.

According to his colleagues and professors, he was the most talented 'designer and creator' of his generation and Ansaldo immediately gave him a contract; in 1932, he joined the *Ufficio*

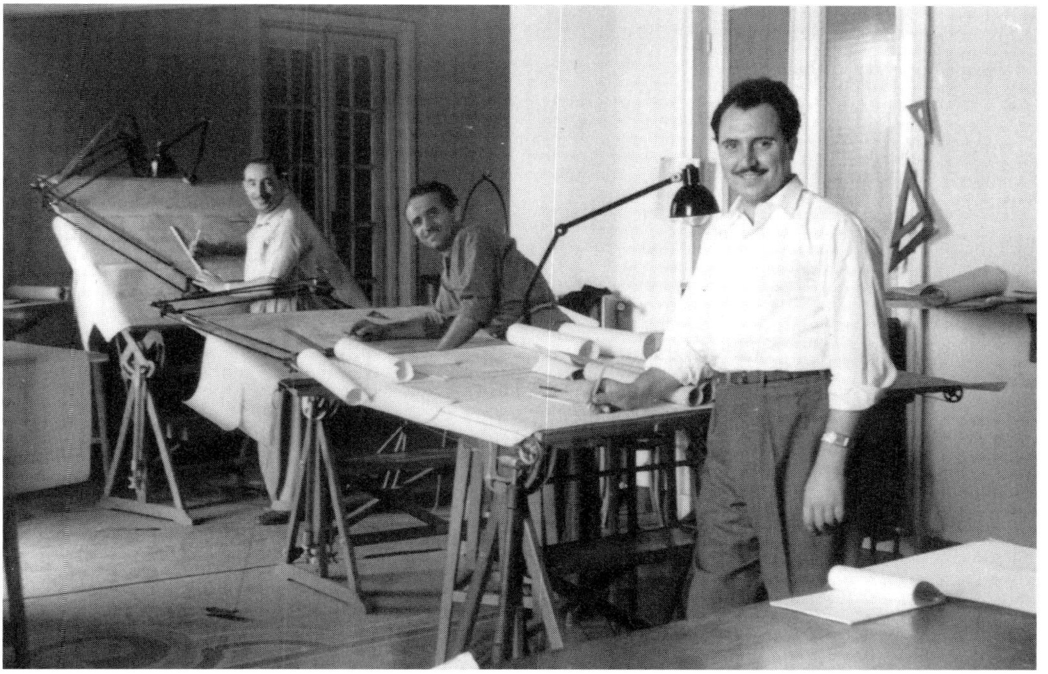

From left to right: Lino Campagnoli, Romano, and Bergamini in 1942, working on the conversion of the RN *Impero* to aircraft carrier. (*Courtesy Archivio Campagnoli*)

Studi Navali (US) under the direction of Achille Piazzai. He would never abandon this office, becoming its director in 1960 until his retirement in 1970.

Once he had finished his studies, he left for military service. At twenty-one years old, he was an excellent naval architect, yet he was dispatched as a reserve officer in the *Regio Esercito*'s infantry, in the 'Bersaglieri' riflemen division.[16]

In the Ansaldo's 'US' during the early '30s, a group was formed with five young architects, all wanted by Piazzai and all in their early twenties. These were Bergamini, Campagnoli, Carlarino, Pero, and Romano, and they produced the most important projects for warships and passenger ships of the 1900s, from the *Littorio* to the great luxury cruise liner of the '60s, the *Michelangelo*.

Forty years of excellence in naval planning led them to professional collaborations with the United States and the major navies in the world. They assumed the name of '*I Ragazzi di Piazzai*' ('Piazzai's Boys') and went through their entire professional lives together.

Lino died at only sixty-four years of age in Genoa, leaving his plans and research to his only daughter, Enrica, and a preliminary work on the *Littorio* battleships as well as the draft of the conversion of RN *Impero* to aircraft carrier.

The *Ufficio Studi Ansaldo* and the '*Ragazzi di Piazzai*' Group

One of the most innovative decisions of director Achille Piazzai, initially criticised by management at Ansaldo, was to create a group of his best young architects and to create a tight-knit team also outside the walls of the shipyard.

In 1938, the 'US' (*Ufficio Studi*) was comprised of the following specialists and architects: Chief 'US' Engineer Ortalda (designer and naval architect trained in the 1910s in Genoa, promoted to general management in Piazzai's staff; in 1939, he was replaced by Luigi Astengo); Chief Specialist cav. Bafico (trained at the Genoese naval school, designer and naval architect), from 1940 was Piazzai's deputy in the Planning Office; Chief Planning and Research Room E. Matucci (a veteran of the group with Ortalda, naval architect and designer,); and the architects-designers known as 'Piazzai's boys'—T. Romano, L. Campagnoli, G. Celesia, Carlarino, Bandinelli, E. Comincini, G. Lertora, Bergamini, F. Arado, A. Massarino, Piccardo, Pero, Ortolani, Pittaluga Fedi, and Marazini.

The philosophy was simple and effective: to create a group of the best students and bring them to a high level of expertise through experiences and training abroad (Great Britain, France, and Germany) and to keep the 'group' close, both outside and within the company, with the opportunity to go on winter vacations in the Alps (Sestriére, Sauze d'Oulz) or to the seaside in high standard accommodations, organised and run by the shipyard.

The group created and raised by Piazzai went on to be the pillar of the shipyard business from the '30s until the beginning of the '70s. This group of architects played a significant role in numerous important projects:

1932 RN *Alberto by Giussano* fitting out
1932 RN *Raimondo Montecuccoli*
1932 RN *Luigi Cadorna*
1933 'P.S. 8' and 'P.S.26' for USSR, Coast Guard vessels
1933 Light Cruiser RN *Eugenio di Savoia*

The 'Boys of Piazzai'. *From left to right*: Bafico, Campagnoli, Bergamini, and probably Comincini and the RN *Alberto da Giussano*. (*Courtesy Archivio Campagnoli*)

1934 RN *Littorio*
1934 RN *Vittorio Veneto*
1936 warship projects for the USSR[17]
1938 RN *Impero*
1941 Aircraft carrier *Aquila*
1941 Aircraft carrier *Sparviero*
1941 Aircraft carrier *Impero* studies

As director of the *Ufficio Studi*, Lino Campagnoli signed off on the following:

Andrea Doria (1951). Transatlantic, Italia di Navigazione S.p.A.
Cristoforo Colombo (1954). Transatlantic, Italia Navigazione.

Federico C. (1958). Transatlantic, Costa Armatori.

Leonardo da Vinci (1960). Turbine-powered ship (transatlantic), Italia Navigazione.

SS *Michelangelo*.

SS *Raffaello*.

Above: The *Andrea Doria*. (*Courtesy 'Commis' via naviearmatori.net*)

Below: The *Cristoforo Colombo*. (*Courtesy Aldo Cavallini via naviearmatori.net*)

Above: The *Federico C.* (*Courtesy Aldo Cavallini via naviearmatori.net*)

Above: The *Leonardo da Vinci.* (*Courtesy Giorgio Ghiglione via naviearmatori.net*)

Above: The *Michelangelo* (above) and the *Raffaello* in New York. (*Courtesy Francesco Mistretta via naviearmatori.net*)

Below: The Ansaldo designers (*from left to right*: Romano, Bergamini, unidentified, Carlarino, and Campagnoli) during *Michelangelo*'s trials at sea. (*Courtesy Archivio Campagnoli*)

RN *Impero*: Fourth *Littorio*-class Battleship

Italy responded to the planning of two more 35,000-ton French battleships, the *Gascogne* and the *Clemenceau*, with two more of the *Littorio*-class units, RN *Roma* and RN *Impero*. The *Roma* was laid down in September 1938 at the shipyard CRDA of Monfalcone and completed in June 1942.

The battleship *Impero*, laid down on 14 May 1938 at the Ansaldo shipyard in Genoa and ready for launch in October 1939, had a completely different story, which has only recently been completely understood thanks to the new documents from the Campagnoli archives.

The start of the construction work on the *Impero* on 14 May 1938 was possible only thanks to the direct intervention of Mussolini with the commissioner general for war manufacturing, who helped obtain the metals needed to launch the hull as they were already in short supply.[18]

The launch date ended up being crucial to the fate of the unit. The Fascist regime wanted the launch to be on 28 October, the anniversary of the March on Rome; however, the ship was already ready for launch on 15 October (also because, according to the contract, delivery was due within forty months from the start of the works and the shipyard had worked at forced rhythm).

The regime intervened to postpone the launch for two weeks, even if this would have increased the risks of encountering unfavourable weather conditions.[19] Genoa was pounded by a series of low-pressure areas that rendered it impossible to proceed with the launch; on 2 November 1939, Cavagnari assured Mussolini that the delay was due exclusively to the inclement weather and not to disagreements with the management of the shipyard and local Fascist authorities.

The ceremony was finally held on 5 November, the sponsor was Her Royal Higness (SAR, *Sua Altezza Reale*), the Duchess Irene of Spoleto, wife of SAR Admiral Aimone of Savoia Aosta. The hull, however, remained on the slipway as the bad weather had once again returned. The *Impero* was launched on 15 November 1939.[20]

At the end of May 1940, when Italy's entrance to the war was imminent, it was decided to transfer the hull to Trieste (where RN *Vittorio Veneto* was almost ready and the *Roma* was almost ready to be launched), being that Genoa was too exposed to French war actions.

RN *Impero* was not able to sail on her own, therefore a complex towing operation, which also included significant reinforcement work to stabilise the incomplete hull of the battleship, was planned; at the time, displacement was 22,000 tons (hull and complete anti-torpedo system, two mounted propellers, internal bulkheads for the most part incomplete, and 2,000 of the 14,000 tons of armour mounted).[21] The transfer began on 1 June, involving several *Regia Marina*'s units and tugboats, and was carried out at an average speed of 4 knots; on 9 June, the *Impero* arrived in Brindisi, the first leg of the transfer.

The onset of war dissuaded the continuation of the slow voyage to Trieste; leaving the unit in Brindisi would have meant giving up on its completion given the impossibility of completing the fitting in that harbour. The delay in launching ended up being fatal to the unit. France's exit from the war would have allowed for the transfer to Trieste or a return to Genoa; however, security conditions for a slow transfer of the unit did not exist.

Thanks to the perseverance of Lt-Col. (NC) Bartolomeo Corradi, it was decided to bring all the necessary equipment to Brindisi to let the unit sail to Trieste securely and to finish the fitting there. This meant transferring armour, turbines, condensers, pipes for the eight boilers,

Left: The RN *Impero* at launch. The flag with the red cross on the white field represents the city of Genoa. (*Courtesy Fototeca Archivo Storico Ansaldo*)

Below: RN *Impero*, before launch. (*Courtesy Rivista Marittima*)

and the main helm from Genoa to Brindisi, as well as the workers who restarted the building in July 1940 (340 specialised workers who stayed on the steamship *Principessa Giovanna*, of 8,955 tsl, then from December 1942 a hospital ship). Moving the turbine reducers required production of a special vehicle, and three homes and two bridges were demolished to transport them.

In January 1942, RN *Impero*, equipped with the turbines, the forward engine groups, and temporary funnels, was judged ready to move. On board there were still sixty carpenters to manage possible damage from the vibrations on the wooden structures built to strengthen internal spaces.[22]

On 22 January 1942, escorted by a formation that included the destroyer RN *Pessagno*, torpedo boats RN *Audace* and RN *Missori*, and gunboats RN *Zagabria* and the RS *Speri* under the command of Capt. Adone del Cima, RN *Impero* left for Trieste.

The *Regia Aeronautica* had guaranteed aerial coverage. The transfer, despite adverse sea conditions, proceeded well with a speed up to 16 knots. On 23 January, RN *Impero* reached Venice, where it remained for ten months; building her was a low priority due to the wartime situation (RN *Impero* was the last in order priority in February 1942) and the difficulties in moving the fittings (by now 90 per cent ready) needed to complete the ship.

In December, the unit finally reached Trieste.[23] In Trieste, RN *Roma*, twin of RN *Impero*,

The hull of the RN *Impero* during German occupation. Note the original bow line planned for units of the *Littorio*-class. (*Wikipedia*)

was completed and delivered to the *Regia Marina*; also ongoing was the refitting and modernisation of RN *Conte di Cavour*, of the anti-aircraft cruisers RN *Etna* and RN *Vesuvio* (previously launched for the Thai Navy) as well as numerous light units.

Work continued until June 1943 when the status was hull 88.00 per cent; engines 76.40 per cent; and fitting 28.15 per cent.[24] By 17 July 1943, there were still 180 workers working on RN *Impero*, of which 150 on the main guns and thirty on the engines. The expected completion date, with an optimum availability of 1,500 workers, was eighteen months from when the order was given to resume work.

The uncertainties and the difficult path of construction of the unit can now be thoroughly explained through the contemporary plans of transformation recovered in the Campagnoli archives.

Campagnoli Archives

The main references outside of the Campagnoli archive (hereinafter AC) concerning the Ansaldo studies on the *Impero* as aircraft carrier are as follows:

1. A 1/200 model preserved at the Italian Navy's Historic Naval Museum of Venice.
2. The conversations regarding the fate of RN *Impero* recorded in the Historic Diary of the Supreme Command.
3. A note reporting the fact that prior to September 1941 the idea of converting the incomplete battleship *Impero* to aircraft carrier was seen in a negative light.[25]
4. The references recorded in the AC regarding facts not concerning the project, which allows relating the material to the historic events in flux.

The first reference by the Supreme Command regarding converting RN *Impero* to an aircraft carrier is from 23 August 1941; this was a conversation between Head Chief of Staff Cavallero and engineer Pegna, with a reference to a 'project of a battleship' and to an 'aircraft carrier'.[26] At that time, there were no plans for battleships and the decision to convert the liner *Roma* to RN *Aquila* had just been made. Previously, on 20 June, a meeting had been held on the topic of 'Aircraft carriers' between the General Chief of Staff and Admiral Foschini.[27]

On 23 September 1941, in a meeting with General De Vito (naval engineer, general director of construction, and director of the projects office at Ansaldo before being recalled to service in 1936) and a member of the management committee at Ansaldo, the subject of the 'usage of the liner *Roma* and of the *Impero* as aircraft carriers' was discussed, and on 27 September, the subject of a second meeting is the *Impero* and the conversion of the liner *Roma* to aircraft carrier.[28, 29, 30] On 4 October, RN *Impero*'s construction schedule was discussed with Admiral Riccardi and the possibility to speed its building as battleship without interfering with other plans.[31]

The archive clarifies that conversion projects were known and followed up by the *Regia Marina*, which required specific Freude tank trials for the *Impero* as aircraft carrier; some activities of the project were continued also after the Armistice of Cassibile on 3 September 1943 (not announced to the Italian public until the 8th), when the entire war industry in North Italy was under German control.[32]

Structure

The Campagnoli archives are represented, as far as the *Impero* is concerned, by typescript paper sheets with the Savoia insignia in the centre, the '*Provveditorato generale dello Stato*' type 4 (CI) watermark, and by a series of technical drawings, both general as well as detailed in various scales (mainly 1:500, 1:200, and 1:100) dated between 1940 and 1943.

Among the typescript papers is a 'general index', which extends for a period of time that begins with the studies for the *Littorio*-class of the early '30s until 1944.

One stamp on two or three lines marks the most relevant drawings:

ANSALDO S. A.—Cantieri Navali
Genova—Sestri
Uff. Studi Lino CAMPAGNOLI

The dating of the documents and plans is in the form day/month/year or month/year/day, eventually separated by periods (for example, '940' is equivalent to 'September 1940').

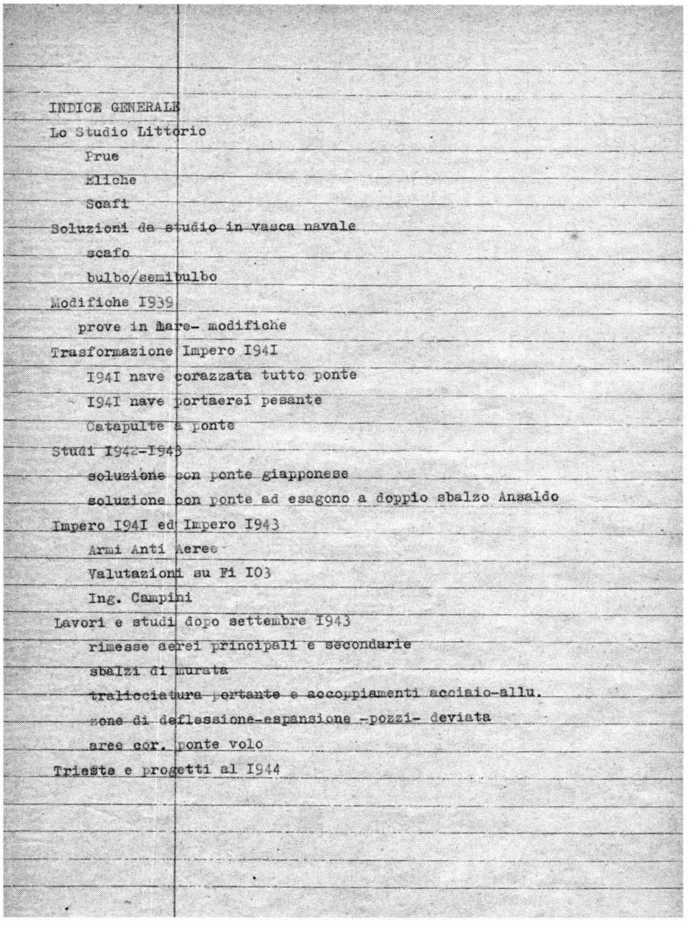
INDICE GENERALE
Lo Studio Littorio
Prue
Eliche
Scafi
Soluzioni da studio in vasca navale
scafo
bulbo/semibulbo
Modifiche 1939
prove in mare- modifiche
Trasformazione Impero 1941
1941 nave corazzata tutto ponte
1941 nave portaerei pesante
Catapulte a ponte
Studi 1942-1943
soluzione con ponte giapponese
soluzione con ponte ad esagono a doppio sbalzo Ansaldo
Impero 1941 ed Impero 1943
Armi Anti Aeree
Valutazioni su Fi 103
Ing. Campini
Lavori e studi dopo settembre 1943
rimesse aerei principali e secondarie
sbalzi di murata
traliccia tura portante e accoppiamenti acciaio-allu.
zone di deflessione-espansione -pozzi- deviata
aree cor. ponte volo
Trieste e progetti al 1944

Archivio Campagnoli—Index.
(*Courtesy Archivio Campagnoli*)

Littorio-class Hull Design

The preliminary project of the units of the *Littorio*-class, which would be built under the Washington Treaty, was requested by then General of the *Genio Navale Umberto Pugliese* in 1932 and reviewed by the Admirals' Committee; its general features were defined in 1935.[33, 34]

The construction contest was launched on 10 April 1934 and its specifications issued in June 1934. The following shipyards participated in the contest: Ansaldo of Genoa, the Cantieri Riuniti dell'Adriatico (CRDA), and the Odero-Terni-Orlando (OTO) of Leghorn—the latter was quickly excluded for the hull, engines, and main helms.

The first tests in the Freude tank were held in Rome beginning from May 1934 on hull design by Ansaldo (Prog. It.214), OTO, CRDA (G 224) and the Ministry of the Navy (Dis. 2/629). The models tested were created by Rome's Freude tank workers from paraffin and then from wood, based on the plans.

From the documents of the '*Vasca navale per le esperienze di architettura navale*', now in the historic archives of INSEAN, it is possible to follow the procedures of the trials. They included the hull modification, if necessary, both upon request of shipyard and by the *Vasca navale* based on experimental evidence, as agreed upon with the shipyard. The results were recorded on diagrams and the model's performance was photographed; everything was transmitted via telegraph and then via courier to the shipyards. Representatives of the companies and the ministry were present during the trials. The trials were conducted under careful secrecy.

The 1934 hull specifications and their trial results at towing are the following:[35]

	Ansaldo C.108 Pg. It.214 1st series June 1934	Ansaldo C.108A 1st series August 1934 mod As on pg.794/107°
Length between perpendiculars (metres)	230	230
Length at waterline	230	230
Max. width	33	33
Width at waterline	31.7	31.80
Draft	9.30	9.34
Volume of displacement (metres^3)	38,206.64	38,536.5
Displacement	39,200	39,500
Wet surface (metres^2)	7,724	7,846
Rudders	Not present	2 in line with hull
Power at 16 knots (CV)	7,380	
18	10,500	
20	14,750	
22	20,400	
24	26,600	
26	38,300	
28	51,800	51,020
29		57,080
30	65,200	63,590
32	87,800	
34	128,700	

Ansaldo C.108A 2nd series August 1934 mod. As on pg.794/107° and stern topside	Ministry of the Navy 1st series C.113 prog. B.190=Dis 2/629	CRDA C.110 Prog. G.224 1st and 2nd series June 1934	CRDA C110 Prog. G.224 3rd series July 1934 Prow mod. Dis. C.110/V PVN)
230	230	230	230
230	230	230	230
33	33.150	32	32
31.80	31.730		31.080
9.34	9.34	9.30	9.30
38,536.5	38,536.5	38,200	38,400
39,500	39,500	39,155	39,360
7,846	7,737.8	7,502.51	7,542.7
2 in line with hull	Not present	Not present	Not present
6,980	7,150		
10,240	10,500	10,790	
14,300	14,800	14,500	
19,600	19,900	19,200	
26,070	26,100	26,200	26,000
36,730	35,850	37,000	36,700
49,920	48,000	49,600	49,000
63,690	62,900	62,400	61,800
84,440	85,000	85,100	

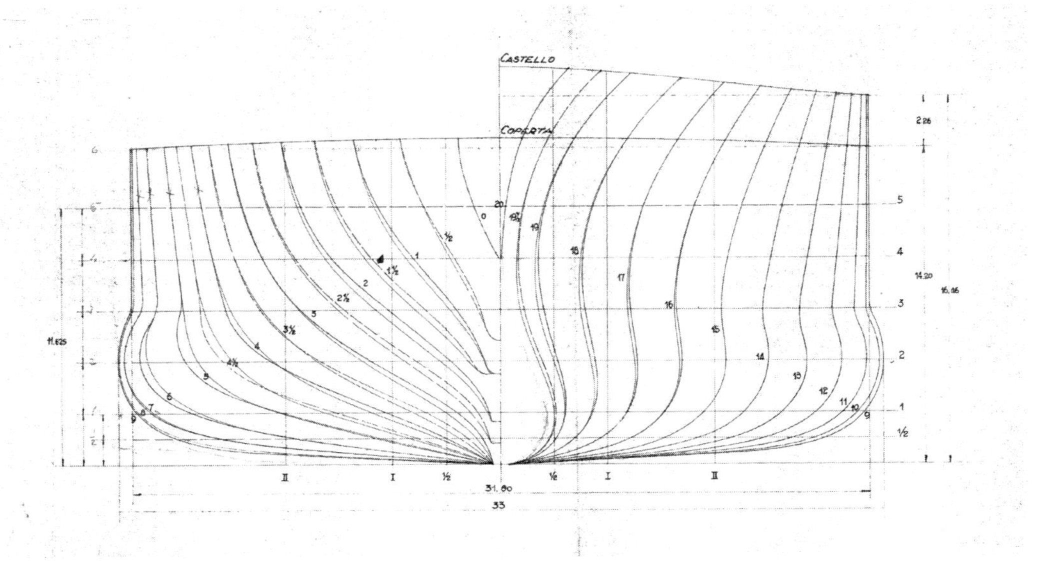

The Ansaldo bulge 188 mod. (*Courtesy archivio storico INSEAN*)

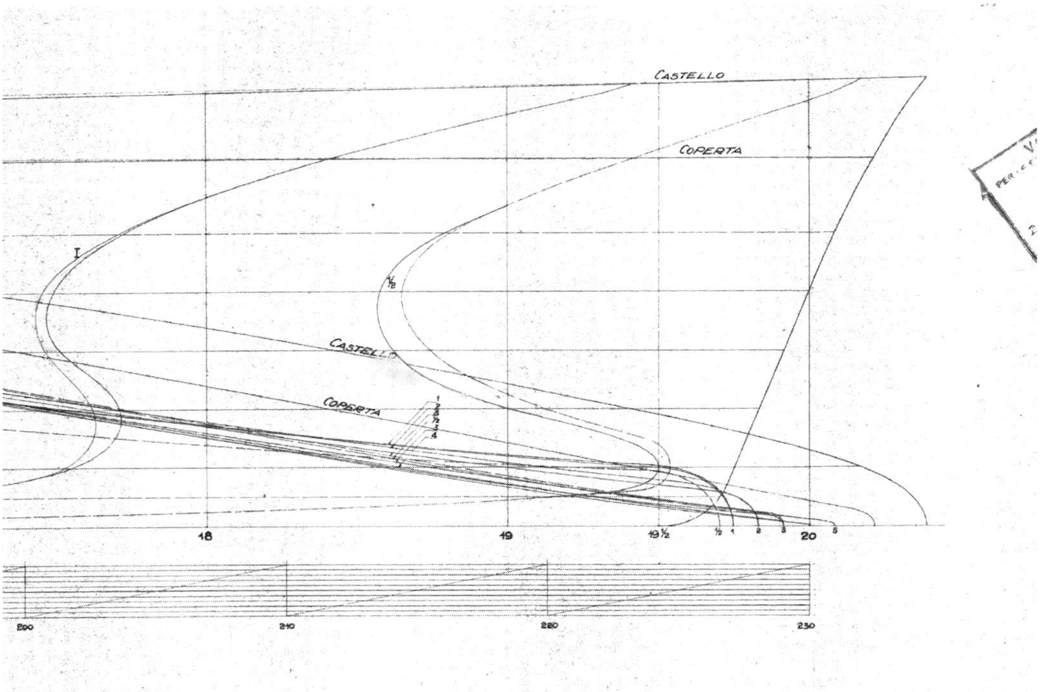

The bulbous hull 188 mod. of Ansaldo. (*Courtesy archivio storico INSEAN*)

The Ansaldo project It.214 presented a significant bulb at bow (not protruding forward). Evidently, the research done in advance with the bulbous bow, as subsequently described, was nixed by the *Regia Marina* at trials in the Naval Military Freude Tank at La Spezia. The Ansaldo designs wave profile was defined by Admiral Rota (Head of Rome's Freude Tank) as perfectly satisfactory; some modifications were requested for the aft area. The planned testing at full load was not held because of model warping due to high temperatures.

The *Regia Marina* would then modify some significant specifications (reducing the number of boilers and adding a further funnel). A new series of trials were carried out in the Freude tank, with modified hulls, and would bring about the choice of 'C.119' CRDA hull. During testing, the Undersecretary of State of the Navy Admiral Cavagnari asked the Director of the National Freude tank General G. N. Rota for the wave profiles for the hulls C.199 (CRDA) and C.123 (Ansaldo) on 13 October 1934.[36] This is significant as the problems recorded during trials at sea involve precisely the wave profiles.

Freud tank towing trials	CRDA C. 118 Dis. 1/18=19 1st Series October 1934	CRDA C. 118 Dis. 1/18=19 2nd Series October 1934	CRDA C. 118 Dis. 1/18=19 3rd Series October 1934 (mod. dis. V.N.4/c.118)	CRDA 119 Dis. 1/21=22 2nd Series October 1934 (bow dis. V.N 4/c.119)	CRDA 119 Dis. 1/21=22 3rd Series October 1934 (*idem*)
Length between perpendiculars (metres)	230	230	230	230	230
Length at waterline	230.191	230.307	230.307	230.163	230.261
Max. width	32.2	33.00	33.00	32.2	32.2
Width at waterline	31.640	31.654	31.654	31.640	31.654
Draft	9.432	9.517	9.517	9.432	9.517
volume of displacement (metres^3)	38,605	39,024.39	39,024.39	38,605	39,024.39
Displacement	39,570.12	40,000	40,000	39,570.12	40,000
Wet surface (metres^2)	7,776.67	7,815.85	7,815.85	7,720.33	7,759.25
Helms	si	si	si	si	si
Power at 16 knots (CV)					
18					
20	14,300			15,500	
22	19,100			20,200	
24	26,700			26,400	
26	36,900			35,400	
27	42,700	43,200	42,800	40,600	41,200
28	48,300	49,100	49,100	46,100	46,500
29	54,100	55,400	55,100	51,600	52,300
30	60,900	62,500	62,000	58,400	59,200
31	69,500	71,500	71,000	67,400	68,700
32	82,800	84,440	85,000	81,400	
34	128,700				

On 12 October 1934 (while comparative trials were still ongoing in the Freude tank), the *Comitato Progetto Navi* approved the definitive features of the new battleships. However, studies on the hull would end up taking a long time—for all intents and purposes, the hull produced was named C.134 of the CRDA, pertaining to RN *Vittorio Veneto*.

It is interesting to follow events as they are directly connected to the material revealed by the AC; plans for the hull C.134 of the CRDA were delivered to the National Freude tank on

CRDA 119 Dis. 1/21=22 5th Series October 1934 (mod. bow e _ Dis. V.N. 6/C.119)	CRDA 119 Dis. 1/21=22 6th Series November 1934 (mod. incl. centre bow and stern bulwarks requested by CRDA)	Ansaldo C.121 Prog. 794 /128 October 1934	Ansaldo C.123 Prog. 794 /132 October 1934 1° Series	Ansaldo C.123 Prog. 794 /132 October 1934 2nd Series (mod. at stern)	Ansaldo C.123 Prog. 794 /132 October 1934 3rd Series (mod.at stern)	Ansaldo C.123 Prog. 794 /133 November 1934 5th Serie
230	230	230	230	230	230	230
230.233	230.233	230.121	230.086	230.086	230.08	230.09
32.312	32.4	32	32	32	32.2	32.2
32.060	32.060	31.405	31.465	31.465	31.645	31.675
9.495	9.495	9.394	9.380	9.380	9.345	9.377
39,024.39	39,024.39	39,024.39	39,034	39,034	39,024	39,024
40,000	40,000	40,000	40,000	40,000	40,000	40,000
7,754.25	7,754.25	7,808.7	7,860	7,860	7,860	7,875.52
si	si	si	si	si	si	si
			10,500			
			14,300			
			19,400			
			26,500			
			37,400			
	41,000					43,100
	46,300	54,200	51,600	51,100	50,000	49,700
51,700	52,400	61,200	58,600	58,100	57,100	56,700
	59,500	68,700	65,500	65,400	64,200	64,000
	68,800					71,800

10 January 1935, and the Freude tank compared the differences with what had been previously experimented on for the 40,000-ton battleship. The stern area and the placement of the rudders (missing from the delivered plans) were certainly modified in the end of January 1935, and again, upon explicit request of the *Regia Marina*, the stern area was lengthened in February 1935.

The placement of the rudders—a main one and two coaxial to the external propellers, very forward compared to the main one, to guarantee independence in case of underwater attacks—was settled by research compiled by Pugliese himself.[37]

The trials were the following (the last one, on 2 April 1935, with a displacement of 43,000 tons):

	CRDA C.134 1st series 1st Feb 1935	CRDA C.134 1st series 8 march 1935 Dis. 1/138=1/139=1/144=1/145 and stern mod. Dis 1/191=1/192=1/193	CRDA C.134 3rd series 22 March 1935 as previous added rudders
Length between perpendiculars (metres)	230	230	230
Length at waterline	230.86	232.414	232.414
Max. width	32.396	32.396	32.396
Width at waterline	32.018	32.005	32.005
Draft	9.357	9.317	9.317
Volume of displacement (metres^3)	39,024	39,024	39,024
Displacement	40,000	40,000	40,000
Wet surface (metres^2)	7,680	7,760.74	7,812.56
Rudders	Not present	Not present	Two side ones and parallel to line of symmetry
Power at 18 knots (CV)		10,700	
18		12,800	
19			
20		15,100	
21		17,100	
22		20,600	20,700
23		23,600	23,800
24		26,700	27,000
25	30,800	30,300	30,600
26	35,800	34,900	35,200
27	41,000	40,000	40,300
28	46,500	45,500	45,800
29	52,100	51,100	51,600
30	58,600	57,700	58,500
31	67,500	66,400	67,900
32		79,800	

CRDA C.134 5th series 30 March 1935 as previous but with inclined auxiliary rudders	CRDA C.134 6th series 2 April 1935 as 4th, profile V.N. 8/C.134 and main rudder	CRDA C.134 6th series 2 April 1935 as 4th, profile V.N. 8/C.134 and main rudder
230	230	230
232.414	232.414	232.732
32.396	32.396	32.396
32.005	32.005	32.2
9.317	9.317	10.059
39,024	39,024	42926.82
40,000	40,000	44,000
7,812.56	7,874.3	8,238.86
Two side ones at 35° at plane of symmetry	Main in axis and two side ones parallel to the plane of symmetry	Main in axis and two side ones parallel to the plane of symmetry
	10,800	11,300
	12,970	13,700
	15,400	16,400
	18,000	19,250
35,100		
40,200		
45,700	46,350	50,550
51,400	52,150	56,950
58,100	59,100	64,600

Final plans were approved in May 1935. As we saw, the modifications introduced change in length (increased to 236.45 metres overall and 232.41 metres at the waterline) and in width (reduced from 33 metres to 32.4 metres), while the speed increased from 29 to 30 knots; the displacement at trials reached 44,000 tons. For the engines, the Ansaldo-Belluzzo-Tosi proposal group was accepted. The Ansaldo project was chosen for heavy calibre weapons, with an agreement of a partial subcontract with OTO.

The AC shows how even in the complex decision-making stage concerning the features of a large and innovative battleship, the innovative shapes of the hull were rejected, perhaps prematurely—such as the bulbous bow protruding from the hull, which did not even reach the trials at the National Freude tank.

On 2 July 1935, the final contracts were signed. The weight of the ships at launch would be of approximately 17,000 tons.

The specification modifications between 1935 and the effective order (which also included type and placement of the air group and of AA, and was originally supposed to include the old 100-mm/45 guns as on the heavy cruisers of the *Zara*-class) are summarised in the following chart:

	Specifications May 1935	*Littorio* 1940
Hull	25.2%	28.1%
Protection	44.5%	36.3%
fitting	9.1%	12.2%
Engines	6.0%	6.1%
Weaponry	15.2%	17.4%
Total	100% (36,450 tons)	100% (37,801 tons)

RN *Littorio*'s and RN *Vittorio Veneto*'s, the first built at Ansaldo and the second at the CRDA, trials at sea in the fall of 1939 showed a set of problems at high speed: strong vibrations, lowering of the bow, and high crests of foam (which reached the bridge and the range finders at the top of the main superstructure).[38] The modifications required the building of a new bow with an overall lengthening of 1.56 metres. The vibrations and bow lowering at speed diminished without completely stopping, notwithstanding the lightening of the weights done in the bow area. The change to the bowlines was extended (together with other more extensive changes) on RN *Roma*, at the time still in the shipyard, while RN *Impero*, already launched, retained the original bow.

Hull, Speed, and Full Bulbous Bow

With the new information made available by the Campagnoli archives, one can now add some considerations on these facts.

The bulbous bows were not new in the '30s. In fact, theoretical studies and practical applications in the Merchant Navy already existed, but they were ignored in military practice.

The AC refers the existence of studies on the subject by Piazzai, the REX naval architect, going back to 1932. The REX (already equipped with a bulbous bow), studied in 1929 in a collaboration between Ansaldo and Hamburg Ship Model Basin (HSVA), a centre of experimental research with a large civil Freude tank, was launched on 1 August 1930.[39, 40, 41]

Additional trials were done in the wind gallery of the Politecnico of Turin. These collaborations certainly continued in the subsequent years, as recorded in the report of the inspection made in Sevastopol at *Sovetskaya Ukraina* battleship.[42]

Advances in the studies of hydrodynamics helped to build a Freude tank inside the Ansaldo facilities in the warehouses next to the large blueprint room. The tank had been wanted by director Piazzai and strongly supported by the members of the *Ufficio Studi*—among them Astengo, thanks to his past experience in the *Genio Navale* and in the military Freude tanks—gave the most significant contribution to the project.

Originally, the venture had an almost '*Carbonaro*' (sort of a secret society) imprint, with only trusted engineers and employees working during the evening and night.

Features of the Ansaldo Freude tank:

Length 10 metres
Width 4 metres
Depth 1.5 metres
One windowed side for visual and photographic access.
Photographic equipment for side shots or from above.
Water flow, in a closed circle, with four propellers powered by electric motors. From 1935, another four motors were added, in order to easily invert the flow and further improve the linearity of the fluid streamlines.

Trials were performed using high-quality wooden models, usually in a scale of 1:200 but also of 1:100, made by a team of artisans from Cornigliano, who produced one model every five to seven days.

On the wooden hull, a series of three fastening points were applied for cotton threads of different colours and lengths; these allowed, when observed and photographed, to evaluate the hydrodynamic performance of the hull being examined.

The first tests (January 1935) were held in secret in the presence of the designers and the director alone. It then became a necessary step in the planning, all the hulls passed through testing in the Freude tank. The tank was in use until 1944—it was ransacked and destroyed in June 1945.

However, the naval architects group (Piazzai, Astengo, Bergamini, Campagnoli, Carlarino, and Romano) was aware that the *Regia Marina* would only consider the results from their own naval tanks.

The *Littorio* Freude Tank Trials and the *Impero* CV

From the same document, we have confirmation that the studies on the *Littorio* hull at Ansaldo in 1934–35, before the trials done by the *Regia Marina*, which was aware of them, were resumed in 1943 for the aircraft carrier *Impero*.[43]

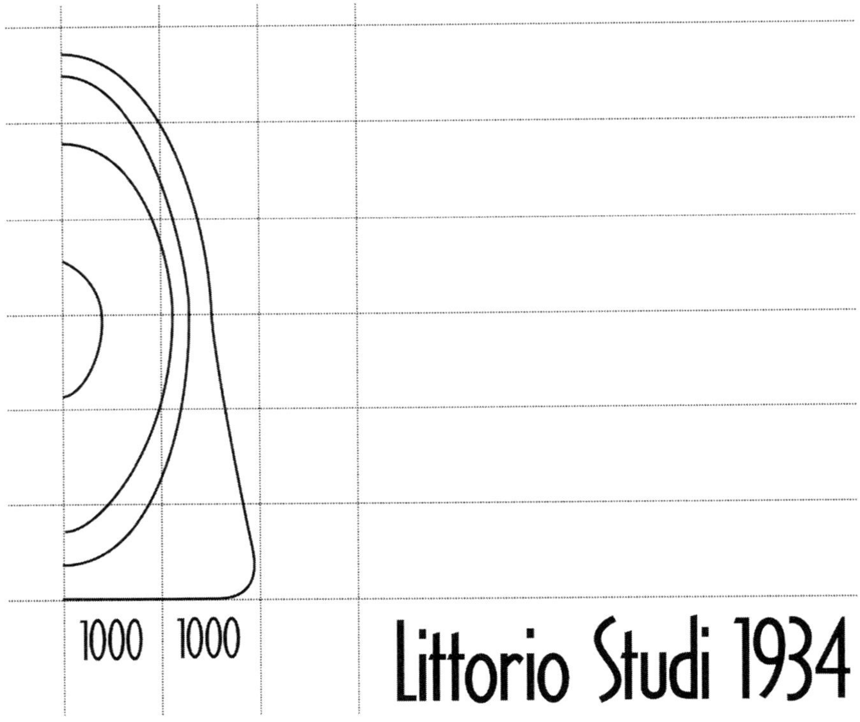

Study of the bulbous bow in the 1934 project for the *Littorio*. (*Courtesy Archivio Campagnoli, drawing Stefano Sappino*)

In the documents, there is reference to trials done in 1934 on a non-identifiable *Littorio*-class project, BU21-US. From the Campagnoli documents, it is clear that there was a certain level of animosity on this occasion (animosity that shows through the number and variations tested in the basin and from the correspondence between the parties). It is written that the then-*Genio Navale* criticised the scale of the models used, the unsteady temperature of the water, unspecified errors of the coefficient correction, the private tank used, and other 'specious and inconsistent criticism against whom the Piazzai's good sense was useless'.[44]

Also recorded in the Campagnoli archives are some ex post notes narrating what occurred during studies for RN *Littorio*:

> Three models at a scale of 1/100 were prepared for testing in the military basin of La Spezia which 'impressed Pugliese' (presumably the same type of the ships 'A', 'B', and 'C', see later).
>
> The results confirmed the strong vibrations and bow heaviness of the semi bulbous hull (this is the solution which was implemented) and of the need to increase manoeuvring space (helms) with the lengthening of the turning range.[45]
>
> Also recorded is how the changes implemented on RN *Roma* did not improve the manoeuvre.

The bulbous bow models alpha and beta (ships 'B' and 'C') were studied at the Hamburg research centre.

However, both the *Regia Marina* and the *Kriegsmarine* did not use the scientific and experimental evidence available; in Campagnoli's words:

Regia Marina's Freude tank at La Spezia, destroyed in the April 1943 bombing. (*Courtesy BAUSMM*)

> The *Genio Navale* and *Supermarina* were deaf to any technical innovation. The Beta bow model plus Alpha had been researched in Hamburg (in a civil Freude tank) and German designers were equally enthusiastic, an enthusiasm which was dampened by their superiors.
>
> The military hierarchy do not want to consider the solutions which evolved from the civil research and consider them alien to their science.[46]

International cooperation in the field of hydrodynamic research was very well developed because of the pressing need to obtain reliable and inspected mathematic models, even though the majority of the Freude tanks were originally military, to the point where, in 1935, the ITTC (International Towing Tank Conference) was founded.[47]

The only class of major military ships planned in the '30s to implement this solution was the *Yamato*-class. The proposals for plans for this class were requested by the Chief of Staff of the Japanese Navy in 1934 and the final design (chosen among twenty-three proposals) was approved in March 1937.[48]

The *Littorio*-class data on the results obtained with the beta bulb (ship 'C') in 1936–7 are as follows:

Rotation radius -18% (compared to the final *Littorio* ship).
Maximum estimated speed 32 knots.
Increase propellant yield 3%.

Above: Placing the cylindrical shell for the triple turret of 152 mm of the RN *Impero*. (*Courtesy Fototeca Ansaldo*)

Below: Section of bow from the 1934 studies for the *Littorio*-class. (*Courtesy Archivio Campagnoli, drawing Stefano Sappino*)

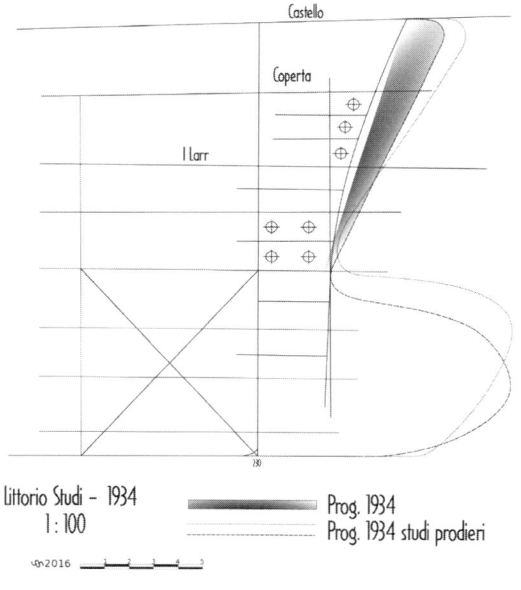

The results were, however, not sufficient to implement the bulbous bow for the two new units of the class, the *Impero* and the *Roma*, even though in the AC there is a very detailed drawing of RN *Littorio* that may be dated to 1938 in a scale of 1:100, and shows a bulbous bow. Evidently, at least for the naval architects, the hope that the solution with the most satisfactory experimental features could be implemented had not been abandoned.

In 1943, the following hull underwent trials, this time upon request of the *Genio Navale*, three models at 1:200 scale:

'A'—*Impero* US 940 semi bulbous bow as in *Littorio* '39.[49]
'B'—*Impero* US 342 bulb alpha.
'C'—*Impero* US 843 bulb beta.

Testing was done with 'naked' hulls, meaning the rudders were present but not the shafts and propellers.

The testing requested by the *Genio Navale* concerned, in particular, the variation of resistance to advancement (total and residual), referencing the work already presented in 1934–35 for the *Littorio*-class design.

Hull 'A'—that is, the *Littorio*—shows a known behaviour:

1. Breakage of the fluid streamlines in configurations that are 'heavily disturbed', today we would say chaotic.
2. Excessive bow wave.
3. Structured centrifuge and centripetal turbulence.
4. Nose-heavy starting from 18 knots.
5. All of phenomena increase with speed.[50]

The noted differences in performance between ships 'B' and 'C' were less than the precision of the coefficients of mathematical corrections, meaning performances that were different between the two solutions in larger quantity because of the uncertainties in the theoretical method applied. The performance of the bulbous bows was at its best the more fully loaded the ships were (estimated at the time at 45,000 tons), meaning the more the bulb was distant from the free surface.

The compared values of all the turbulence phenomena, assigning the value 1 to the *Littorio* '39 were 0.43 for 'B' hull and 0.38 for 'C' hull, for all speeds from 18 to 35 knots, with clear evidence of the positive effects of a full bulbous bow compared to the original half bulb.

The streamlines instability always present when testing the RN *Littorio* hull did never appear under any load condition when the full bulbous bow was tested; also, at minimal load, the values of instabilities never got close to those produced by the 'A' hull.

The perception of the value of the Ansaldo studies on the *Genio Navale*'s part should have changed radically over the course of the intervening years, given the evidence of the accuracy of the observations made in 1934–35 as it precisely spotted the problems during trials at sea done with RN *Vittorio Veneto* and RN *Littorio*.

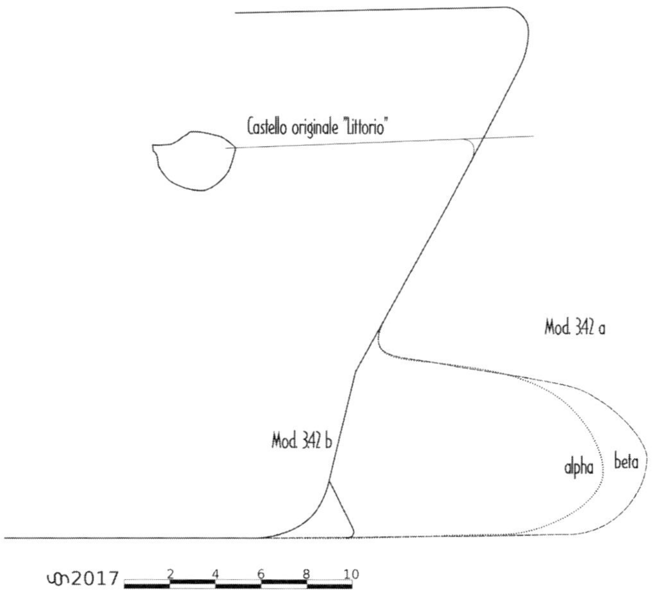

Studies of the *Impero*'s bow, tested in the Freude tank; note the difference with the *Littorio* studies of 1934. (*Courtesy Archivio Campagnoli, drawing Stefano Sappino*)

Early Thoughts

The first drawings in the archive, which probably date back to 1940 and to preliminary studies, shows a solution very similar to what planned for the conversion of the cruiser *Bolzano* to an aircraft launch ship.

A catapult, using the already available aeronautic facilities for RN *Impero* (the Gagnotto catapult with a crane) was placed bow near centreline. The construction height is only a bit higher than the original forecastle deck, so no a hangar underneath it was possible.

The position of the catapult on the centreline is a sign of the lack of a flight deck—this position was necessary due to machinery needed for its use.

The sketch of the aircraft on the catapult is interesting: a biplane fighter that is not identifiable, but with floats (meaning deck landing is not planned). It could be a Fiat ICR.42 seaplane (experimental version of the CR.42), or one of the many prototypes that were planned but never produced by aeronautic firms in those years.

From these initial studies, it is hard to speculate on the placement and the number of vehicles expected, considering that the main guns and turrets for RN *Impero* had already been produced. It is possible—hypothetically speaking—that the intention was to create a small deck devoted to the air group, perhaps by removing the first 381 turret to create a hybrid unit of battleship-aircraft carrier, essentially intended to assure some air coverage to the fleet.

A second drawing, not dated but closely related to the previous one, shows a marked leap in the conversion: a flight deck is visible, with an elevator of approximately 14 × 15 metres, and the catapult, about 29 metres in length, is moved to port. The crane, if considered of the same

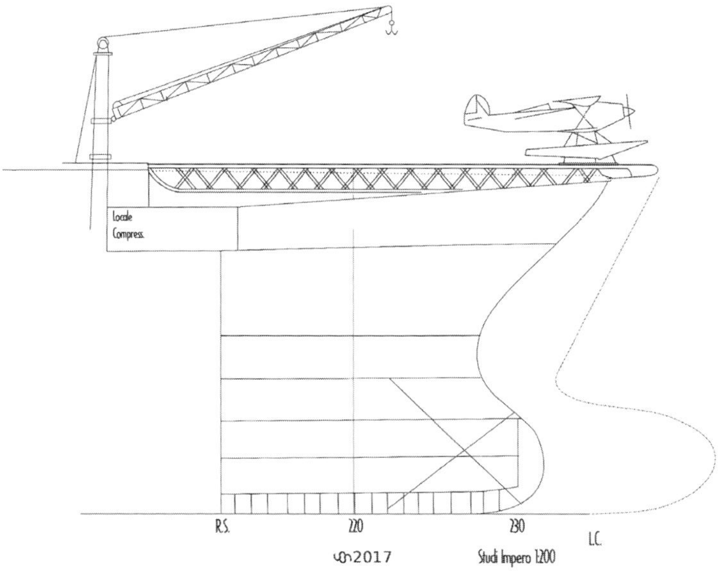

Bow catapult. (*Courtesy Archivio Campagnoli, drawing Stefano Sappino*)

Launch of a Re.2000 from the RN *Miraglia*, a solution similar to that planned in the first drawings of the RN *Impero*. (*Courtesy Rivista Marittima*)

The ICR.42 experimental seaplane Fiat CMASA. (*Italo De Marchi: CR. 42 'l'ultimo biplano'. 'AEREI', anno II, n.7, Ermanno Albertelli editore, courtesy Angelo Taverna*)

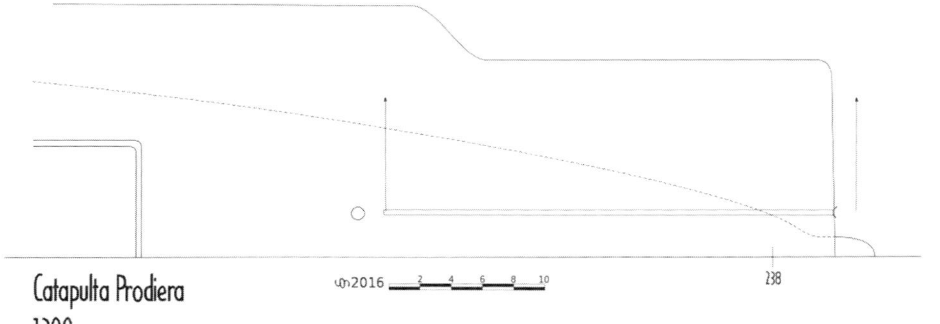

First flight deck. (*Courtesy Archivio Campagnoli, drawing Stefano Sappino*)

design as the *Littorio*-class, needs 5 metres of deck level, so a hangar level is certainly present, as well as the mandatory upper hull modifications to accommodate it.

1940 Campini's DAAC: First Surface to Surface Guided Rocket Weapon?

The history of the Ansaldo and RN *Impero* as aircraft carriers intertwine often with that of Campini. The projects of engineer Secondo Campini (Bologna 28 August 1904–Milan 7 February 1980) are known for having been ahead of their time for jet- and rocket-propulsion engines both in the naval and aviation fields.

With his company, VENAR (*VEicoli e NAtanti a Reazione*), he produced and demonstrated in 1932 a rocket-propelled motorboat (on assignment by the Ministry of Aviation). Between 1931 and 1934, he developed a jet motor for aircraft with which, in collaboration with Caproni, the Campini-Caproni C.C.2 was produced. Several flights were successfully flown including a Milan–Rome flight in 1941. The tests done by the *Regia Aeronautica* between January and August 1942 did not lead to the development of the project.

Campini was very active in the international field, and after the war, he moved to the United States to work.

The AC also sheds light on another important contribution of Campini in the field of rocket propulsion, the DAAC (*Dispositivo Anti Aereo Campini*, Campini AA device) and documents the developments from his plans that later led to the development of one of the last German anti-aircraft weapons, the Henschel Hs 117 Schmetterling.

German Pre-War Developments

Campini had collaborated with the German firm Argus until 1939, working on the development of jet-propulsion aircraft guided by radio.[51] The cooperation ended after the start of the war, however, some of the Argus projects did come into effect in the Fi 103 known as the V-1.

The story of the DAAC, of the V-1, and of the Hs 117 intertwine in a new way thanks to the AC; it is thus necessary to give some brief historical notes on the development of non-conventional weapons in Germany.

The Argus Motoren GmbH (specifically Fritz Gosslau) developed a small propelled drone (first test flight in June 1937) and, after a successful test flight guided by radio in May 1939 of the Flakzielgerät 43, received an order for 100 reconnaissance drones in October 1939 (these were delivered from 1942). With the outbreak of the war, the German Ministry of the Air Force requested a project for a remote-controlled weapon capable of transporting a warhead load of 1,000 kg to a distance of 500 km.

The design was actualised by Argus in a joint venture with Arado *Flugzeugwerke* and Lorentz AG. Its outcome, the enormous '*Fernfeuer*' was equipped with a propelled motor Argus; the projects were refused by the *Luftwaffe* in August 1940.

On 11 September 1942, Hitler ordered the suspension of all developments on weapons that could not be produced immediately. Included in these suspensions were the developing anti-aircraft German rocket weapons: an Italian DAAC would have belonged to this set.

With the collaboration of Paul Schmidt, who had started to work on pulse jets from 1928, Argus produced the Argus-Schmidt pulse engine in 1941. After tests held in January and April 1941 with the first pulse jet that would have equipped the V-1, Robert Lusser, aeronautical engineer of Fieseler, joined the design group and the first complete project of the future V-1 was developed. The P 35 'Erfurt' followed and was presented to the *Luftwaffe* on 5 June 1942 and then renamed, after various modifications, among which a single helm instead of the two-sided ones, as Fi 103.[52]

In June 1942, Fieseler (which had developed the failed Fi 157 before the war) became prime contractor for the Fi 103, now no longer guided by radio; the Fi 103 was developed at the *Luftwaffe* centre in Karlshagen. The first launch of the prototype was done from an aircraft on 20 October 1942 and from a launching ramp on 24 December 1942.[53]

A launching ramp of 55 metres was envisaged, for a breakaway speed of 322 km/h.[54]

1940 Campini's DAAC

Prior to 1940 in Italy, Campini developed the DAAC (acronym for *Dispositivo Anti Aereo Campini*), a rocket-propulsion weapon with anti-aircraft goals.[55] The weapon was radio guided and was experimented in five units in April 1940 in Libya (Tripolitania) against captive balloons, with success.[56]

Campini's interest in innovative anti-aircraft and anti-ship weapons is often reported in the AC:

> The weapon [this is in reference to the intelligence received regarding the German V1 development included in the 'Gunnarson document', see later] was interesting to us as related to the development of an anti-aircraft and anti-ship weapon already being researched by Campini.[57]

The technical specifications of the DAAC, version 1940, were the following:

Range	38 km
Launch system	Modified Vickers-Armstrongs naval carriage, solid propellant booster hooked to fuselage
Length	420 cm
Width of fuselage	44 cm
Wing span	252 cm
Speed	500 km/h
Weight when empty	135 kg
Weight when loaded	480 kg
War load	125 kg
Engine	Campini '40 three phases mixture of kerosene, catalyst and nitric acid (model 1943)
Guide	Two radio operators

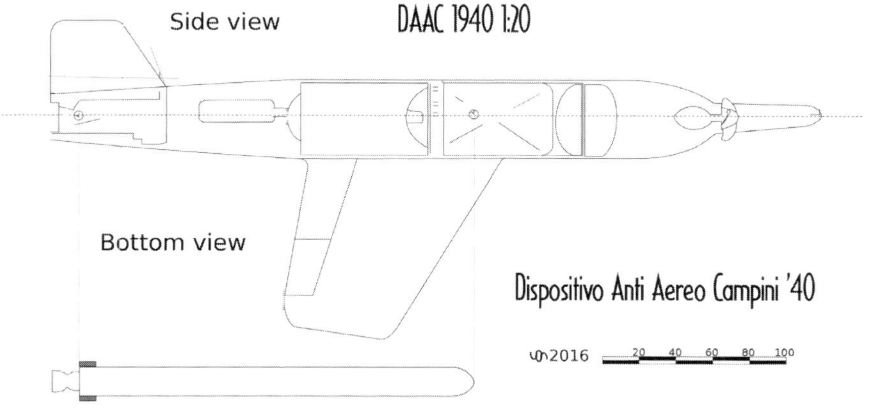

DAAC. (*Courtesy Archivio Campagnoli, drawing Stefano Sappino*)

The Ansaldo designers immediately recognised the excellent potential of the DAAC as an anti-ship weapon.[58] Its range was larger than the big calibre guns and it could be launched from simply modified naval gun carriages (big or medium units). It also had the ability to be radio guided and its speed made it much more interesting, in terms of damage caused, than the naval shells. The explosive charge was, also in the 'light' version, five times greater than the charge in one 381-mm shell (but obviously with very different penetration capabilities).

The loaded weapon weight (approximately a half of a 381-mm shell) made it easy to be moved on board. However, securing the engine's liquid fuels on-board still remained a problem.

In the AC, there is mention of various contacts regarding the DAAC with the *Regia Marina* and the *Regia Aeronautica*, probably starting in 1940; however, in Campagnoli's words, 'there is lack of interest to continue'—probably the General Staff (in the original text, it says SM, it could also be referring to *Supermarina*) adduced the issues to budget problems, operational difficulties, and, again in Campagnoli's words, 'inability to foresee its potential'.[59]

In 1942, after inconclusive negotiations with the *Regia Marina*, Campini was directed by engineer Astegno of Ansaldo to contact the *Kriegsmarine* for the development of small watercrafts with water-jet propulsion, which had already performed excellently during trials.

A contract was closed for 50,000 Reichsmarks (approximately 600,000 Euro in 2016, using gold as an exchange medium) with the *Kriegsmarine*, and the development facility was placed, upon request of the Germans, at the Garda Lake, with the goal of keeping it near the Caproni plants and safe from aerial raids.

However, Campini 'was anyway convinced that the collaboration with the *Kriegsmarine* was one-sided and in fact, it was'.[60] Presumably, the scepticism of the possibility of a loyal and equal collaboration with the Germans led Ansaldo (in 1942) to consider other ways to achieve their goals, thus acquiring the 'Gunnarson document'.

German DAAC Incarnation: Henschel Hs 117 Schmetterling

After the trials in Tripolitania in 1940, engineer Campini decided to continue the development of the weapon with German BMW, which, according to him, had a more advanced engine.[61, 62] In 1943, this collaboration led to the German Henschel Hs 117 Schmetterling ('butterfly').

In September 1942, Göring approved, after Hitler's approval on 1 September 1942, the restart of the programme of anti-aircraft rocket weapons, given the impossibility for the *Luftwaffe* to block Allied access to German skies. In the document of technical specifications of 25 September 1942, the first reference to what would eventually become the Henschel 117 can be found. Its development occurred despite numerous difficulties in building the testing location and assuring the required manpower.

The Hs 117 was one of the anti-aircraft weapon among the many developed in Germany during the war, without a centralised coordination (rivalries and competition among different industrial firms were common) until at least 1944. The tactical aim was the necessity to intercept enemy aircraft at altitudes not reachable by anti-aircraft artillery.

Between May and July 1944, only five Henschel 117 test models were produced. The expectation of being able to produce initially 3,000 units a month and 5,000 with a tuned production cycle was pure fantasy, given the conditions of the war and the industrial supplies at the time.

The specifications, as well as the lines and technical solutions of the Hs 117, closely follow those of the DAAC 1940 with the difference being that it has two solid combustible boosters for take-offs instead of one and a higher top speed due to its intended use as anti-aircraft weapons. The two boosters were meant to be unhooked after 600 metres of flight—cruising speed is 210 metres per second.

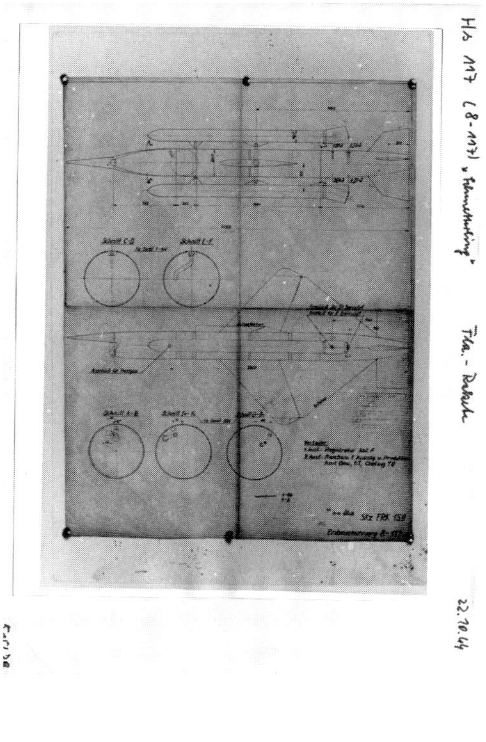

The Hs 117 in 1944.
(*Courtesy www.deutscheluftwaffe.de*)

	DAAC 1940	HS 117 1944
Range	38 km	32 km anti-aircraft at altitude 16 km anti-aircraft at low altitude
Launcher	Vickers-Armstrongs modified naval carriage, one solid booster hooked to fuselage	37 mm modified carriage, two Schmidding 109-553 boosters with solid di-glycol hooked to fuselage
Length	420 cm	429 cm
Fuselage width	44 cm	35 cm
Wing span	252 cm	200 cm
Speed	500 km/h	756 km/h
Weight when empty	135 kg	180 kg
Weight when loaded	480 kg	420 kg (two boosters of 90 kg each)
Useful war load	125 kg	23 kg, proximity fuse
Engines	Campini 40 combustion a mixture of kerosene, catalyst and nitric acid in three phases (model 1943)	Wasag 109-512 (nitric acid/gasoline) or BMW 109-558 (hypergolic combination of nitric acid and Tonka 250)
Guides	Two radio operators	Radio guide from ground, visual control and joystick; from 1944 via radar guide
Maximum useful altitude		9 km
Duration of thrust		50 seconds

For a battery of eight launch points and two radio control stations, a total of 151 men were expected; this estimate gives an interesting assessment of a full compatibility with the use on board, even in small units with one or two launch points. The time between the go order and launching was calculated in 180 seconds.[63]

The direct derivation of the German weapon from the Campini studies is recorded in the AC: 'Campini developed two devices, a first one in 1940 and a second in Germany in 1943 with BMW'.[64]

1941 designs: Decks

For 1941, the AC reports the studies underway for a 'full-deck battleship' followed by an aircraft carrier 'with Japanese deck'. Unfortunately, there are not too many drawings available that can be traced with certainty to 1941.

The first illustration that seems to be related to the full-deck battleship shows a simple fine-tuning of the positioning of the catapult and the crane, already seen in preliminary illustrations. A flight deck is also seen with a bow elevator, approximately 15 metres wide.

A second illustration of the bow section of the deck provides more details regarding the architectural choices contemplated; above all, it is the first important clue regarding the aerial component that was being considered. There are two catapults of different lengths (27 metres

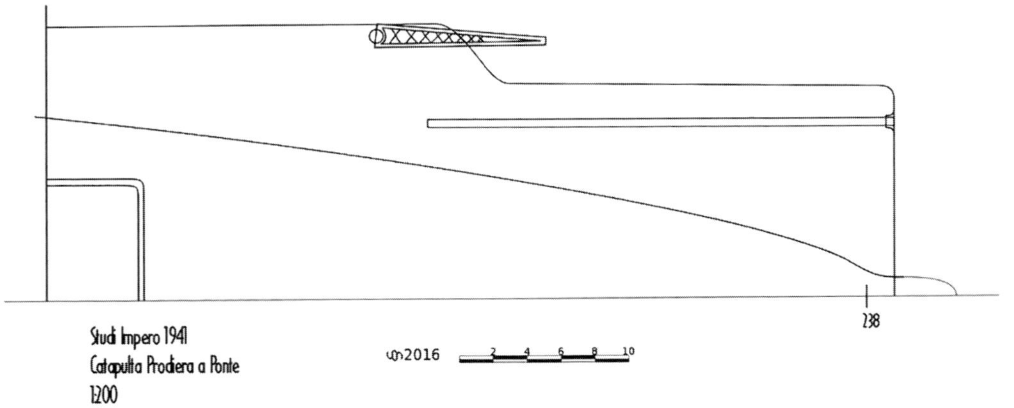

Solution with hangar and flight deck. (*Courtesy Archivio Campagnoli, drawing Stefano Sappino*)

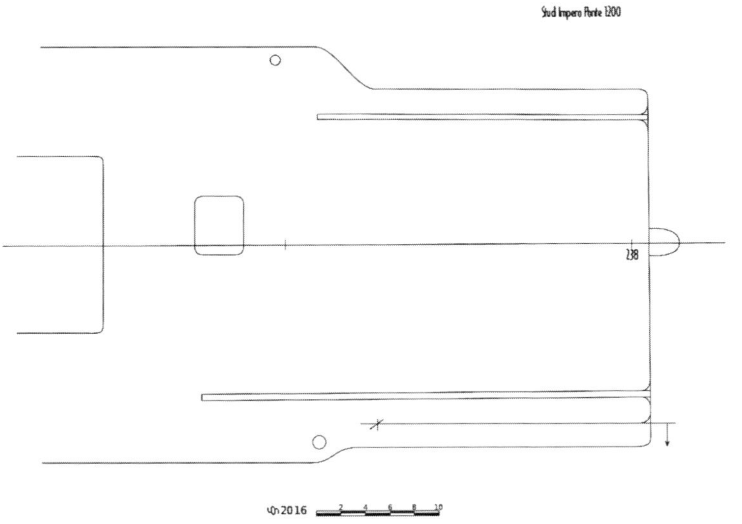

Flight deck, bow section. (*Courtesy Archivio Campagnoli, drawing Stefano Sappino*)

and 36.5 metres) linked to two cranes in different dimensions and ranges. The bow flight deck is asymmetrical and the take-off area to starboard was widened by 3 metres. The port crane was placed in a more rational position.

Apparently, the placement of the catapults did not block the possibility of take-off directly from the deck for lighter vehicles. The main bow elevator was 15 × 14 metres.

The most important clue from this drawing is the distance between the crane and the axis of the starboard catapult, which, as we have seen, is of an unusual length. This distance is insufficient to guarantee passage of any aircraft available at the time, being only 3 metres. It is instead sufficient to guarantee passage of a rocket-propelled weapon such as the DAAC, which had a wing span of 2.5 metres. The secondary elevator of 5 × 4 metres, otherwise hard to explain, is compatible and presumably aimed to the lifting of this type of weapons.[65]

Island and 'Japanese Deck'

The second series of 1941 drawings is instead connected to a different project. Even though it is not possible to recreate the overall concept, a deck that stops well before the bow is shown and the bow itself is raised in a conspicuous way. A prominent full bulbous bulb, similar to one of the two experimented on for the *Littorio*-class of 1934, is shown.

The deck construction height is 23.6 metres, and this is the height for all the following projects. The island appears not to be placed in the best position—one level under the deck. We cannot, however, exclude the possibility that the bow includes a sky jumper, given the lack of catapults and the height of the bow. The usefulness of an anti-aircraft artillery that cannot operate at transverse would otherwise be limited (the new 120-mm L. 50 guns are represented).

It is also possible that the hangar was opened and the take-offs, perhaps with catapults, were possible from bow as in the pre-war Japanese solutions.

The island, which would remain stable in overall design in the following drawings, called for a bridge, and an admiral's bridge house overlooked by what is probably the headquarters of aerial operations. Beneath them, one structure on three levels possibly hosted the rooms for the air group.

The funnel's line is close to the design followed by the large *Regia Marina* warships.

The 120 L. 50 DP Gun

The single 120-mm/50 gun is represented in single turrets of a slightly different design compared to the well-known stabilised 90-mm AA.

Until the availability of the AC, it was commonly believed that the 120-mm planned for the 1939 destroyer-class were housed in the same turrets used for the 90-mm.

Specifications of the naval 120-mm:[66]

Initial speed 800 m/s
Projectile weight 32.15 kg

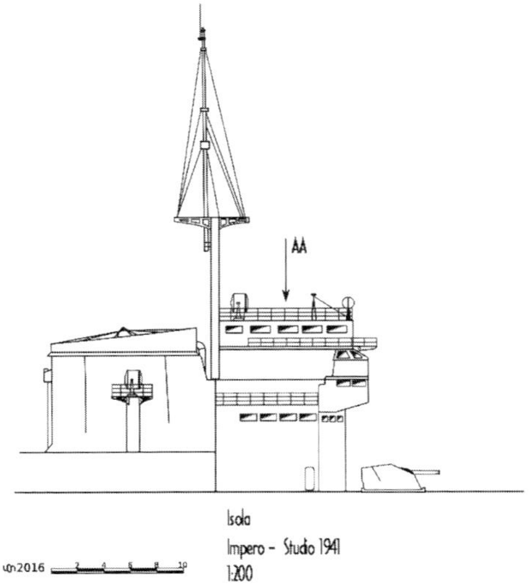

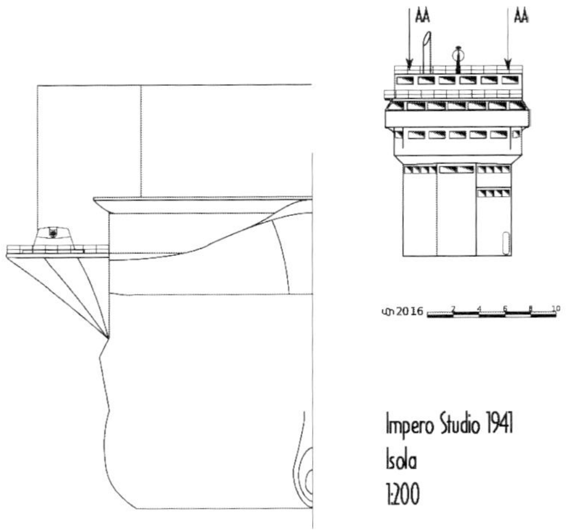

Above left: Island, side view. (*Courtesy Archivio Campagnoli, drawing Stefano Sappino*)

Above right: Front view, island, hangar, and flight deck. (*Courtesy Archivio Campagnoli, drawing Stefano Sappino*)

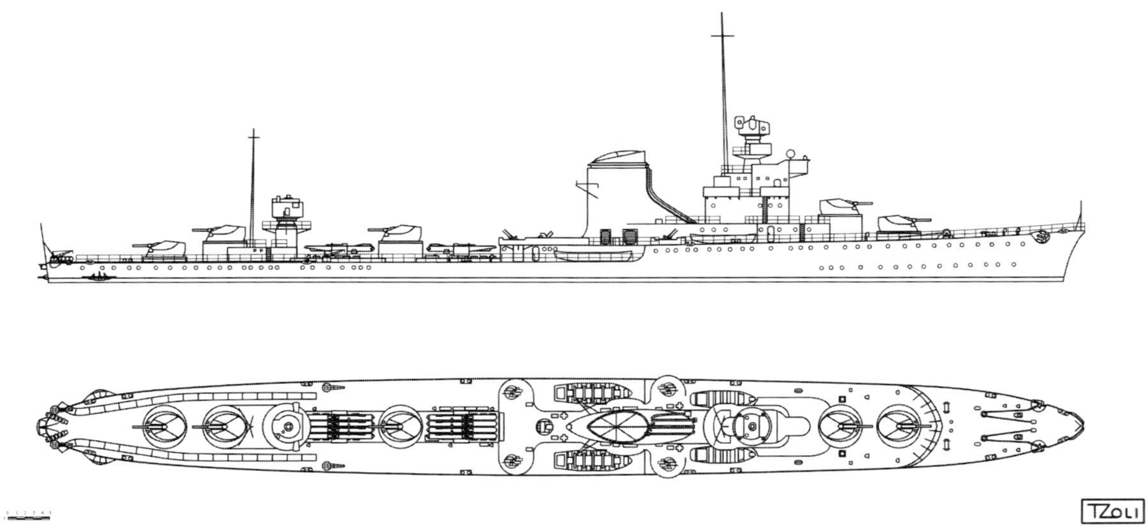

1939 programme destroyer. (*Drawing by Tzoli*)

Cartridge length 1,200 mm
Elevation from -5° to + 85°
Range: 20,000 metres
At least 12 rounds/minute at any elevation

The 120-mm/50s in stabilised turrets were supposed to replace the 135-mm, originally expected for the *Comandanti Medaglie d'Oro*-class, were produced at Ansaldo, a production that would continue throughout the entire war.[67]

The *Regia Marina*'s 1943 plan included the installation of the 120-mm L. 50 on the existing fleet of destroyers and the dispatch of the previously planned 135-mm to the coast defences.

1939's Building Plan for Destroyers

Possible aspect and specifications based on partial originals:[68]
Length: 117 metres waterline, 119.75 metres overall
Beam: 11.5 metres
Displacement: estimate is 2,200–2,500 standard 2,800–3,000-ton full load, which makes it similar to the USN's *Gearing*-class
Draught: estimate is 4.2–4.25 metres

1942 Projects

In 1942, the term 'study' disappears from the drawings. It is possible that this indicates a transition to a more advanced phase closer to the actual start of the conversion.

The first full drawings of the flight deck are available: one at large scale (1:200) of the entire deck, dated '2-1942', allows us to deduce its main specifications.

The deck measures 240 metres in length and its maximum width is 42.7 metres. The island is cantilevered on starboard and, excluding the pads, it is approximately 28 × 10 metres. The weaponry includes six pieces (probably 120-mm L. 50) in singles, two different types of twin AA and numerous AA pieces that are unidentifiable.

The island's levels are compatible with the 1941 drawing; the funnel is at the same height as RN *Impero* bow engine area.

Missing are the cranes, previously always present. It could be that a different method of aircraft handling and launch was envisaged and that different types of aircraft were taken into consideration (in 1942, tests for take-offs and deck landing for RN *Aquila* air group were in full swing), with two catapults of which one was apparently designated to the launch of heavy aircraft due its length and available space. The length of the catapults was indeed 48 metres and 32 metres. The 48-metre catapult is also compatible with the launch of rocket weapons; the 'Gunnarson document' was received precisely from 1942.

The ship was expected to have a pronounced bulbous bow.

Four elevators are present, two for the aircraft and two, presumably, for torpedoes and bombs. The bow elevator was 16 metres long and 14 metres wide, and it was placed immediately from the centre of the original large calibre turret number 3. An elevator of 9 × 9 metres was placed between the original stern 152-mm turrets.

The next drawing, dated '3-42', represents the deck in small scale as well as the details of the three alternative bows and the main rudder design. The latter is detailed in a 1:100 drawing, containing the main rudder for the *Littorio*-class and the one designed for RN *Impero* as aircraft carrier. A reduced surface is noticed and the rudder is identical to that present in the aircraft carrier model preserved in Venice. The reduced surface is possible thanks to the improved manoeuvrability and better hydrodynamics of the ship, as discussed above. This rudder will then be reported in detail in 1943 RN *Impero* drawings.

The three bows of March '42 are consistent with previous studies: the first represents an extension of the existing bow; the other two are two bulbous bows of different size, marked as alpha and beta as in the studies of 1934 for the *Littorio* ships. In both cases, the flight deck is 23.6 metres from the construction line.

The placement of the anchor stations remains in the original location planned for the battleship.

A complete sketch of the deck at a scale of 1:500, dated '3-42', presents a re-examination of the project, probably determined by an analysis of weights balancing. The island is moved tangential to the original bulwark line.

The weaponry was reduced to four pieces of 120-mm in single turrets and to two large AA twin turrets, perhaps of 65-mm L. 64 guns. The drawing also offers the best available view of the island from above, with two AA pods, the disposition of the platforms on flight deck side, and what could be a platform designed for a range finder.

The overhang sections of the deck are larger, arriving up to the same height as the catapults given the decrease of the area designated for the handling the take-off operations.

The elevators are reduced to two, one of 15 × 14 metres and one apparently of 14.5 × 14.5 metres. The bow elevator is moved to the position previously occupied by a third large-calibre turret, a third elevator (for aircraft ammo handling) is 5 × 5 metres.

The cranes near the two catapults are again represented. The catapults are 28 and 23 metres long; two arresting gears, apparently too close to the start of the landing deck, are present. Two platforms for AA weapons are on both sides of the bow, probably one level below the flight deck.

1943 Projects

In 1943, the planning outlines of the conversion of RN *Impero* into an aircraft carrier split. The first followed the outline of a fleet aircraft carrier, while the second concentrated on the embarkation of jet-propulsion or rocket-propelled weapons.

V-1 on RN *Impero* CV

The following series of illustrations introduces an unexpected element in the evolution of the study of the conversion of RN *Impero*: the presence of embarked jet-propulsion or rocket-propelled weapons.

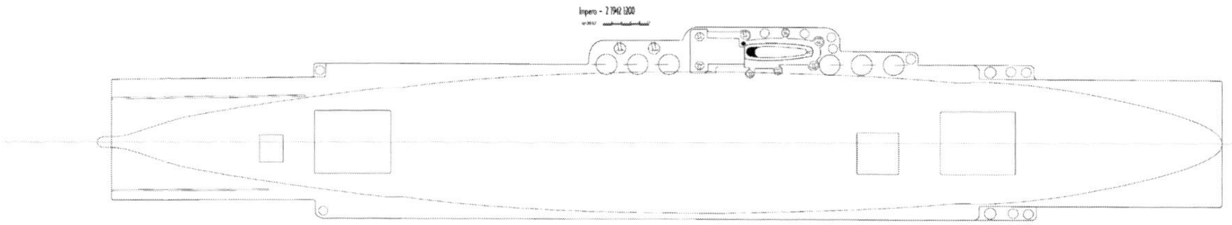

Above: January 1942 flight deck. (*Courtesy Archivio Campagnoli, drawing Stefano Sappino*)

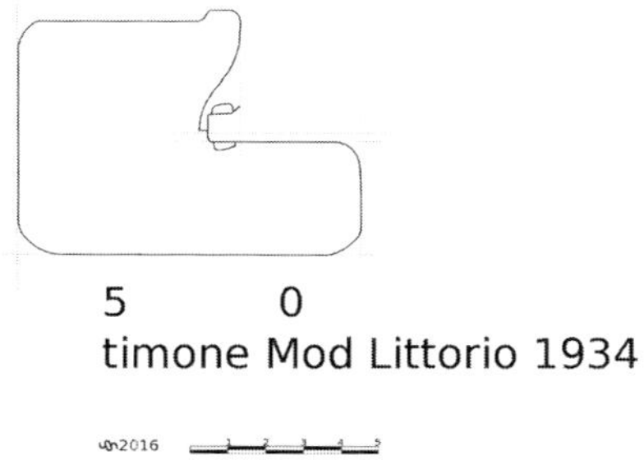

Right: Main rudders, RN *Littorio* 1934 and RN *Impero* NPA 1943. (*Courtesy Archivio Campagnoli, drawing Stefano Sappino*)

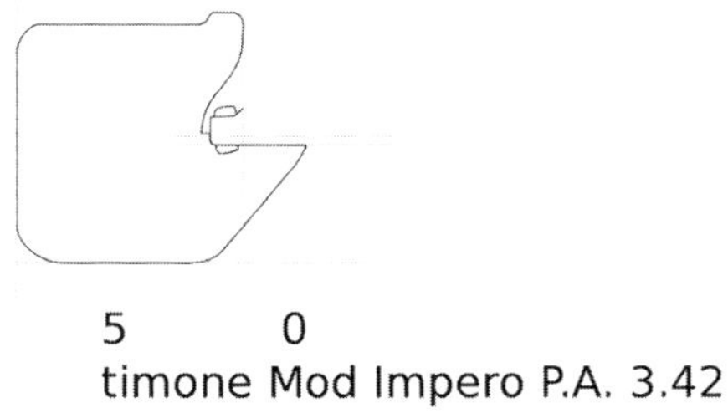

Below: RN *Impero* flight deck, March 1942. (*Courtesy Archivio Campagnoli, drawing Stefano Sappino*)

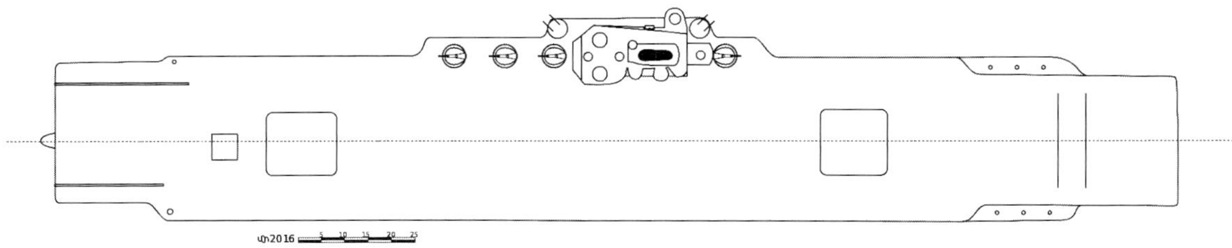

As is evident from the documents, Ansaldo already knew the details of one of the most secret German retaliatory weapons, the V1, before 1943 and was, in any event, searching for an innovative solution for the anti-ship armament of its major ships, studying the matter in conjunction with Campini since 1939.[69] We already summarily examined the developments that led to the V-1 in Germany.

The Ansaldo company purchased, in several steps, the so called 'Gunnarson document' in Switzerland, with an operation of industrial intelligence that Piazzai sponsored at the board of directors. The document, available as photo negatives, was obtained through funds drawn from a secret bank account also located in the Helvetian Confederacy; the total amount was 150,000 Lire in gold marks (approximately 240,000 Euro in 2016 as a reference to the gold).

The 'Gunnarson document' was composed of a series of intelligence reports, which were sent by Danish sources via Sweden to Great Britain from 1942 and, in the process, intercepted and sold. Sweden was neutral; however, it had maintained contacts with Italy because of the past military collaboration and the Swedish land was directly overlooking the German base of Peenemünde where experiments for secret German military weapons were being developed.[70, 71]

The analysis of the 'Gunnarson document' was done jointly by engineers Piazzai, Astengo, and Campini in the *Ufficio Studi* Ansaldo.[72] The presence of the latter is important because of his experience in the production of innovative aero-naval devices, particularly with rocket motors.

The last section of the document (or its final version) arrived in Genoa between August and fall of 1943; in the last segment, there is a detailed description of the weapon that fell on the island of Bornholm (Danish island, but occupied by the Germans during the war) and it is derived from the report made by a Danish naval official, Lt-Cdr Hasager Christiansen to the British intelligence on the V-1, which plummeted on the island on 23 August 1943.[73] The 'Bornholm incident' is known in detail in literature on the subject.[74]

The Bornholm device info was related to an unmanned jet craft, as seen in several non-technical photographs of every part of the vehicle.

Described as coming from south-south-east, it was flying at high speed at low altitude with a strong hiss, it then hit, crawling in the residential area. The meteorological conditions at the time of the accident were wind from the south, strength 0.1, cloudy, hot, and foggy.

The object was yellow, in the shape of an aeroplane, with a few wooden parts, no canvas, and the surfaces were thin metal sheets. It was 4 metres long and weighed 400–500 kg, the diameter of the fuselage was 0.8 metres. The engine was 2 metres long and 0.5 metres diameter, without a main control surface and with steering gear in the tail; when it was recovered, it was misshapen by the impact.[75]

The object was marked as 'Ser. V8E', and the absence of radio guidance devices was noted. There was, therefore, proof of the practical actualisation of one of the Argus projects known to Campini, simplified by the absence of any radio steering device. Campini was of the opinion that rocket propulsion in small vehicles was advantageous compared to other solutions, even though volatile combustibles in liquid phase caused big concerns if embarked.

Campini was also of the opinion that radio guidance had been abandoned by the Germans since 1939. The joint analysis done on the information made available by the 'Gunnarson document' brought about the following conclusions by the Ansaldo specialists:

1. Test flights were underway.
2. It was a simple ballistic device.
3. It was without radio guidance.
4. It was without self-destruction mechanisms.
5. It had a range of 200–250 km.
6. It was less advanced than the DAAC.

The AC includes a series of drawings related to the on-board placement on the aircraft carrier *Impero* of objects classified as Fi 103 (namely V-1). From the analysis done, they do not appear to perfectly match the German weapons, even if they are based on them.

The first drawing shows the launch ramp (41 metres long) and a jet-propelled weapon in a rather different shape from the V-1, even if labelled as 'Fi 103'. The ramp was placed at bow in a side position, with support joints distributed throughout the main frames of the ship. It is possible that a stabilising mechanism for the ramp was included.

The weapon appears to be equipped with a vertical tail, though it is not possible to determine whether it also has helms and whether it was radio guided or not. The main body is 7.5 metres long with a diameter of approximately 1.3 metres. The engine is approximately 5 metres long, with a diameter of approximately 60 cm, and a total length of approximately 8.8 metres.

It seems probable—as in the case of the weapons that will be analysed hereafter—that these plans were produced in Italy based on the information deducted from the intelligence documents, plans which can likely be attributed to Campini.

A series of views of particular interest follow, where it is possible to completely verify the planned on-board layout for the jet-propulsion weapons facilities and some of their specifications.

Based on the plans of the 3.42 flight deck, a new design was developed to support the new weapons. Its most interesting feature is the starboard flight deck enlargement, probably because of the necessity to make space in the hangars for jet weapons without hindering the air group too much. Two elevators are added, one dedicated to jet-propulsion weapons and the other to equipment for the liquid propellants, which evidently were going to be handled on deck because of their dangerousness.

The length of the flight deck is always 240 metres, but it goes up to 50 metres at its widest point.[76] The launch ramp (30 metres long) reserved for the new weapons was moved to the port and a specific deflector shield, which can be elevated, was added at its end with the purpose of blocking and dispersing the high-temperature jet flow.

Attributable to the same project is the portrayal of the bow with a view of the elevated flame shield. Also portrayed are the levels of the original *Littorio*-class forecastle deck as well as the profiles of the modified bows for the two *Littorios* and RN *Roma*. It is worth noting that in no instance is the original *Littorio* bow, as actually built, used as a reference; rather, the bow profile originally suggested by Ansaldo.

The elevator for jet and rocket weapons was 15 × 12.5 metres, and the one designated to serve the launch preparation station approximately 8 × 7 metres. This area is detailed in a 1:100 drawing of the ramp (apparently with a rail guide 1.1 metre wide) and of the weapon. A hydraulic elevated shield 8 metres wide and 4.4 metres long is placed 5.5 metres from the launching point of the weapon.

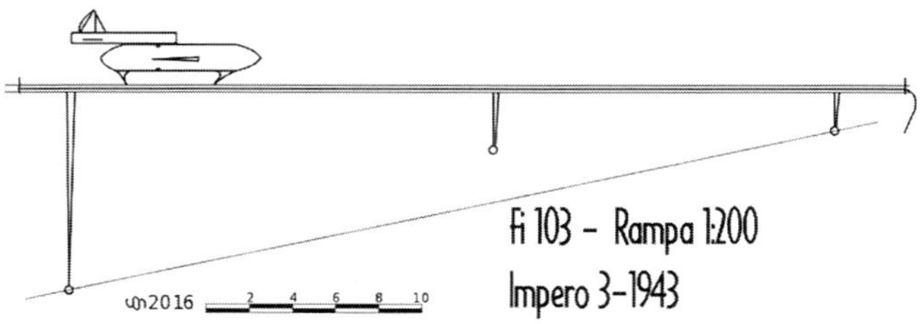

The first launching ramp for non-conventional weapons. (*Courtesy Archivio Campagnoli, drawing Stefano Sappino*)

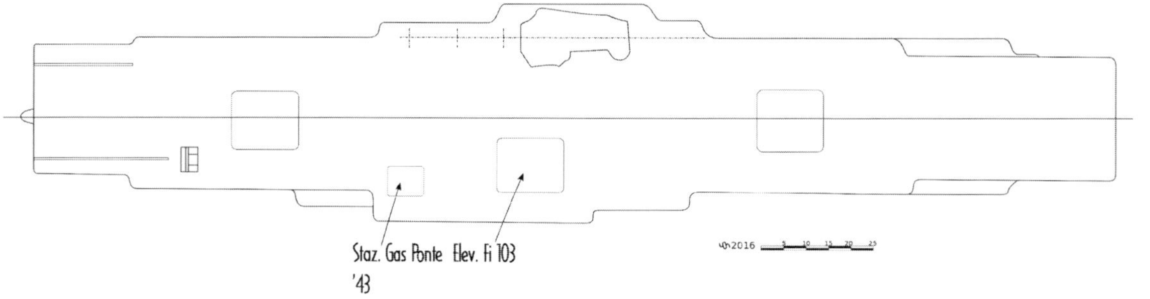

Above: The March 1942 flight deck, with the jet-powered weapons facilities. (*Courtesy Archivio Campagnoli, drawing Stefano Sappino*)

Below: Bow profiles. (*Courtesy Archivio Campagnoli, drawing Stefano Sappino*)

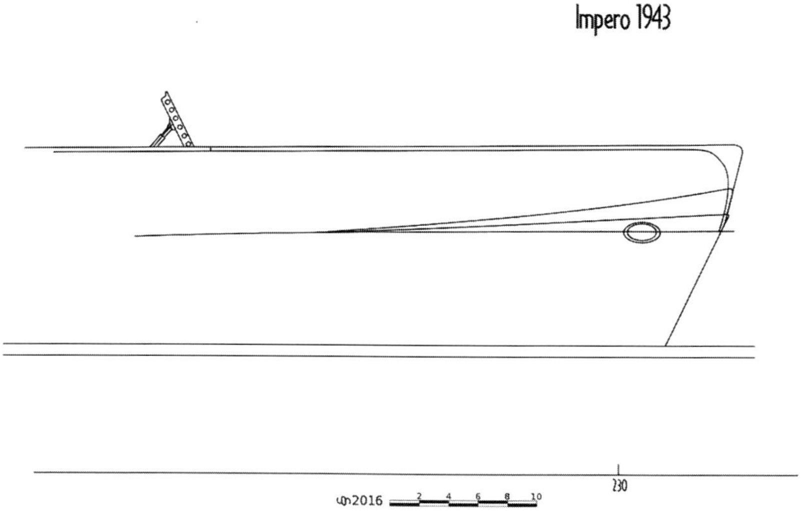

The depicted weapon is 6.9 metres long, with a wingspan of 5 metres, a diameter of the fuselage of 1.1 metre, and 0.5 metre for the jet engine. The weapon shape is noticeably different from the V-1, both in its dimensions and its aerodynamics. Some of the elements give the impression that the weapon in question may have been of mixed propulsion, with a pulse engine as with the V-1 (certainly present) and a jet engine (particularly given the tail nozzle shape). The wing surface is much smaller compared to the V-1 and appears not to be compatible with a take-off with the thrust of a jet pulse only. Unfortunately, a side view, which would allow solving this issue with certainty, does not exist.

A topside drawing shows the detail of the planned procedures for the jet weapons launch: they were brought on deck in groups of three via the main elevator, then loaded and calibrated for the target (assuming that they had not been designed to be used for a double scope, radio guided anti-ship weapons similar to the DAAC), and moved to launch position on the ramp.

The presence of what appears to be an elevator for fuel leads one to believe that it was normally kept in appropriately protected areas due to its dangerousness. However, considering the slowness of set up operations typical at that time for these weapons, the presence of a main elevator of that size appears overabundant.

The illustration at a scale of 1:100 of the launch ramp planned in 1943 for jet weapons allows for a verification of the level of aerodynamics associated with them.

The well-known lack of horizontal stability of this type of aerodynamic requires a stabilised launch ramp (probably with hydraulic actuators) in order to constantly maintain the vertical position the ramp during rolling. The maximum manageable inclination angle seems to be determined by the necessity to avoid contact between the deck and the wing tips. The diagram also allows appreciating the dihedral angle of 5 degrees, useful to improve stability during rolling.

The ramp seems to be positioned close to deck edge and therefore not inclined horizontally.

Based on the gathered information and of the low military value of an embarked weapon of this type, Ansaldo considered abandoning the Fi 103, while the research on the DAAC continued, considering a longer launch ramp to increase the war load.

Below is a complete description of the final evaluation of the 'Fi 106', in its entirety:[77]

> Targeting: complex, unmanageable on board;
> Accuracy: unknown;
> Range: 300 km declared;
> Propellant Managing: to be done on deck;
> Ramps: cannot be stabilised, unmanageable;
> Launch cycle: declared 30 min., not less than 50 minutes from data.
> We are using useful space in the hangar for unknown devices which according to the data only offer a strong psychological impact but do not have practical feasibility.
> A large unit which gets within to 250 km of the target is seriously engaged, it is better to have a bombing air group.
> Piazzai received even more critical data regarding feasibility.
> Developments are being prepared with deck '43 with two catapults of 50 and 38 m.
> Vatura will report on the subject.

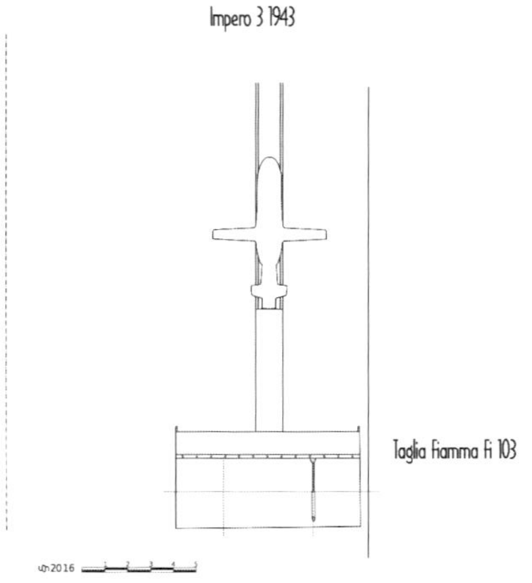

Above: Launch ramp with fire shield. (*Courtesy Archivio Campagnoli, drawing Stefano Sappino*)

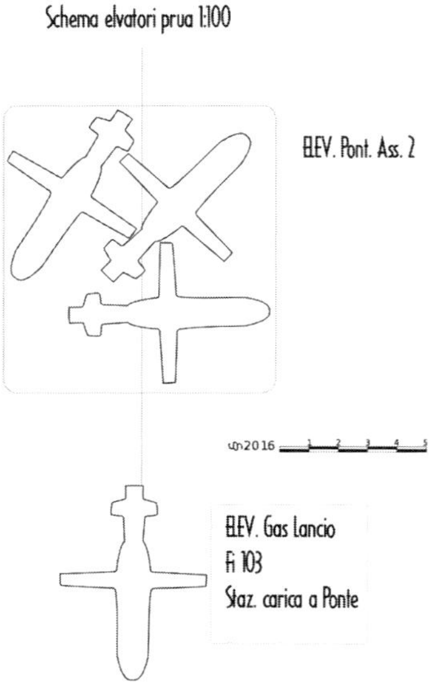

Left: Fi 103 elevator and pre-flight station. (*Courtesy Archivio Campagnoli, drawing Stefano Sappino*)

Below: The stabilised ramp, front view. (*Courtesy Archivio Campagnoli, drawing Stefano Sappino*)

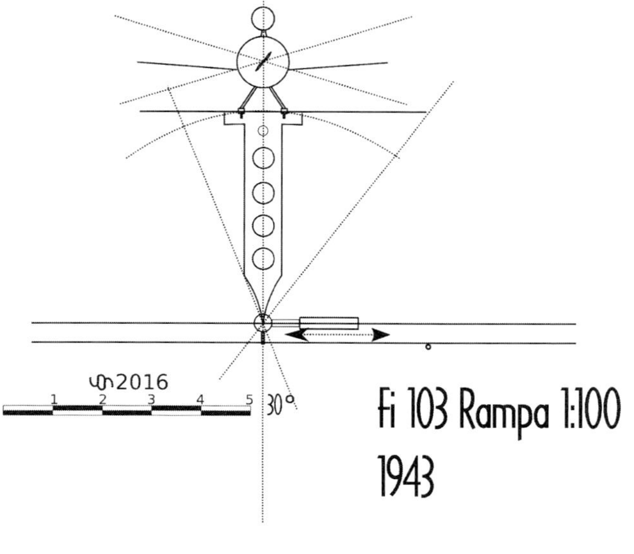

RN *Impero* 1943

The series of drawings available for the 1943 aircraft carrier *Impero* version has a higher level of detail compared to the previous ones, and allows analysis of a few more architectural elements.

This version presents a unique feature for aircraft carriers of the time (in addition to the exceptionally wide deck), namely the equivalent of modern sky jumpers. A further unique characteristic in the western designed aircraft carriers is visible, a funnel is sloping outwards to divert the smoke from the flight deck.

The series of drawings (now once again classified as studies) brings us from the deck already examined in 1942 to the final version.

NPA *Impero*, 443

An important intermediate step is seen in version 443, the best documented project, with complete side and top views at a scale of 1:200, showing the modifications of the 1942 project those of the last project, 843.

Starboard View

The drawing is labelled *Impero* 4.1943. The island includes 443 modifications to a previous version and a sloping funnel is introduced. A Gufo III radar, with a parabolic antenna, is shown placed at a height of approximately 32 metres above the waterline.

Comparing the plans with those of RN *Roma*, it can be noticed that the hangar deck is placed at the level of the forecastle deck of the battleship. The height of the hangar is approximately 6.5 metres—probably allowing for the hooking of airplanes at the hangar ceiling, as in RN *Aquila*.

The propeller blades are not depicted, or rather, they are only hinted in the drawings as hydrodynamics trials led the Ansaldo designers to identify four-blade propellers as optimal.[78]

The bow, as already discussed, recaptures the lines of the 1934 plans modified as per the new Freude tank trials results. It therefore differs from all of the other bow profiles of that class, both from the original RN *Littorio* at launch as of the modifications, which were later applied, and from the bow of RN *Roma*. The bow area was closed aft up to the flight deck and open at starboard immediately after, where an AA weapons platform is present, one level under the deck.

The reduced dimensions of the inclined connector between armoured belt and bulwark led to the deduction that the main armoured belt was to be reduced, probably removing the decapping plate and its support, for a total of 22 cm of thickness.

On the flight deck, one catapult and one inclined ramp are present. The latter, an exceptional design for the time, includes a catapult (or a guide); it is 47 metres long, with a maximum height from the flight deck of 3.6 metres.

Descending towards the stern, the beginning of the hangar area includes openings for the boats with their cranes. A 10-metre deck overhang accommodates the anti-ship and anti-aircraft artillery and the island. It then tapers down to 7.8 metres at the funnel and to 4 metres at the stern 120-mm gun.

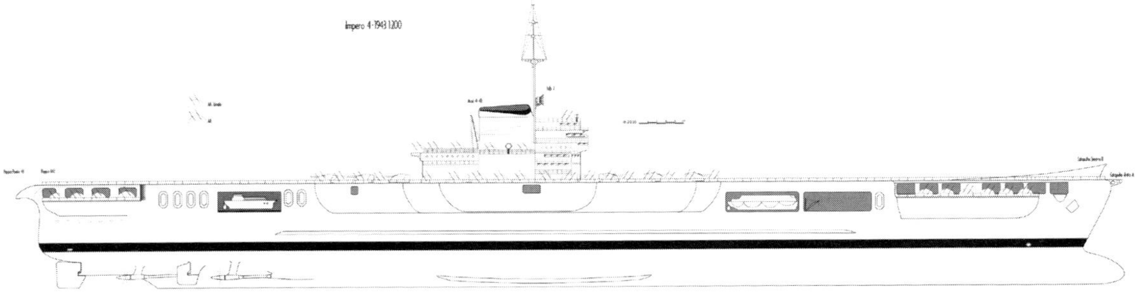

Above: April 1943 starboard view. (*Courtesy Archivio Campagnoli, drawing Stefano Sappino*)

Below: March 1943 launching ramp. (*Courtesy Archivio Campagnoli, drawing Stefano Sappino*)

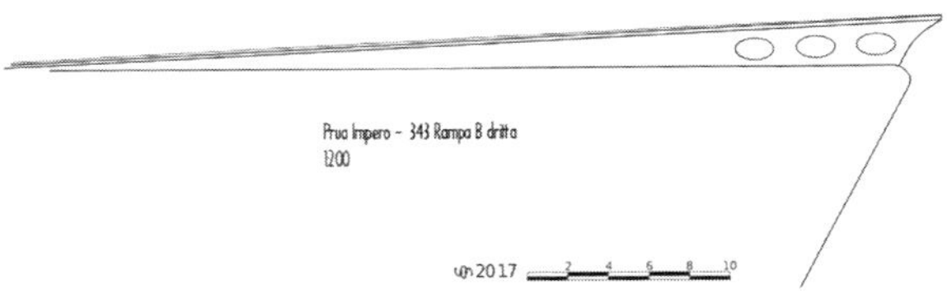

The stern area, after another boat bay, probably with a platform protruding out of the bulwark, presents an AA platform one level below the deck. The inclined overhang to the landing deck is longer than the one in the 1942 design. The island, on six levels in its highest point, is 35 metres long and 14 metres high.

The weaponry, aside from the six 120-mm L. 50 in single turrets, is not otherwise defined; the AA weapons are all twins, even if of two different types (even though for the *Aquila*, sextuplets were expected, a sign that in 1943 the hope for such AA complexes had possibly permanently been abandoned).

A previous diagram, from March 1943, shows a starboard ramp sloped at 3 degrees, 46 metres long, and 2.5 metres high in its highest point, without any other data. It could be a first draft of a ski jumper or a rigid ramp for jet weapons.

Deck and Port Side 443-843

Possibly the most interesting drawing of the AC is dated '*Impero* 443 Mod. 843-13 Studio', with a note: 'superstructure moving at stern Mod. 843.13 on deck 443 and hull 443'.

This is a design change decided after the end of the Fascist regime, which occurred on 25 July 1943, a few days before the Armistice with the Allies. The reintroduction of the word 'study' clearly shows that any realistic possibility of actually building was over.

The deck has a very 'modern' design with a double deck enlargement at starboard and to the port; the island is moved 15 metres astern in comparison to the 342 version and has slightly different dimensions (36.5 metres long and 7 metres wide for the main structure).

The reasons that led to this significant variation are not known; the advantage must have been noteworthy, perhaps connected to hangars widening at starboard, to the resulting weight redistribution and an increased longitudinal stability. What is noticeable in this version is a tendency to be cautious with weight, also given the decrease of AA weapons previously placed on the island. The diagram also portrays the possible position of the range finder, added in August 1943. The starboard side seems to be a logical consequence of the ideas adopted during the design of the jet-powered weapons accommodations, reconverted and extended to aeronautical use only. The bow overhang is increased by 5.2 metres compared to the 1942 drawings.

The dimensions of one of the elevators are significantly larger than those planned in 1942 (16.5 metres long and 17 metres high), allowing for simultaneous movement of two fighters or one larger plane. The aircraft depicted have a profile and dimensions compatible with the Re 2001 OR (in the drawings), the fighter already being manufactured for RN *Aquila*, which would have been equipped with bombs or torpedoes as also specified by the name of the elevator devoted to their movements.

The deck area above the starboard overhang was likely reserved for aircraft fittings before take-off as indicated by the placement of the aircraft on deck and the presence of a nearby elevator for weapons.[79]

As far as the AA weapons are concerned, even though the nomenclature in the drawing does not list them, the weapons on the starboard side of the deck are labelled as the retractable 37-mm singles as on the bow of the *Littorio*-class ships: therefore, that part of the flight deck could have been made entirely flat.

The top view shows a catapult or guide, which runs along the take-off ramp. There are no details for the left catapult except for the length—36 metres. The shape of the final sustaining frame for the take-off inclined ramp hints to the fact that it could be lowered, thus leaving the take-off deck entirely flat.

The bow appears entirely closed, even if openings to the manoeuvring area appear dotted in the picture. Platforms for anti-aircraft weapons are missing from the starboard side.

The last drawing, in a scale of 1:200 and dated 443 with 843 modifications, offers the only bow and stern views of RN *Impero* as aircraft carrier. The paper is deformed due to time and

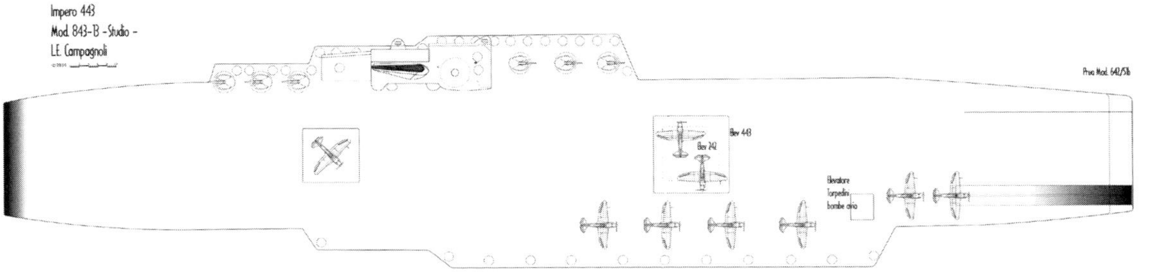

Flight deck, August 1943. (*Courtesy Archivio Campagnoli, drawing Stefano Sappino*)

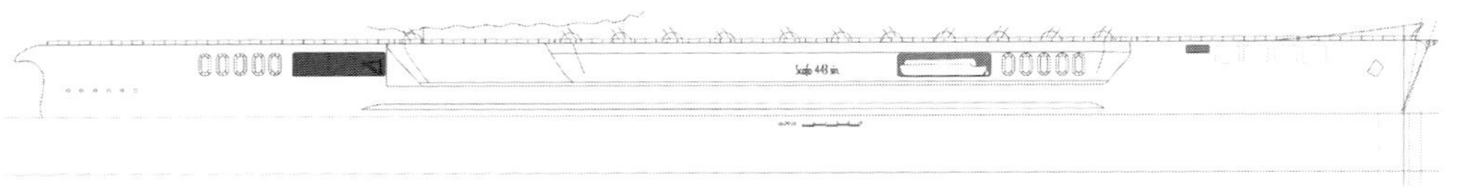

August 1943 port view. (*Courtesy Archivio Campagnoli, drawing Stefano Sappino*)

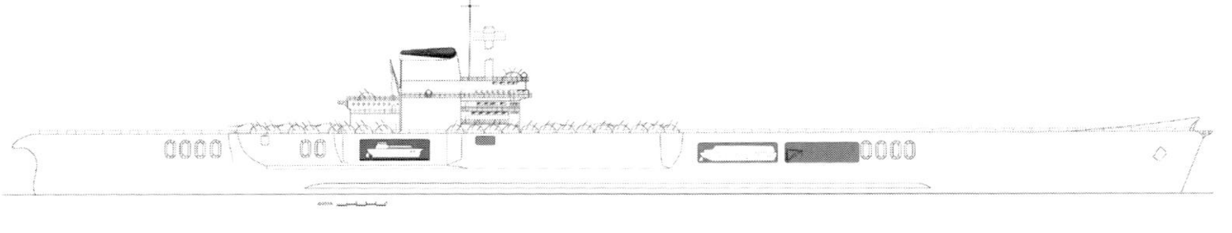

A reconstruction of the starboard side after the island aft moving. (*Drawing Stefano Sappino*)

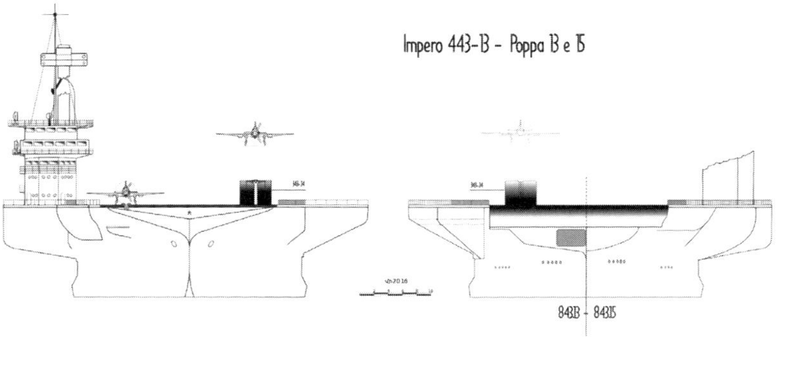

RN *Impero*, bow and stern views. (*Courtesy Archivio Campagnoli, drawing Stefano Sappino*)

humidity; therefore, the drawing has been reconstructed using the port and starboard side view as guides

The views allow us to appreciate the shape and dimensions of the stanchions, particularly the fact that the hangar spaces, aside for the space necessary for the exhaust gas ducts, were almost certainly extended under the island.

The bow is completely closed with a 'hurricane' configuration, while at stern, in one of the two versions present, 84313 and 84315, there is an opening to the manoeuvring space.

The island has one bridge level missing compared to the previous designs and shows a tubular structure to support two 5-metre range finders (probably those earmarked on the original RN *Impero* for the 152-mm guns), similar to what in use for the main range finders of the '*Littorio*-class. It is possible to also observe the curvilinear funnel shape.[80]

None of the AC drawings depict the island from the flight deck. The radar is not present in this version and would have probably been placed on top of the range finder structure, which could also be an armoured conning tower. The mast is reduced to a small signal one just forward the funnel.

A catapult and a flight jumper are present on the flight deck. The latter seems to be shaped into a differentiated structure, stiff to support the wheels of the fighters and light on the sides. The maximum height was reduced to 2 metres from the previous 3.6 metres; however, this modification was marked 34324—in other words, it preceded the 443 drawings.

There is a bare hint to what could be an auxiliary bridge on the two ends of the starboard stanchion.

1943 Ansaldo's 'Hexagonal Hull'

The AC does not contain a detailed description or drawings of the internal layout of RN *Impero* as aircraft carrier, although it is known that the drawing of the hangars was realised and much can be deduced from the elevators and the island's position. Two sheets include a concise description of some of the features of the planned solution.

The design activities concerning this part of the project seem to have been continued even after the Armistice of 3 September 1943.[81]

The presence of a partially armoured flight deck is reported, assisted by what is defined as 'the hexagonal hull' solution. It was essentially an area connected to the side armour support frames (with a 30-degree angle with respect to the vertical), which includes the hangars, and what were probably oblique lateral armoured bulkheads. It is possible that the armoured area was increased, on the deck, to cover the steam pipes and the elevators.

The starboard view gives a good estimate of the dimensions of the hangar, which is about 173 metres long. The profile of the overhang has a 2-metre rim, enough to guarantee space for the hiding mechanism of the sets of single AA guns on the deck and for potential storage, in the ceiling, of the Re 2001 OR.

An air group estimate based on the available spaces, in case the hangar was subdivided in three main compartments, is about forty-five fighters in the main hangars and about twenty-five hooked to the hangar ceiling—this not considering folding wings aircraft.

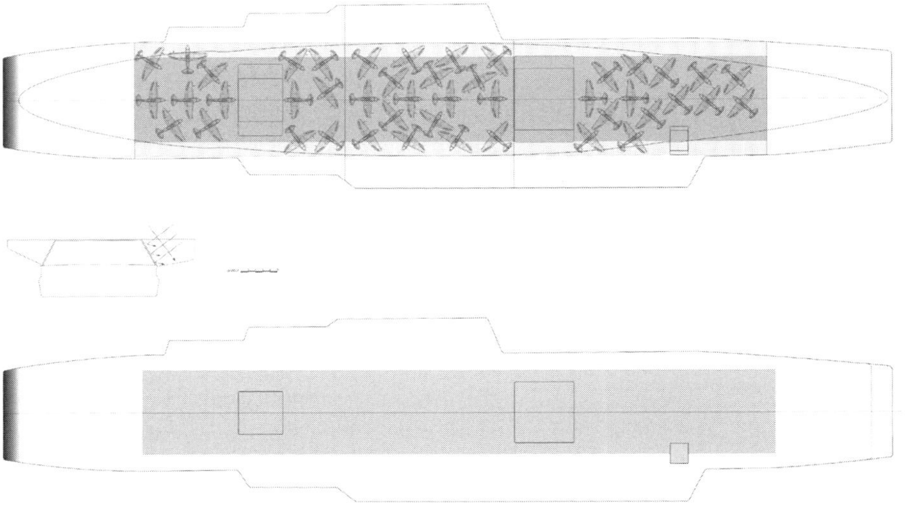

A general diagram of the partially protected areas, in view and in section; in grey is the protected area of the hangars, in darker grey is the armoured area of the deck, reconstruction by S. Sappino. Amidships section. (*Courtesy Archivio Campagnoli, drawing Stefano Sappino*)

Aircraft storage on hangar's ceiling, planned for the RN *Aquila*. (*Courtesy Rivista Marittima*)

A light material (aluminium) was planned for the area of the overhangs as programmed failure areas in case of explosions, acting as vents for collisions and gases.

The deck is in aero-naval profiled aluminium, 16–18 cm thick with self-fastening elements in the underneath steel frames. The solution is described as being easy to maintain and replace, as well as very light.[82]

The chosen solution is not far from those adopted for the British aircraft carriers, such as HMS *Victorious*, which had an armoured deck (62 per cent of the surface) protected by 3 inches of nickel-chromed steel, and the hangars were protected on all sides by 4.5 inches of nickel steel.[83]

The engines are the same that were planned in 1938 (in any event, already fitted) even though there was a hypothesis to evaluate a Diesel Fiat or Man propulsion.

The engines would have to operate on four-blade propellers, which appeared to be the optimal solution based on the studies in the Freude tank.

'Gufo 2' Radar

In the 843 plans of the Campagnoli archives, there is a radar labelled 'Gufo 2', with a parabolic antenna, installed at a height of approximately 32 metres at waterline. The diameter of the dish is 2.6 metres.

At the time, the *Regia Marina* was already embarking nationally produced radar, particularly the 'Gufo' EC-3bis and ter, developed in Leghorn by Ugo Tiberio, and other types produced in Germany.

The dimensions of the 'Gufo 2' perfectly coincide with the 'Gufo G.III', a 'Gufo' evolution, at that time available from the SAFAR Company of Milan.

The naval architects probably used the classification 'Gufo 2' in order to emphasise the clear separation of the specifications from the preceding version.

The dish of the G.III, a metre long, was cut below and above for a height of 2.6 metres.[84] The technical specs, which included the ability to direct naval fire, are listed in detail in a document of the SAFAR archive:[85]

Range: function of height on sea level, e.g.:
- motorboat of 200 tons with superstructure 4 metres high appreciable at approximately 30 km;
- heavy aircraft at altitudue 1,000 metres appreciable at approximately 30 km;
- minimum operational distance 800 metres;
- precision: 50 metres;
- angular precision: +-0.5°, with average trained crew;
- beam angular aperture: 10–11° depending on the frequency

Production of this model continued, for the Germans, after the Armistice and was used onboard on light units of the *Kriegsmarine*.[86]

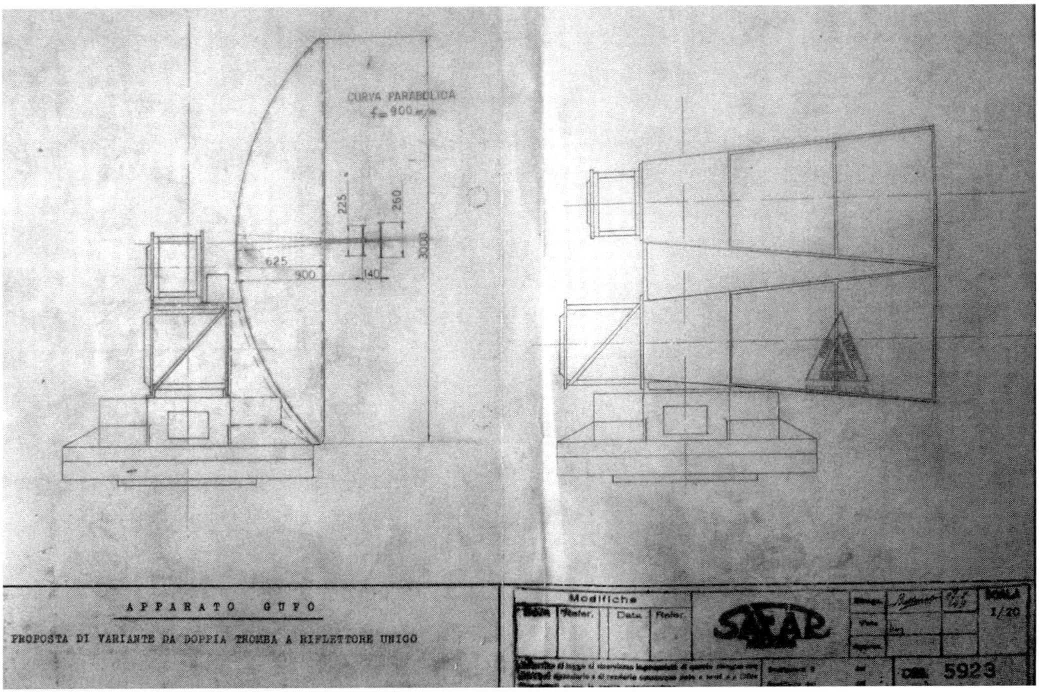

Safar design for G.III. (*Courtesy G. Galati's 'Cent'anni di Radar', ARACNE 2012, p. 39*)

Final Evaluation

Despite the fact that planning for the aircraft carrier RN *Impero* continued for around three years, the material available does not allow to affirm with certainty that executive plans were drawn. It is, however, certain that the work by the Ansaldo designers was done with full awareness of the *Regia Marina* and its technical corps.

It is possible that more detailed material is present in not yet classified sections of the Ansaldo or CRDA archives, given that many documents of the Genoese shipyard were transferred initially to Rome and then to Trieste during and after the Armistice.

The AC bears witness to the status of activity at Ansaldo, and particularly of the *Ufficio Allestimenti* (in charge for warships' fitting out), during German occupation. Since 1942, engineer Piazzai ordered that the most relevant documents had to be put in safe places 'in case of a future change of circumstances'.[87] It is probably due to this statement that we owe the existence of the AC.

During 1943, activities were already reduced to a minimum, mainly 'emergency', given the scarcity of materials, huge war damage, and the lack of qualified personnel. After the Armistice, the *Ufficio Allestimenti*, by then practically idle, passed under the *Kriegsmarine* control, which used the police of the Republic of Salò for internal control.

Some designers were moved to the CRDA in Trieste; the *Ufficio Allestimenti* documents were first moved to Rome at the end of August 1943 and then to Germany. They were then seen again by the Ansaldo architects in Trieste. The 'Gunnarson document', which by now included material considered very dangerous, was in the possession of engineer Astengo, who directed the *Ufficio Allestimenti* at the time.[88]

RN *Impero* as a battleship was not modified during the plan of transformation into an aircraft carrier, except for what described for the bow, steering gear, propellers, and armoured belt; of course, the internal arrangement of the section, free of the turrets and the ammo deposits was different (probably used as the bomb and torpedo magazines and aviation fuel storage). The displacement is 45,000 tons.[89]

No information is available for the lesser fitting layout and AA, as well as night rangefinders. The final placement of the AA weapons is, in the last design, unbalanced on the left side and leads one to assume that a series of platforms were possibly reintroduced on the starboard side.

The embarked aircraft, although not explicitly mentioned in the AC, would have been Re 2001/OR ('Falco II'), under development for RN *Aquila* or the Re 2005 ('Sagittario'), planned for RN *Sparviero*, whose main features were as follows:

Bomber Re 2001/OR	Re 2005
Single-engine, single-seater	Single-engine, single-seater
Fixed wing	Fixed Wing
Retractable landing gear	Retractable landing gear
All metal construction	All metal construction
Length 8.36 metres	Length 8.73 metres
Wing span 11 metres	Wing span 11 metres
Height 3.15 metres	Height 3.15 metres
Alfa Romeo Motor A.1000 RC twelve cylinders on line (under license of Daimler Benz 601), 1,175 cv	Fiat 1050 RC.58 Motor twelve cylinders inverted V, 1,475 cv
Maximum speed 545 km/h at 5,470 metres altitude	Maximum speed 628 km/h a 6,950 metres altitude
Highest altitude 11,000 metres	Highest altitude 12,000 metres
Autonomy 1,175 km at 4,800 metres altitude and 470 km/h (without auxiliary tanks)	Autonomy 1,250 km at 515 km/h
Unloaded weight 2,806 kg	Unloaded weight 2,600 kg
Weight at take-off 3,890 kg	Weight at take-off 3,610 kg
Armament: 20-mm Mauser in the pod and two Breda-SAFAT in the fuselage, bombs/torpedoes up to 600 kg	2 12.7-mm Breda-SAFAT in fuselage, 3 MG 151/20, bombs/torpedoes up to 1,160 kg.

The presence of an elevator of larger dimensions in the 1943 drawings could accommodate a heavier aircraft, but there is no information about it. The use of catapults for take-off was by then obsolete, but there is reason to believe that it was not the only option, as with RN *Aquila*.

From a military viewpoint, we already discussed how the window of opportunity to have an aircraft carrier-based naval aviation closed by the first half of the '30s; this assuming that a decisive political intervention would force the *Regia Aeronautica* to overcome its aversion to naval aviation, an intervention which did not materialise even during the war.

From an industrial point of view, aside from the insufficient standardisation in the aeronautic field, the resources necessary to build a class of aircraft carriers, particularly the metallurgic ones, were already scarce at the time of the planning of RN *Impero* as battleship.

From a political viewpoint, it has already been discussed that Mussolini did not choose a side, until after a prolonged erratic political strategy, a very last-minute one based on superficial considerations and this did not allow to set up a strategy of a balanced naval construction programme.

In the same way, he, encouraged by evidence of the war events, made impulsive decisions for prestige reasons more than for accurate planning, here too earmarking important resources and activities without any military value.

Furthermore, the 'Fascistisation' of the state and of its industries never led to the standardisation of manufacturing: the interests of individual industrialists remained unchanged, leading to an increase of prototypes (particularly in the aeronautic field) and to a waste of already scarce resources.

The story of the *Impero* project as an aircraft carrier confirms that a conversion was considered and discussed at the highest military level in 1941. Following the line of thought of the designers of the time, the group of the Ansaldo's *Ufficio Studi* and Campini, allows to verify the distance from what was already known and experimented on scientifically to what was considered useful on a military level (one should only consider the different strategic scenarios which would have happened if rocket, radio-guided weapon such as the DAAC would have been available in the Mediterranean in 1941); the intelligence story between allies narrated by the AC shows how low the level of collaboration and trust between allies was.

This lack of trust took on an absurd slant with the reiterated accusations by the Germans of weakness in integrity of the Italian chain of command, alleging the presence of spies, in particular with regards to the 'battle of convoys': it was precisely the German cryptographic device that was the Achille's heel of the Mediterranean operations, without this hypothesis ever being taking into consideration by the two commands, even though there was no lack of clues that pointed to where to look for the source of the information leak.

The news of the existence of ULTRA, which was kept secret by the British Government for decades after the end of the war, elicited an increase in naïve and not well-documented literature, particularly Italian, concerning the existence of 'traitors' in the *Regia Marina* and allowed for a big portion of the British literature to depict a series of episodes as a product of 'brilliance and superiority' and Italian inability, instead of as surprise operations based on detailed information.[90]

The importance given to the information provided by ULTRA for the Mediterranean theatre is clear according to the following data. A total of 185 merchant ships, plus nine *Regia Marina* warships, were sunk at sea due to direct ULTRA information, for a total of 356,698 tons (46.5 per cent of the lost ships and 49.4 per cent of the total tonnage).[91]

This table summarises the contribution of ULTRA to the *Regia Marina* losses (sixteen German ships lost in convoys due to ULTRA action are included, for a total of 50,574 tons):

Losses at Sea by Enemy Actions (Excluding Mines, Accidents, and Units<500 tons)

	Lost ships	tons	Documented ULTRA losses (ships)	ULTRA losses (tons)	Lost, % ships	Losses % tons
Libya, total	153	613,792	54	222,578	35.3	36.3
Libya, ULTRA (2,4)	122	489,429	54	222,578	44.3	45.5
Tunisia (3)	63	232,310	32	134,120	50.8	57.7
Total	216	846,102	86	356,698	39.8	42.2
Total, ULTRA	185	721,739	86	356,698	46.5	49.4

(1) Two cruisers and seven escort units were also lost on the Libyan route due to ULTRA instructions (RN *Da Mosto*, *Da Barbiano*, *Di Giussano*, *Pessagno*, *Polluce*, *Da Verrazzano*, and *Lupo*).
(2) Thirty-one ships were lost in the period when ULTRA was not working in the Mediterranean theatre. The first ULTRA attempt (which failed) on 23 June 1941 (*Oceania* convoy).
(3) Plus the escort units *Folgore* and *Perseo*.
(4) Tonnage, linear estimate linear/tons.

Finally, from the point of view of naval architecture, the *Impero* project, although it was tied to the plans of an existing ship and structures, shows some true innovations:

1. The embarkation of rocket/jet weapons, probably radio guided.
2. The inclined ramp for take-off.
3. The use of light pre-programmed failure areas and light materials.
4. A flight deck layout very similar to the large USA aircraft carriers of the '60s.
5. An advanced hydrodynamics.

RN *Impero*'s Distant Relatives

The Shinano

The *Shinano* is the only example of ship set up as a battleship and launched as an aircraft carrier during the Second World War, in circumstances and with decisions similar to those that distinguished the *Impero* project.

Notwithstanding that the final project was not a fleet aircraft carrier, but a warehouse supporting other aircraft carrier units, the *Shinano* called for maintaining the side armour, even if in reduced amounts compared to the original, and an armoured flight deck.

Laid down in May 1940, the conversion order came after the loss of four carriers in the Battle of Midway, in mid-1942. While the outfitting was still under completion, she was hit by four torpedoes from the USS *Archefish*. While she was headed towards Kure to finish the fitting, she sunk because the watertight compartments had not yet been entirely installed and because of the inadequate training of the crew and the decisions (apparently reckless but perhaps guided by the clear knowledge of the ship's readiness status) of the Commander (who had tried to push off the voyage).

USN's V-1 Version

The USA quickly built a copy of the V-1 from salvaged German pieces. The United States built over 1,000 JB-2s (this was the name for the weapon, also known as LTV-N-2 Loons), but at a certain time, researched the possibility of building 1,000 units per day.[92]

A certain number of these weapons were embarked on a USN aircraft carrier in case of possible use against Japan; the USA had requested fifty-one weapons for experimental use on aircraft carriers.[93]

The USN sea-launched their first Loon from the deck of a modified submarine, the USS *Cusk*, in February 1947.[94] Interestingly enough, the USN considered converting other vessels to JB-2 carriers in June and July 1946, specifically one *Essex*-class aircraft carrier and one battle cruiser.[95]

Hitler's H-44 Paper Battleship

As much as the first research work by Italians and Germans on rocket-propulsion weapons was directed to naval use, for the *Kriegsmarine* the only clue of embarkation of these weapons on-board units were the non-realistic series of drawings of enormous battleships made by the *Schiffsneubaukommission* (not by the K-amt (Office of the Naval Construction of the *Kriegsmarine*), in the last years of war, culminating in the H-44 drawing.

The H-44 would have been a battleship of 139,272 tons at maximum load, 345 metres long, 51.5 metres wide, and have 13.5 metres of full-load draft. The engine system of 280,000 cv would have pushed her to a maximum speed of 30.1 knots, with a 20,000-mile range of action at 19 knots.[96]

This plan never went past the sketch stage.

Pugliese TDS System: German Trials and *Sovetsky Soyuz*-class

The AC also offers information regarding the Pugliese system as it was designed and implemented by the Soviet Navy on the units of the *Sovietsky Soyuz*-class and how to interpret the results of the large-scale testing held by them before the final approval of the plans.

The Pugliese system is largely underestimated in the naval literature, both in terms of efficiency and because of a mistaken identification of the areas damaged by torpedoes, as well as for wrong damage assessment: S. Breyer attributes the sinking of RN *Conte di Cavour* in Taranto to the Pugliese system, due to a 'large leak under the armoured belt'—actually, the torpedo exploded under the keel;[97] Breyer also states 'it was now clear that the system did not live up to expectations' referring to the damage of RN *Littorio* in Taranto—actually the only torpedo, out of three, which hit the area protected by the Pugliese system, did not cause any problems;[98] and W. H. Garzke and R. O. Dulin state that 'its complex shape must have made the repair of battle damage particularly difficult', while the analysis regarding repair times contradicts this statement and that 'the loss of the battleship *Roma* revealed the vulnerability of the system to the near-miss detonation of large explosive charges', maintaining that the system 'demonstrated effectiveness against contact detonation, but vulnerability to heavy non-contact explosions due to stress concentrations in the structure that joins the cylindrical system to the hull girder'.[99]

RN *Roma* did not suffer any hit in the Pugliese system and sunk due the deflagration (not the explosion) of the forward 152 and 381 deposits.

RN *Italia* (former RN *Littorio*) suffered the close underwater explosion of a PC 1400 X without any trouble—the explosion was completely absorbed by the Pugliese system.

Bagnasco and De Toro, in the reference volume dedicated to the *Littorio*-class, came to the conclusion that 'the *Littorio* showed a substantial structural solidness which compensated for a few inadequacies in the underwater protection': this conclusion, drawn after having discussed comparatively and positively *Littorio*-class TDS performance compared to torpedo damage suffered by the *Scharnhorst*, the HMS *Nelson* and the HMS *Price of Wales* seems not based on evidence.[100]

The system called for the following layout: external plating 14–15 mm, double bottom of 9–11 mm, and distance of 1–1.5 metres. The curvilinear armoured bulkhead, 40 mm thick, was completely welded from the start of the 1934 conversion of the *Conte di Cavour*-class, a remarkable innovation for the time.

The bulkhead was positioned beyond the Pugliese cylinder. The connector of the bulkhead towards the double bottom was 28 mm. The absorbing cylinder was amidships, 3.8 metres in diameter and 6 mm thick. Beyond the armoured bulkhead, another bulkhead (at a minimum distance of 1 metre from the armoured one) of 7–9 mm isolated ship compartments from the Pugliese system.[101]

Proceeding from outside to inside, the system had a first level of dry cells then a cylindrical area entirely and always filled with liquids, which surrounded a small cylinder, always kept empty, of the optimal diameter of 3.8 metres. The system was then separated from the ship compartments by an armoured curvilinear bulkhead, followed by an additional bulkhead buffer. The resulting cells were divided each three or four frames.

The Pugliese protection system was developed and tested from the 1920s. The system is based on the physics concept of the instantaneous distribution of the pressure wave caused by the explosion of the torpedo on the entire resistant bulkhead, thanks to the presence of liquid that surrounded the Pugliese cylinder, and on the simultaneous absorption of energy, thanks to the destruction of the cylinder itself (on which the same pressure operates).

Trials at a scale of 1:1 had been carried out in La Spezia in 1932 on sections corresponding to the rebuilt *Giulio Cesare*-class, charges equivalent to those of a torpedo head were used, registering pressures for 100 kg per square centimetre. In order to assure a complete and uniform distribution of pressure on the internal bulkhead, vital for the correct operation of the system, a large-scale welding system was implemented—a definite innovation for those times.[102]

In addition to the advantages of the lesser weight compared to the bulges or the multi-level cellular structures used by the other navies, the system did not modify the hull lines, thus not interfering with the speed and manoeuvrability. It nevertheless occupied quite a lot of space, thus rendering it suitable only for units with large displacements.

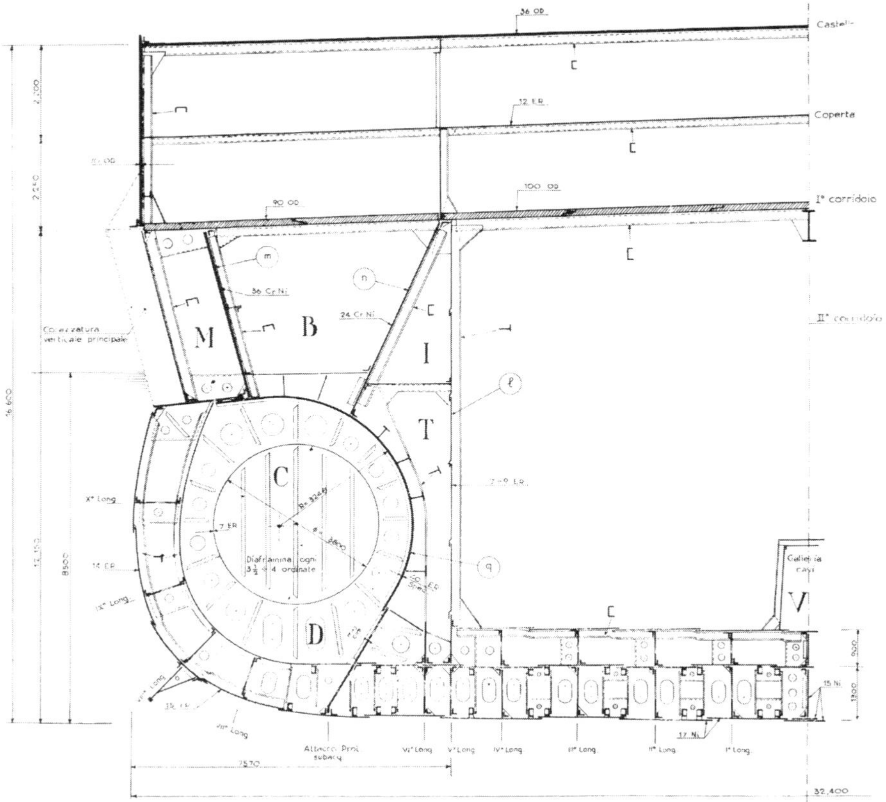

Above: Protection of the *Littorio*-class and Pugliese System. Note the absence of rivets on the internal bulkhead, which was welded. (*Corazzate classe Vittorio Veneto, parte prima, Roma 1973*).

Left: A good view of the Pugliese system as built on the RN *Littorio*. (*Courtesy Vittorio Catalano Gonzaga*)

Upon the explosion of a torpedo or the concussion as a result of a nearby explosion, the external cells were immediately destroyed and the shock wave would almost instantly spread (since the liquids are uncompressible) on the entire contact surface between the structure of the ship and the liquid (therefore on the internal resistant bulkhead and on the central empty cylinder), weakening its impact. The central cylinder, purposely built for a programmed failure, would homogenously collapse, absorbing a large part of the explosion energy with its deformation.

The water would enter the TDS cells, an automatic balance system, through the triple bottoms of the hull, which would bring it to an automatic balance. If necessary, this could be further corrected with the cases of ballast.

The system, after many tests, was built on the two tank ships *Brennero* and *Tarvisio* in 1921 and 1928 (they did not suffer any damage during the war), and implemented on a reduced (due the hulls' size) scale on the four battleships rebuilt in the '40s of the *Conte di Cavour*- and *Andrea Doria*-classes and with complete dimensions on the four *Littorio*-class units.

Pugliese System War Effectiveness

Damage to the Pugliese system during the war.[103]

RN Littorio (later RN Italia)

12 November 1940: Of the three Mk XII torpedoes with 176 kg of TNT explosives that hit RN *Littorio* in Taranto on 12 November 1940, only one of the three hit the Pugliese system in the area between Turret 1 and Turret 2, opening a leak of 10 × 7.5 metres. This did not cause serious problems as the explosion was well absorbed by the system, even if the internal compartment had flooding (in the munitions warehouse of tower 1, possibly caused by seepage from the big leak at bow) behind the armoured bulkhead. The ship was placed in the basin after a complex operation of lifting the bow from the clayish seabed on 11 December and left it on 19 March 1941.[104]

9 September 1943: A German aerial attack, explosion of a German PC 1400 X with explosive charge of 320 kg of high explosives, blew up at approximately 6 metres from the hull.[105] The bomb pierced the decks at starboard between Turrets 1 and 2, exiting and exploding at sea. The leak was 7.5 × 6 metres and deformations to the plating were 24 × 9 metres squared. Two bulges were destroyed and one flooded, and six double bottomed bulwarks flooded. The automatic counterbalance worked adequately. Two absorbing cylinders completely collapsed. The ship was not flooded in the protected areas, embarked a total 1,246 tons of water, including the water for balance, and continued navigating without problems. Repairs were expected to last one and a half months.[106]

The study of damage suffered due to the explosion of the charge of PC 1400 X on the *Alexandria*, show the efficiency of the Pugliese system for absorbing non-contact explosions

RN Vittorio Veneto

A Mark VIII submarines torpedo, with a war load of 340 kg of TNT on port side abreast of Turret 3, in an area where the Pugliese system started to taper off. The armoured bulkhead and one

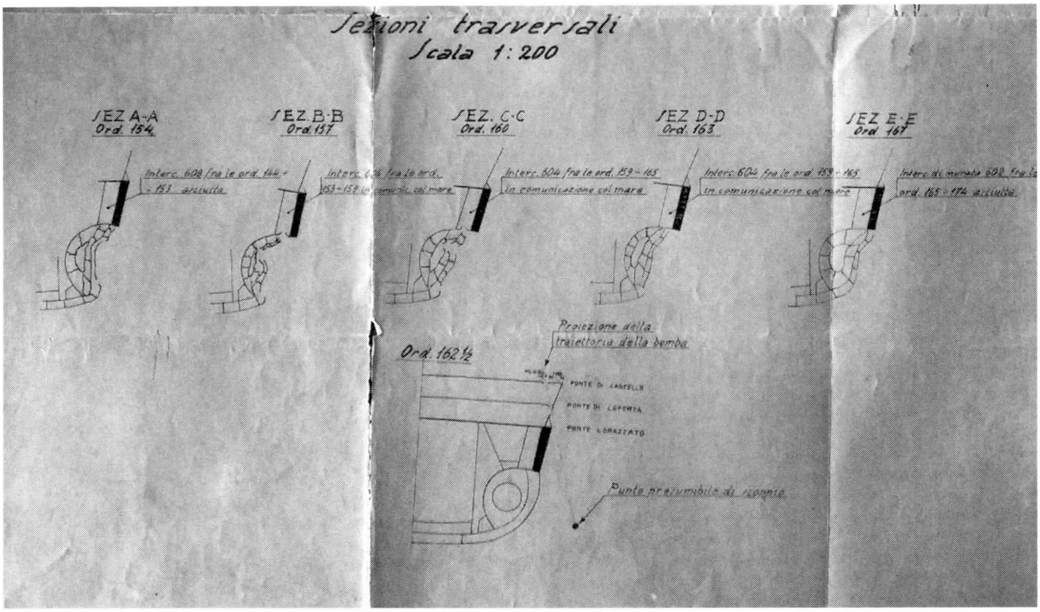

RN *Italia* (former RN *Littorio*) PC 1400 X damage as asserted in Alexandria. (*Courtesy USMM*)

longitudinal bulkhead collapsed with fast and large leaks, with about 3,000 tons of water entering the ship. Listing was reduced to 1 degree, and speed was easily maintained at 23.5 knots. The ship stayed in basin from 1 January 1942 to 4 March 1942, and eight absorbing cylinders were rebuilt.

On 5 June 1943, an armour-piercing bomb of 908 kg, which passed through the entire ship without exploding, went through a Pugliese cylinder (another identical bomb at bow exploded in the water after having gone through the ship). With little damage, the ship entered the basin on 16 June and left on 1 July.[107]

RN *Roma*

On 9 September 1943, the damage endured is reported from a direct testimony of what occurred to RN *Roma*, even if not of interest for the evaluation of the Pugliese system, to attest the fact that its sinking has nothing to do with what W. H. Garzke and R. O. Dulin asserted:

> … the *Roma* experience confirmed the susceptibility of the (Pugliese Author's note.) system to failure under heavy loadings from non-contact detonations, due to the inadequacy of the riveted joint joining the protective system to the bottom structure of the hull girder.[108]

A German aerial attack, with more PC 1400 X with a blast charge of 320 kg of high explosives. The first bomb had, in the words of Arturo Catalano Gonzaga di Cirella, commander of one of the complexes of 152 at stern on-board RN *Roma*, the following result:

> … the bomb had hit the ship at a point that was quite distant from my position, precisely more than half the ship on the starboard side, piercing through little more than a meter from the

> starboard bulkhead of the ship at the height of the anti-aircraft pieces of 90 mm n.9 and n.11. The recoil of the crash on the ship had destroyed the gabion of the range finder radio and the range finder of the anti-aircraft 'centre of shooting'. Basically, the bomb had passed through from one side of the ship to the other eventually exploding under the hull breaking through it and flooding the four stern boilers and the stern engines. The explosion under the hull also blocked two of the four propellers. The ship's speed immediately lowered to under 16 knots.[109]

The second bomb caused the deflagration of the charges in the 381 forward magazine, which caused the loss of the ship:

> … the second bomb had perforated the weather deck of the ship, as did the first, but this time it exploded inside the ammunition magazine of medium calibre barbette n. 2 at bow. The explosion smashed the boilers nearby generating a huge wave of vapour which easily ignited the explosion of the munitions magazine of main calibre barbette n. 2. The strength of the explosion had been so strong that it all at once threw at sea the entire turret n. 2 of 381 mm. Other explosions followed for the magazines of medium calibre barbette n.2 on the left side of the ship.[110]

RN Conte di Cavour and RN Caio Duilio

Contrary to what is often reported in the literature on the subject, none of these units suffered damage to the Pugliese system during the night of Taranto. The torpedoes that hit RN *Conte di Cavour* and RN *Caio Duilio* both exploded. As they were equipped with magnetic ignition, when they connected under the hulls of both ships, they were not within the Pugliese system's area of absorption.[111]

RN Giulio Cesare

RN *Giulio Cesare* TDS was damaged while at anchor in Naples, on 8 January 1941 by a 250-kg bomb (by the British 148 Squadron based in Malta) detonating 4 metres from the hull about 4 metres deep, in correspondence to the forward engine rooms. Damage was examined by General (NC) Pugliese and General (NC) Rotundi. A hole about 12 square metres in the bulkhead was present, 4.5 metres below the waterline. One cell of the auto balancing double bottom was flooded. The Pugliese cylinder was found entirely collapsed, while the armoured, welded, curved internal bulkhead (40 mm, according to the trials done in La Spezia in 1932) was found intact. RN *Giulio Cesare* moved to Genoa and repairs lasted twelve days.[112]

Kriegsmarine Testing on RN *Impero*'s Pugliese System

Recently, a *Kriegsmarine* report has come to light about the trials done by the *Kriegsmarine* in July 1944 on the hull of RN *Impero*. These trials were done with the goal of testing the performance of the Pugliese system.[113]

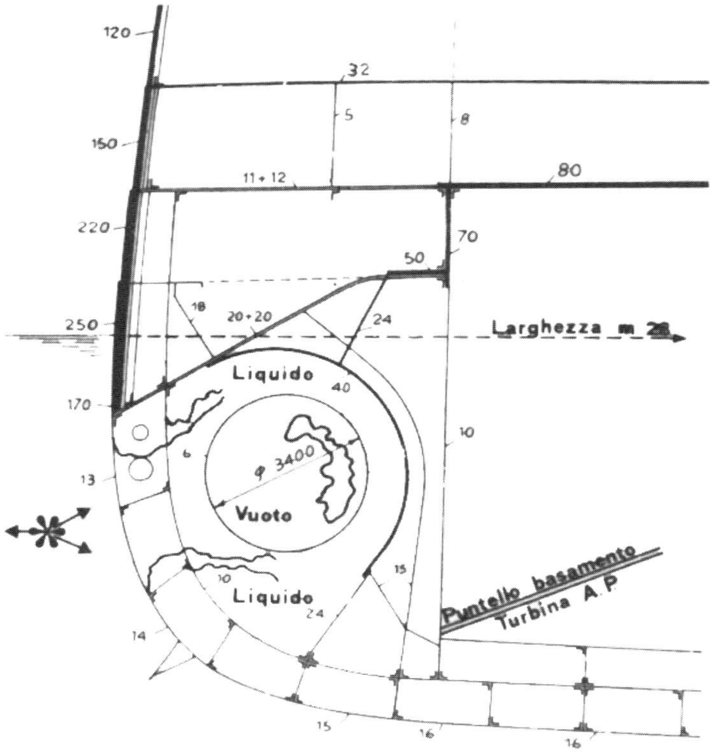

8 January 1941, damage to the RN *Giulio Cesare*. (*Courtesy Rivista Marittima*)

RN *Impero*'s Status at German Trials, 1944

The report, discovered by *Dipl.-Ing.* (FH) Dieter Thomaier, gives an accurate description of the status of RN *Impero* at the time of the German experiments. The ship was completed up to the first armoured deck and the armoured plates were mainly welded.

The armoured hatches were absent, and doors and hatchways under the armoured deck were only temporarily waterproof. Armoured plates for the forecastle lay on the deck. Turrets for large calibre artillery 1 and 2 were mounted but without cradles and guns. The n.3 HCG Turret was being mounted on land. The main armoured belt was mounted on both sides.

The bow turbine compartment was almost complete, the stern one was 40 per cent complete. Maintenance aboard ship was good and the compartments in excellent shape.

Kriegsmarine Trials

Four tests were carried out using *Kriegsmarine* explosives, of which the equivalent in TNT will be reported. The trials were done in the Capodistria bay with a sea depth of 19–20 metres.

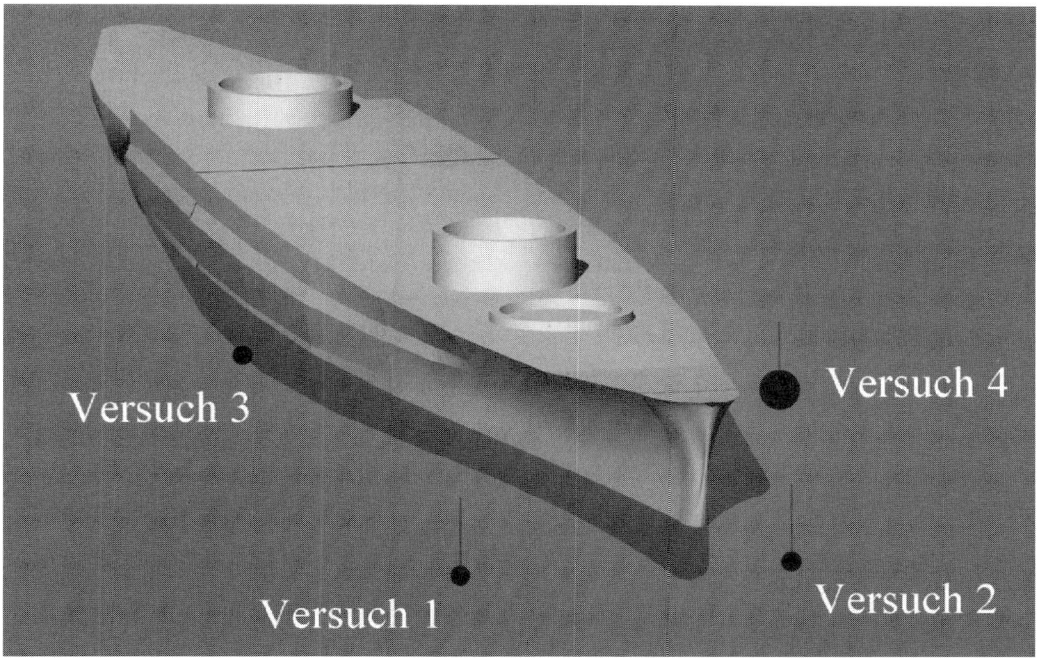

Kriegsmarine's trials, charges position. (*Courtesy Dieter Thomaier*)

During the testing on 18 July, the cells around the Pugliese cylinder were left empty instead of full as required during operational conditions.

18 July 1944

300 kg of explosives S2 (567 kg TNT), placed at starboard at the level of the ordinates 208–209, 8 metres depth.

Results of the underwater inspection: limited damage, buckling of around 16 cm to 5 metres in depth and a few metres in length. Some of the planking plates distorted and there was light leaking. Some deformation of frames and decks.

Around 200–300 kg of explosive S3 (459 kg TNT) on the port side at 10 metres from the hull at the level of frame 209 at 8 metres depth. Underwater inspection showed two vertical tears in the hull a metre from each other, and 2.3 and 3.5 metres high. In between the tears, the hull was very deformed towards the interior. Two compartments flooded.

20 July 1944

This test had been designed in order to directly test the Pugliese system. A total of 330 kg of type S1 (511.5 kg TNT) was applied on the hull at starboard on the ordinate 112 at a depth of 4 metres. The Pugliese system was in compliance with the operational conditions. A leak of 8 × 8 metres was formed, with a bad distortion of the hull around the leak.

Two bulkheads were flooded, but the longitudinal bulkhead was intact. Boiler rooms were dry, infiltration from below was from the balance ducts. The evaluation of the *Kriegsmarine*'s technicians was very positive compared to the testing previously done on the equivalent German systems.[114]

21 July 1944

Three charges of 300-kg type S3 (1,377 kg TNT) 17 metres to the port of the hull at 7 metres depth, ordinate 127. The internal bulkheads were flooded between ordinates 123 and 129. Upon inspection, buckling of the hull up to 80 cm deep and about 30 metres long between armoured belt and bilge keels was discovered.

After the trials were concluded, RN *Impero* should have been demolished, this did not happen due to the war situation.

Soviet Project 23 and Ansaldo Inspection

In the period between 1929 and 1936, Italy and Russia actively collaborated in the naval field, regardless of the ideological differences of both governments.

In the naval field, the Russians maintained a substantial and steady presence in Italy with the goal of trying to seize the technology and innovative solutions, emphasising the opportunity of opening their markets and supply to Italy, and received great assistance, in particular from Ansaldo, which designed the following plans for the Soviet Navy:[115, 116]

Year	Type	Details
1934	Cruiser	187 metres long
1936	Scout cruiser	4,500 tons
1936	Armoured Cruiser[117]	19,000 tons, 254-mm HCG
1936	Armoured Cruiser[118]	22,000 tons, 254-mm HCG
1936	Battleship	28,000 tons, 29.5 knots, 9 343 mm
1936	Battleship	UP41, 45,000 tons
1936	Fast seaplane carrier[119]	Probably with 'seaplane-fighters'

It is often reported in naval literature that the Soviets received the Pugliese system specifications and projects with the plans for the UP41, but this is not confirmed by the drawings of the unit, which instead show the three layers Ansaldo TDS.[120]

It is only thanks to a special agreement between the governments that Italy gave information regarding an underwater protection system 'similar to the Pugliese one'.[121]

In his text, dedicated to plans of Soviet battleships of the '30s, A. M. Васильев writes that the Soviets received 'almost complete' information on the Pugliese system from Italy.[122]

The Soviets, before choosing the TDS for the new units of *Советский Союз*-class (*Sovetsky Soyuz*), Project 23 according to Soviet classification, performed a series of comparative trials on different underwater protection systems, on models of a scale of 1:5; from these results, the best ones were the 'West Virginia' system, implemented in seven layers in the Soviet version, and the 'Pugliese'.[123]

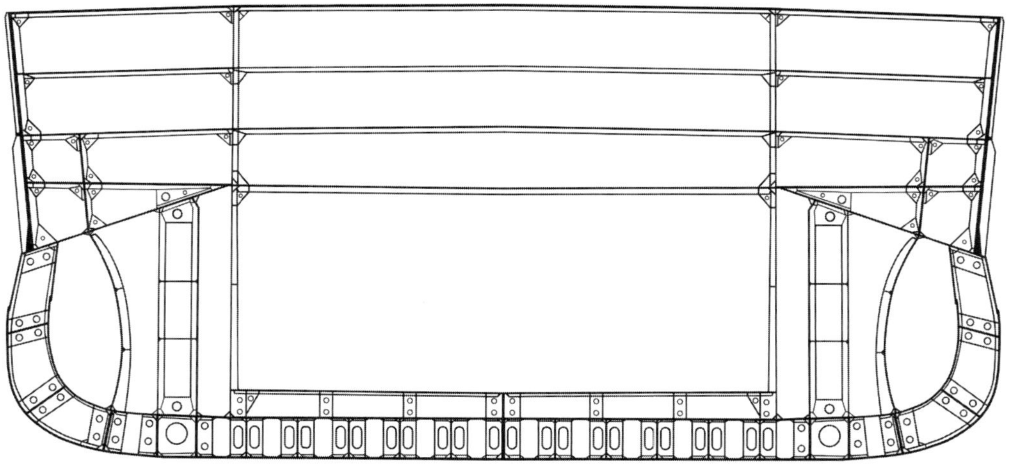

Section of UP41. (*Drawing by Tzoli, based on original blueprints*)

Based on considerations concerning the building complexity, it was proposed to substitute the Pugliese system with the USA version; however, the decision was postponed until a revision of plans decided for 'Project 23bis' battleships.[124, 125]

A second comparative series of tests between the two systems was performed in Sevastopol in October 1938 on a scale of 1:5 and then on a specifically built ship on a 1:1 scale. This contained two compartments with a total length of 50 metres and a width of 30 metres, on which both protection systems were placed for a total width 7.5 metres each. The explosive charges of 400 kg (USA system) and 500 kg (Pugliese system), in both cases, left the internal compartments intact.[126]

One of the ships of *Советский Союз*-class, the *Советская Украина* (*Sovetskaya Ukraina*) was under construction at the plant shipyard, number 198 named after André Marty in Nikolaev on the Black Sea, when the German troops occupied the city in August 1941. She was captured with little sabotage damage when she was technically 17.5 per cent ready—the hull was 65 per cent complete and 13,000 tons of material were assembled.

Had the war not erupted, the Soviets' estimate for the end of the construction work was for 1945.[127] This unit was accurately examined by German technicians and, in August 1942, by the naval architects of Ansaldo (Campagnoli and Carlarino), who wrote a concise technical report.[128, 129] Construction of the ship, interrupted after the capture of the city for lack of plans, slowly restarted in 1943.[130] The ship was then completely destroyed by the Germans in March 1944, when they abandoned the area.

The Italian analysis of the Soviet unit under construction occurred after a remarkable war experience had already been accumulated and available also from the perspective of responses of the implemented designs to the war damage.

The AC's technical note refers to the 'preparation ['*impostazione*' in the original] of a battleship project 21-3 on specifics of project ss39'. It is possible that a plan was developed

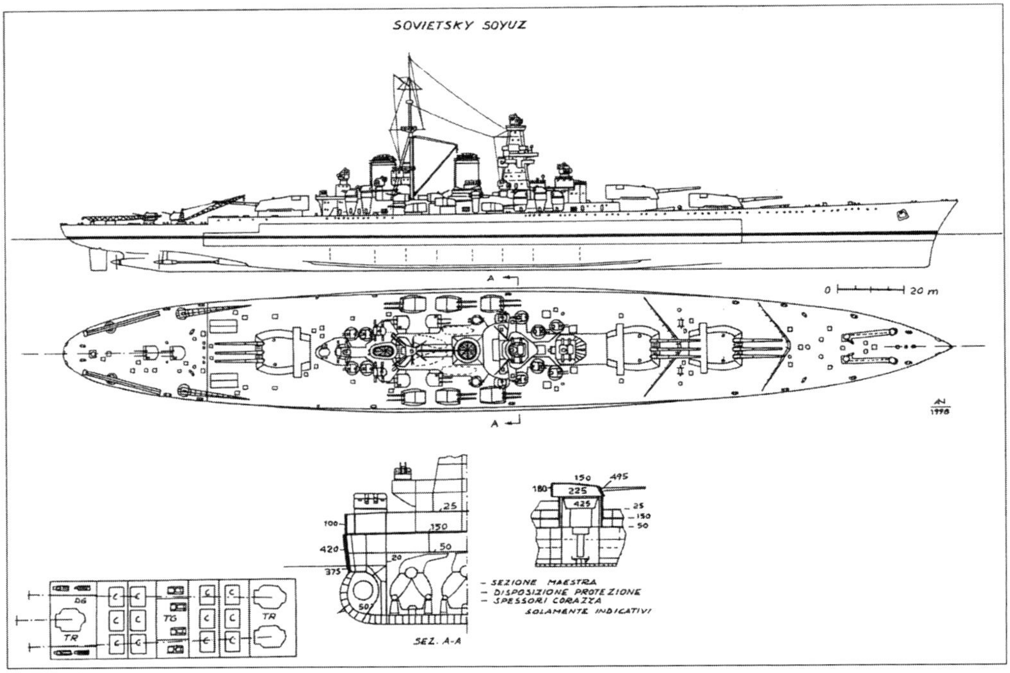

Line drawing of the *Sovetsky Soyuz*. (*Courtesy Rivista Marittima*)

to continue the work on the *Sovetskaya Ukraina* based on plans recovered in Sevastopol or perhaps already available at Ansaldo.[131]

The term '*impostazione*' in Italian is usually used to refer to a new design, and since the parts of military interest had already been stripped off by the Germans, it seems likely that a different project than the original, developed by Ansaldo, was being considered.

As far as the Soviet Pugliese system implementation, as it was examined in the Soviet shipyards, the analysis resulted in the following elements:

Component	Opinion	Notes
Internal cylinder (armoured bulkhead)	Built in a technically erroneous way, with welded points and heat riveted sections.	The mandatory continuous welding was ahead of its time for the Soviets.[132] This solution compromises the optimal system functioning.
Bulkhead thickness	30 and 35 mm, not compliant	As seen, these are decisions taken by the Soviets after testing on a scale of 1:1.
TDS anchoring to the hull	Modified anchoring points	

Certainly the highlighted constructive defects, presumably present also when the comparative trials were done by the Soviets, are elements of a reduction of the system's performance during the trials.

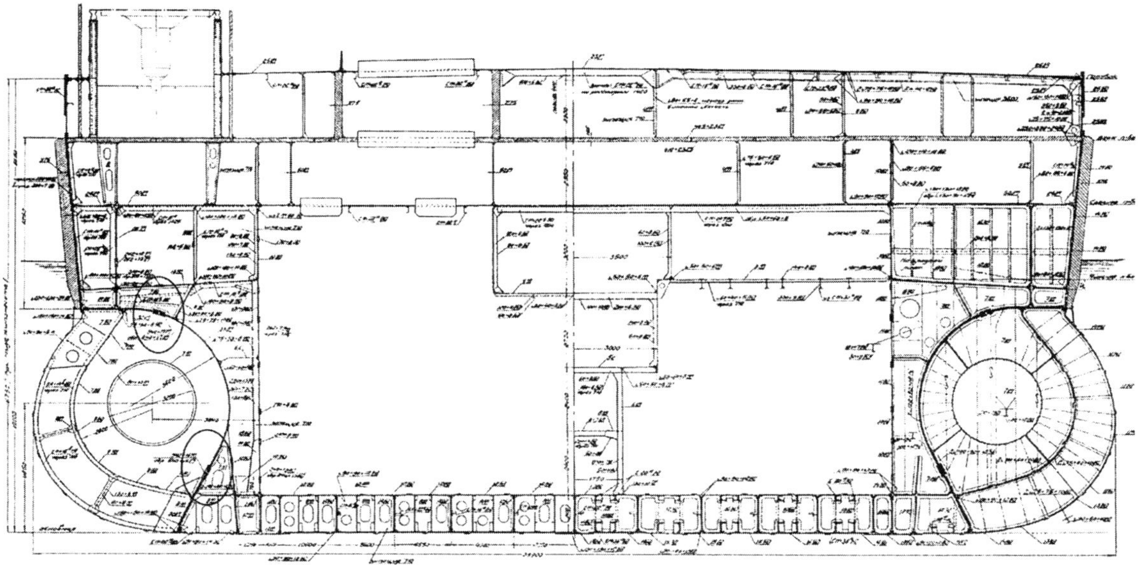

Section of the *Sovetsky Soyuz*. The rivet points of the internal bulkhead of the Pugliese system are marked, the absence of a triple bottom evident. (*Courtesy* Васильев, А. М., Линейные корабли типа, Советский Союз)

The other observations contained in the document 'Sevastopol 1942' are as follows:

	Sevastopol 1942	Project ss39
Overall length	271 m	269.4 m
Maximum width	38.7 m	38.9 m
Inclined splinter armour	28 mm measured on the first corridor	36 mm
Side armour	250 × 100 × 10 × 16 high resistance steel and 220 × 75 – 0.5/1.0 NiCr (not compliant)	375-420 + 25 mm (amidships) 180 mm
Internal side armour	150 mm mono not compliant	
Bulwark belt	Bulwark armour—deckhouse 18 mm + 45 mm—not compliant Bulwark armour—Side 1st corridor 60 mm in mono (? Probably a comment on steel composition)—not compliant	
Double bottom	Cellular compartmentalisation largely reviewed.	
Frames	Noted missing reinforced framework at the second frame	

Hull	Wrong half bulb with increased block coefficient;	
Rudder	Very large, partially compensated, two auxiliary ones; electro-hydraulic-pneumatic.	
Boilers	Under dimensioned; 200,000 HP; better Diesel with Man c 9 × 12⊠elect. transm. Sv. 1937	
Propellers	Triple blades: not optimal as for *Littorio*, better four or five blades as per 1935–1937 studies	
Workshop status	Heavily damaged	

The AC refers to the ex-Soviet ship as a unit for which it was necessary to resume planning, referring also to the opportunity of restarting research on the bow area given what was resulted from the inspection (incorrect bulb, with increase of the coefficient of the hull and subsequent tendency to go down by nose). There is a reference to the previous work done in collaboration with the *Vasca Navale* of Hamburg in the mid '30s.

Pugliese System Final Assessment

Based on the evaluation done by Ansaldo in 1942, with war experience available, and by the performance of the Pugliese system both in Russian and German testing, in addition to sustained war damage, the critique against the system appear to be without basis, as well as based on insufficient research.

The opinions made by W. H. Garzke, R. O. Dulin, and Norman Friedman (Friedman: 'in practice the system actually built suffered from poor structural connections') regarding the supposed critical point of the TDS design and the long repair times, appear to be proven wrong both by the war experience (also for systems produced at more modest dimensions such as on RN *Giulio Cesare*) and by the trials done in a scale of 1:1 by three different Navies.[133, 134, 135] The Pugliese system appears to comparable in performances to the latest multi-layer system in use at the USN, and better than any other.[136]

RN *Impero*'s Fate

In November 1942, orders were given that the 152-mm complexes of the *Impero*, ready and available at the OTO in La Spezia, should remain in La Spezia and should not be transported to Trieste (given the difficulties of transport during winter in the Apennine passes and the lack of materials needed to complete the ship) and the request was given to 'disperse them' so as not to expose them to bombings.[137]

After the end of the war, the *Impero*'s hull became object of diplomatic controversy as she was declared 'war prize' by the Yugoslav authorities. Therefore, on Allied orders, in July 1946, she was lifted and towed to Vallone di Muggia, and at the end of August 1947, she was moved

RN *Impero* at launch. (*Courtesy Archivio Ansaldo*)

The former RN *Impero*'s hull in Venice before scrapping. (*Courtesy Fototeca USMM*)

to Venice for demolition. At the time of the transfer, the hull weighted about 20,000 tons and had a light listing (4 degrees). The ship ran aground and was once again lifted and towed to Porto Marghera for demolition in February 1949.

Thus ends the complex story of the last battleship of the *Regia Marina*, which could have become a large and modern aircraft carrier.

Epilogue

Still in 1942, the aero-naval actions in the Pacific, well-known to those in charge of the *Regia Marina* and *Regia Aeronautica* thanks to meetings with the Japanese Navy's representatives in Europe, fully proved their feasibility and efficiency, and while the *Roma*'s conversion into RN *Aquila* was ongoing, the *Regia Aeronautica* continued to state that it was futile and impossible to utilise aircraft on board of an aircraft carrier.

They further maintained that it was impossible for a fighter to land on the flight deck (and the resulting need to limit the range of action of the aircraft carrier to 220 miles from the airports to allow for the fighters to return), due to the limited possibility of success of an air–sea cooperation even for aircraft on aircraft carriers and that the best solution both for the offense and the defence was to rely on ground-based, twin-motor fighters with great autonomy.

According to the *Regia Aeronautica*, the current situation was the best one (ground-based aircraft); in fact, the general opinion was as follows:

> … even if (the bombers) could depart from on board an aircraft carrier no operational advantages would be obtained compared to the current situation since the range of action of our bombers is such to permit to act, leaving from our actual bases, over the entire Mediterranean and the reconnaissance crafts allow to explore, from ground bases, the entire eastern Mediterranean and western until the meridian of Orano.[1]

Regarding the torpedoes, it was said:

> … we have the types S 79 and S 84. Neither one would be able to depart from the flight deck … the R. Aeronautica does not have any type of vehicle available that could be embarked, the plan for such an aircraft … would require a solution to the problem of the torpedo launch, which is set up for a different vehicle and speed.[2]

The 'new solution [of the carrier] presents the uncertainty of the experiment, while that which was implemented to this date has given a certain and high result'.

Evidently, the analysis of the repeated failures during the war events did not bring about a change of mind of convictions based on motives of prestige and political power, even the collaboration demanded by the 'upper echelons' for the creation of the *Aquila*'s air group was going forward with the greatest mental reservations.

Further, some of the choices made were contradictory to the abundant information obtained from the Japanese, represented by Admiral Nomura, Admiral Abe, Commander Toyoda, and Commander Mitsunobu, who many times made their experience available both to the *Regia Aeronautica* and the *Regia Marina*; instead of relying on the Japanese operational and war experience, *Regia Marina* chose to 'verify' the information the Japanese Navy supplied with what the Germans were thinking of going with the yet not operational *Graf Zeppelin* (which incidentally had enjoyed, as already explained, a wide support from the Japanese Navy).[3]

Even though late for practical purposes, Commander Toyoda's analysis sounds like a perfect acknowledgment of the reasons for the lack of efficient aero-naval operations for Germany and Italy:

> ... the recent Japanese military mission, which visited Italy and Germany, reported the impression that both the *Regia Aeronautica* and the *Luftwaffe* do not have a high enough level of preparation for the current war at sea: according to his opinion this is because of the lack of a naval aviation. He points out that the high command of the Japanese Navy is very satisfied to have strongly opposed the creation of an independent Japanese air force, similar to what was done in Germany and Italy.[4]

Toyoda's opinion is confirmed by the uncertainty which had distinguished German plans for the naval aviation and the aircraft carrier. In addition to the never-operative *Graf Zeppelin* and its soon-to-be dismantled twins, the ships considered for conversion to aircraft carrier during the war were the battleships *Scharnhorst* and *Gneisenau*, the *Lutzow*, the *Admiral Scheer*, the liners *Europa* and *Potsdam*, and the heavy cruiser *Seydlitz* (already 90 per cent ready as heavy cruiser).

By mid-1942, the conversion of three passenger ships was approved and the transformation of the French cruiser *De Grasse* was also taken into consideration. For the *Europa* and *Potsdam*, work was cancelled in November 1942, for the last one, as for *De Grasse*, Hitler's order on 30 January 1943 to dismantle the German surface fleet ('The cheapest victory Great Britain ever obtained', in the words of Admiral Raeder) came to interrupt any further development.

In any event, the Italian military situation had already been compromised, even though in January 1943, *Supermarina* still stated that the aircraft carriers were essential to the war at sea and irreplaceable in the event of action on the oceans.[4] The naval plans were revised, placing the *Aquila* as ready for summer of 1943, the *Sparviero* in spring of '44, the transformation of the *Bolzano* for spring '43, and the salvage and transformation of the French Navy cruiser *Foch*, sunk in Toulon, for spring 1946 (probably with a solution similar to that planned for the *Bolzano*).

Beyond the optimistic predictions, the reality of the war situation and the difficulties encountered while fine-tuning the deck landing systems being done in Perugia, caused the *Regia Aeronautica* to earmark RN *Aquila*'s air group for national defence. At the same time, it asked the *Regia Marina* when RN *Aquila* would actually be ready and whether the situation of the naval forces would be adequate enough to run the joining of an aircraft to the fleet.

Admiral Riccardi's answer confirmed the start of flight trials on RN *Aquila* for October 1943 and asked the *Regia Aeronautica* to continue with the plan, eventually in limited form. This answer was supported by the positive evolution of the trials in Perugia, of the positive trials of the on-board catapults, and of the static tests of RN *Aquila*'s turbines.[5]

In the end, on 22 June 1943, the Chief of Staff of the Navy ordered the interruption of the work being done on the major units being fitted; manpower and materials would be allocated to the escort units and the submarines.

For RN *Impero*, work had already been interrupted with the exception of the installation of the heavy artillery for their preservation. The status of readiness for the large units was as follows:

RN *Impero*, hull 88 per cent, engines 76 per cent, and fitting 28 per cent (underway were the assembly of the No. 2 381-mm turret and the assembly of the basic structures of the other turrets).

RN *Conte di Cavour* end of rebuilding expected within 1943

AA cruisers RN *Etna* and RN *Vesuvio*, hull 78 per cent, protection 88 per cent, engines 75 per cent, and fittings 18 per cent—six or eight months to readiness.[6]

Regia Marina's crest. (*Courtesy Archivio Centrale dello Stato, Roma*)

APPENDIX I

RN *Impero* Model at Venice's Navy Museum

The Campagnoli archives confirm the attribution (and explain some peculiar features) of a model of an aircraft carrier preserved at the *Museo Storico Navale della Marina* of Venice.

This model, in a scale of 1:200, was labelled for a long time as a preliminary study for conversion to aircraft carrier of the *Roma* liner—that is, RN *Aquila*—and had been exhibited at the *Accademia Navale* in Leghorn and then moved to the Museum of Venice in the '60s.

An investigation held in 2006 on the model, proceeding with the measurement of its dimensions, ascribed it with certainty to a hypothetical conversion to an aircraft carrier of a battleship of the *Littorio*-class, without determining its historical context.[1]

The measurements inferred from the model are the following:

Overall length:	238 m
Length at waterline:	231 m
Max. flight deck width	32 m
Island dimensions	50 × 10 m
Width at waterline:	32 m
Height of flight deck waterline	20 m
Height at hangar deck	12 m
Max. draft	10.4 m
Displacement (block coefficient of the *Littorio*)	45,000 tons
Power and speed (estimate)	130,000 cv, 30 knots
Armament (from model)	4 triples 152mm L. 55, 24 presumably 65mm L. 64 1939 singles
Air group (estimated)	50 or more aircraft

The elements in the Campagnoli archives that connect and help identify this model as an elaboration of the *Impero* project US 940 (*Impero*, *Ufficio Studi* Ansaldo, September 1940) are the following:

The 1:200 model of the RN *Impero* as aircraft carrier, Venice. (*Stefano Sappino*)

1. Results of trials in the Ansaldo Freude tank regarding three models, of which the US 940 with the semi-bulbous bow as the *Littorio*, like in the model.[2]
2. The usual production of models at a scale of 1:200 with rudders and shaft support, but without propellers and shafts for the trial in the Ansaldo Freude tank, as in the model.
3. The presence of a main rudder with a different design from the final version of the *Littorios* and identical to what was documented in the AC for the conversion of the *Impero*.[3]
4. The presence of an exceptionally long (more than 50 metres) launch placed unusually on the side of the flight deck (designated to jet propulsion or rocket weapons, not suitable for aircraft).

The model does not include important features such as the elevators. The connection to the *Impero* as aircraft carrier projects offers an interpretation key for the ramp at starboard in the model, of an unusual length and uncommonly close to the edge of the deck. The studies concerning the DAAC (dated 1940) clarify that, from the beginning, the aircraft carrier *Impero* was thought of as a carrier of innovative weapons (anti-aircraft, but especially anti-ships). There is proof of this in the Campagnoli archives: 'the use of DAAC from a long ramp in order to obtain a better thrust and to increase the war load, maintaining [launch from] the gun posts for minor units'.[4]

Furthermore, the model shows a much more approximate concept compared to the AC projects, like the island placed directly on the flight deck and similar in design to that of the *Aquila* and completely different from the drawings, which remained stable in time, of the island of the *Impero* in the detailed plans offered by the AC. The presence of the four 152-mm turrets on the fight deck is an outdated concept only possible with the idea of using something already available. The model shows a unique height of the flight deck on the waterline and the absence of visible elevators.

Model's flight deck, stern view. Notice the long take off ramp. (*Stefano Sappino*)

A possibility remains that this is, for the superstructures, a 'show' model produced by the shipyard, based on already available elements. This model could be temporarily placed in the very first planning stages of the planned conversion or, more likely, as 'an emergency' solution speculated upon after the Armistice of 8 September 1943, given the unusual height of the deck that hints to the presence of two superimposed hangars, and the use of turrets and barbettes of 152 mm, which we know where completed and available in La Spezia.

APPENDIX II

1922–1943 Stakeholders' Table

Ministry of the Navy

Minister		Undersecretary	
Paolo Ignazio Thaon di Revel	21.10.1922–8.5.1925	Costanzo Ciano	31.10.1922–5.2.1924
Benito Mussolini	8.5.1925–11.9.1929	Giuseppe Sirianni	14.5.1925–11.9.1929
Giuseppe Sirianni	12.9.1929–5.11.1933	Domenico Cavagnari	6.11.1933–7.12.1940
Benito Mussolini	6.11.1933–25.7.1943	Arturo Riccardi	8.12.1940–25.7.1943

Ministry of Aviation

Minister		Undersecretary	
Benito Mussolini (as Commission Head)	24.1.1923–29.8.1925	Aldo Finzi	24.1.1923–29.8.1925
Benito Mussolini	30.8.1925–11.9.1929	Alberto Bonzani	14.5.1925–5.11.1926
		Italo Balbo	6.11.1925–12.9.1929
Italo Balbo	12.9.1929–5.11.1933	Raffaello Riccardi	12.9.1929–6.11.1933
Benito Mussolini	6.11.1933–25.7.1943	Francesco Pricolo	31.10.1939–15.11.1941
		Rino Corso Fougier	15.11.1941–27.7.1943

APPENDIX III

The *Regia Marina*'s Ship Naming

In Italian, the warship names are always male. Therefore, '*il*' article is used, which is the male version of '*the*'—*il Roma*, *il Littorio*, *il Saetta*, etc.

However, the correct way to refer to a *Regia Marina* warship is to label it with the words '*Regia Nave*', abbreviated as R. N. or RN. It represents the Italian equivalent of the British HMS—in other words, it means 'King's ship'.

If RN is present, the article assumes the gender of '*Nave*', which is feminine, therefore '*la*', the female version of 'the'—*la* RN *Roma*, *la* RN *Littorio*, *la* RN *Saetta*, etc.

If the ship type precedes the name, the article assumes the gender of the type of ship. Usually, if the type of ship is present, the 'RN' prefix is not used.

It is not rare for the type of ship to be implicit while leaving its article gender before the ship name.

To complicate matters further, some ships, usually smaller ones, have the prefix 'R' (King's) followed by their type—for example, *Regio Sommergibile* (Submarine (RS)), *Regio Caccia Torpediniere* (destroyer (RCT)), *Regio Incrociatore* (cruiser (RI)), *Regia Torpediniera* (torpedo boat (RT)). These abbreviations can also be found on the ribbons of the caps of those embarked on the ships. In this case, the article assumes the gender of the type of ship, whichever it may be.

By 1931, the types of official ships were 'Ships of the line (*Navi da Battaglia*)', cruisers, scout, cruisers, destroyers, torpedo boats, submarines, auxiliary craft, and craft for local use.[5] In 1939, the classification was changed as follows: battleships (*Corazzate*), cruisers, destroyers, torpedo boats, submarines, gun boats, MAS, auxiliary ships, and ships for local use.[6] The plans for aircraft carriers and aircraft carriers under construction were referred to as '*Nave Porta Aerei*', aircraft carrier ship, or (NPA). The fleet organisation included:[7]

Squadron: consistent formation of at least four units of light ships (of which one in the role of flagship)—destroyers, torpedo boats, submarines or MAS. The units would preferably be of the same class or at least have nautical and military features as similar as possible.

Flotilla: it was a formation of two or more squadrons (whose commander was usually embarked on a unit not belonging to the squadrons; that was initially a scout cruiser and after the reclassification, a destroyer leader.

Division: a formation of two or more large ships (cruisers or battleships) of which one may have functioned as flagship. Usually one or more squadrons (destroyers or torpedo boats) joined the division as escorts.

Fleet (part '*Squadra Navale*' or the entire fleet '*Armata navale*'): consisted of the grouping of two or more divisions. The command roles of the fleet were taken by a flagship that could belong to one of the divisions or be independent.

Groups were formed on a temporary basis for operational needs according to what was needed at a given time.

APPENDIX IV

The 'Radar' Connection

The lack of radar and the *Regia Marina*'s alleged lack of attention to the subject are often considered among the key elements impacting the evolution of operations. Since the Campagnoli archives document the presence of a state-of-the-art radar apparatus (the 'Gufo III') on the 1943 aircraft carrier *Impero*, it is appropriate to focus on what happened in the field.[8]

In 1934, Ensign Ugo Tiberio, an engineer, was tasked by General Luigi Sacco, who had seen Guglielmo Marconi's demonstrations, with starting a research project with the objective of determining the maximum range a radar device could achieve, based on the transmission power and signal reception capabilities available at the time.[9]

In 1936, Tiberio (by then, the German *De.Te.* had already passed the prototype stage) warned about the possibility that the *Regia Marina* would find itself facing an enemy 'equipped with devices for night firing of anti-aircraft naval artilleries at a great distance'.[10]

His report resulted in two different proposals: the first called for the allocation of a substantial budget (comparable to the cost of a 10,000-ton cruiser) for further R&D and requiring the mobilisation of the whole national electronics industry; the second proposed to entrust a small group of scientists with the task of staying abreast of the advances of the technology, while monitoring developments in foreign navies.[11]

Adding insult to injury, bureaucratic difficulties prevented the *Accademia* from hiring a qualified technical staff to support Tiberio, while strict Ministry of Finance rules negated him an appropriate salary. To circumvent this, Tiberio was hired as a teacher in the Academy, a role that obviously took away a lot of time from his research.

Tiberio was recalled into active duty in the Navy in June 1936, and assigned to the *Accademia di Livorno*, the *Regia Marina*'s Officer Academy, with a yearly budget of 20,000 Lira (approximately 21,500 in 2017 Euros). His role was to design, build and test the new devices.

Work at the *Accademia di Livorno* was hindered by the inability of the national industry to provide the necessary electronic components for the very shortwave radar, forcing designers to work with commercial material from the USA and Germany, although locally it was considered obsolete.

The first prototype could only generate 150 watts of power and could detect a motorboat at a range of 2,000 metres. The *Regia Marina*'s efforts to ascertain the development status of radar technology in foreign navies (British, German, and American) did not obtain significant information, partly due to the lack of expertise of the intelligence personnel.[12]

In 1938, the Naval Weapons Directorate of the Navy, eager to obtain a working prototype, awarded a contract to Milan-based company SAFAR, completely lacking qualified personnel (to the point where it asked the *Regia Marina* for technicians[13]) and was at such an early stage of research for developing television that, by the war's outbreak, they had not yet produced the two requested prototypes.[14]

Despite the trials carried out on the Ec.3 and Ec.3bis prototypes in Leghorn during 1939–41, development of production lagged very much behind compared to other naval forces who, in 1937, had already developed technology for very short waves.[15] The satisfying results of the prototypes were therefore useless given the inability of the Italian industry to develop serial production of components smuggled from the USA.[16]

Did their German ally not have radar well before the war?[17] In truth, in June 1940, Admiral Raeder expressed the necessity to set aside all reservations concerning the secret devices and provide their ally with 'decisive tools with the goals of running the war'.

Such resources were made available to the *Regia Marina* at the meeting of Friedrichshafen on 20 and 21 June 1939, between Admirals Cavagnari and Raeder. Following that meeting, from which Italy returned convinced that there would be no war earlier than 1942, a series of operational meetings originated, and on the very day when Italy joined the war (June 1940), Raeder ordered to share the relevant information to the ally.

In the pictures of the German battleship *Graf Spee* that was scuttled in December 1939 in front of Montevideo, the antenna of the first German naval radar apparatus, the Funkmessgerät FuMO 21 (also called *De.Te.*, with a range of 15–18 km) was indeed very visibly deployed on top of the conning tower.

The *Regia Marina* promptly dispatched a team of naval technical officers to Germany from 14 to 28 June 1940 to discuss, among other subjects, the 'devices for the long-distance discovery of aircraft in flight', connected to a ground radar called Freya.[18]

The supply of naval radar by the Germans was not without problems. The Italians' request of July 1940 for two full sets of ultra-shortwave air traffic detectors received an inconclusive response. In December 1940, the request was submitted to at least receive a prototype to eventually duplicate, with the same result.[19]

Without getting into all the details of this complex story, where a key role was played by General of Naval Weapons Carlo Matteini (who by the end of 1940 had confirmed the strong evidence that the Royal Navy already possessed devices capable of locating vessels by radar[20]), suffice it to say that when the time came to move to Sicily in February 1941, the *X Fliegerkorps* was already equipped with a device for aerial detection with features that were unknown to Italy.[21] The pressing requests to examine the device were refused by Colonel Stange, commander of the anti-aircraft regiment of the *X Fliegerkorps*. We now know that the two devices deployed to Sicily were a Würzburg and a Freya radar.

The complete lack of collaboration between the two allies on the development of radar is confirmed by Ugo Tiberio himself: 'The first exchange of information took place with the German Navy, shortly after the night battle mentioned earlier (Cape Matapan, March 28–29, 1941)'.[22]

Conclusive confirmation of the availability of radar by the British occurred via the decoding of the British communications at Matapan, following which, strong pressure was

Ugo Tiberio. (*Courtesy Rivista Marittima*)

put on the small research group in Leghorn [23] On 20 April 1941, Tiberio demonstrated to the ministerial commission that the EC.3ter apparatus could successfully detect merchant ships of medium tonnage at 10,000–12,000 metres.[24]

Finally in April 1941, Germany communicated its willingness to send a naval radar of the type *De.Te.*, on the condition that it be kept entirely secret and that it would not be duplicated, also outlining the possibility, considering the needs of Germany and the manufacturing speed of devices, to start full-scale deliveries to Italy starting from the first half of 1943.[25] Hence the necessity to continue driving to launch local production in the shortest possible time.

A German board of experts in the field of radio ranging, invited to Italy, ascertained that the technical solutions adopted by Germany and Italy were almost identical with the only basic difference being in power output, the Germans having developed the generator with specific components, while Italy, due to the aforementioned limitations of the national industry, had had to rely on commercial components of German manufacture dating from a few years earlier.[26]

The EC.3ter prototypes, which had by now been named Gufo (owl), were installed on RN *Littorio*, where they demonstrated excellent ranging capabilities, but also dismal detection performance, and on RN *Carini*, a destroyer very busy with convoy escort service, which, for this reason, could not run significant tests until September 1941, when the device was finally removed.[27]

In September 1941, the *Regia Marina* finally accepted the German conditions for supplying the *De.Te.* However, Admiral Iachino opposed its installation on the *Regia Marina* flagship and insisted instead—to the puzzlement of *Supermarina*—that it be installed on the destroyer *Legionario*, then under construction in Leghorn.[28]

In the meantime, the *Regia Aeronautica* was proceeding independently to obtain from Germany twelve each of the Freya and Würzburg devices.[29]

Unbeknown to the Axis commands, the British system of decoding messages transmitted with the German ENIGMA device was proving deadly efficient, prompting the German Navy to scathingly criticise the strategy, training, and equipment of the *Regia Marina*.[30]

These criticisms, even though not justified (in fact, the Axis commands failed to realise that those convoys that did not follow the established route and timetable were rarely attacked), would find a response in a series of actions launched by the *Regia Marina* in the development of reduced-flare munitions (the lack of which was also shared by the German Navy, which at the time only employed reduced-flare-charges only up to the calibre of 105 mm) and of long-range tracer rounds, and in the purchase of very bright binoculars and night range finders.[31, 32]

During the skirmish at Cape Bon on 21 December 1941, four British destroyers sank Italian cruisers *Da Barbiano* and *Di Giussano*, in an action that took the Axis forces completely unawares, and was only possible thanks to the enemy's perfect knowledge of the position of the Italian vessels acquired through ULTRA.[33] This episode highlights the dramatic impact of the lack of radar on the Italian ships, especially considering the circumstances of the nightly surprise engagement.

One could think that in such a critical situation, the Italian-German collaboration in the radar field would have quickly gotten to a good point, as was the case with the *Regia Aeronautica* (in that case, however, entire *Luftwaffe* units had been moved to Italy and therefore their assignment to the Italians was functional for the *Luftwaffe*'s needs).

Instead, while the *Regia Marina* was able to order fifty devices before 11 February 1942 thanks to the Italian industry finally managing to develop the necessary electronic power components, and the single German *De.Te.* delivered proved itself on the destroyer *Legionario*, the requests for *De.Te* to the German Navy went unanswered.[34, 35]

On 1 May 1942, General Matteini asked the naval *attaché* of the Italian embassy in Berlin to submit a request to the German Navy for the purchase of more *De.Te.*s, three of which were identified as 'absolutely urgent'. The reply of the OKM (*Oberkommando der Kriegsmarine*—Supreme Command of the Navy, the German equivalent of *Supermarina*), written in a letter of 23 May 1942, was negative as the supplies under development were essential to other particularly urgent uses.[36]

In a written reply on that same day, Admiral Riccardi wrote Grand Admiral Raeder, requesting, in addition to the fuel oil issue, that they urgently provide the three *De.Te.*s.[37] The letter reached the OKM on 12 June and, notwithstanding the *Kriegsmarine*'s acknowledgment of the need to improve patrols on the Mediterranean, the response was negative, again mentioning the urgent needs of the German Navy and of its coastal commands (defined as 'extraordinarily numerous'), while the possibility for delivering three devices 'in late autumn' was left open.[38]

During the successful counteraction to the Royal Navy's Operation Vigorous, the *De.Te.* embarked on the destroyer *Legionario* proved its worth, prompting positive comments from Admiral Iachino.[39]

Delivery of the promised three De.Te.s was delayed to the point where Admiral Riccardi sent a note to Grand Admiral Raeder on 8 October 1942 reminding him of his promise.[40] In January 1943, the first four sets of six eventually provided by Germany arrived. In January 1943, nine Gufo devices were also available, three on the battleship *Littorio*, two on destroyers *Fuciliere* and *Carabiniere*, two in Leghorn and four in various testing stages; the manufacturing capacity of the industry was three to four devices a month.[41, 42]

We have already described how compartmentalisation and competition among the different armed forces was strong both in Italy and in Germany: the devices for ground defence, necessary to naval bases, were part of the exclusive negotiations between the German and Italian Aviation.[43]

In the meantime, the operational Gufos were causing serious trouble. Finally, on 5 July 1943, the Gufo III was made available, with a parabolic reflector. This is the radar model that was uncovered in the Campagnoli archives for the project of converting the *Impero* to a fleet aircraft carrier.[44]

Features of the radars of the *Regia Marina*:[45]

Model	First appearance	Wavelength	Peak power	Frequency Hz	Anti-ship range	Anti-aircraft range
EC.3bis	5.1941	72 cm	5	500	6 miles	16 miles max.
EC.3ter	9.1942	60 cm	10	500	16 miles on BB 8 miles on destroyer	43 miles max.
G.III	7.1943	65–80 cm	10	500	16 miles on small targets >16 miles large targets	24 miles max.

In conclusion, the *Regia Marina* was indeed interested in radar technologies and actually developed them. Alas, it was not in a position to influence Italian industry's priorities, and, more generally speaking, the industry itself was not as advanced as the industries of contemporary USA, Germany, and the Netherlands. If anything is to be blamed on the *Regia Marina*, it is how it underestimated the progress status of potential enemies (and allies alike) before the war, and how it misinterpreted the data from the first battles. German behaviour was formally open to collaboration, but in practice, no real effort was made to share radar technology until it was too late.

APPENDIX V

Ansaldo's 1931–1945 Shipbuilding

Ansaldo Warship Production 1931 to April 1945 [46, 47]

Production number	Type of ship	name	buyer
297	Light Cruiser	*Raimondo Montecuccoli*	*Regia Marina*
298	Coastguard cutter	P.S. 8	URSS
299	Coastguard cutter	P.S. 26	URSS
300	Light Cruiser	*Eugenio di Savoia*	*Regia Marina*
301	Battleship	*Littorio*	*Regia Marina*
302	Torpedo boats	*Aldebaran*	*Regia Marina*
303	Torpedo boats	*Andromeda*	*Regia Marina*
304	Torpedo boats	*Antares*	*Regia Marina*
305	Torpedo boats	*Altair*	*Regia Marina*
306	Tug boat	*Rapallo*	*Regia Marina*
307	Tug boat	*Taormina*	*Regia Marina*
308	M/Refrigerated ship	*Ramb I*	*R. Azienda Monopolio Banane*
309	M/ Refrigerated ship	*Ramb III*	*R. Azienda Monopolio Banane*
310	Torpedo boats	*Alcione*	*Regia Marina*
311	Torpedo boats	*Airone*	*Regia Marina*
312	Torpedo boats	*Aretusa*	*Regia Marina*
313	Torpedo boats	*Ariel*	*Regia Marina*
314	Torpedo boats	*Clio*	*Regia Marina*
315	Torpedo boats	*Calliope*	*Regia Marina*
316	Torpedo boats	*Calipso*	*Regia Marina*
317	Torpedo boats	*Circe*	*Regia Marina*
318	Tanker	*Giulio Giordani*	*Agip*
319	Not built		
320	Warship	*Impero*	*Regia Marina*
321	Light cruiser	*Cornelio Silla*	*Regia Marina*
322	Light cruiser	*Paolo Emilio*[48]	*Regia Marina*

aid down	launch	delivery	displacement (tons) or tonnage	Weight naked hull (t)	Power motor device (cv)
931	1934	1935	7,052	1,850	105,000
933	1934	1934	850	306	4,500
933	1934	1934	850	306	4,500
933	1935	1936	7,400	2,090	105,000
934	1937	1940	35,560	9,850	160,000
935	1936	1936	652	245	19,000
935	1936	1936	652	245	19,000
935	1936	1936	652	245	19,000
935	1936	1936	652	245	19,000
936	1936	1937	280	81	650
936	1936	1937	280	81	650
936	1937	1937	3,667 tsl	1,481	6,800
936	1938	1938	3,667 tsl	1,481	6,800
936	1937	1938	690	257	19,000
936	1938	1938	690	257	19,000
936	1938	1938	690	257	19,000
936	1938	1938	690	257	19,000
936	1938	1938	690	257	19,000
937	1938	1938	690	257	19,000
937	1938	1938	690	257	19,000
937	1938	1938	690	257	19,000
938	1939	1940	10,534 tsl	4,791	7,800
938	1939		35,560	9,850	160,000
939	1941		2–3 × 3,416 t	12/14 x 1,239 t	110,000
939			3–5 × 3,074 t	7/12 x 668 t	110,000

323	Cargo Motor vessel	*Nino Bixio*	*Società cooperativa Garibaldi*
324	Cargo Motor vessel	*Luciano Manara*	*Società cooperativa Garibaldi*
325	Cargo Motor vessel	*Rosolino Pilo*	*Società cooperativa Garibaldi*
326	Cargo Motor vessel	*Agostino Bertani*	*Società cooperativa Garibaldi*
327	multipurpose ship	*Amerigo Vespucci* (later *Giuseppe Majorana*)	*Società di navigazione Italia*
328	multipurpose ship	*Marco Polo* (later *Niccolò Giani*)	*Società di navigazione Italia*
329	multipurpose ship	*Antoniotto Usodimare* (later *Vittorio Moccagatta*)	*Società di navigazione Italia*
330	multipurpose ship	*Ugolino Vivaldi* (later *Ferruccio Buonaparte*)	*Società di navigazione Italia*
331	multipurpose ship	*Sebastiano Caboto* (later *Marco Visentin*)	*Società di navigazione Italia*
332	multipurpose ship	*Paolo Toscanelli*	*Società di navigazione Italia*
333–334	Not built		
335	Tanker	*Pozarica*	*Petroleos Mexicanos*
336	Tanker	*Panuco*	*Petroleos Mexicanos*
337	Tanker	*Minatitlan*	*Petroleos Mexicanos*
338	Undelivered Tanker (see 354)		Union Molasses
339	Pontoon cranes	*IX Febbraio*	Ansaldo S.A.
340	Floating basin, not built		
341–342	2 anchor winch pontoons	GAS 268-269	*Regia Marina*
343	Escort vessel	*Ardito*	*Regia Marina*
344	Escort vessel	*Animoso*	*Regia Marina*
345	Escort vessel	*Ardente*	*Regia Marina*
346	Escort vessel	*Ardimentoso*	*Regia Marina*
347	Tug boat	*Giasone*	*Regia Marina*
348	Torpedo boat	*Ariete*	*Regia Marina*
349	Torpedo boat	*Arturo*	*Regia Marina*
350	Torpedo boat	*Auriga*	*Regia Marina*
351	Torpedo boat	*Dragone*	*Regia Marina*
352	Torpedo boat	*Eridano*	*Regia Marina*
353	Torpedo boat	*Rigel*	*Regia Marina*
354	Tanker	*Fede*	Achille Lauro - Naples
355–360	6 torpedo boats not built		
361	Tanker	*Punta Vagno*	Shipowner Ravano
362	Tanker	*Ombrina*	La Polena Company
363	Tanker	*G. Matteotti*	Garibaldi Company
174–185	12 guard ships	A.S. 301–312	*Regia Marina*
186	Corvette	*Gabbiano* C. 11	*Regia Marina*
187	Corvette	*Procellaria* C. 12	*Regia Marina*
188	Corvette, not built		
189	Corvette	*Cormorano* C. 13	*Regia Marina*

1939	1940	1941	7,136 tsl	3,154	5,900
1939	1941	1942	8,103 tsl	3,154	5,900
1939	1941	1942	8,325 tsl	3,154	5,900
1940	1941	1942	8,328 tsl	3,154	5,900
1940	1942	1949	7,400 tsl	3,550	7,500
1940	1942	1948	7,400 tsl	3,550	7,500
1940	1942	1949	7,400 tsl	3,550	7,500
1940	1945	1947	7,400 tsl	3,550	7,500
1942	1946	1947	7,400 tal	3,550	7,500
1942	1947	1948	7,400 tsl	3,550	7,500
1939	1940	1941	7,800 tsl	3,158	2,800
1939	1940	1941	7,800 tsl	3,158	2,800
1939	1941	1941	7,800 tsl	3,158	2,800
	1941	1942	384 tsl	300	
1942	1942	?	709	659	360
1941	1942	1942	869	385	16,000
1941	1942	1942	869	385	16,000
1941	1942	1942	869	385	16,000
1941	1942	1942	869	385	16,000
1941	1941	1941	1,210	625	2,500
1942	1943	1943	696	284	22,000
1942	1943	1943	696	284	22,000
1942	1943	1943	696	284	22,000
1942	1943	1944	696	284	22,000
1942	1943	1944	696	284	22,000
1942	1943	1944	696	284	22,000
1941	1943	1943	7,800 tsl	3,283	5,800
1943	1945	1946	6,300 tsl	3,824	4,000
1943	1945	1947	6,300 tsl	3,824	4,000
1943	1946	1946	6,300 tsl	3,824	4,800
1942-43	1942-43	1942-44	85	30	1,300
1942	1942	1942	600	211	3,500
1942	1942	1942	600	211	3,500
1942	1942				
1942	1942	1943	600	211	3,500

190	Corvette	*Pellicano* C. 14	*Regia Marina*
191–193	3 Corvette, not built		
194	Steamship	*Mrassafell*	*Samband Islanda*
195	Steamship	*Titania*	*L. Pittaluga*
559–560	2 Steamships	K.T. 1-2	OKM (Germany)
561	Corvette	*Tuffetto* C. 51	*Kriegsmarine*
562	Corvette	*Marangone* C. 52	*Kriegsmarine*
563	Corvette	*Strolaga* C. 53	*Kriegsmarine*
564	Corvette	*Ardea* C. 54	*Kriegsmarine*
565	Corvette	*Cicogna* C. 15	*Regia Marina*
566	Corvette	*Folaga* C. 16	*Regia Marina*
567	Corvette	*Ibis* C. 17	*Regia Marina*
568	Corvette	*Gru* C. 18	*Regia Marina*
569–587	19 construction of the mechanical department		
588–605	18 construction of the Carpentry department		
606–613	8 rafts	M.z. 742–749	*Regia Marina*
614–615	unassigned numbers		
616–619	4 Steamships	K.T. 13–16 (later *Monte Cengio*)	OKM (Germany)
620–621	2 Steamships	K.T. 9-10 (later *Monte Grappa*)	OKM (Germany)
622–627	6 floats		*Regia Marina*
628	Tug boat	*Cremona*	Spading Firm
629	Aircraft carrier	*Sparviero* (*Augustus* conversion)	*Regia Marina*
630–697	68 constructions of the Savoia shipyard before its merging with Ansaldo		
698–701	4 unbuilt destroyers		
702–703	2 Steamships	K.T. 31-32	*Kriegsmarine*
704–708	Not built		
709–714	6 Rafts	M.z. 595-598; M.z. 553-554	*Kriegsmarine*
715–725	11 Steamship	K.T. 35-36; K.T. 43-51	*Kriegsmarine*
726–734	Unassigned numbers		
735–742	8 Unbuilt torpedo boats		
743–748	6 Rafts	M.z. 514-513; M.z. 503; M.z. 432-433; M.z. 450	*Kriegsmarine*
749	River boat		A. Spada–Pavia
750–759	10 tug boats not built		Finmare–Trieste
760	River boat		A. Spada–Pavia
761	River boat		Vinelli and Caffè
762–765	4 unbuilt motor river boats		
766–768	3 unbuilt tankers		

1942	1942	1943	600	211	3,500
1942	1942				
1942	1943	1946	1,664 tsl		1,550
1942	1943	1946	1,650 tsl	765	1,660
1942	1942	1942	700	330	2,400
1943	1943	1944	600	211	3,500
1943	1943	1944	600	211	3,500
1943	1943	1944	600	211	3,500
1943	1943	1944	600	211	3,500
1942	1942	1943	600	211	3,500
1942	1942	1943	600	211	3,500
1942	1942	1943	600	211	3,500
1941	1942	1943	600	211	3,500
1942	1942	1942	125	90	
1942	1942	1942-43	700	330	2,400
1942	1942	1943	700	330	2,400
1942-43	1943-47	1944-47			
1943	1943	1943	700	330	2,400
1943	1943	1943	125	90	
1943-44	1944	1944			2,400
1943	1943	1943	125	90	200
		1945			

769–793	25 unbuilt rafts		
794–803	10 unbuilt torpedo boats, *Ariete*-type		
804–833	30 ships type 'S.23'—assembly not done		
834–839	6 unbuilt rafts		
840	River boat		Vinelli and Caffè
841–843	River boat	*Ina II*; *Ina III*; *Ina IV*	Montecatini–Milano
844	Unbuilt river boat		
845	River boat		*ing.* Segalini - Pavia
846	Wine tanker	*Alleanza*	All. vini - Genova
847	Cargo boom	*M. Isabella*	Comp. del Mare
848	Cargo Boom	*Bianca Maria*	Comp. del Mare
849	Wine tanker	*Alice Maria Pina*	Trascovin–Milano
850	Wine tanker	*Unione*	E Polotto–Genova
851–852	2 tug boats	*Cina I*; *Cina II*	C. Ind. Nav. Arm.
853–854	2 tug boats	*S. Caterina*; *S. Francesco*	Ansaldo S.A.
855	tug boat	*Etral*	Etral–Lisbona
856	tug boat	*S. Giorgio*	Ilva Alti Forni

1945	1947				80
		1946			
1945	1945	1945	140 tsl		
1945	1945	1946			
1945	1946	1946			
1945	1945	1946	140 tsl		150
1945	1946	1946	140 tsl		150
1945	1945	1945			160
1945	1945–46	1947			160
1945	1947	1947			160
1945	1947	1947			160

APPENDIX VI

Regia Marina Ranks (1923–1943)

Since there is often reference to the *Genio Navale*, Naval Corps of Engineers, this table lists the corresponding ranks between embarked officials and those of the Naval Corps, Royal Navy ranks listed as reference.

Ufficiali di Vascello	Engineer Officers	Naval Corps	Royal Navy
Grande Ammiraglio			Admiral of the Fleet
Ammiraglio			Admiral
Vice Ammiraglio			Vice-Admiral
Vice Ammiraglio di Squadra	*Tenente Generale Macchinista*	*Tenente Generale Genio Navale*	Squadron Vice-Admiral
Contrammiraglio di Divisione	*Ispettore Generale Macchinista*	*Ispettore Generale Genio Navale*	Rear Admiral
Contrammiraglio	*Vice Ispettore Generale Macchinista*	*Vice Ispettore Generale Genio Navale*	Counter-Admiral/Rear Admiral
Capitano di Vascello	*Colonnello Macchinista*	*Colonnello Genio Navale*	Captain
Capitano di Fregata	*Tenente Colonnello Macchinista*	*Tenente Colonnello Genio Navale*	Frigate Captain (Commander)
Capitano di Corvetta	*Maggiore Macchinista*	*Maggiore Genio Navale*	Corvette Captain (lieutenant-commander)
Tenente di Vascello	*Capitano Macchinista*	*Capitano Genio Navale*	Lieutenant (senior)
Sottotenente di Vascello	*Tenente Macchinista*	*Tenente Genio Navale*	Lieutenant (junior)
Guardiamarina	*Sottotenente Macchinista*		Sub-Lieutenant

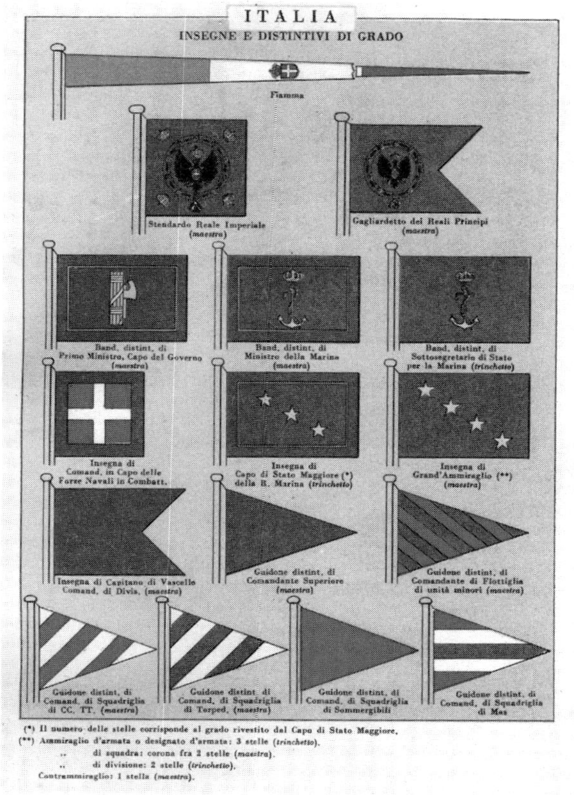

RM Flags. (*Almanacco Navale 1942-XX*)

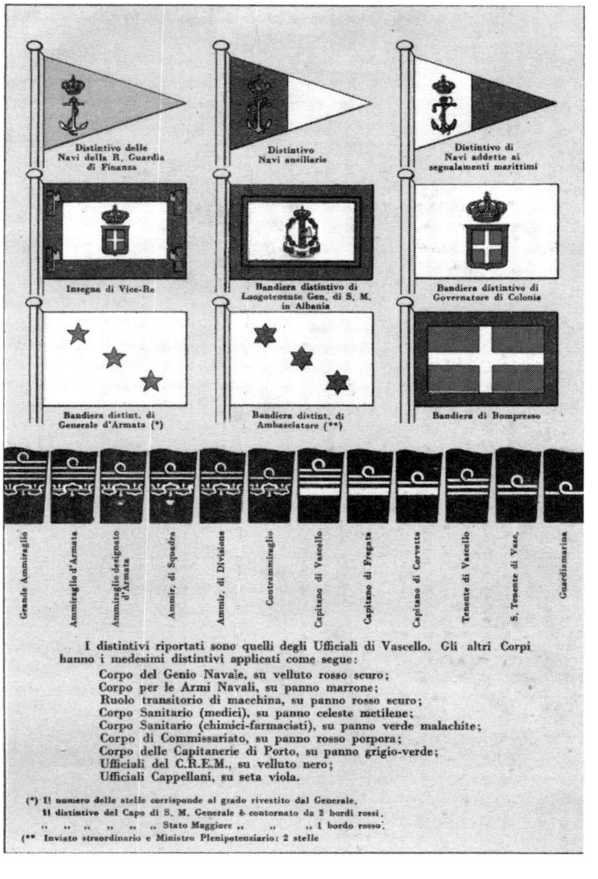

RM Insigia. (*Almanacco Navale 1942-XX*)

Endnotes

Chapter 1

1. The attempt to annex Corfu (1923) was Mussolini's first attempt of 'Exquisitely Fascist foreign policy', in other words the use of 'armed diplomacy'. K. MacGregor, *Destino comune, Dittatura, politica estera e guerra nell'Italia fascista e nella Germania nazista* (Torino: Einaudi, 2003), p. 137.
2. Regarding the unpopularity and mistakes of the commander of the Italian army, General Luigi Cadorna, see the writings of Keegan and Rochat: J. Keegan, *La prima guerra mondiale, Una storia politico-militare* (Roma: Carocci, 2000), pp. 394-395; G. Rochat, *L'esercito italiano, da Vittorio Veneto a Mussolini* (Bari: Laterza, 2006), pp. 321-327. Regarding President Wilson's stance on the condemnation of the London Pact of 1915 and on the splitting up of German properties in Africa done in Paris by the Allies in 1919, which did not consider Italy at all, see M. Isnenghi, G. Rochat, *La grande guerra* (Bologna: Il Mulino, 2008), pp. 480-484.
3. E. Gentile, *Il fascismo in tre capitoli* (Bari: Laterza, 2004), p. 8. One of the most fascinating definitions of Fascism—that of totalitarian Caeserism—is given by Gentile in the next page, in other words: 'a charismatic dictatorship Caesar style, integrated in an organizational structure built in compliance with a totalitarian myth, consciously implemented and functioning concretely as a code of conduct and benchmark for the actions and organization of the State and the masses. Also see the skillful book by Mosse on Fascism'. G. L. Mosse, *Il fascismo, verso una teoria generale* (Bari: Laterza, 1996).
4. E. Gentile, *op. cit.*, p. 32.
5. In the case of the British Empire and France, the non-intervention policy lasted at least until the status quo ended.
6. K. MacGregor, *op. cit.*, p. 80.
7. M. Miegge, *Che cos'è la coscienza storica?* (Milano: Feltrinelli, 2004), p. 162.
8. E. Mawdsley, *World War II, a new history* (Cambridge: Cambridge University Press, 2009), p. 7.
9. F. Mattesini, 'Il blocco navale italiano nella guerra di Spagna', BAUSMM December 1997, pp. 123-174 and G. Giorgerini, *Da Matapan al golfo Persico, la marina militare italiana dal fascismo alla repubblica* (Milano: Mondadori, 2003), p. 355. Regarding the 'good performance' of the *Regia Aeronautica* in Spain, this was determined by the not excessive competitiveness between Spanish republican aircraft rather than by the *Regia Aeronautica*, this caused delusions at a command level as they were not able to see the innovations achieved by the Germans during that. Regarding this subject, see G. Rocca, *I disperati, La tragedia dell'aereonautica italiana nella seconda guerra mondiale* (Milano: Mondadori, 1993), pp. 82-91.
10. Commenting on the fall of the Spanish capital in Franco's hands, Mussolini is reported to have said, pointing to the atlas open to Spain's page, 'It was open in this manner for three years, now enough. But I already know that I have to open it on another page'. G. Ciano, *Diario 1937–1943* (Milano: Rizzoli, 1980), p. 273.
11. E. Di Nolfo, *Storia delle relazioni internazionali 1918-1992* (Bari: Laterza, 1994), pp. 50-57.

12. *Ibid.*, pp. 26-30.
13. *Ibid.*, pp. 155-162.
14. In this aspect, among the various theories that convinced Mussolini to join the war, we reject the one suggested by Vincent P. O'Hara who proposed the idea of the economic 'embargo' imposed on Italy by Great Britain: 'Britain's power to strangle Italy's economy justified war in the context of the spring of 1940 more than did the prospect of snatching Tunisia or Nice'. V. P. O'Hara, *Struggle for the Middle Sea, The Great Navies at War in the Mediterranean Theater, 1940-1945* (Annapolis: Naval Institute Press, 2009), p. 3. What should be instead considered one of the reasons for Italy's approach to Germany is the idea suggested by Santoni, who writes:

    > The Italian aggression on Ethiopia of 3 October 1935 is commonly assumed to be a determining factor in the mentioned change of direction of Italian politics, even though the first split of the so-called Front of Stresa was precisely the work of the British who on 18 June of that year had signed a little known pact with Germany, the Hoare-Ribbentrop. Based on this agreement, London gave Hitler, who was working on the re-armament of his country, the authority to build a fleet 35% of the British Empire's with the exception of submarines for which the quota went up to 45% and in certain circumstances, subject to prior agreement with Great Britain, it could even reach 100%. The clause was invoked from Berlin in December 1938.

    A. Santoni, F. Mattesini, *La partecipazione tedesca alla guerra aeronavale nel Mediterraneo* (1940-1945) (Parma: Albertelli Edizioni Speciali, 2005), p. 7. In the following pages, Santoni himself recognises the importance of the Ethiopian war as it affected the deterioration of Anglo-Italian relations and underlines Mussolini's responsibility, who, according to him, could have disengaged at least until the 1938 conference in Monaco. Santoni, Mattesini, *op. cit.*, p. 8.
15. A. Hitler, *Il mio testamento politico, prefazione di Giorgio Galli* (Milano: Rizzoli, 2016), pp. 106-107.
16. Several books recently helped understand how the German ally was disliked by most of Italian society and by the majority of Italian career military officers. Among these, Simona Colarizi's written work takes into consideration the reports of public security. The academic analysis police documents starting from the signature of the Pact of Steel. In one of these reports regarding the presence of German tourists in some vacation spots in Italy, it is written: 'The disgust and hostility for that which is German is becoming more defined in deeper and complete ways in Italy. In spite of all the trips, the overtures, the visits exchanged between recreational groups of the nations, one cannot see even a bit of fondness for the Germans at all'. S. Colarizi, *L'opinione degli italiani sotto il regime, 1929-1943* (Bari, 2000) p. 299. We also cite Field Marshal Kesserling who, while expressing a negative opinion on the Italians' shortcomings in military terms, subsequently reflects on a different matter:

    > Because Mussolini had not been able to change the deep aversion of the people for the war itself, he should have abstained from joining the conflict. The fact however that the partisans who participated in the battle against German armed forces did so with passion gives one to suppose that the population was not devoid of a fighting spirit.

    A. Kesserling, *Soldato fino all'ultimo giorno* (Gorizia: LEG, 2007), pp. 117-118. As far as Hitler's analytical ability, the Führer was considered such a bad strategist that an operation to kill him was cancelled as 'strictly from a military point of view it was almost an advantage that Hitler continue to maintain control of German military strategy, considering the coarse errors that followed'. I. Kershaw, *Hitler 1936–1945* (Milano: Bompiani, 2001), p. 1,143. Regarding the veracity of the writings, Fest reports:

    > Since the notes are not available in their original text at this time, what is presented here are retranslations from the French, thus it follows that part of the propositions have a significance, formal and pertaining to content, which for the most part was a defect on Hitler's part. One also has to keep in mind that without a doubt it is a reworked manuscript and that the passages mentioned here are, once again, a type of extract of a rambling text, full of outbursts and tangents. For this reason, Albert Speer communicated to the author that he believes Goebbels

was largely involved in the editing of the text, and perhaps even formulated it himself, at least partially; in any event, in his opinion the idioms are more typical of the style of the minister of propaganda than Hitler's.

J. C. Fest, *Hitler* (Milano: Rizzoli, 1974), pp. 925-926.

17. On the date of the declaration of war, the Italian navy possessed one of the biggest submarine fleets in the world: "with 115 boats in service, she was preceded in terms of numbers only by the Soviet navy which had about 160. It is necessary to point out though that the Soviet units were for the most part small coastal boats and they were divided in four different theatres [...], while the Italian submarines were all located in the Mediterranean, with the exception of eight assigned to the Red Sea.

E. Bagnasco, *I sommergibili della Seconda Guerra Mondiale* (Parma: Ermanno Albertelli Editore, 2008), pp. 178-179.

18. The possibility for the *Regia Marina* to equip itself with aircraft was always opposed by the management of the *Regia Aeronautica*. On this subject, see Rochat, *Le guerre italiane 1935–1943* (Torino: Einaudi, 2005), pp. 216-217.
19. Recently, Professor Santoni's conclusions on ULTRA received some criticisms; in fact, these criticisms on the real advantage offered by the decoding, weakly rely on points that have already been emphasised by most of the military historiography and by Santoni several decades prior:

> In truth, as we shall see, also the very valuable ULTRA had its serious limitations, particularly in the form of the time necessary to decode and divulge the news extracted from enemy radio messages and which would vary from a minimal average of twenty-four, forty-eight hours and a maximum of even forty-five days.

A. Santoni, *Il vero traditore*, il ruolo documentato di Ultrà nella guerra del Mediterraneo (Milano, 1981), p. 7. Also Keegan emphasises the value of information received from ULTRA and of the 'services' bringing the opinion of Sir Henry Hinsley, an official historian of British intelligence during the Second World War who, commenting on the role of British intelligence, maintains that 'It did not win the war, as it resolutely maintains, but it reduced its duration'. J. Keegan, *Intelligence* (Milano: Mondadori, 2006), p. 231.

20. See chap. 'Operazione Judgment'.
21. In the days preceding Italy's entrance into the war, Balbo presented what in his opinion were the vehicles and materials needed for the Libyan front. At the end of the request for material, Graziani singled out Mussolini feeling it was appropriate that not only should he be aware of the situation, but that he should personally follow the expeditions: 'Duce, permit me to implore you that the programme you yourself have outlined and for which cutbacks are not acceptable, be applied in its entirety so that Libya will be able perform its duty in the great picture of the new European war'. M. Montanari, *Le operazioni in Africa Settentrionale, Vol. I–Sidi El Barrani (Giugno 1940–Febbraio 1941)* (2 ed., Roma: Ufficio Storico dell'Esercito, 2000), p. 32.
22. *Ibid.*, p. 72.
23. The resignation was presented by Graziani himself on 8 February 1941 and immediately accepted by Mussolini who ordered an inquest on the General's behaviour. www.treccani.it/enciclopedia/rodolfo-graziani_%28Dizionario_Biografico%29/ (seen on 7 July 2015).
24. Messe's opinion regarding Anglo-Italian relations after the formation of the 'Italian-Ethiopian' Empire is well summarised in these words:

> Our foreign policy [...] inevitably brought us, after the conquest of the empire, to the conflict with Great Britain [...] In truth, according to British mindset, the new Italian-Ethiopian empire cut off the way to the Indies from England, who could not tolerate the formation of a strong dominion of millions of Italians on the Ethiopian plateau which dominates the Red Sea and the African shore of the Indian Ocean from where it would have been possible to attack India and threaten to overrun the entire British empire in Asia and Africa.

G. Messe, *La mia armata in Tunisia, come finì la guerra in Africa* (Milano: Mursia, 2004), pp. 20-21.

25. It is worth noting the story of the historian Dan Segre about the resistance done beyond enemy lines by irregulars commanded by an Italian official since October 1941 in the book V. Dan Segre, *La guerra privata del tenente Guillet, La resistenza italiana in Eritrea durante la seconda guerra mondiale* (Milano: Corbaccio, 1993).
26. '... Amedeo Duca d'Aosta, the only prince of the house of Savoia able to emerge from anonymity'. Rochat, *op. cit.*, p. 87. In the page, there is also a brief biography.
27. From the moment when Italy attacked Greece, Prime Minister Churchill told his General Chief of Staff John Dill to assist the Greeks to the utmost extent in any possible way. In 1939, Neville Chamberlain (the previous British Prime Minister) assured Greece of Great Britain's support against an attack. Now Churchill felt that the lack of intervention on Greece's behalf would cause a very bad impression on the United States, where many were asking themselves if Great Britain would indeed be able to conduct war against Nazi Germany. Max Hastings, *Winston's War: Churchill 1940-1945* (New York: Knopf, 2010), p. 105.
28. On the contribution of the Germans to the aero-naval war with Italy in the Mediterranean see: Santoni, Mattesini, *op. cit.*
29. *Ibid.*, p. 29.
30. The 'parallel war', which was autonomous and with goals that were exclusively Italian, had as its main goal control of the Mediterranean, firstly by conquering the Suez Canal, an objective that failed because of the absolute unpreparedness of the Italian military. And yet it was Badoglio who, in his memo of 1 April 1940, advised Mussolini against receiving assistance from the Germans, despite having acknowledged the lack of preparedness of the armed forces (preparation for war was not more than 40 per cent). In the cited memo, Badoglio warned Mussolini:

    > Our intervention should have been done with our own forces and vehicles, because the result that we could accomplish should be attributed exclusively to us and not diminished by German aid.

    Santoni, Mattesini, *op. cit.*, p. 19.
31. As per Hitler's wishes, the composition of the first German units, which arrived in Libya to assist the Italians, was developed in this manner:

    > ... from the 3rd Panzer Division unit, on 14 January 1941 the following unit was formed and named *Leichte Divisionen* Funck from its commander's name (the *Leichte Divisionen*, or light divisions, were initially comprised of one battalion of Panzer and one cavalry regiment; in 1940, they were all changed to Panzer divisions). Immediately afterwards, the unit was renamed 5th *Leichte Divisionen*. On 14 January 1941, its first divisions ... arrived in Tripoli; four days later, Hitler gave the order to reinforce the German presence in northern Africa sending a second division, in this case Panzer (the 15th), and with the creation of an army corps command that of the *Deutsches Afrika Korps*.

    P. P. Battistelli, *Afrika Korps 1941–1943* (Gorizia: LEG, 2012), pp. 9-10.
32. Despite the fact that the war against the Italian-Germans was using up the major resources of the British Empire, the British High Command was forced to maintain significant resources in Asia because of an ever-increasing Japanese aggressiveness, towards the defence of key locations such as Singapore and Burma. In fact, from the first months of 1941, relations between Japan and the British Empire had deteriorated to the point where a conflict appeared to be inevitable. The battalions already present in the area were increased from nine to thirty-two to defend Malaysia–Singapore, and sending two battleships (HMS *Prince of Wales* and HMS *Repulse*) was judged sufficient as a deterrent for the Japanese against British interests in the area. Also, strongholds such as Hong Kong, considered indefensible, received reinforcement from the Commonwealth (Canada). B. Lai, *Hong Kong 1941–45: First Strike in the Pacific War* (Oxford: Osprey Publishing, 2014), pp. 29-32.
33. On Tobruk, see R. Lyman, *The Longest Siege: Tobruk, the Battle that Saved North Africa* (London: Pan Books Ltd, 2009).
34. The historian of the Army Chief of Staff Mario Montanari in his description of the chain of command of the Italian Army wrote about 'an atavistic narrow-mindedness'. K. MacGregor, *Destino*

Comune, Dittatura, politica estera e guerra nell'Italia fascista e nella Germania nazista (Torino: Einaudi, 2003), p. 175.

35. MAE, Affari Politici 1931-1945, b. 30, file 2 Japan and England, folio 2 recto, Prime Minister Winston Churchill to Japanese Minister of Foreign Affairs Yosuke Matsuoka, Moscow, 1941, April 12.
36. *Ibid.*
37. 'In a letter to Hitler, Mussolini remembered the promise not to unleash a European war before 1942 and that nonetheless Italy would honour the pact of Steel, intervening immediately if Germany would provide the needed raw materials'. A. Santoni, F. Mattesini, *La partecipazione tedesca alla guerra aeronavale nel Mediterraneo (1940 – 1945)* (Parma: Ermanno Albertelli Editore, 2005), p. 15.
38. Document no. 8 of 14 April 1940 / XVIII; Note to the Head of Government by the Chief of General Staff of the *Regia Marina*.
39. G. Rochat, 'Militari e politici nella preparazione della campagna d'Etiopia' (Milano: Franco Angeli Editore, 1971), pp. 225-226.
40. R. Quartararo, 'Imperial Defence in the Mediterranean on the eve of the Ethiopian Crisis (July–October 1935)', *Historical Journal*, 20-1-1977, pp. 192-193.
41. G. Rochat, 'Militari e politici nella preparazione della campagna d'Etiopia', pp. 226-228.
42. G. Giorgerini, '*Le costruzioni navali italiane nel periodo bellico con specifico riferimento al 1942*', B.A.U.S.M.M., December 1992, p. 311.
43. D. Mack Smith, *Le guerre del duce* (Bari: Laterza, 1976), p. 231.
44. *Ibid.*
45. *Ufficio Storico della Marina Militare*, '*La Marina Italiana nella seconda guerra mondiale IV Le azioni navali in Mediterraneo*' (3 ed., Roma 1976).
46. D. Mack Smith, *A proposito di Mussolini* (Bari: Laterza, 2004), p. 11.
47. Rochat, *Le guerre italiane 1935–1943*, p. 152. On the difference of the two regimes during wartime (Fascist and Nazi) see K. MacGregor, *Destino comune.*
48. *Senato*, 29 March 1935, pp. 936-8; Canevari, *La guerra*, vol. I, p. 381; DDF, 1/4/283.
49. Rochat, *op. cit.*, p. 228.
50. Rocca, *op. cit.*, p. 104.
51. J. Gooch, *Mussolini and his Generals, The Armed Forces and Fascist Foreign Policy, 1922-1940* (Cambridge: Cambridge University Press, 2007), p. 479.
52. For a description of the progress of Italian-German naval relations, see chapter 'Matapan'.
53. Santoni, Mattesini, *op. cit.*, pp. 18-20. Mussolini's cited words are brought down in G. Ciano, *Diario 1937-1943* (Milano: Rizzoli, 1980), p. 441.
54. A. Hillgruber, *Storia della Seconda Guerra Mondiale, Obiettivi di guerra e strategia delle grandi potenze* (Bari: Laterza, 1989), p. 110.
55. In addition to the Italian ships, the German contribution should be mentioned, and especially that of the British. On this matter, see M. Stille, *The Imperial Japanese Navy of the Russo-Japanese War* (Oxford: Osprey Publishing, 2016), pp. 20-21.
56. F. Pike, *Hirohito's War: The Pacific War 1941–1945* (London: Bloomsbury, 2016), pp. 60-64; E. J. Drea, *Japan's Imperial Army: Its Rise and Fall, 1853–1945* (Lawrence: Kansas, 2009), pp. 190-194.
57. Last, but not least, the military mission to China on orders of General Scaroni should also be mentioned. S. Scaroni, *Missione Militare Aeronautica in Cina* (Roma: Ufficio Storico Aeronautica Militare, 1970).
58. Renzo De Felice, *Mussolini l'alleato, I. L'Italia in guerra 1940-1943, 1. Dalla guerra «breve» alla guerra lunga* (Torino: Einaudi, 1996), pp. 400-411.
59. *Ibid.*
60. Gooch, *op. cit.*, pp. 354-355.
61. A certain hostility and distrust towards the Italians persisted until 1937, above all because of the military mission to China (present since 1933). Scaroni writes:

> In diplomatic ways the Japanese are pleased to ask us the itinerary of our exit from China. They would like to avoid, so they say, a similar mistake as what happened with the British ambassador who was erroneously machine-gunned by their fighters. Perhaps they simply want to be certain that we are leaving. And that our safety has little or no importance at all we

> see from the aerial bombing of our train from Canton to Kowloon (Hong Kong). From our windows we saw very well the aerial bombs falling on the tracks in front of our train … was it an unfortunate coincidence this time as well? Yet the Japanese pilots must have seen the Italian flag painted on the roof of the wagons.

Scaroni, *op. cit.*, p. 73. The Tripartite Pact was an alliance:

> … political and military signed in Berlin on 27 September 1940 by Germany, Italy and Japan, which called for mutualy assisting each other in case one of the parties would be attacked by a power not yet involved in the European war of the Chino-Japanese.… It was based on the premise of recognition of the Italian-German project to establish a new order in Europe and of the Japanese to do the same in Eastern Asia.

As seen on 14.01.2017, www.treccani.it/enciclopedia/patto-tripartito_(Dizionario-di-Storia)/.

62. '… Taranto, which the Japanese had used as a blueprint for Pearl Harbor'. J. R. Cox, *Rising Sun, Falling Skies, The disastrous Java Sea Campaign of World War II* (Oxford: Osprey Publishing, 2014), p. 95. In opposition to common belief, Evans and Peattie stated:

> The Japanese navy's use of shallow torpedo attacks on 'Battleship Row' at Pearl Harbour was supposedly prompted by the British attack on the Italian Fleet at Taranto in November 1940. The British assault may well have strengthened Japanese interest in such a tactic, but in fact the Japanese had already practiced this tactic in 1939 against their own fleet units anchored in the shallow water of Saeki Bay in Kyushu. At that time, they did not have Pearl Harbor specifically in mind.

D. C. Evans, M. R. Peattie, *Kaigun, Strategy, Tactics, and Technology in the Imperial Japanese Navy 1887–1941* (Annapolis: Naval Institute Press, 2012), pp. 344-346.

63. ACS, Min. Aer. Gab. 1941–42.
64. Following is a copy of the entire list of the group as it appears in Italian diplomatic papers (some names have been corrected): Vice-Adml Nomura Naokumi; Rear-Adml Mito Yosihiko; Rear-Adml Abe Katsuo; Rear-Adml Irifune Naosaburo; Rear-Adml Sakamaki Munetaka; Capt. Sato Namizo; Capt. Nishina Kozo; Col. Army Navy Rai Jungo; Capt. Matsuo Minoru; Col. of *Genio Navale* Yokota Toshio; Capt. Mitsunobu Toyo; Frigate-Capt. Nagai Taro; Lt-Col. Naval Aviation Ito Yozo; Frigate-Capt. Kobayashi Yoshito; Lt-Col. *Genio Navale* Yamada Seizo; Lt-Col. *Genio Navale* Minami Siniti; naval engineer Nisi Takeo; Frigate-Capt. Naito Yu; Lt-Col. *Genio Navale* Atobe Tamotu; Lt-Col. Commissioner Inaba Masaki; Maj. Naval Aviation Iku Tuneyo; Maj. Naval Aviation Yosikawa Haruo; Corvette-Capt. Yamanaka Dengo; Maj. Medic Sugita Tamotu; Maj. Naval Aviation Iwaya Eiiti; Maj. Naval Aviation Shoji Genzo; Corvette-Capt. Fujimura Yoshikazu; Maj. Naval Engineer Kasai Seiiti; Maj. Naval Engineer Inouye Kenzo; Corvette-Capt. Morinaga Kenzo; Naval Engineer Abe Suehiti; Naval Engineer Uriu Tomoziro.
    ACS, SPD, CO, b. 1571, *Missione Giapponese della marina e dell'esercito* in Roma.
65. In Giuseppe Fioravanzo's article, Vice-Adml Nomura Kichisaburo is mistaken for Nomura Naokuni; as a matter of fact, at the time of the visit of the Japanese Mission to Italy, the former was ambassador to the USA. G. Fioravanzo, 'The Japanese military mission to Italy in 1941', in *US Naval Institute Proceedings*, Jan. 1956, Vol. 82, Issue 1, p. 24. Correct information can be found in R. Fuller, *Japanese Admirals 1926–1945* (Atglen, Pa, USA: Schiffer Military History, 2011), pp. 174-175; P. Herde, *Pearl Harbor* (Milano: Rizzoli, 1987), p. 40.
66. Fioravanzo, *op. cit.*, p. 24.
67. *Ibid.*
68. It is worth noting that soon after the raid, Lieutenant Commander Naito, the Japanese naval *attaché* in Berlin, was sent to Italy with instructions to visit Taranto and report what he could about the way the attack was carried out. The report was duly passed on to Admiral Yamamoto for evaluation. At the time Yamamoto was the commander of the Japanese Combined Fleet, and the architect of the plan to attack Pearl Harbor. Also, upon his return to Japan, Naito personally briefed Commander Fuchida on the Taranto raid. Fuchida would go on to lead the attack on Pearl Harbor.

A. Kostam, *Taranto 1940, The Fleet Air Arm's Precursor to Pearl Harbor* (Oxford: Osprey Publishing, 2015), p. 91. For more detailed information on this matter, see G. W. Prange, *At Dawn We Slept: The Untold Story of Pearl Harbor*; Revised Edition (London: Penguin Books, 1991), p. 320.

69. Fioravanzo, *op. cit.*, p. 27.
70. When the ships are out of firing range of both fleets.
71. For the operational aspect and the documents connected to the Japanese naval mission and the technical questions, see the paragraph in this book at p. XXX.
72. C. W. Spang, R.-H. Wippich, *Japanese-German Relations, 1895-1945: War, Diplomacy and Public Opinion* (New York: Routledge, 2006), p. 47.
73. 'Admiral Abe and I often expressed our opinions to top officers of the armed forces of the Axis, regarding the importance of operations in the Mediterranean, particularly on the capture of Malta.... The above opinion was not respected much'. '*Osservazioni sulla guerra in Italia dal 1940 al 1944 dell'addetto navale giapponese presso il governo di Roma*', in *Il movimento di liberazione in Italia*, 1956 n. 44/45, p. 33 (as seen on 06-01-2017, www.italia-resistenza.it/wp-content/uploads/ic/RAV0068570_1956_40-45_27.pdf).
74. M. Stille, *Malaya and Singapore: The Fall of Britain's Empire in the East* (Oxford: Osprey Publishing, 2016), p. 45. On the underestimation of the Japanese force, see also Jeffrey R. Cox, *Rising Sun, Falling Skies* p. 94; John W. Dower, *War Without Mercy, Race and Power in the Pacific War* (New York: Pantheon Books, 1986), pp. 77-117.
75. *Osservazioni sulla guerra in Italia dal 1940 al 1944 dell'addetto navale giapponese presso il governo di Roma*, pp. 31-38.
76. *Ibid.*, p. 32.
77. *Ibid.*

Chapter 2

1. F. Cardoni, '*Il problema aeronavale italiano*', BAUSMM, Year I N° I, September 1987, p. 108.
2. E. Bagnasco, "La portaerei nella marina italiana", Rivista Marittima, Roma 1989, p.16.
3. E. Cernuschi, V. P. O'Hara, 'Search for a Flattop: the Italian Navy and the aircraft carrier 1907-2007' Warship (2007), p. 63.
4. M. Angelozzi, U. Bernini, 'Il problema aeronavale italiano, aspetti storici ed attuali', *Livorno*, 1981, p. 25.
5. On the matter, see also BAUSMM, Year I N° I, September 1987, F. Cardoni, '*Il problema aeronavale italiano*', chap. I, p. 109. *Ibid.*, '*Douhet e le aviazioni ausiliarie*', *relazione del comando Ufficio Storico Marina Militare al Congresso internazionale di studi su Douhet*, Caserta 12-14 April 1987, p. 117. In A. Rastrelli, '*La portaerei Italiana*' (Milano: Mursia, 2001) reports on the same topic 657 aircraft in service, 42 seaplane bases, 5 airports, 38 fighter and reconnaissance seaplane squadrons, 8 squadrons of ground-based fighter and bomber aircraft.
6. Bagnasco, *op. cit.*, p. 27.
7. Cardoni, *op. cit.*, p. 109.
8. The debate was obviously ongoing in the armed forces of all nations. The performance of the different countries' air forces at sea during the Second World War depended on its final outcome.
9. *Gazzetta Ufficiale*, *Regio Decreto* n. 1438, 30 September 1920.
10. F. Cardoni, '*Il problema aeronavale italiano (Capitolo II)*', BAUSMM, Year I, N° 2, December 1987, p. 219.
11. Report of 16 May 1922 to the Minister of the Navy by the *Comitato Ammiragli*, in Rochat, Italo Balbo, *aviatore e Ministro dell'aeronautica* 1926-1933, (Ferrara: Bovolenta, 1979), pp. 6-17.
12. Cardoni, *op. cit.*, pp. 224-225.
13. She was the only one among four units of its class to launch on 12 May 1920.
14. N. Friedman, *British Carrier Aviation, The Evolution of the Ships and their aircraft* (London: Conway Maritime Press, 1988), p. 60. The first aircraft carrier was supposed to have a speed and autonomy such that it would operate with the battle cruisers and the second would operate with the battle fleet. The flush deck without superstructures would have been 240 metres long.
15. *Ibid.*, p 62.
16. HSS *Argus*, HMS *Hermes*, and HMS *Eagle*, operational; HMS *Furious* undergoing conversion, HMS *Glorious* and HMS *Courageous* with almost complete plans.

17. … the Wakamiya participated in the naval manoeuvres off Sasebo that year, and in 1914, the ship was sent to waters off Kiaochow Bay, where its seaplanes operated against the German naval base at Tsingtao. During these operations the Japanese aircraft made fifty reconnaissance and bombing sorties over the base while also undertaking search operations at sea.

    Evans, Peattie, *op. cit.*, p. 180.
18. … in 1920 the Navy (Japanese) sent a representative to Britain to observe air operations off the decks of Furious. Finally, in 1921, the Japanese government requested that the British naval air service dispatch a naval air mission to Japan in order to provide a professional edge to this newest arm of the Japanese Navy. The Sempill Naval Air Mission of 1921–22 marks the true beginning of an effective Japanese naval air force.

    Ibid., p. 181.
19. Cardoni, *op. cit.*, p. 215.
20. *Ibid.*, p. 214.
21. The King, fearing a civil war, refused to sign the decree to militarily face fascist forces. Similar to what occurred later in Germany, many personalities believed Mussolini could be 'manoeuvred' according to their interests.
22. *Gazzetta Ufficiale*, *Regio Decreto* n. 62, 24 January 1923.
23. Rochat, *Le guerre italiane*, p. 221.
24. Regarding the metaphorical transference of Fascism with aviation, the aviation historian Eric Lehmann quote Mario Isnenghi:

    > There is an aviation ideology according to which, to the Italians in between the two wars, the aerial Army presents itself as typically Fascist and the Regime's favourite; Italo Balbo is boss of the organization of Fascists in the Po valley and from 1929 Minister of Aviation, its prophet, impresario and main personality; the raid, the undertaking, the flyover are its setup and apex is in the presence of Italy and the entire world. This propensity comes from a variety of reasons, not only of a military nature. One could think that aviation, the aviation of the time, actualises a type of metaphor of Fascism, of its myth, of the identity which it idealises and promotes itself; of its story (only partially true, and for the most part imaginary); of the tension between transgression and organisation. Thus, speaking of aviation will mean speaking of Fascism, in general terms.

    E. Lehmann, *Le ali del potere, La propaganda aeronautica nell'Italia fascista* (Torino: Utet, 2010), p. XIII.
25. AUSMM, folder 2411, file 2 '*aviazione* 1923, letter sent to Navy officials.
26. Cardoni, *op. cit.*, p. 239-241.
27. *Gazzetta Ufficiale*, *Regio Decreto* n. 645, 28 March 1923.
28. The agreement reached is very similar to the one that would be reached a year later in Great Britain (the Trenchard-Keys agreement, July 1924), with the big difference that the budget for embarked aircraft in Italy was *Regia Aeronautica*'s one, while in Great Britain, it was in the Royal Navy's. S. W. Roskill, *The War at Sea, Vol. I, The Defensive* (London: HMSO, 1954), p. 29.
29. With the *Regio Decreto* 3482 of 30.12.1868 instead of the '*Consiglio di Ammiragliato*' of the Order of the Sardinian Navy, the '*Consiglio Superiore di Marina*' was established, and appointed to provide the Minister with technical opinions on the new rules and regulations. However, over time, its arrangement varied, usually the greatest experts in the various fields of administration were part of it and it was presided by the most senior ranked vice-admiral, who was not a minister. By law, he was required to ask the Council's opinion on numerous subjects even though the opinion was not binding. In the beginning of the twentieth century, the need was felt to place some committees side by side with the aforementioned Council, committees in which the heads of the Armed Forces would be best represented and that not only the Minister but also the General Chief of Staff could use all of the opinions of high political-strategic value who would represent the ideas of the most highly qualified important officials and thus, the entire institution. With law 404 of 27.6.1907, the advisory bodies were thus reorganised, establishing the constitution of a '*Comitato degli Ammiragli*' made

up of the President and the Vice-President of the Superior Council, the Commanders at the helm of the Department and the Naval Forces, by the General Chief of Staff and by the President of the '*Comitato per l'esame dei Progetti di Navi*' ('Committee for the examination of naval plans'). The latter in turn shaped by those in charge of planning and construction of the new units (General officials of the corps of GN or Machinists) and by one or more officials of the Head of Staff responsible for design of artillery and weapons (Admiral officials or superior specialists). The Planning Committee had a 'Technical Office' that generally developed the planning for the new units and machines. P. P. Ramoino, 'La *Regia Marina* tra le due guerre mondiali', *Rivista Marittima*, settembre 2011, (Livorno: Ministero della Difesa, 2011), p. 24.

30. AUSMM, folder '*Portaerei*', Minutes of the Assembly of the *Comitato Ammiragli* of 12 June 1923.
31. *Ibid.*
32. *Ibid.*
33. *Ibid.*
34. Friedman, *op. cit.*, pp. 100-103.
35. F. Cardoni, '*La questione della nave portaerei nella Regia Marina nel 1923-1925 ⊠ difficoltà finanziarie ed incertezze tecniche e dottrinarie*' in BAUSMM, June 1991, p. 71.
36. *Atti Parlamentari, Camera dei Deputati, Discussioni*. Session of 10 December 1924, pp. 1,352-1,353.
37. *Biblioteca dell'Istituto di Guerra Marittima di Livorno, posizione* 2479, entry number 16.07.48.
38. As it clearly emerged during British manoeuvres of March 1925, see G. Till, *Air Power and the Royal Navy, 1914-1945: A Historical Survey*, (Northampton: Jane's, 1979), p. 164 and those of the USN in January 1929 (see A. D. Turnbull, C. L. Lord, 'History of United States naval aviation', Newhaven, 1949, p. 271).
39. Till, *op. cit.*, pp. 142-143.
40. The *Regia Marina* considered launching raids against British units at anchor in Alexandria and Haifa, using light and heavy cruisers, which would occur with a timeframe of twenty-four hours from the declaration of war: M. Gabriele, *Mediterraneo* 1935-36, *La situazione militare marittima nella visione britannica*, *Rivista Marittima*, maggio 1986, pp. 24-31.
41. The Grand Admiral considered intolerable the fact that the Army had established coordination powers over the Navy and predicted a 'purely terrestrial' war theory; the subsequent events would prove him right given the inability of the Supreme Command to establish priorities and ccordinate the different armies. Mussolini was taken completely by surprise by the resignation, to the point where he initially thought that it it was caused by the merging of the *Regia Marina*'s air force with the new *Regia Aeronautica*.
42. Giorgerini, *op. cit.*, p. 203.
43. F. Cardoni, 'Il problema aeronavale italiano', BAUSMM, Year I N° 2, December 1991, p. 73, note 6.
44. AUSMM, Folder '*Portaerei*', *Comitato Ammiragli*, *Quesito* '*Nuove Costruzioni*', minutes of the afternoon assembly of 11 August 1925, p. 2.
45. Clearly stated, these proposals were a way to circumvent the limits of Washington Treaty for the heavy cruiser. *Ibid.*, p. 13.
46. AUSMM, Folder '*Portaerei*', *Comitato Ammiragli*, *Quesito* '*Nuove Costruzioni*', minutes of the afternoon assembly of 11 August 1925, p. 3.
47. Till, *op. cit.*, pp. 72, 117, 148.
48. AUSMM, Cartella '*Portaerei*', *Comitato Ammiragli*, *Quesito* '*Nuove Costruzioni*', minutes of the afternoon assembly on 11 August 192, p. 7.
49. Alan D. Zimm, 'The USN Flight deck cruiser', *Warship International*, N°3, 1979.
50. *Gazzetta Ufficiale*, *Regio Decreto* n. 1513, 2 September 1925.
51. *Ibid.*, pp. 78-122.
52. F. Caffarena, *Dal fango al vento, Gli aviatori italiani dalle origini alla grande guerra* (Torino: Einaudi, 2010), p. 187.
53. Rochat, *Le guerre italiane*, p. 222.
54. *Rivista Marittima*, February 1923, p. 150.
55. G. Rochat, 'Mussolini e le Forze Armate', in *Il Regime Fascista* (Bologna, 1974), p. 166.
56. Thaon di Revel, Parliamentary Acts, Chamber of Deputies, Discussions, Session of 20 December 1924, p. 1, 353.

57. *Ibid.*, Session of 10 December 1924, p. 909.
58. Cernuschi and O'Hara, 2007, p. 67.
59. 'Sulla opportunità della costruzione di navi portaerei oppure di incrociatori del tipo Trento', invitation to tender by the Navy Chief of Staff. Winning response by Commander Fioravanzo, *op. cit.*
60. Georges Leygues declared in 1923: 'We refuse parity with Italy because France is surrounded by three seas and owns a vast empire only eighteen hours from Marseille and communications with it must be heavily protected…', G. Bernardi, 'Il disarmo navale tra le due guerre mondiali', Roma, USMM, 1975.
61. A. de Toro, '*Le origini politico-diplomatiche delle navi da battaglia Littorio e Vittorio Veneto*', BAUSMM, Year XI, March 1997, pp. 67-151.
62. M. Cosentino, *op. cit.*, p. 67.
63. P. P. Ramoino, 'La "Minaccia" navale francese negli anni venti e trenta del XX secolo', BAUSMM, June 2011, pp. 9-10. The names of the French units are underlined. Not including MN *Pluton* (1928) and MN *Jeanne d'Arc* (1928).
64. On Douhet and his theories, see E. Lehmann, *La guerra dell'aria* (Bologna: Il Mulino, 2013).

Chapter 3

1. E. Bagnasco, '*La portaerei nella marina italiana*', *Rivista Marittima*, December 1989, pp. 14-15.
2. *Ibid.*, pp. 19-20.
3. Cernuschi, O'Hara, 2007, p. 63.
4. E. Bagnasco, 'Una portaerei mancata: la "Francesco Caracciolo"', *Rivista Marittima*, p. 21.
5. *Ibid.*
6. Cernuschi, O'Hara, 2007, p. 67.
7. G. Rabbeno, 'Studio di massima di un nuovo tipo di nave portaeroplani per una Marina oceanica', *Rivista Marittima*, January 1923.
8. Cosentino, *op. cit.*, pp. 34-35.
9. AUSMM, Cartella 'Portaerei', Comitato Ammiragli, Query 'Nuove Costruzioni', minutes of the afternoon assembly of 11 August 1925, f. 5.
10. *Ibid.*
11. Parliamentary Acts, Chamber of Deputies, Discussions, Session of 10 December1924, pp. 1,352-1,355.
12. AUSMM, Minutes of the assembly of the *Comitato Ammiragli* on 8 March 1924.
13. Cosentino, *op. cit.*, p. 39.
14. Washington Treaty's wording brought about a full set of hybrid 10,000-ton warship designs, see R. D. Lyman and Stephen McLaughlin, *The Hybrid Warship: The Amalgamation of Big Guns and Aircraft* (London: Conway Maritime Press, 1991).
15. See chapter on 'Douhet, Fascism and the rise of *Regia Aeronautica*'.
16. Cosentino, *op. cit.*, pp. 57-59.
17. C. Ressmann, 'La nave portaveivoli di Alessandro Guidoni', *Rivista Marittima*, February 1977. Complete information on this projects is available at: www.alieuomini.it/pagine/dettaglio/uomini,5/la_porta_aerei_italiana_in_un_progetto_del_generale_alessandro_guidoni,20.html on 12.03.2017.

Chapter 4

1. Rochat, *Italo Balbo, aviatore e Ministro dell'aeronautica 1926-1933* (Ferrara: Bovolenta, 1979), p 201.
2. F. Botti, 'La strategia Marittima degli anni venti', BAUSMM, September 1988, p. 253.
3. Rochat, *op. cit.*, pp. 50-52.
4. F. Cardoni, 'Il problema aeronavale italiano Parte 5°: la nomina di Italo Balbo a capo dell'Aeronautica e la sua battaglia contro le aviazioni ausiliarie', BAUSMM, Year VI, June 1992, p. 200.
5. The problem of 'Dual control' of air force personnel at sea was not unique to the Italians: the British Empire, where 70 per cent of the pilots were in the Navy and 30 per cent in the Air force, had so many problems that in 1934 the Admiralty started a campaign to regain complete control of the embarked air force: 'Deeply concerned by the general crisis in manning and exasperated by

institutional instability to solve it, the Admiralty had already decided to reopen the campaign to regain control of the FAA'. Till, *op. cit.*, p. 48.

6. Cardoni, *op. cit.*, pp. 201-202.
7. *Ibid.*, p. 204.
8. Bernardi, *op. cit.*, p. 53.
9. R. Bernotti, *Cinquant'anni nella Marina Militare* (Milano: Mursia, 1971), p. 208.
10. *Regio Decreto* of 6 February 1927, n° 68.
11. Bernotti, *op. cit.*, p. 186.
12. The same discussions and the same outcome occurred in Germany, in the thirties: the *Kriegsmarine* was defeated by a politically stronger Head of *Luftwaffe*. On this see E. Raeder, *La mia vita* (Milano: Baldini e Castoldi, 1960), pp. 367-368; it is common to underestimate the political weight in making military decisions, particularly with dictatorships: in fact, what appear to be meetings with an 'open' outcome are in reality already decided before the meetings unfold.
13. 'I insist with my reservations concerning the necessity to build an aircraft carrier, particularly in the reduced or experimental design which Bernotti recommends', Mussolini's letter on 23 October 1927 to Vice Minister Sirianni, reported in Bernotti, *op. cit.*, p. 172.
14. AUSMM, 'La nostra politica marittima', memo for admirals, folder 2516, file 4.
15. AUS Aer. Cart. 'Relazioni di Bilancio' 1928-33.
16. A. Curma, Giancarlo Garello, 'L'aviazione ausiliaria per la Regia Marina fra le due guerre (1923-1940)' *Rivista Marittima*, ag-set. 1985, p. 78.
17. *Ibid.*, p. 79-80.
18. Cardoni, *op. cit.*, p. 207.
19. The maximum level of consistency we are certain of during Balbo's management was of 911 in 1933 according to Rochat, Italo Balbo, Appendice IV, column 13.
20. AUSMM, Folder 2659, '*Aeronautica* 1932-33', Valle Memorandum of 7 April 1932.
21. AUSMM, Folder 2650, '*Aeronautica* 1932-33', letter of the *Ufficio del CSM della Marina al Ministro 'Aviazione per la Regia Marina'*, 13 February 1933.
22. Rochat, *op. cit.*, p. 228.
23. Curma, Garello, *op. cit.*, p 80.
24. AUSMM, folder 2571, file 1, *Direttive per l'addestramento all'impiego della Aviazione per la R. Marina*, *Regia Marina*'s Chief of Staff 21 July 1931.
25. G. Fioravanzo, 'L'aviazione navale per la Marina, 1940-1943', *Rivista Marittima*, November 1963, p. 29.
26. 'The decision revived the hope that the Premier might also change his mind and be persuaded in favour of a naval air arm; it was evident that a carrier programme implied the necessity of having a fleet air wing available', Admiral Bernotti, Naval Institute Proceedings, July 1956, p. 728.
27. On the development of Japanese naval aviation in the thirties, see M. Peattie, *Sunburst: The Rise of Japanese Naval Air Power 1909-1941* (Annapolis, Maryland, USA: Naval Institute Press, 2007), pp. 21-51.
28. Cosentino, *op. cit.*, p. 97.
29. Giorgerini, *op. cit.*, pp. 304-306.
30. *Ibid.*, p. 105.
31. A. Rastrelli, *La portaerei Italiana* (Milano: Mursia, 2001), p. 107.
32. Cosentino, *op. cit.*, p. 100.
33. F. Cardoni, 'Il problema aeronavale italiano—Conclusione: 1935-1939. L'incerto riorientamento della politica navale e il fallimento finale della portaerei', BAUSMM, December 1992, pp. 29-30.
34. 27 June 1935, Badoglio-Gamelin agreement.
35. See R. Quatarnaro, 'Roma tra Londra e Berlino. La politica estera fascista tra il 1930 e il 1940', Roma 1980, and R. De Felice, 'Alcune osservazioni sulla politica estera mussoliniana', AA VV., in *L'Italia fra tedeschi e alleati*, Imola, 1973, pp. 57-74.
36. E. Pellegrini, 'Le implicazioni navali della conquista dell'Impero' (1935-1941), Roma 2003, p. 46.
37. After the Conference of Stresa on 12–14 April, Mussolini was certain of the friendship of the British and therefore of the continuation of traditional naval politics: see C. J Lowe and F. Marzari, *Italian Foreign Policy 1870-1940* (London: Routledge, 1975), pp. 263-264.
38. G. Rochat, 'Militari e politici nella preparazione della campagna d'Etiopia', Milano 1971, pp. 225-226.

39. R. Quartararo, 'Imperial Defence in the Mediterranean on the eve of the Ethiopian Crisis (July–October 1935)', *Historical Journal*, 20.1.1977, pp. 192-193.
40. It is interesting to note that the *Regia Marina*'s plans envisaged surprise shelling of the ports of Alexandria and Haifa to be executed at dawn with light cruisers of the *Condottieri*-class (*Haifa*) and heavy cruisers of the *Trento*-class (*Alexandria*), and possibly 'in the first hours after the declaration of war' (general order of operations n.1 Op. N.A.), Giorgio Giorgerini, *Da Matapan al golfo Persico, la marina militare italiana dal fascismo alla repubblica*, (Milano: Mondadori, 2003), pp. 323-325.
41. Till, *op. cit.*, p. 166.
42. G. Rochat, 'Militari e politici nella preparazione della campagna d'Etiopia', Milano 1971, pp. 226-228.
43. Marder, "The Italian Navy and the Ethiopian crisis of 1935-36", *American Historical Review*, LXXV, n.5 giugno 1970, p. 1339; and R. Quartararo, 'Imperial Defence in the Mediterranean on the eve of the Ethiopian Crisis (July–October 1935)', *Historical Journal*, 20, I, 1977, pp. 202-203.
44. S. Tur, *Plancia Ammiraglio* (3 vols., vol. III, Roma: Edizioni Moderne, 1963), p. 150.
45. M. Angelozzi and U. Bernini, 'Il problema aeronavale italiano, aspetti storici ed attuali', Livorno 1981, p. 46; in the same directive, instructions were given to develop plans for a battleship of 26,500 tons.
46. AUSMM, folder *Portaerei*, Letter from Undersecretary Cavagnari to the *Comitato Progetto Navi* of 23 September 1935.
47. Letter from Adml Ducci to Adml Bernotti, 1956, 28 August, in Bernotti, *op. cit.*, p. 234.
48. The questions of the *Comitato Progetto Navi* concerned the length of the deck and the opportunity to feature arrest cables; the length of the deck necessary for take-off; if the flight deck had to be entirely free, with smokes unloaded at stern or on the sides and if an island was possible; and if an auxiliary deck and catapults for fighter launches was appropriate.
The answers of the Navy aero-naval Office were depending on the arrest system (which required trials) not less than 100 metres, better 120–130; island is permissible and useful, if conveniently outlined; catapults are beneficial for aircraft with heavy loads and for the simultaneous take-off of fighters and bombers; and opportunities to prearrange retractable screens to protect the various sections of the flight deck from the wind.
In any event, these subjects had already been dealt with and solved by the Royal Navy (see N. Friedman, *British Carrier Aviation: The Evolution of the Ships and their Aircraft*, (London: Conway Maritime Press, 1988).
49. AUSMM, Folder *Portaerei*, Report of General Pugliese of 27 July 1936, pp. 2-3.
50. AUSMM, Folder *Portaerei*, folio B5248 of 15 August 1936 and memorandum for SE: of 1 August 1936.
51. F. Cardoni, 'Il problema aeronavale italiano—Conclusione: 1935-1939. L'incerto riorientamento della politica navale e il fallimento finale della portaerei', BAUSMM, December 1992, pp. 39-40.
52. AUSMM, Folder *Portaerei*, report of General Umberto Pugliese, 27 June 1936.
53. In December 1937, the planned 'Norme la navigazione degli aerei di conserva con una formazione navale' procedures for an air group to escort naval units at sea were still missing, AUSMM *Cartella Portaerei, Ufficio di SM della Regia Marina, reparto o.a. ufficio aeronautica, pro-memoria a S.E. Pini del capo ufficio aeronautica dello Stato Maggiore della Marina* f. 20 December 1937.
54. AUSMM, Folder *Portaerei, Ufficio di SM della Regia Marina, reparto o.a. ufficio aeronautica, pro-memoria a S.E. Pini*, 1 August 1 1936.
55. Cardoni, December 1992, p. 43.
56. AUSMM, Folder *Portaerei*, Minutes of the Assembly of the *Comitato Progetti Navi* of 4 August 1936.
57. Giorgerini, *op. cit.*, p. 355.
58. AUSMM, *Raccolta di Base*, b2715, f 6 '*il nostro problema militare nel Mediterraneo*'.
59. F. Cardoni, 'Il problema aeronavale italiano, parte sesta: I rapporti tra Marina ed Aeronautica dal 1929 al 1935—Anni di stasi', BAUSMM, September 1992, p. 44.
60. *Ibid.*, p. 45.
61. *Ibid.*, p. 46; the 'torpedo bomb' was developed by the *Regia Aeronautica* as 'Motobomba FF', utilised for the first time in the battle in mid-August (11–14 August 1942) see: Riccardo Nassigh, *Operazione Mezzo Agosto* (Milano: Mursia, 1976), pp. 60-61.
62. Letter of Arturo Ciano, President of the torpedo factory in Fiume to Mussolini 27 May 1937, duplicated in USMM, '*La marina italiana della seconda guerra mondiale*', XXI, Tome I, Roma, p 43.

63. *Ibid.*, p 44; the idea will subsequently make a comeback and be used during the war, using 381 naval shells as armour-piercing bombs.
64. Ufficio Storico Stato Maggiore dell'Esercito, minutes of the meetings held by the General Chief of Staff (26 January 1939 to 29 December 1940), Roma 1983, pp. 11-13; on this occasion, Admiral Cavagnari said that the torpedo (which could be launched from an altitude of 120 metres and at a speed of 300 km/h) was to be considered final and not experimental
65. Letter of Arturo Ciano, President of the torpedo factory in Fiume to Mussolini 27 May 1937, duplicated in USMM, 'La marina italiana della seconda guerra mondiale', XXI, Tome I, Roma, memorandum of Marinarmi, 25 November 1937, p. 44.
66. E. Cernuschi, *Domenico Cavagnari, storia di un ammiraglio*, (Roma: Rivista marittima, 2011), p. 186.
67. Cardoni, September 1992, p. 49.
68. Ufficio Storico Stato Maggiore dell'Esercito, minutes of the meetings held by the General Chief of Staff vol. I (26 January 1939 to 29 December 1940), Roma 1983, p. 30.
69. Letter of the head of SMG to Admiral Cavagnari on 7 December 1938, reproduced in USMM, '*La marina italiana della seconda guerra mondiale*', XXI, Tome I, Roma, p 48.
70. Rastrelli, *La portaerei nella Marina Italiana*, p. 185.
71. Tur, *op. cit.*, p. 265.
72. F. Pricolo, *La Regia Aeronautica nella seconda guerra mondiale, novembre 1939–novembre 1941* (Milano: Longanesi, 1971), p. 115. Besides, General Pricolo maintained already in 1927 about the 'uselessness of the aircraft carriers' even affirming the uselessness of marine reconnaissance in *Rivista Aeronautica*, year III, March 1927, pp. 5-14.
73. Till, *op. cit.*, p. 87.
74. *Ibid.*, pp. 88-89.
75. N. H. Gibbs, *Grand Strategy, vol. I, Rearmament Policy* (London: HMSO, 1976), p. 367.
76. S. W. Roskill, *op. cit.*, p. 30.
77. S. W. Mitcham Jr, *Eagles of the Third Reich: Leaders of the Luftwaffe in the Second World War* (Manchester: Stackpole Books, 2010), pp. 23-25.
78. M. Williamson, *Strategy for Defeat: The Luftwaffe 1933-1945* (London: Eagle Editions, 2001), pp. 11-29.
79. Like the *Regia Aeronautica*, the *Luftwaffe* had control not only of the anti-ship air groups and coastal patrols, but even of the aircraft embarked on the ships. While the first organisation of naval aviation since 1939 had fourteen *Küstenfliegerstaffeln* (coastal aviation squadron) and one *Bordfliegergruppe* (ship-based aviation group), the subsequent reorganisation 'resulted in the formation of two *Fliegerdivisionen—Fliegerdivisionen Luft West* and *Fliegerdivisionen Luft Ost*, acting as aerial support to the *Kriegsmarine*'s *Marineoberkommando West* and *Ost* respectively'. C. McNab, *The Luftwaffe 1933–45: Hitler's Eagles* (New York: Chartwell Books, 2014), p. 294.
80. *Ibid.*
81. On Fw 200 Condor, see J. Scutts, *The Focke-Wulf Fw 200 Condor: A Complete History* (Manchester: Crecy Publishing, 2009); C. Goss, *Fw 200 Condor Units of World War 2* (Oxford: Osprey Publishing, 2016).

Chapter 5

1. M. Cosentino, *La portaerei scomparsa del Generale Bonfiglietti* (Milano: Jouvence, 2016), p. 64.
2. *Ibid.*, pp. 41-44.
3. *Ibid.*, p. 36.
4. *Ibid.*, pp. 69-77.
5. *Ibid.*, pp. 87-88.
6. E. Bagnasco, 'Una portaerei mancata: la "Francesco Caracciolo"', *Rivista Marittima*, maggio 1991, p. 52.
7. AUSMM, *fondo MARISTAT*, Rep. *Mobilitazione, Difesa e Servizi*, envelope 250, dossiers 4699 and 4700.
8. M. Cosentino, *op. cit.*, pp. 96-97.
9. AUSMM, *Raccolta di base*, Folder 2631, File 1, '*Riunione comitato Ammiragli*', March 1934.
10. AUSMM, *Comitato Ammiragli*, minutes of the meetings of 1926-1931. There is mention of the proposal for a diesel cruiser, presumably for raider war, proposed by engineer Calzavara, armed with 9 pieces of 152.

11. AUSMM, *Raccolta di base*, Folder *Portaerei*, Report to the Committee of General Pugliese, 27 July 1936.
12. M. Cosentino, *op. cit.*, pp. 113-114.
13. *Ibid.*, pp. 115-118.
14. E. Cernuschi, V. P. O'Hara, 'The Breakout Fleet: The Oceanic Programmes of the Regia Marina, 1934-1940', *Warship*, 2006 (London: Conway Maritime, 2006), p. 90.
15. *Ibid.*, p. 71.
16. Report of the *Comitato Progetto Navi* of 27 July 1937, quoted in '*La portaerei nella marina italiana*', E. Bagnasco, *Rivista Marittima*, Roma 1989, p. 53.
17. Cernuschi, O'Hara, *op. cit.*, pp. 86-101.
18. See: '*Studio sulla preparazione*', *Ufficio di Stato Maggiore della Regia Marina, promemoria sul programma anno XVII e seguenti*, January 1939 in Ernesto Pellegrini, *Le implicazioni navali della conquista dell'Impero* (1935-41), USMM, Roma, 2003, *allegato* 5 '*Studio sulla preparazione*', pp. 196-205.
19. Cosentino, *op. cit.*, pp. 125-126.

Chapter 6

1. U. H. J. Israel, *Einziger deutscher Flugzeugtraeger Graf Zeppelin* (Herford: Koehler, 1994), p. 98.
2. *Ibid.*, pp. 87, 98.
3. *Ibid.*, p. 88.
4. S. Breyer, *Flugzeugtrager Graf Zeppelin* (Dorheim, 1988), p. 7.
5. H. Jentschura, D. Jung, and P. Mickel, *Warships of the Imperial Japanese Navy, 1869-1945*, pref. (London, 1999).
6. Israel, *op. cit.*, p. 41.
7. AUSMM, *Raccolta di base*, b 2698, f '*Forniture navali al Governo Russo – 1937*'.
8. Rastrelli, *La portaerei nella marina italiana*, p. 127.
9. Rocca, *op. cit.*, p. 84.
10. AUSMM, Folder 2688 File 5. *Promemoria del capo di SM della Marina al Capo di SM generale*, 18 November 1937, p. 1.
11. Cosentino, 2016, pp. 121-122.
12. F. Cardoni, 'Il problema aeronavale italiano—Conclusione: 1935-1939. L'incerto riorientamento della politica navale e il fallimento finale della portaerei', BAUSMM, December 1992, p. 46.
13. Author's note: given the problem of building the aircraft carriers.
14. Parliamentary Acts, Chamber of Deputies, discussions, session of 15 March 1938, p. 4,696.
15. AUSMM, Minutes of the Assembly of the *Comitato Ammiragli* no. 51 of 26 July 1938.
16. Cardoni, December 1992, p. 49.
17. Cosentino, *op. cit.*, p. 134.
18. AUSMM, 9 September 1938, Pro-memoria, *Osservazioni sulle direttive e norme dell 'impiego in guerra della 2° squadra.*
19. G. Bernardi, *Il disarmo navale tra le due guerre mondiali (1919-1939)* (Roma: USMM, 1975), pp. 670-690.
20. M. Mazzetti, *La politica militare italiana fra le due guerre mondiali (1918-1940)* (Salerno: Edizioni Beta, 1974).
21. Cosentino, *op. cit.*, p. 126.
22. E. Pellegrini, *Le implicazioni navali della conquista dell'Impero (1935*-41) (Roma: USMM, 2003), pp. 213-215.
23. Mussolini was so convinced that he had made it clear with the Germans, in the conference of Milano, that it was necessary to wait for the 1942, to the point of mentioning the reasons in the memorandum sent to Admiral Cavagnari on 27 May 1939: 'In a memo to Von Ribbentrop, at the time of the conference in Milano, I explained the reasons for which Italy needs a period of preparation so that everything should go in order in 1942'.

Chapter 7

1. ACS, R. Marina, busta 88 and D. S. Landers, *The Unbound Prometheus* (Cambridge: Cambridge University Press, 1972), p. 459.
2. R. Romeo, *Breve storia della grande industria in Italia 1861-1961* (first ed. 1961, Milano, 1988), pp. 151-152 and passim.
3. Personal folder of Senator Admiral Ducci, Senate: '*Richiesta di revocazione del provvedimento di decadenza da Senatore*'" of 28 March 1946, pp. 2-3.
4. The Japanese pilots would enter the operational air groups after 800 hours of training, R. Overy, *The Air War 1939-1945* (New York: Stein and Day, 1985), pp. 382-401.
5. For the strategic military plans in agreement with the ever-changing political decisions, see F. Minniti, 'Gli obiettivi di guerra nella pianificazione operativa (1938-1940)' in *Commissione italiana di storia militare 'L'Italia in guerra—il primo anno—1940'*, Roma 1991, pp. 11-17.
6. A concise description of the organisation and the responsibilities of command and its consequences can be found in G. Giorgerini, '*La guerra italiana sul mare La Marina tra vittoria e sconfitta 1940-1943*' (Milano: Mondadori, 2001), pp. 105-123.
7. P. Bertinaria, 'Il Comando Supremo e la Guerra – Preparazione e ritardi', in Commissione italiana di storia militare 'L'Italia in guerra—il primo anno—1940', Roma 1991, p. 80.
8. Mussolini was convinced that the military was not for the Fascism but for King and Country, and that many of their objections came from 'professional bias' and 'stonewalling'. E. Faldella, *L'Italia nella seconda guerra mondiale, Revisione di Giudizi* (Bologna: Cappelli, 1967), p. 58. He was also intolerant towards any opposition, as seen with the removal of General Baistrocchi, a proven Fascist who had opposed the war in Spain. This is a mental attitude not different from that of other dictators across time, and is well documented.
9. A. Santoni, 'Strategie politiche e militari del fascismo dalla Conferenza di Stresa all'intervento in guerra', BAUSMM, March 1994, pp. 7-24.
10. In April 1943, Mussolini would still have the following response sent to whomever asked to interrupt the useless refitting of RN *Conte di Cavour* to use the much-needed material to real emergencies: 'would there be political and prestige needs towards the ally and the enemy which require the speedy return to service of the R. Nave *Cavour* … as a result no diversion of materials can be authorised as per express order of His Excellency the Minister'. G. Giorgerini, 'Le costruzioni navali italiane nel periodo bellico con specifico riferimento al 1942', BAUSMM, December 1992, p. 311.
11. As Alberto Santoni summarises: '… the delusions suffered by Italy … had distant reasons.… In fact a large part of their source was from outdated strategic and tactical concepts, from wrong choices in military preparation of all three Armed Forces, of the inadequacy of the scientific and industrial apparatus of the country, of an adventurous foreign policy and by the illusions of grandeur fomented by the regime'. A. Santoni, 'Strategia marittima e operazioni navali nell'anno 1940', BAUSMM, March 1991, p. 126.

Chapter 8

1. USMM, *La Marina Militare nella seconda guerra mondiale*, vol. XXI, Roma 1972, pp 38-39 e pp. 238-239.
2. Once apprised of the declaration of war (of which he had not been informed), Giovanni Host Venturi, Minister of Communication who was also responsible for the Merchant Navy, ran to Mussolini to protest '"for this act of guilty short-sightedness" which allowed the enemy to seize a very large part of our ships, but received this answer: "There is nothing to worry about, in a few days your ships will be returned to you, tripled in number with French and British ships"'. D. Grandi, *Il Mio Paese. Ricordi autobiografici* (Bologna: Il Mulino, 1985), p. 586.
3. USMM, *La Marina Italiana nella seconda guerra mondiale, vol. IV Le azioni navali in Mediterraneo* (3 Ed., Roma: USMM, 1976) pp. 99-100.
4. *Ibid*., pp. 84-90.
5. C. de Risio, '*Punta Stilo: una chiara lezione dalla Storia*', *Rivista Marittima*, June 1985, p. 33: 'Commander in Chief Mediterranean Fleet at Warspite Command—Command Group cruisers (…)—(…)—(…) Stop time (…) 9 July. Force A miles … Capo Spartivento—Stop Force B … Stop'.

6. USMM, *La Marina Italiana nella seconda guerra mondiale IV*, pp. 106-107.
7. *Ibid.*, pp. 108-109.
8. *Ibid.*, p. 113.
9. *Ibid.*, p. 114.
10. *Ibid.*, p. 116.
11. For a complete view of the action, see F. Mattesini, *La battaglia di Punta Stilo*, USMM (Roma, 2001) and E. Cernuschi and A. Tirondola, *Quando tuonano i grossi calibri, Punta Stilo, 9 luglio 1940*, (Roma: USMM, 2016).
12. USMM, *La Marina Italiana nella seconda guerra mondiale, IV*', pp. 127-128.
13. *Ibid.*, p.133.
14. *Ibid.*, p.138.
15. Enrico Cernuschi writes, analysing British documents (TNA ADM 267/111) that the damage officially reported as an aerial bombing of the HMS *Warspite* (reports of damage repair of 20.7.1940 and of 31.7.1940) are in truth caused by hits or splinters on board received during the naval battle. E. Cernuschi, 'Punta Stilo 19 July 1940—Carta (inglese) canta', *Marinai d'Italia*, August–September 2014, pp. 29-33.
16. Damage sustained from near misses should have prevented the HMS *Eagle* from participating as planned in the attack on Taranto. B. B. Schofield, *La notte di Taranto* (Milano: Mursia, 1974), p.31.
17. USMM, *La Marina Italiana nella seconda guerra mondiale IV Le azioni navali in Mediterraneo* 3th Ed. (Roma: USMM, 1976), pp. 134-135.
18. Evidence of the problems encountered was given by General Tedeschini-Lalli, Commander of the second air fleet. Before the action, he recommended extreme care in identifying the enemy before an attack, hoping for the on-board presence of a Navy observer. In his final report, he wrote: '... in the following very important reason: the offensive actions of the enemy aircraft departed from the aircraft carrier ships, which carrier ... is always present in the battle theatre and gives, compared to the ground bases, the privilege of a rapid intervention', continuing to assert that this privilege revealed itself also in optimal conditions (for the *Regia Aeronautica*) of action near ground fighter bases and that it would always be present in the future. ('*Alcune precisazioni sull'intervento aereo nella battaglia di Capo Stilo*', brought down in Carlo de Risio, '*Punta Stilo: una chiara lezione dalla Storia*', *Rivista Marittima*, June 1985, p. 39).
19. *Ibid.*, pp. 140-141.
20. F. Mattesini, *La battaglia di Punta Stilo*, USMM (Roma: USMM, 2001), attachment 36: Report on the war mission of days 7–9 July 1940 of fleet Admiral Inigo Campioni, Protocol 1/396 SRP, August 17, 1940, pp. 197-198.
21. *Ibid.*, p. 154.
22. G. Santoro, *L'aeronautica italiana nella seconda guerra mondiale* (Roma: Esse, 1950).
23. Note of 13 July 1940. Ciano, *op. cit.*, pp. 451–452.
24. The reference for the military operation, unless otherwise specified, is USMM, '*La Marina Italiana nella seconda guerra mondiale IV*', pp. 184-189.
25. The night of 16 August, a torpedo attack was launched against Alexandria with five aircraft; it failed because of the violent British reaction and for the difficulties encountered in identifying the targets. Rocca, *op. cit.*, pp. 129-130; on 17 September, the cruiser HMS *Kent* was torpedoed next to Bardia, and then towed to Alexandria.
26. The reference for the operation, unless otherwise specified, is *Ufficio Storico della Marina Militare*, '*La Marina Italiana nella seconda guerra mondiale IV*', pp. 219-262.
27. Originally requested by Admiral Dudley Pound in 1935, subsequently resumed in 1938 by Captain Arthur L. St. George Lyster when took command of the *Glorious*; in September 1940, Lyster presented the updated plan to Cunningham at a meeting in Alexandria. T. P. Lowry and J. W. G. Wellham, *Attack on Taranto* (Mechanisburg, PA: Stackpole Books, 1995) p. 58. The original plan called for the participation of two aircraft carriers; however, HMS *Eagle* was out of service because of the damage suffered during the bombing on 11 July after the action at Punta Stilo.
28. Admiralty Historical Section, Naval Operations off Dakar: July–September 1940, Battle Summaries No. 3 and 20 (London: HMSO, 1959), p. 13.
29. Three aeroplanes had been lost in the preceding days because of contamination of the fuel at the depot it came from. Schofield, 1974, pp. 33-35.

30. Another 2,900 metres were available but yet to be installed while to arrive to the planned 12,800 metres, they had to wait for production to be completed. Production reached capacity of 3,600 metres per month in September.
31. M. Simpson, ed., *The Cunningham Papers, vol. 1, The Mediterranean Fleet, 1939– 1942. Selections from the Private and Official Correspondence of Admiral of the Fleet Viscount Cunningham of Hyndhope, O.M., K.T., G.C.B., D.S.O. and Two Bars* (London: Ashgate, 1999), p. 188.
32. 'In a total flying time of about six hours, twenty aircraft had inflicted more damage on the Italian Fleet than was inflicted on the German High Seas Fleet in the daylight action at the battle of Jutland'. O. Warner, *Cunningham of Hyndhope: Admiral of the Fleet* (London: Camelot, 1967), p. 114. Churchill enthusiastically declared to the British House of Commons, 'The result affects decisively the balance of naval power in the Mediterranean and also carries with it reactions upon the naval situation in every quarter of the globe'. D. A. Thomas, *Malta Convoys 1940–1942: The Struggle at Sea* (Barnsley, U.K.: Leo Cooper, 1999), p. 41.

    There can be little doubt that the crippling of half the Italian battlefleet is having, and will continue to have, a marked effect on the course of the war. Without indulging in speculation as to political repercussions, it is already evident that this successful attack has greatly increased our freedom of movement in the Mediterranean and has thus strengthened our control over the central area of this sea.

    Simpson, *op. cit.*, p. 180.
    S. W. Roskill wrote: 'Thus was British maritime power reasserted in the central basin and By the air attack at Taranto and by the two surface ship encounters with the Italian Fleet, Admirals Cunningham and Somerville had established a clear moral ascendancy within the Mediterranean' (*The War at Sea 1939–1945*, vol. 1, The Defensive (London: Her Majesty's Stationery Office, 1956), pp. 301 and 419, respectively) in *Air Power and the Royal Navy,* Geoffrey Till states that Taranto transformed the strategic situation in the Mediterranean (*Air Power and the Royal Navy 1914–1945: A Historical Survey* (London, 1979), p. 179). In 2004, Michael Simpson states that 'the crippling of half the Italian battle fleet was of infinite value' and that by December 1940 'well might Cunningham conclude that 'our control of the Mediterranean was close on being re-established'. M. Simpson, *A Life of Admiral of the Fleet Andrew Cunningham: A Twentieth-Century Naval Leader* (London: Psychology Press, 2004), pp. 74-75.
    The German naval command suggested that the British would now have complete freedom to reinforce their positions in the Mediterranean and Middle East, transfer ships to the Atlantic, and mount offensive operations that would place the Italian land operations in Egypt in jeopardy (Greene and Massignani, *Naval War in the Mediterranean*, pp. 107-108).
33. Ufficio Storico della Marina Militare, *La Marina Italiana nella seconda guerra mondiale IV*, p. 289.
34. G. A. Titterton, *Royal Navy and the Mediterranean* (vol. 2, London: Whitehall History Pub., 2002), p. 72.
35. *Ibid.*, p. 22.
36. *Ibid.*, p. XVI.
37. *Ibid.*, p. XIV.
38. G. Gorla, 'L'italia nella seconda guerra mondiale', Milano, 1959, p. 123; *Commissione italiana di storia militare*, '*L'Italia in guerra. Il 2° anno. 1941*', Roma, 1992. p. 495.
39. Unless otherwise indicated, the reference for the action is *Ufficio Storico della Marina Militare*, '*La Marina Italiana nella seconda guerra mondiale IV*', pp. 345-388.
40. S. O. Playfair, *The Mediterranean and Middle East vol. I* (London: Naval and Military Press, 1954), p. 329.
41. AUSMM, Memorandum 34 bis '*Azione navale nel Golfo di Genova*' of 19 February 1941, AUSMM, Folder '*Promemoria di Supermarina, 1941*', brought down in F. Mattesini, '*Il bombardamento navale di Genova del 9 Febbraio 1941*', BAUSMM, giugno 1990.
42. F. Mattesini, 'Il bombardamento navale di Genova del 9 febbraio 1941', BAUSMM, giugno 1990, pp. 93-98.
43. The Africa Korps was entirely transported to Tripoli by March 1941, with a loss of 3.7% of men and of 5% of material. *Ibid.*, p. 397.
44. USMM, *La Marina Italiana nella seconda guerra mondiale IV*, pp. 389-528, to which one is referring unless otherwise indicated.
45. *Ibid.*, p. 411.

46. Aerial explorations on day X-1 for identification of convoys and enemy units, from 10 of day X-1 escort of the Italian units for aerial protection and to prevent their sighting.
47. CR.43 in the cited text of USMM.
48. Not able to be intercepted by ULTRA.
49. On the matter, see: F. Mattesini, 1998.
50. The availability of this information to the British through ULTRA intelligence, confirmed through direct observation of Cunningham's operational order given two days prior to the operation by Frigate Captain Silvano Brengola, who was taken prisoner on board the HMS *Jervis*, caused an endless controversy and literature on the subject of inexistent traitors: A. Santoni, *Il vero traditore—il ruolo documentato di ULTRA nella guerra del Mediterraneo* (Milano, 1981), pp. 80-81; P.R.O. , ADM 223/76, document F.260, dispatch of 10.07 on 26 March 1941; P.R.O., ADM 199 folder 781, folio 107; P.R.O., ADM 199 folder 781, folio 107 dispatch of 18.20 on 26 March 1941; P.R.O., ADM 199 folder 781, folio 107 dispatch of 18.22 on 26 March 1941; similar decodings gave information on the Axis' estimate of the position and size of the British forces.
51. USMM, *La Marina Italiana nella seconda guerra mondiale IV*, pp. 421-422.
52. The practice of sending reconnaissance planes to cover for the ULTRA's source of information was the norm for British Command.
53. In AUSMM, IAM b. 39 f. 596, there is a request from the *Deutsche Botschaft der Marine attaché* B. Nr. Gkdos 980/41 of 31 May 1941 to the chief of Cabinet of the Minister of the Navy, which asked for information on the type of shells used by RN *Vittorio Veneto*: 'In a report published by the British regarding the daytime battle at Cape Matapan there is the story of the Commander of a British cruiser who said that heavy shells of the *Vittorio Veneto* passed the bulwark [that is how it is written in the text], without exploding'. The research done by other authors: V. P. O'Hara, *Struggle for the middle sea*, pp. 85-91; F. Mattesini, *L'Operazione Gaudo e lo scontro notturno di Capo Matapan* (Roma: USMM, 1998), pp. 137-148) did not bring to light further documentation on the subject.
54. A. Iachino, *Gaudo e Matapan. Storia di un'operazione della guerra navale nel Mediterraneo 27-28-29 marzo 1941* (Milano: Mondadori, 1946), pp. 128-129.
55. F. Mattesini, 1998, pp. 167-182.
56. USMM, *La Marina Italiana nella seconda guerra mondiale IV*, p. 520.
57. The HMS *Prince of Wales* was lost due to damage in the same area.
58. The document, from 1942 (ACS, *Ministero dell'Aeronautica*, Gabinetto, '*Navi Portaerei*', 2.VIII.15) is instead dated 9 July 1941 in Michele Cosentino, *op. cit.*, pp. 166-167.
59. Order of Supreme Command 7726 of 31 March 1941: 'Communication of an order personally given from the Duce-the Regia Marina, until new orders are given, will not undertake actions which will be done beyond the limit of protection of our fighter airplanes'; an order which echoes, in manner and consequences, that of Hitler when he ordered to dismantle the German surface Navy after the battle of the Barents Sea on 31 December 1942.
60. Only after Operation Gaudo was the supply of the first German *De.Te.* unblocked; there were several occasions when it had been possible to reflect on the nighttime performance of the British fleet, such as the battle that took place the night of 11–12 October 1940 between HMS *Ajax*, HMS *Orion*, and HMS *Sydney* and a light Italian formation; RN *Artigiere* and RN *Airone* and RN *Ariel* were sunk and minor damage was inflicted on HMS *Ajax* (which had radar) regardless of seven hits on board.
61. The information on Operation Halberd, unless otherwise specified, is from F. Mattesini, '*L'Operazione Halberd—Cronistoria di una mancata battaglia navale*', BAUSMM, December 1990, pp. 137-218.

Chapter 9

1. Cernuschi and O'Hara, 2007, p. 72.
2. E. Bagnasco and E. Cernuschi, 'La portaerei Impero?' *Storia Militare* (Parma: Albertelli, May 2006), pp. 51-59.
3. *Ibid.*, pp. 138-139.
4. G. Giorgerini, '*Le costruzioni navali italiane nel periodo bellico con specifico riferimento al 1942*', BAUSMM, December 1992, p. 308.

5. 20 January 1941, assigned to MARCOMINAV, Michele Cosentino, *Le portaerei italiane* (Parma, 2011), p. 144.
6. AUSMM, *Raccolta di base, Cartella Portaerei*, '*Progetto di trasformazione del piroscafo Roma in Nave portaerei*', 6 June 1941.
7. To be collected from those of the six light cruisers of the *Capitani Romani*-class, suspended at the start of war.
8. Cosentino, *op. cit.*, p. 145.
9. *Ibid.*, p. 147.
10. ACS, *Ministero dell'Aeronautica*, '*Nave Portaerei*', 1942, 2.VIII.3.
11. Cosentino, *op. cit.*, pp. 149-162.
12. AUSMM, *Nave 'Aquila'*, Folder n.1, '*Carteggio relazioni missioni in Germania, visita n.p.a "Graf Zeppelin"*', 1941–43. As a major of the *Genio Navale*, engineer Astengo of Ansaldo participated in the missions, he then played a crucial role in the incident of the V-1. The *Kriegsmarine* made available, in addition to the complete plans of the *Graf Zeppelin*, the precious experience of the 2,200 deck-landing trials done on the ground.
13. AUSMM, *Nave 'Aquila'*, Folder n.7, meetings of 5 March 1942 and of 9 March 1942.
14. AUSMM, *Nave 'Aquila'*, Folder n.4, memorandum15 October 1942, '*Nave portaerei Aquila e Sparviero*'.
15. *Ibid.*, '*Informazioni—NPA Estere NPA Giapponesi 1942-43*', 3/B, memorandum for his Excellency Navy Undersecretary of State of 14 October 1942.
16. Cosentino, *op. cit.*, p. 187.
17. AUSMM, *Nave 'Aquila'*, Folder n.3/f, '*Apparecchi rilevamenti r.t. Radiotelemetri Radiolocalizzatori*'.
18. *Ibid.*, *Navi portaerei- Radiotelemetri del 9 gennaio 1943 da Ispettorato Artiglieria e Munizionamento a Marinarmi*; it is interesting to note how in a memorandum of 19 March 1942, the *Kriegsmarine* specified that the rangefinders aboard the ships of the KM could locate aircraft at low altitude at a distance of 7 km and aircraft at high altitude at 35–45 km without being able to detect the actual altitude. Based on these feats, considered equal to the Italian apparatus, the choice of radar devices to be installed on RN *Aquila* was postponed (*ibid.*, '*Installazione radiolocalizzatori su N.P.A.*' of 17 March 1942 from the Office of Chief of Staff of the *Regia Marina* to Marinavia).
19. AUSMM, *Nave 'Aquila'*, Folder n.7, '*Promemoria per l'Ecc. l'Ammiraglio Riccardi, Capo di Stato Maggiore della R. Marina, n.90*', 28 January 1943.
20. E. Bagnasco, '*La portaerei nella marina italiana*', *Rivista Marittima*, Roma 1989, p. 71.
21. E. Bagnasco and A. Rastrelli, '*L'affondamento' della portaerei Aquila a Genova nel 1945. Un avvenimento storico controverso avviato a soluzione attraverso l'analisi di fotografie ed un "confront" internazionale*', BAUSMM, Year VI, June 1992, pp. 219-252.
22. It is usually reported that the charge exploded, with scarce damage: *Ufficio Storico della Marina Militare*, '*La Marina Italiana nella seconda guerra mondiale XIV—I mezzi d'assalto*' 4th Ed. (Roma 2001) pp. 259-260.
23. Reynolds, C. G., *Hitler's Flattop: The End of the Beginning*. (Annapolis: United States Naval Institute Proceedings, January 1967), p. 47.
24. Cosentino, *op. cit.* pp. 180-182.
25. According to '*Programma Navale 1943—Armamento*', AUSMM, MARISTAT IAM, b24 f360; Cosentino states 24.
26. Cosentino, *op. cit.*, pp. 183-185.
27. AUSMM, Base Archive, Folder *Portaerei*, *Trasformazioni di P/fi in Navi P.A.*, 11 November 1942.
28. Cosentino, *op. cit.*, pp. 185-186.
29. E. Bagnasco, 'La portaerei nella marina italiana', *Rivista Marittima*, Roma, 1989, p. 83.

Chapter 10

1. Although Ansaldo's economic output in its first thirty years of operations was mediocre, within the company, there accumulated practical knowledge and technical expertise that made it into a unique experience in the unified Italy's industrial landscape. The Ansaldo manpower, comprised of turner workers, repairers, assemblers, boilermakers, smelters, and power hammer workmen, had been

shaped by British 'master of art' and was so rare that the company would pay them even during times of reduced activity to avoid the risks to having them emigrate. Ansaldo. *Organizzazione e lavoro di Roberto Tolaini*, February 2008, in Testo for Storiaindustria.it (as seen 20.10.2017).

2. In this aspect, the first to protect their workforce, of which we have definite information, were the Venetians, who guaranteed the salary of the '*arsenalotti*' (the workers of the Venice Arsenal), also during times when there was no work.
3. A general-purpose manpower team, from which there emerged those foremen who had excellent technical experience and were in charge of the hiring of new workers, contracted the salary of newly hired workers with the engineers, had a say in the matter of fixing piece rates and side by side with the engineers but often with a superior authority, which came from their 'know how', had the responsibility of organizing the work. In actuality, there were limited options of control on cost production because the foremen, careful with the quality of production but less careful with the total costs, imposed the time and manner of work. In terms of employed workers, the workforce jumped from 500 units in the '50s to 700 at the beginning of the '80s. Ansaldo. *Organizzazione e lavoro di Roberto Tolaini* February 2008 in Testo for Storiaindustria.it (as seen 20.10.2017).
4. Organisational changes were proposed with the goal of consolidating the hierarchical outlooks and coming up to the war, the Taylor system was carefully studied. With the start of the war, employment notably increased and this caused related organisational problems because there were men, women, and young people who needed to be trained quickly in order to fill the war commissions. In this context, Perrone family energetically proceeded to introduce new work methods derived from the Taylor method. Ansaldo. *Organizzazione e lavoro di Roberto Tolaini*, 2008 (as seen 20.10.2017).
5. With employees numbering approximately 1,000 managers and office workers and a maximum of 13,000 blue-collar workers. G. de Rosa, *Storia dell'Ansaldo—6. Dall'IRI alla guerra 1930-1945* (Bari: Laterza, 1999), p. 39.
6. *Ibid*., pp. 44-45.
7. The hiring of young technicians with degrees and engineers was necessary in order to rejuvenate and update the technical aspects of the production structure, as their manufacturing process was still largely based upon the discretion of workshops foremen. *Ibid*., p. 69.
8. *Ibid*., p. 79.
9. The piece rates were often adjusted to force the workers to intensify their work pace. At the same time, however, the company introduced welfare and recreational activities and opened a school for apprentices, the Ansaldo-Siac, which proved to be an efficient training tool.
10. In 1936, the intra-firm school of apprentices Ansaldo-Siac was created. From it emerged, in the words of Rocca, 'the aristocracy of our employees'. de Rosa, *op. cit*., p. 184.
11. *Ibid*., pp. 171-176.
12. Achille Piazzai was the most forward thinking and brilliant director of the years 1930–40, a native of Città di Castello, he was educated in the Genoese Naval School, from there, he joined Ansaldo immediately. He promoted the establishment of specialised schools for the Ansaldo staff. He left the company in 1940 because of the discontent caused by the introduction of new work methods to the shipyards and died in Genoa in 1955.
13. Marcenaro, M. E. Tonizzi, *Dalla Regia Scuola Superiore Navale alla Facoltà di Ingegneria 1870-1935—Fonti e studi per la storia dell'università di Genova* (Genova: 1997).
14. The *Regia Navale* High School, established in June 1870, is an integral part of a national programme to promote technical-scientific education. Vittorio Emanuele II defined the Statute and Regulation of the *Regia Scuola Superiore Navale* with decrees n. 5749 of 25 June, and n. 6170 of 4 December 1870. At the time, only three other such institutions existed in Europe: in Berlin, Paris, and Kensington. The Genoese school's charter was inspired by that of the Berlin school, which had educational traditions similar to Italy's.
15. The titles awarded by the school were as follows:

    Diploma of engineer of naval construction in wood and iron (triennial class). In addition to technical subjects also planned were courses on economy, Italian literature, English language and literature, and marine law.
    Diploma for eligibility for teaching in the institutions of the navy for secondary education.

The diploma of engineer, equivalent to a degree, allowed admission to the contests for entering the *Genio Navale*, while that for the eligibility to teach was only a preferential title for nomination of professor in the nautical institutions (www.storiain.net/storia/la-regia-scuola-superiore-navale-di-genova/).
This is the sequence of denominations:
1870–1905 *Regia Navale* High School.
1905–1932 *Regia Navale* School of Engineering.
1932–1936 *Regia* School of Engineering.
1936–1972 Department of Engineering—Institutes of Naval Architecture and of Construction of Naval commercial ships,
The academic course of specialisation, after two common years of mathematics and engineering included:
First year: Thermodynamics and technical physics, mechanics applied to the machinery with design, mechanics applied to construction with design, construction of naval merchant vessels with design, mechanic technology chemistry, applied to machinery design (elective subject).
Second year: Hydraulics and hydraulic machinery with practical exercises, thermal steam machines with design, construction of machinery with design, construction of boilers with design, construction of naval merchant vessels with naval architectural design, warship construction (elective subject).
Third year: Electrical engineering and naval magnetism with practical exercises, internal combustion motors, naval architecture, construction of military vessels, maritime law and industrial economy. www.storiain.net/storia/la-regia-scuola-superiore-navale-di-genova/ (as seen 18.08.2017).

16. He would humorously comment 'they did not send me to the Alpini (mountain troops) because they realised just in time that I knew how to ski well and that I was a good rock climber'.
17. See *Sovetsky Soyuz* chapter.
18. G. Giorgerini, '*Le costruzioni navali italiane nel periodo bellico con specifico riferimento al 1942*', BAUSMM, December 1992, p. 307.
19. F. Ceccarelli, '*La corazzata Impero: storia di una nave mai nata*', BAUSMM, June 1992, p. 255.
20. *Ibid.*, p. 256.
21. *Ibid.*, pp. 257-260.
22. *Ibid.*, pp. 260-262.
23. *Ibid.*, pp. 263-264.
24. *Ibid.*, p. 265.
25. E. Bagnasco, E. Cernuschi, '*Capitani Romani*', *Storia Militare*, February 2015, pp. 17-19.
26. Stato Maggiore Esercito—Ufficio Storico, *Diario storico del Comando Supremo*, Volume IV (1.5.1941-31.8.1941) Tome I (Roma, 1992), p. 652.
27. *Ibid.*, p. 369.
28. Between 1921 and 1924, he was also a member of the *Regia Marina*'s '*Comitato Progetti Navi*', developing research on an aircraft carrier of 8,000 tons.
29. Stato Maggiore Esercito—Ufficio Storico, *Diario storico del Comando Supremo*, Volume V (1.9.1941-31.12.1941) Tome I (text) (Roma, 1995), p. 100.
30. *Ibid.*, p. 164.
31. *Ibid.*, p. 240.
32. AC, '*Relazione sui risultati in vasca navale int.* 1943/8' (date added in pen), f. 1.
33. Pugliese was responsible for General Management of Naval Construction and Mechanics (Maricost).
34. *Comitato Ammiragli*, 21 and 22 March 1934. The preliminary plan presented included nine pieces of 381 in triple towers, 12/152 in twin towers and 30 knots. The admirals, while approving the proposal in principal, asked to examine the possibility of installing ten pieces of 381 (in two quadruples and one twinned or two triples and one quadruple—in both cases, the quadruple would be at stern); for the AA armament, at least four quadruple 60 mm AA. Only Admiral Foschini expressed his preference for an armament of 8/406 with two triples and one twinned. More details were brought to the attention of the *Comitato Ammiragli* on 5 July 1935.
35. Wave profile along the ship are also available.
36. Insean Archive, Folder C.123.

37. Insean Archive, C.134, Letter of 9 March 1934.
38. In February 1942, Marinalles (ship outfitters) asked if it was necessary to proceed with the bow modification for RN *Impero*: in the response to the Office of General Staff of the *Regia Marina*, it is specified: 'The necessity to raise the bow of all units of the *Impero* type came about through trials at sea during which it was established that with bow waves and high speed, the fire direction of the heavy artillery and the surveillance of the lookouts was strongly disturbed'. AUSMM, '*Impero*', 1942, communication of 10 February 1942.
39. CA, 'Note'.
40. de Rosa, *op. cit.*, p. 161.
41. HSVA tested hulls for the fast ocean liners *Europa* and *Bremen*. Additionally, studies on the ship hull form (1931), on propeller cavitation (1933), as well as on wake measurements (1935–36) were carried out for the French fast steamship *Normandie* (1935).
42. AC, '*Note ed osservazioni tecniche Sebastopoli,* August 1942: [for the bow] *Riprendere studi prodieri, p. 305-350, 1934-5—su correzione ex p.509 sub 235-271 Amburgo—Campagnoli /Carlarino*".
43. AC—*Relazione sui risultati in vasca navale int.*
44. There is a reference here to a document by engineer Piazzai '*Incontri con il GN 1934-35*', ff. 22-26, evidently available at the time of the writing of engineer Campagnoli's notes.
45. This note can explain the difference found between the rudder used for the *Littorio*-class and that found in the project *Impero* as aircraft carrier, which show a slightly smaller rudder it is also depicted in the model at the Museum of Venice, testifying to its provenance from the Ansaldo offices.
46. Studies and applications in civil use had already been done. Non-specified United States studies are cited in the Campagnoli archives, for a summary see Allington, P., & Greenhill, B., *The First Atlantic Liners: Seamanship in the Age of Paddle Wheel, Sail and Screw* (London, 1997), pp. 35-47.
47. C. Boccalatte, '*La vasca navale della Spezia e la nascita della moderna architettura navale in Italia*', BAUSMM, September 2013, p. 60.
48. A. Yoshimura, *Battleship Musashi: The Making and Sinking of the World's Biggest Battleship* (Tokyo, 1999), p. 30; J. Skulski, *Anatomy of the Ship: The Battleship Yamato*, (London, 1995), p. 8.
49. It is possible that it is the hull used for the model preserved in the Historic Naval Museum of Venice.
50. All of the energy that goes to produce whirlwinds and waves is dispersed and is distanced from running the ship and the efficiency of the motor thrust.
51. AC—'*Sui lavori Campini*', f.2.
52. B. J. Ford, *Secret Weapons: Death Rays, Doodlebugs and Churchill's Golden Goose*, (Cambridge, 2013); Steven J. Zaloga, Jim Laurier, *V1-V2-V3, volume 3; V-1 Flying Bomb 1942–52: Hitler's Infamous 'Doodlebug'* (Oxford, 2005), p. 6.
53. A. Thomas, *V1 Flying Bomb Aces* (Oxford, 2013), p. 7.
54. K. P. Werrel, *The Evolution of the Cruise Missile* (Maxwell, Air Force Base, 1985), p. 42.
55. AC—'DAAC 40 Campini'.
56. *Ibid.*
57. AC, '*Sui lavori Campini Sul finire 1941*', f. 2.
58. AC, 'DAAC 40 Campini'.
59. *Ibid.* In a pencilled note, engineer Campagnoli mentions a comment of engineer Piazzai from 1943: 'Campini, the only true genius albeit misunderstood!' Not a small acknowledgement from a group of experimenters and doers with great experience and innovation such as the engineers at Ansaldo.
60. *Ibid.*, '*Per Richin, dei progetti dopo il 1942*', f. 1.
61. *Op. cit.*, 'DAAC 40 Campini'.
62. *Ibid.*
63. Information from www.deutscheluftwaffe.de (as seen 10.04.2017), which has a large selection of original documents.
64. AC, 'DAAC 40 Campini.
65. See chapter '1940 Campini's DAAC'.
66. AUSMM—MARISTAT IAM 39, b. 25, f. 380.
67. Ansaldo Archive—Work in progress 1941–44, heavy artillery factory, six turrets and six gun mounts of 120/50 single, by 31 August 1941; fifteen single complexes by 31 March 1943.
68. A. de Toro, '*Il programma navale italiano del 1939*', *Storia Militare*, November 2013.

69. AC, '*Sui lavori Campini nel finire 1941*', p. 2.
70. *Ibid*., f.1.
71. Incidentally, Sweden had acquired four ships from the *Regia Marina*, which had been confiscated (and then released after a diplomatic crisis between Sweden and Great Britain) by the Royal Navy in 1939 while *en route*, under Swedish flag, for the new ports, invoking on the British side the Law of Angary towards two non-belligerent powers.
72. AC, '*Sui lavori Campini nel finire 1941*', f. 3.
73. *Ibid*., f. 1.
74. '*Bornholmske Samlinger*', vol. 9, Rønne 1976, pp. 80-90. The illustrations and photographs taken by the Danes and also sent to Danish authorities in Copenhagen were smuggled in to the Allies through different channels; a first attempt was discovered by the Germans at Elsinore and Lieutenant Christiansen (who was head of the resistance on the island, strategic for its position of closure of the Baltic, therefore with excellent the excellent possibility of observing the *Kriegsmarine*'s movements) was harshly tortured before the Danish Government was able to transfer him to Sweden. A second copy arrived in Great Britain through the embassy in Sweden. On the island, the Germans had installed observation stations for the test flights of the V-1s.
75. AC, '*Sui lavori Campini nel finire 1941*', ff. 1-2; Danish reports specify that the warhead, substituted with cement, had broken up during impact; from the condition of the remains, it is easy to deduce the causes of the mistaken placement of the jet motor during reconstruction.
76. It is a curiosity to note that her dimensions are very close to those of the modern aircraft carrier Nave *Cavour* (C 550) 244 metres long overall and 51 metres of maximum width.
77. AC, 'Fi 106'; is the only place in the AC documents where 'Fi 106' is used.
78. AC, '*Sulle eliche Impero da studi Littorio*': related are the technical discussions previously held with Pugliese and the Commission for the contest for the *Littorio* project and regarding the choices 'issued from the Commission' concerning the propellers, ignoring the experimental results presented by Ansaldo, which showed far inferior mechanical losses. The best configuration of RN *Impero*, according to Campagnoli, as aircraft carrier version 843 is with four-blade propellers.
79. Reggiane Re 2001 OR drawings by M. L. Watts (own work) (CC0), via Wikimedia Commons.
80. On the original, the funnel appears of a much larger width, positioned more towards the external side of the island. It was preferred to keep it in this configuration as coherent with other available designs.
81. AUSMM, Archive 37 L6, *Archivio* 37, V3 and V3bis.
82. The use of composite and light materials, such as the large-scale use of welding for hulls and superstructures, is part of the noteworthy effort product by the Italian shipyards, with a total of 620,000 tons of new construction, both military and civil. See BAUSMM, G. Giorgerini, '*Le costruzioni navali italiane nel periodo bellico con specifico riferimento al 1942*', December 1992.
83. R. Watton, *The Aircraft Carrier Victorious* (London: Conway Maritime Press, 1991), p. 8.
84. G. Galati, *100 Years of Radar* (Springer, 2016), Complement L, p. 36.
85. *Ibid*., pp. 46-47.
86. E. Cernuschi, *Marinelettro e il radiotelemetro italiano—Lo sviluppo e l'evoluzione del radar navale (1933-1943)* (Roma, 1995), p. 127.
87. To be consistent with the position taken by AD (CEO), Rocca regarded potential orders to destroy the machinery both in case of Allied invasion and—after 25 July 1943—to avoid it being used by ex-German allies: '... any order for self-destruction will not be carried out except through directives and authorisation of the AD himself'. Rocca's attempt to keep Ansaldo out of politics, particularly the RSI, becomes strained at the end of 1943, when it was forced by events starting from half of 1944; de Rosa, *op. cit*., pp. 233-234, 237-238, 241-245.
88. AC, '*Per Richin*', ff. 1-2; engineer Astengo was subsequently arrested and deported in Germany.
89. AC, '*Relazione sui risultati in vasca navale int. 1943/8*', f. 1.
90. A. Santoni, *Storia e politica navale dell 'età contemporanea* (Gaeta, 1993), pp. 163-164, correctly cites the arrogant assurance constantly being placed in proper methods by authoritarian regimes, who, in this particular case, never abandoned their complete faith in the impenetrability of the cyphering machines ENIGMA and HAGELIN.
91. Analyses on the data in Santoni, *Il vero traditore*, Milano, 1981.

92. Werrel, *op. cit.*, p. 63.
93. George Mindling, Robert Bolto, *US Air Force Tactical Missiles 1949–1969: The Pioneers*, (Morrisville: Lulu, 2011).
94. Werrel, *op. cit.*, p. 67.
95. *Ibid.*, p. 68.
96. E. Gröner, 1990, p. 38.
97. S. Breyer, *Battleships of the World* (London, 1980), p. 282.
98. *Ibid.*, p. 296.
99. W. H. Garzke and R. O. Dulin Jr, *Battleships: Allied Battleships in WWII* (Annapolis, 1980), p. 328.
100. E. Bagnasco, A. de Toro, *Le Navi da Battaglia classe Littorio, 1937-1948* (Parma: Ermanno Albertelli Editore, 2008), pp. 260-261.
101. Data reported for RN *Impero* in D. Thomaier, *Unterwasser-Ansprengversuche am Schlachtschiff IMPERO in der Bucht von Capodistria, 42° Deutsche Gesellschaft fuer Schiffahrts-u. Marinegeschichte Acta*, (Berlin 2013). These differ slightly from what is reported in the designs for the *Littorio–Vittorio Veneto* pair.
102. B. Corradi, 'La protezione subacquea tipo "Pugliese"', *Rivista Marittima*, February 1982, pp. 91-93.
103. AUSMM, *Archivio* 37 L6, *Archivio* 37 V3 e V3 bis.
104. AUSMM, *Archivio* 37 L6, *Corazzata Littorio (poi Italia)—Danni riportati l'11 novembre 1940 durante incursione aerea su Taranto*.
105. AUSMM, *Archivio* 37 L6, *Comunicazione da* RN *Italia a Nave Eugenio di Savoia per FF.NN. del 17 settembre 1943 'Avarie causate da offesa nemica nella navigazione da La Spezia a Marsa Scirocco'*.
106. Nicknamed Fritz X, the FX 1400 was the world's first precision guided weapon deployed in combat.
107. AUSMM, *Archivio* 37 V3, 'RN *Vittorio Veneto Servizio del Genio Navale—Relazione circa i danni subiti dalla nave a causa del bombardamento del 5 giugno 1943 XXI*'.
108. W. H. Garzke and R. O. Dulin, *Battleships: Axis and Neutral Battleships in World War II* (Annapolis: Naval Institute Press, 1985), p. 427.
109. A. Catalano Gonzaga di Cirella, *Per l'onore dei Savoia*, (Milano: Mursia, 1996), p. 91.
110. *Ibid.*, p. 93.
111. The damage and salvage operations and transport to Genoa of RN *Caio Duilio* are described in detail by Rear-Admiral Armando Andri in A. Andri, E. Andri, 'Recuperi navali in basso fondale—Leonardo da Vinci Duilio—Corazziere—Pontone posa massi', Genoa 2015, pp. 75-97.
112. B. Corradi, 'La protezione subacquea tipo "Pugliese"', *Rivista Marittima*, February, 1982, pp. 91-93.
113. D. Thomaier, *Unterwasser-Ansprengversuche am Schlachtschiff IMPERO in der Bucht von Capodistria, 42° Deutsche Gesellschaft fuer Schiffahrts-u. Marinegeschichte Acta*, (Berlin 2013).
114. Courtesy of Dieter Thomaier. The mentioned tests 3, 4, and 6 refer to the test pontoon II (*Sprengziel II*). This test pontoon II were the adapted middle part of the old German battleship *Preussen*. The test section represents always a 1–1 part of the torpedo defence system of a new German ship, each test with 300 kg of S1 (equivalent of 465 kg of TNT) explosive:
    Test 3 refers to *Admiral Scheer, Admiral Graf Spee*
    Test 4 refers to *Scharnhorst, Gneisenau*
    Test 6 refers to *Bismarck, Tirpitz*
    In each test, the internal bulkhead was cracked or damaged; the anti-torpedo systems were anyway narrower than the Pugliese on board RN *Impero*.
115. L. Zani, 'La marina italiana e l'unione sovietica tra le due guerre'—Parte Prima 1929-1933', BAUSMM, June 1994.
116. Insean Archive.
117. 22,000 tons fully loaded, according to J. Rohwer, M. S. Monakov, *Stalin's Ocean-Going Fleet*, (London, 2001), p. 63.
118. The following specifications are available regarding this project: standard displacement 22,000 tons, fully loaded 26,700 tons, length 241.5 metres, breadth 28 metres, draught 7.45 metres, 240,000 hp, 37 knots, range 7,000 nmi at 20 knots, 3 × 3 250 mm, 6 × 2 130 mm, 6 × 2 100 mm, 32 × 45, 2 × 3 533-mm TT, two catapults, and four aircraft. *Ibid.*, p. 96.
119. Cernuschi, 2001, p. 152.
120. Breyer, *op. cit.*, p. 374; Rohwer, Monakov, *op. cit.*, p. 96.

121. Васильев А. М., and Морин А. Б, *Суперлинкоры Сталина.* (*Советский Союз, Кронштадт: Сталинград*, 2008), p. 65.
122. Васильев, А. М., '*ЛИНЕЙНЫЕ КОРАБЛИ ТИПА СОВЕТСКИЙ СОЮЗ*', *Санкт-Петербург*, (2006), p. 69.
123. The tested systems were the USA model used for the *West Virginia*-class, the Pugliese model used for the *Littorio*, the 'Pugliese' model used for the *Brennero* tankers and the Ansaldo model with three compartments, used in the UP41, the model used on the HMS *Hood* and two Soviet designs. *Ibid.*
124. 'The antitorpedo system adopted in the project 23 had been very difficult to manufacture. In addition, a series of experimental explosions completed in autumn 1939 on 1:1 project 23 sections has identified advantages in the USA system'. Васильев А. М.,Морин А. Б, *Суперлинкоры Сталина.* (*Советский Союз, Кронштадт: Сталинград*, 2008), p. 135.
125. Richard Worth instead records 'The Pugliese system, revealed as defective, gave way to a more conventional layered system' for the next units. There is no confirmation for this statement in Vasiliev's text, nor in the trials done; we will see later that the Soviet design of the system, as much as it was positive during trials, did have design and manufacturing problems and defects. R. Worth, *Fleets of World War Two* (Boston: Da Capo Press, 2001), p. 243.
126. It is interesting to note that during these trials the Pugliese system had its original design with 40 mm of thickness of the resistant bulkhead, and that, in 1939, it was decided to reduce it to 35 mm in the areas where the system was at its largest and 30 mm to the lower section. Васильев, А. М., *ЛИНЕЙНЫЕ КОРАБЛИ ТИПА СОВЕТСКИЙ СОЮЗ*, (*Санкт-Петербур*, 2006), p. 69.
127. *Ibid.*, p. 117.
128. *Ibid.*, p. 188.
129. AC, '*Note ed osservazioni tecniche Sebastopoli, August 1942*'.
130. E. Gröner, *German Warships 1815-9145 Volume One: Major Surface Vessels* (Annapolis: Naval Institute Press, 1990), p. 38.
131. 'There were Italian builders in Soviet shipyards up to the declaration of hostilities in June 1941'. S. McLaughlin, Russian www.amazon.com/Russian-Soviet-Battleships-Stephen-McLaughlin/dp/1557504814/ref=la_B001K8OBSS_ Soviet Battleships (Annapolis: Naval Institute Press, 2003), p. 363.
132. The difficulty of the Soviet shipbuilding methods in following more advanced standards had already been seen for the planned responses of *Tashkent*'s sister ships, which wear never built J. Rohwer, M. S. Monakov, *op. cit.*, p. 46.
133. W. H. Garzke and R. O. Dulin, *op. cit.*, pp. 422-423.
134. N. Friedman, *Battleships: Design and Development 1905-1945* (New York: Mayflower, 1978), p. 83. Friedman offers a better view of the physics beneath of the underwater protection system compared to Garzke and Dulin.
135. The Royal Navy also carried out experiments at a scale of 1:1 in Chatham, for the HMS *Nelson* (protection for a charge of 750 lb (340 kg) of TNT at contact with the ship); protection of the HMS *King George V* (based on three levels of bulkheads) was planned as protection for a load of 1,000 lb (450 kg) of TNT. *The Design and Construction of British Warships, 1939-1945: The Official Record: Major Surface Warships*, (London: HMSO, 1995), pp. 24, 31.
136. The Russian tests referred to the outline used for the West Virginia; without getting into the details of construction, the *North Carolina* had five bulkheads, the *South Dakotas* and the *Iowa* had four, with an inclined armoured belt in the system. Warship International N°2, 1994, W. H. Garzke, E. O. Dulin Jr, *The Bismarck's Final Battle*, p. 190; the system of underwater protection of the Bismarck, on two levels, is defined by the authors themselves as 'poor design practice'. *Ibid.*
137. AUSMM, Folder *Impero*, Communication of 21 November 1942, 'RN *Impero—impianti da 152/55 da trasportare da La Spezia a Trieste*'.

Epilogue

1. ACS, *Ministero dell'Aeronautica*, Gabinetto, '*Navi Portaerei*', 2.VIII.15.
2. See '*Promemoria per il Sig. Colonn. G.N. Gagnotto in occasione della missione in Germania*' of 20.1.1942, AUSMM, '*Nave P.A. Aquila*', folder n°1, correspondence reports of missions in Germany.

3. AUSMM, '*Risposte al questionario per l'impiego notturno della aviazione imbarcata sulla N.P.A. Giapponesi*' (from Commander Toyoda in the meeting of 11.3.1942 at the Ministry of the Navy), f. 5.
4. AUSMM, '*La Marina Italiana nella seconda guerra mondiale, vol. XXI, tome 2*'.
5. M. Cosentino, *op. cit.*, pp. 191-192.
6. AUSMM, *Cartella 'Impero'*, Memorandum for CSM of the Navy 17 July 1943.

Appendix

1. E. Bagnasco and E. Cernuschi, 'La portaerei Impero?', *Storia Militare*, May 2006 (Parma: Ermanno Albertelli Edizioni, 2006).
2. AC, '*Relazione sui risultati in vasca navale int.* 1943–8'.
3. AC, '*Timone modello Impero 3.42*'.
4. AC, '*Sui lavori Campini*', f. 2.
5. Office of the Chief of Staff of the *R. Marina, Ufficio Storico*, '*Onomastica navale—Studio di massima per l'assegnazione dei nomi alle unità della nostra Marina Militare*', Roma 1931.
6. A. da Zara, *Pelle di ammiraglio* (Milano: Mondadori, 1949), pp. 197 and 262.
7. *Regio Decreto Legge* 19/5/1938 n. 782
8. AC, '*Impero*' 4-1943.
9. P. Tiberio, *L'invenzione del radar: il contributo di Ugo Tiberio dal 1935 al 1943* (Pianeta Galileo 2012), p. 219.
10. U. Tiberio, 'Sullo sviluppo delle cognizioni radar italiane durante la guerra', *Rivista Marittima*, April 1951, p. 42.
11. *Ibid.*, p. 219.
12. *Ibid.*, p. 220.
13. U. Tiberio, *op. cit.*, April 1951, p. 44.
14. F. Galati, '100 Years of Radar', Switzerland 2016, pp. 33, 34; and Francesco Mattesini, '*I radiolocalizzatori della Regia Marina*', BAUSMM, September 1995, pp. 106-107.
15. F. Mattesini, 'I radiolocalizzatori della Regia Marina', BAUSMM, September 1995, pp. 107-109.
16. *Ibid.*, p. 112.
17. For the development of radar theory and technology, see G. Galati, 'Lo sviluppo del Radar in Italia e all'estero' in *Storia delle telecomunicazioni*, vol. II, Firenze 2001, pp. 589-607.
18. *Ibid.*, pp. 115-118.
19. AUSMM, *Ispettcrato Artiglieria e Munizionamento*, b.23
20. *Ibid.*
21. Maristat, *Reparto Mobilitazione—Difesa e Servizi*, b.155.
22. U. Tiberio, 'Some Historical Data Concerning the First Italian Naval Radar', IEEETrans. AES, vol. 5, 1979, p. 734.
23. F. Mattesini, 'I radiolocalizzatori della Regia Marina', Bollettino d'Archivio USMM, September 1995, pp. 124.
24. *Ibid.*, p. 125.
25. AUSMM, *Ispettorato Artiglieria e Munizionamento*, b.23
26. *Ibid.*
27. F. Mattesini, September 1995, p. 126.
28. *Ibid.*, pp. 128-130.
29. *Ibid.*, pp. 130-136. This, despite the fact that the organisation Ra.Ri. was operational and was supposed to coordinate the entire complement of Italian military and industry radio detection (author's note).
30. AUSMM, *Marina Germanica in Italia*, b.1: *conversazione tra Ammiraglio Löwisch e Comandate Tallarigo*.
31. F. Mattesini, September 1995, p. 139.
32. *Ibid.*, p. 129. Also in this instance, the national industry was pointing out the impossibility of developing the technology requested due to already existing commitments.
33. Santoni, *Il vero traditore*, pp. 130-136.

34. F. Mattesini, September 1995, p. 145. Includes a memorandum from Admiral Riccardi (*Archivio Ufficio Storico Esercito*, historic diary of Marshal Cavallero, b.1346).
35. *Ibid.*, pp. 146-149.
36. *Ibid.*, pp. 149-150.
37. *Ibid.*, pp. 150-155.
38. Letter of 15 June, 1942, prot. Skl Qu A III 2015/42, brought down in F. Mattesini, September 1995, pp. 196-198.
39. AUSMM, *Scontri navali ed operazioni di guerra*, b. 57. '*Rapporto Operazione Mediterraneo Orientale 14-15-16 giugno 1942-XX*'.
40. F. Mattesini, 'I radiolocalizzatori della Regia Marina—parte seconda', BAUSMM, December 1995, p. 27.
41. *Ibid.*, p. 29.
42. *Ibid.*, p. 54.
43. *Ibid.*, p. 30.
44. *Ibid.*, p. 58-60.
45. E. Cernuschi, *Marinelettro e il radiotelemetro italiano – Lo sviluppo e l'evoluzione del radar navale (1933-1945)* (Roma: Rivista Marittima, 1995).
46. de Rosa, *op. cit.*, tab. 6.
47. Sources: *Registro delle costruzioni dal 1873 al 1970* (*Archivio privato* A. Rastelli, Milano); Note *sull'attività dei cantieri navali Ansaldo S.A.*, ASA, FE, 266/1. Production numbers in cursive, from 174 to 195, refer to the items manufactured in the Cerusa yard after it transferred to Ansaldo. From n. 559, double numbering was eliminated. Some figures of the *Registro* are illegible. From the latter there are 2. 21 K.T. built, while the 'Notes' mention 32, including 20 units under construction by 8 September. We have not been able to determine the fate of 11 of these units. Also mentioned in the 'Notes' are the following minor construction jobs (within the period of 10 June 1940 to 8 September 1943): a) 6 barges for the Navy, 2 work pontoons, 2 pontoons for Army tanks, 2 floating cranes for the Air Force, 2 ferry pontoons for the Military, 2 pump boats for the Navy, 2 floating structures for accumulator chargers; b) commercial units: 2 Finmare ships that can be disassembled (started before transferring to the Ansaldo shipyard); 4 S. Antonio floating structures for accumulator chargers and motorboats, under construction the end of September 1943.
48. Corrected a likely transcription error present in the original, where the following was written: 3/5 × 3.416 tons and 7/12 × 1239 tons.

Bibliography

Archives

Ministero degli Affari Esteri (MAE), Affari Politici 1931–1945, Busta 30.

Archivio INSEAN (Istituto Nazionale per Studi ed Esperienze di Architettura Navale), Cartella C.123, Cartella C.134.

Archivio Fondazione Ansaldo, Lavori in corso 1941-44.

Archivio Centrale dello Stato (ACS), Ministero dell'Aeronautica, Gabinetto 1941, Busta 155.

Archivio Centrale dello Stato (ACS), Ministero dell'Aeronautica, Gabinetto 1942, Busta 108.

Archivio Centrale dello Stato (ACS), Regia Marina, Busta 88.

Archivio Centrale dello Stato (ACS), Segreteria Particolare del Duce, Carteggio ordinario MI, P.S. 1943, Busta 8.

Archivio Storico Aeronautica Militare (AUSMA), Fondo Diari Storici II Guerra Mondiale, Diario 32 Gruppo BT 1941; Diario 32 Gruppo BT 1942; Diario 20 Gruppo CT 1942.

Archivio Privato Campagnoli (AC).

Archivio Ufficio Storico dello Stato Maggiore della Marina (AUSMM), Comitato degli Ammiragli e Commissione Suprema di avanzamento: Verbali di sedute del Comitato degli Ammiragli 1920–1922; Verbali di sedute del Comitato degli Ammiragli 1924–1925; Verbali delle sedute anno 1926-31: Verbali delle adunanze 1933–1940.

Archivio Ufficio Storico dello Stato Maggiore della Marina (AUSMM), Consiglio Superiore di Marina: Vol. 7 Verbali dal n 13981 al n 14340; Vol. 8 Verbali dal n 14341 al n 14610; Vol. 9 Verbali dal n 14611 al n 14880.

Archivio Ufficio Storico dello Stato Maggiore della Marina (AUSMM), Fondo Marina Germanica in Italia, bb. 35 (1938–1946).

Archivio Ufficio Storico dello Stato Maggiore della Marina (AUSMM), Fondo Maristat Reparto Mobilitazione, Difese e Servizi, Busta 155.

Archivio Ufficio Storico dello Stato Maggiore della Marina (AUSMM), Fondo Maristat Reparto I.A.M., Busta 23; Busta 24; Busta 25; Busta 29; Busta 39.

Archivio Ufficio Storico dello Stato Maggiore della Marina (AUSMM), Nave Aquila, bb 12 (1938–43), Carteggio relazioni missioni in Germania, Busta 1; Busta 3/f; Busta 4; Busta 7; Busta 10; Busta 11; Busta 12; Busta 20.

Archivio Ufficio Storico dello Stato Maggiore Marina (AUSMM), Nave Impero.

Archivio Ufficio Storico dello Stato Maggiore Marina (AUSMM), Nave Portaerei.

Archivio Ufficio Storico dello Stato Maggiore Marina (AUSMM), Naviglio Militare bb 167 (1940–1949).

Archivio Ufficio Storico dello Stato Maggiore Marina (AUSMM), *Supermarina* Patto Tripartito b1, Busta 1 (1941–1943).

Archivio Ufficio Storico dello Stato Maggiore Marina (AUSMM), *Supermarina* Armera, bb 18 (1940–43).

Archivio Ufficio Storico dello Stato Maggiore Marina (AUSMM), Scontri navali ed operazioni di guerra, Busta 57.

Published Documents

Biagini, Frattolillo F. (a cura di), *Verbali delle riunioni tenute dal capo di Stato Maggiore Generale* (4 voll., Roma, 1983–1985).

Bottai, G., *Diario 1935–1944* (Milano: Rizzoli, 2006).

Cavallero, U., *Comando Supremo* (Bologna: Cappelli, 1948); *Diario 1940 -1943* (Roma: Ciarrapico, 1984).

Ciano, G., *Diario 1937–1943* (Milano: Rizzoli, 1980).

Mattesini, F., Cermelli, M. (a cura di), *Le direttive tecnico-operative di Superaereo* (2 vols., Roma, 1992).

Gazzetta Ufficiale.

Regio Decreto n. 645, 28 March 1923.

Regio Decreto n. 1438, 30 September 1920.

Regio Decreto n. 1513, 2 September 1925.

Regio Decreto n. 3482, 30 December 1868.

Regio Decreto Legge n. 782, 19 May 1938.

Regio Decreto Legge n. 68, 6 February 1927.

Books

Aga Rossi, E., *Una nazione allo sbando. L'armistizio italiano dell'8 settembre* (Bologna: Il Mulino, 2003).

Aichner, M., *Il gruppo Buscaglia* (Milano: Mursia, ed. 2008).

Andri A., Andri E., *Recuperi navali in basso fondale—Leonardo da Vinci Duilio—Corazziere—Pontone posa massi* (Genova: Eidon, 2015).

Badoglio, P., *L'Italia nella Seconda Guerra Mondiale* (Milano: Mondadori, 1946).

Bagnasco E., de Toro A., *Le Navi da Battaglia classe Littorio, 1937-1948* (Parma: Albertelli Editore, 2008).

Bagnasco, E., *La portaerei nella marina italiana* (Roma: Rivista Marittima, 1989).

Barnett, C., *I generali di Hitler* (it. ed., Milano: Rizzoli, 1991).

Bernotti, R., *Cinquant'anni nella Marina Militare* (Milano: Mursia, 1971).

Borghese, J. V., *Decima Flottiglia Mas. Dalle origini all'armistizio* (Milano: Garzanti, 1950).

Bornholms Historiske SaMediterranean Fleetund, *Bornholmske Samlinger* II RAEKKE - vol. 9 (Rønne 1976).

Breyer, S., *Battleships of the World* (London: Conway Maritime Press, 1980).

Brown, D. K. *The Design and Construction of British Warships, 1939-1945 the Official Record—Major Surface Warships* (London: Conway Maritime Press, 1995).

Canevari, E., *La guerra italiana* (Roma: Tosi, 1948 – 1949).

Catalano Gonzaga di Cirella, A., *Per l'onore dei Savoia* (Milano: Mursia, 1996).

Cernuschi, E., *Domenico Cavagnari, storia di un ammiraglio*, (Roma: Rivista Marittima, 2011).

Ceva, L., *Africa Settentrionale 1940–1943* (Roma: Bonacci, 1982); *La condotta italiana della guerra: Cavallero e il Comando Supremo 1941/1942* (Milano: Feltrinelli, 1975); *Le forze armate* (Torino: Utet, 1981); *Guerra Mondiale, Strategie e industria bellica 1939 – 1945* (Milano: Franco Angeli, 2000).

Ceva, L., Curami A., *Industria bellica anni trenta* (Milano: Franco Angeli, 1992).

Commissione italiana di storia militare, *L'Italia in guerra. Il 2° anno. 1941*, (Roma: USMM, 1992).

Cosentino, M., and Bonfiglietti F., *La portaerei scomparsa del Generale Bonfiglietti* (Milano: Jouvence, 2016).

Cosentino, M., *Le portaerei italiane* (Parma: Albertelli Edizioni Speciali, 2011).

Crociani P., Battistelli P., *Italian soldier in North Africa 1941–1943* (Oxford: Osprey Publishing, 2013); *Italian Army Elite Units & Special Forces 1940–43* (Oxford: Osprey Publishing, 2011); *Italian Navy & Air Force Elite Units & Special Forces 1940–45* (Oxford: Osprey Publishing, 2013).

Da Matapan al golfo Persico, la marina militare italiana dal fascismo alla repubblica (Milano, 2003).

Da Zara, A., *Pelle di ammiraglio* (Milano: Mondadori, 1949).

De Felice, R., Mussolini l'alleato, 1. *L'Italia in guerra 1940–1943, Tomo primo, Dalla guerra «breve» alla guerra lunga* (Torino: Einaudi, 1996); Mussolini l'alleato, 1. *L'Italia in guerra 1940–1943, Tomo secondo, Crisi e agonia del regime* (Torino: Einaudi, 1996).

De Risio, C., *Generali, servizi segreti e fascismo* (Milano: Mondadori, 1978).

de Rosa, G., *Storia dell'Ansaldo – 6. Dall'IRI alla guerra 1930-1945*, (Bari: Laterza, 1999).

Friedman, N., *British Carrier Aviation, The Evolution of the Ships and their Aircrafts* (London: Conway Maritime Press, 1988); *Battleships: Design and Development 1905-1945* (New York: Mayflower Books, 1978).

Galati, F., *100 Years of Radar* (Cham, Switzerland, Springer International Publishing AG, 2016).

Garzke, W. H., and Dulin Jr, R. O., *Battleships: Allied battleships in WWII* (Annapolis: Naval Institute Press, 1980); *Battleships: Axis and Neutral Battleships in World War II*, (Annapolis: Naval Institute Press, 1985).

Gentile, E., *Fascismo. Storia e interpretazione* (Bari: Laterza, 2008); *Il fascismo in tre capitoli* (Bari: Laterza, 2004).

Georg, F., *Hitler's Miracle Weapons, The Secret History of the Rockets and Flying Craft of the Third Reich Volume 2:From the V-1 to the A-9: Unconventional short- and medium-range weapons* (Solihull, West Midlands, UK: Helion, 2005).

Gibbs, N. H., *Grand Strategy, vol. I, Rearmament Policy* (London: HMSO, 1976).

Giorgierini, G., *Uomini sul fondo* (Milano: Mondadori, 1994).

Gooch, J., *Mussolini and his generals* (Cambridge: Cambridge University Press, 2007).

Greene, J., Massignani, A., *The Naval War in the Mediterranean 1940–1943* (London: Chatham Publishing, 1998).

Gröner, E., *German warships 1815-1945, volume I: Major Surface Vessels* (Annapolis: Naval Institute Press, 1990).

Hillgruber, A., *La Strategia militare di Hitler* (it. ed., Milano: Rizzoli, 1986).

Hinsley, F. H., *British Intelligence in the Second World War* (2 voll., London: HMSO, 1979–1990).

Israel, U. H. J., *Einziger deutscher Flugzeugtraeger Graf Zeppelin* (Herford: Koehler, 1994).

Kahn, D., *Hitler's Spies, German Military Intelligence in World War II* (Cambridge, Mass, USA: Da Capo Press, 2000).

Keegan, J., *La seconda guerra mondiale* (it. ed., Milano: Rizzoli, 2002); *Intelligence, Storia dello spionaggio militare da Napoleone ad Al Qaeda* (Milano: Mondadori, 2006).

La guerra italiana sul mare La Marina tra vittoria e sconfitta 1940-1943 (Milano: Mondadori, 2001).

La marina italiana della seconda guerra mondiale XXI—L'organizzazione della Marina durante il conflitto (Roma: USMM, 1972-78).

Landers, D. S., *The Unbound Prometheus* (Cambridge: Cambridge University Press, 1972).

Lehmann, E., *Le ali del potere, La propaganda aeronautica nell'Italia fascista* (Torino: Einaudi, 2010).

Lyman R. D., and McLaughlin, S., *The Hybrid Warship: The Amalgamation of Big Guns and Aircraft* (London: Conway Maritime Press, 1991).

MacGregor, K., *Destino comune, Dittatura, politica estera e guerra nell'Italia fascista e nella Germania nazista* (it. ed.,Torino: Einaudi, 2003); *Alleati di Hitler, Le régie forze armate, il regime fascista e la guerra del 1940-1943* (Milano: Garzanti, 2002).

Mack Smith, D., *A proposito di Mussolini* (Bari: Laterza, 2004); *Mussolini* (Milano: Rizzoli, 2008); *Le guerre del duce* (Bari: Laterza, 1976).

Maiolo, J., *Cry Havoc, The Arm Race and the Second World War, 1931–41* (London, John Murray, 2010).

Malaya and Singapore, The fall of Britain's empire in the East (Oxford: Osprey Publishing, 2016).

Mattesini, F. *L'operazione Gaudo e lo scontro notturno di Capo Matapan*, (Roma: USMM, 1998); *La battaglia di Punta Stilo*, (Roma: USMM, 2001).

Mattioli, M., *Savoia: Marchetti S.79 Sparviero Torpedo—Bomber Units* (Oxford: Osprey Publishing, 2014).

McLaughlin, S., *Russian & Soviet Battleships* (Annapolis: Naval Institute Press, 2003).

Mindling G., Bolton R., *U.S. Air Force Tactical Missiles 1949–1969 The Pioneers* (Morrisville: Lulu, 2011).

Montanari, M., *Le operazioni in Africa Settentrionale, Vol. I—Sidi el Barrani (Giugno 1940–Febbraio 1941)* (2 ed., Roma: Ufficio Storico Stato Maggiore dell'Esercito, 2000); *Le operazioni in Africa Settentrionale, Vol. II—Tobruk (Marzo 1941–Gennaio 1942)* (2 ed., Roma: Ufficio Storico Stato Maggiore dell'Esercito, 1993); *Le operazioni in Africa Settentrionale, Vol. III—El Alamein (Gennaio–Novembre 1942)* (2 ed., Roma: Ufficio Storico Stato Maggiore dell'Esercito, 2006); *Le operazioni in Africa Settentrionale, Vol. IV—Enfidaville (Novembre 1942–Maggio 1943)* (Roma: Ufficio Storico Stato Maggiore dell'Esercito, 2005); *La Campagna di Grecia* (Roma: Ufficio Storico Stato Maggiore dell'Esercito, 1980); *L'Esercito italiano alla vigilia della 2ª guerra mondiale* (Roma, Ufficio Storico Stato Maggiore dell'Esercito, 1982).

Mori Ubaldini, U., *I sommergibili negli oceani* (Roma: Ufficio Storico della Marina Militare, 2002).

Nassigh, R., *Guerra negli abissi, I sommergibili italiani nel secondo conflitto mondiale* (Milano: Mursia, 1971); *Operazione Mezzo Agosto* (Milano: Mursia, 1976).

Neulen, H. W., *In the Skies of Europe: Air Forces Allied to the Luftwaffe 1939–1945* (Ramsbury, UK: Crowood, 2005).

O'Hara, V. P., *Struggle for the Middle Sea, The Great Navies at War in the Mediterranean Theater, 1940-1945* (Annapolis: Naval Institute Press, 2009).
Overy, R., *Why the Allies won* (London: Pimlico, 2006).
Peattie, M., *Sunburst, The rise of Japanese Naval Air Power 1909-1941* (Annapolis: Naval Institute Press, 2007).
Pegolotti, B., *Uomini contro navi* (Firenze: Vallecchi Editore Firenze, 1967).
Pellegrini, E., *Le implicazioni navali della conquista dell'Impero (1935-1941)* (Roma: USMM, 2003).
Playfair, S. O., *The Mediterranean and Middle East*, vol. I (London: HMSO, 1954).
Pricolo, F., *La Regia Aeronautica nella seconda guerra mondiale, novembre 1939-novembre 1941* (Milano: Longanesi, 1971).
Quatarnaro, R., *Roma tra Londra e Berlino. La politica estera fascista tra il 1930 e il 1940* (Roma, Bonacci, 1980).
Rastrelli, A., *La portaerei Italiana* (Milano: Mursia, 2001).
Rocca, G., *I disperati, La tragedia dell'Aeronautica italiana nella seconda guerra mondiale* (Milano: Mondadori, 1991).
Rochat, G., *Le guerre italiane 1935-1943, Dall'Impero d'Etiopia alla disfatta* (Torino: Einaudi, 2005); *L'esercito italiano da Vittorio Veneto a Mussolini* (Bari: Laterza, 2006); *Italo Balbo, aviatore e Ministro dell'aeronautica 1926-1933* (Ferrara: Bovolenta, 1979).
Rohwer, J. S., and Monakov, M., *Stalin's ocean-going fleet*, (London: Routledge, 2001).
Roskill, S. W., *The War at Sea, Vol. I, The Defensive* (London: HMSO, 1954).
Santoni A., and Mattesini, F., *La partecipazione tedesca alla guerra aeronavale nel Mediterraneo (1940–1945)* (Parma: Albertelli Edizioni Speciali, 2005).
Santoni, A., *Il vero traditore, Il ruolo documentato di ULTRA nella guerra del Mediterraneo* (Milano: Mursia, 1981); *Guerra segreta sugli oceani. L'ULTRA britannico e i corsari tedeschi* (Milano: Mursia, 1984); *Storia e politica navale dell 'età contemporanea* (Gaeta: USMM, 1993).
Schofield, B. *La notte di Taranto* (Milano: Mursia, 1974).
Stille, M., *Italian battleships of world war II* (Oxford: Osprey Publishing, 2011).
The Imperial Japanese Navy of the Russo-Japanese War (Oxford: Osprey Publishing, 2016).
Thomaier, D., *Unterwasser-Ansprengversuche am Schlachtschiff IMPERO in der Bucht von Capodistria, 42° Deutsche Gesellschaft fuer Schiffahrts-u. Marinegeschichte Acta*, (Berlin: 2013).
Thomas A., *V1 Flying Bomb Aces*, (Oxford: Osprey Publishing, 2013).
Till, G., *Air Power and the Royal Navy, 1914-1945: A Historical Survey*, (London: Jane's, 1979).
Tur, S., *Plancia Ammiraglio*, (Roma: Canesi, 1963).
Ufficio Storico della Marina Militare, *La Marina Italiana nella seconda guerra mondiale IV Le azioni navali in Mediterraneo*" (Roma: USMM, 1976); *La Marina Italiana nella seconda guerra mondiale XIV—I mezzi d'assalto* (Roma: USMM, 2001).
Watton, R., *The Aircraft Carrier Victorious* (London: Conway Maritime Press, 1991).
Werrel, K. P., *The Evolution of the Cruise Missile* (Maxwell: Air University Press, 1985).
Yoshimura, A., *Battleship Musashi: The Making and Sinking of the World's Biggest Battleship* (Tokyo: Kodansha International,1999).
Zaloga S. J., and Laurier, J., *Hitler's Infamous "Doodlebug"* (Oxford: Osprey Publishing, 2005).
Васильев А. М., Линейные корабли типа «Советский Союз», (Санкт-Петербург, 2006).
Васильев А. М.,Морин А. Б, Суперлинкоры Сталина. «Советский Союз», «Кронштадт», «Сталинград» (2008).

Articles and Chapters

Bagnasco, E., and Cernuschi, E., La portaerei *Impero*? *Storia Militare* (Parma: maggio, 2006), pp. 51-59; Capitani Romani, *Storia Militare* (Parma: febbraio, 2015).
Bagnasco, E., Rastrelli, A., *L'affondamento' della portaerei Aquila a Genova nel 1945. Un avvenimento storico controverso avviato a soluzione attraverso l'analisi di fotografie ed un 'confronto' internazionale* (Roma: BAUSMM, Year VI, giugno 1992).
Bagnasco, E., Una portaerei mancata: la "Francesco Caracciolo, *Rivista Marittima*, maggio, 1991, pp. 95-107.
Boccalatte, C., *La vasca navale della Spezia e la nascita della moderna architettura navale in Italia*" (Roma: BAUSMM, settembre 2013).

Cardoni, F., *Il problema aeronavale italiano*, (Roma: BAUSMM, Year I N° I, settembre 1987).

Ceccarelli, F., *La corazzata Impero: storia di una nave mai nata*, (Roma: BAUSMM, giugno 1992).

Cernuschi, E. P., and O'Hara, V., 'Search for a Flattop: the Italian Navy and the aircraft carrier 1907-2007' (Annapolis: Naval Institute Press, 2007), pp. 61-80.

Ceva, L., 'Italy' in I.C.B. Dear e M.R.D. Foot (ed.), *The Oxford Companion to the Second World War* (Oxford: Oxford University Press, 1995), pp. 580-603.

Corradi, B., La protezione subacquea tipo "Pugliese", *Rivista Marittima*, (Roma, febbraio 1982), pp 91-93.

Curma A., Garello, G., L'aviazione ausiliaria per la Regia Marina fra le due guerre (1923-1940) *Rivista Marittima*, (Roma: aug-set. 1985), pp. 71-86.

de Toro, A., *Le origini politico-diplomatiche delle navi da battaglia Littorio e Vittorio Veneto*, (Roma: BAUSMM, marzo 1997).

Fioravanzo, G., L'Aviazione per la Marina (1940-1943), *Rivista Marittima*, (Nov., 1963), pp. 6-46.

Giardinieri, V., 'L'attacco a Pantelleria', *Storia Militare*, 9 (Parma: 1994), pp. 32-42.

Giorgierini, G., *Le costruzioni navali italiane nel periodo bellico con specifico riferimento al 1942* (Roma: BAUSMM, dicembre 1992).

Hervieux, P., 'I sommergibili della classe "Calvi" del 1936', *Storia Militare*, 8 (Parma, 1994), pp. 26-34.

Il problema aeronavale italiano Parte 5°: la nomina di Italo Balbo a capo dell'Aeronautica e la sua battaglia contro le aviazioni ausiliarie, (Roma: BAUSMM, Year VI, giugno 1992).

Il problema aeronavale italiano parte II, (Roma: BAUSMM, Year I N° 2, dicembre 1987).

Il problema aeronavale italiano, parte sesta: I rapporti tra Marina ed Aeronautica dal 1929 al 1935—Anni di stasi", (Roma: BAUSMM, settembre 1992).

Il problema aeronavale italiano—Conclusione: 1935-1939. L'incerto riorientamento della politica navale e il fallimento finale della portaerei, (Roma: BAUSMM, dicembre 1992).

Jabes, D. F., 'Macchi C-202 Folgore. Il caccia italiano di maggior successo durante la seconda guerra mondiale: un punto di vista anglosassone', *Ricerche Storiche*, XLII, 1 (Firenze: Edizioni Polistampa, 2012), pp. 149-156.

La questione della nave portaerei nella Regia Marina nel 1923-1925–difficoltà finanziarie ed incertezze tecniche e dottrinarie, (Roma: BAUSMM, giugno 1991).

Marcon, T., 'Le difese costiere della piazzaforte di Augusta—Siracusa negli anni 30–40', *Storia Militare*, 2 (Parma: 1993), pp. 24-32.

Mariano, G., 'Mediterraneo 1935-36, La situazione militare marittima nella visione britannica', *Rivista Marittima* (Roma, maggio 1986), pp. 24-31.

Mattesini, F., *Il bombardamento navale di Genova del 9 Febbraio 1941*, (Roma: BAUSMM, June 1990); *Il blocco navale italiano nella guerra di Spagna* (Roma: BAUSMM, December 1997); *I radiolocalizzatori della Regia Marina*, (Roma: BAUSMM, September and December 1995); *L'Operazione Halberd—Cronistoria di una mancata battaglia navale*, (Roma: BAUSMM, December 1990).

Minniti, F., 'Aspetti organizzativi del controllo sulla produzione bellica in Italia', *Clio*, VI (Roma: Elsinore, 1977), pp. 305-340; 'Profilo dell'iniziativa strategica italiana dalla «non belligeranza» alla «guerra parallela»', *Storia contemporanea*, XVIII, 6 (1987), pp. 1113-1195; 'Gli obiettivi di guerra nella pianificazione operativa (1938-1940)' in "*L'Italia in guerra—il primo anno—1940*" (Roma: Stato Maggiore Difesa Ufficio Storico, 1991); Santoni, A., *Strategia marittima e operazioni navali nell'anno 1940* (Roma: BAUSMM, March 1991).

Ramoino, P., *La "Minaccia" navale francese negli anni venti e trenta del XX secolo* (Roma: BAUSMM, giugno 2011).

Schmider, K., 'The Mediterranean in 1940–1941: Crossroads of Lost Opportunities?' in *War and Society*, 15, n. 2 (1997), pp. 19-41.

Tiberio, P., L'invenzione del Radar: il contributo di Ugo Tiberio dal 1935 al 1943, Rivista semestrale dell'Accademia Nazionale di Scienze Lettere ed Arti di Modena, Serie 8, XIII, pp. 217-229.

Tiberio, U., "Sullo sviluppo delle cognizioni radar italiane durante la guerra", *Rivista Marittima* (Roma: aprile 1951); Some Historical Data Concerning the First Italian Naval Radar, *IEEETrans. AES, vol. 5, 1979.*

Zani, L., *La marina italiana e l'unione sovietica tra le due guerre—Parte Prima 1929-1933* (Roma: BAUSMM, giugno 1994).